HOMICIDE AND THE POLITICS OF LAW REFORM

Homicide and the Politics of Law Reform

JEREMY HORDER

OXFORD
UNIVERSITY PRESS

OXFORD
UNIVERSITY PRESS

Great Clarendon Street, Oxford, OX2 6DP,
United Kingdom

Oxford University Press is a department of the University of Oxford.
It furthers the University's objective of excellence in research, scholarship,
and education by publishing worldwide. Oxford is a registered trade mark of
Oxford University Press in the UK and in certain other countries

© J. Horder, 2012

The moral rights of the author have been asserted

First Edition published 2012
Impression: 1

Crown copyright material is reproduced under Class Licence
Number C01P0000148 with the permission of OPSI
and the Queen's Printer for Scotland

British Library Cataloguing in Publication Data
Data available

Library of Congress Cataloging in Publication Data
Library of Congress Control Number: 2012937858

ISBN 978-0-19-956191-9

Printed in Great Britain by
CPI Group (UK) Ltd, Croydon, CR0 4YY

To colleagues and friends across the world, whose advice
I should have followed and not just listened to.

General Editor's Introduction

The law of homicide has received considerable scholarly and political attention over the years, but this original study takes a different approach. It re-examines the recent history of proposed and actual reforms of the law of homicide, charting and assessing the forces that shaped (or failed to shape) the law. The focus is on the law of England and Wales, but there are frequent comparisons with other jurisdictions. However, the monograph contains more than a political history of homicide law reform. It probes the constitutional and theoretical arguments that underpin many of the debates about the approach to law reform, adapting two models of legal rationality as explanatory tools. The study deals not just with the contours of the offences of murder and manslaughter but also, in some depth, with other important sites of debate such as corporate homicide, joint criminal ventures, and (partial) defences. Unique to the study is an insider's view of the processes of proposing and accomplishing law reform, stemming from Professor Horder's work as a Law Commissioner, which brings critical reflections on the role of academic commentators and the role of public opinion. The result is a fascinating monograph that challenges many received ideas and tendencies, and puts forward a nuanced view of the forces that should ideally operate to shape the law of homicide. It is a pleasure to be able to commend such a scholarly study.

Andrew Ashworth

Preface and Introduction

In this book I seek to do two things: to tell a story, and to criticize various manifestations of a widely held thesis about the criminal law (the two tasks will turn out to be linked). The story is the subject of Parts I and III, and each Part deals with a different aspect of the whole. In Part I, I tell the story of law reform efforts bearing on the substantive offences of homicide (and on murder, in particular) from the early nineteenth century to the present day. This involves, I hope, no mere recounting of key events or developments, fascinating though many have been. In Part I, and especially in Chapter 1, I look at efforts to reform homicide law—and the resistance to them—from the perspective of those historically confined, and still largely confined, to be onlookers in the process: the citizens of the state. The citizen's role in homicide law reform still remains, metaphorically, that of standing with his or her nose up against a heavily protected glass window, watching, whilst behind the window political and legal elites squabble over whose expertise and (inevitably) whose views should most heavily influence the law reform process. Efforts to consult (but not involve) the public have not progressed, even with the advent of new technology, beyond a limited 'interest group' model first employed to legitimize changes to road traffic legislation in the 1930s.[1] The situation needs to change. This should be something accepted even by those—myself included—who deplore the disproportionate influence on legislators of hastily devised but lurid newspaper editorials calling for ever harsher laws and more draconian punishment, and the (phony) backing those newspapers claim to have for their views from their own crude opinion polling. The public deserves better; but they will not get what they deserve, in that respect, until properly conducted and wide-ranging research into their views becomes a focal point for—if not a determining influence on— reform of what I will call 'violative' crimes such as homicide.

Even that is not enough. Whilst homicide law is not as such constitutional law, constitutional conventions concerning the legislative process have adversely im-pacted on the way in which changes to the law of homicide can be sought. There is, for example, no convention that morally or politically controversial aspects of homicide law will be reviewed on a regular medium- to long-term basis. This is so, even when it is known at the time legislation is passed that new research, new medical advances, or new thinking may change the landscape that formed the backdrop to the legislation, and even when the law's opponents are motivated by profound dictates of conscience or concern for human rights.[2] The result is that, whilst re-consideration of some controversial features of the law, such as the blanket

---

[1] The 'bureaucratic-administrative' cast of thought influencing the law of homicide, as it has developed in relation to road traffic law and corporate manslaughter, is the subject of Ch 2.

[2] Similarly, there is, of course, no constitutional convention that common law development of homicide and homicide-related rules be reviewed by the legislature on a regular basis.

prohibition on euthanasia, is indeed from time to time on the legislative agenda, this happens in a haphazard way dependent largely on political opportunism. By contrast, why should we not contemplate as a matter of constitutional principle—writing this into the legislation itself—a full-scale debate every twenty years on, say, the right to an abortion? I argue that the constitutional importance of a commitment to periodic reconsideration of controversial aspects of homicide law is that it shows proper legislative humility and respect for citizens who have the 'effrontery' to disagree with (amongst other things) the cherished nostrums of the legal and political elite. After all, suppose that it is true (and I sincerely hope and believe that it is true) that there is widespread public support for, for example, a woman's right to an abortion, and, in exceptional circumstances, for the lenient treatment of those who assist in another's suicide. If so, then those who support such positions have little to fear from periodic *bona fide* reconsideration through public debate of these issues. To say that such reconsideration merely wastes time, or is a foregone conclusion and so pointless in the first place, is to display a profound cynicism about politics and the use of legislative power. Even in the unlikely event that support for these views turns out not to be widespread, a minority opinion—whether or not correct—can over time become a majority one to which conscientious and humble legislators may eventually have to defer, even if they disagree. Above everything else, though, legal politics and reform processes should from top to bottom be about finding ways to engage with all citizens, leaving no one out. The viewpoint of a dominant political or legal elite on some aspect of homicide law should not be allowed indefinitely to prevail purely through carefully cultivated legislative inertia.

Part III tells the story of the post-war reforms to defences to murder, through a re-consideration of the reforms proposed by Royal Commission on Capital Punishment (1953). We will see how the favoured recommendations of the Royal Commission would have given an important and wide-ranging discretionary role in sentence mitigation to the judge and jury acting together, in individual murder cases. These recommendations were rejected by a Government fearful of the public's reaction to the shrinking scope for the death penalty that such change would obviously have involved. Instead, the Government cherry-picked some of the Royal Commission's less favoured reform options, hence embracing a strategy that would reduce in a less dramatic—and less obvious—way the scope for the application of the death penalty. The Government brought in new but narrowly focused defences capable of reducing murder to manslaughter, and only slightly (albeit, as things turned out, significantly) broadened the old defence of provocation. The occasional success of such defences to murder in individual cases would reduce the overall number of instances in which the death penalty had to be applied. The narrowness and specialized focus of the defences would ensure, though, that the reduction would be achieved without it becoming a matter of easily accessible public record or seen as the product of deliberate Government strategy. The result was a much more heavily doctrinal approach to the circumstances in which murder could be reduced to manslaughter than was favoured by the Royal Commission. Predictably, this approach mired the law in a bog of ever-thickening legal complexity from which, following the coming into force of the Coroners and Justice Act 2009, there is now little hope of escape.

Part II of this book is founded on essays previously published elsewhere, with the exception of Chapter 5 which is new. Even so, each essay has been re-worked, sometimes (as with Chapter 4) very substantially, and replies to critics have been added in Chapters 3 and 7. In Part II, I examine the boundaries of murder and manslaughter as substantive offences. In that respect, one task I undertake, ex-emplified by Chapters 3 and 6, is to defend from attack (some of) the existing law, and (many of) the Law Commission's recommendations in the period 2005–07 to reform it. Principally the criticism has come from those (so-called 'subjectivists') who would like to see liability for homicide, and criminal liability more generally, depend on culpability in the way that the accused—'D'—saw events unfolding. Subjectivists would have the law disregard, in point of liability, what D ended up doing having failed—however culpably—to see it coming. Killers-who-did-not-see-it-coming are particularly the subject in Chapter 5 of a re-worked thesis (originally developed in 1995 and 1997[3]), defending the legitimacy of what has come loosely to be known as 'one-punch' manslaughter. At the heart of Chapter 6, where the subject is murder arising out of a joint criminal enterprise, is also a critique of 'subjectivism' (the insistence that the law make liability hinge on how D saw events unfolding). Now, though, at issue is the restricted—'individualist'—basis on which subjectivists regard D's liability for the homicidal acts of another as justified. For subjectivists, very broadly, if I am to be criminally liable in respect of your homicide,[4] either I must play a role in shaping your homicidal action, by assisting or encouraging it, or I must agree with you that we (you, or me, or one of the others in the agreement, or some of us together) will perform the action. That restricted basis for liability leaves out of the picture a more contextual account of individual responsibility for the criminal conduct of others. This is an account that includes some of the cases where I engage in a criminal enterprise with you of a kind well known to involve a risk of other offences—homicide, in particular—being committed by one or more members of the enterprise. Some subjectivists resist the common law conclusion that I should be liable for those other offences arising out of the joint enterprise, in such circumstances. They resist that conclusion even if, ironically, I satisfy a subjectivist requirement for liability, in that I realized at the time that there was a realistic chance that those other offences might be committed in the course of the joint enterprise. My argument is that the intellectual energy put into this resistance is misdirected, and that the common law rules—and the Law Commission recommendations that broadly track them—are essentially sound. Even so, in Chapter 7, I argue that there may be some scope for a subjectivist approach to means, as opposed to ends. In discussing the doctrine of 'transferred malice', I suggest that when the way in which a murder came about was very remote from the way in which D intended it to come about, there may be—by analogy

---

[3] See Horder (1995); Horder (1997a).
[4] Putting aside the case of corporate manslaughter, discussed in Ch 4.

with certain doctrines of remote causation—a fair labelling reason to relieve D of liability for what would otherwise be murder.

Part II is not wholly pre-occupied with a focus on individual criminal liability. In Chapter 4, I turn my attention to so-called 'corporate' manslaughter. My concern will be to develop a critique of the Marx-inspired focus in left-liberal scholarship on the liability of commercial organizations for deaths caused to employees through the negligence of employers. I will concentrate on what I argue is a far more significant problem addressed by the Corporate Manslaughter and Corporate Homicide Act 2007. This is the scandal of deaths caused to at-risk users of public services, by the combined negligence of employers *and* employees who together unjustifiably imperil those users. This manifestation of organizational negligence has led to a death toll in comparison with which the number of employee deaths at the hands of employers almost pales into insignificance, tragic and inexcusable though the latter may equally be. An unholy combination of right-wing concern to shield from liability the police and the army, and left-wing concern to do the same for NHS Trusts and social services more generally, has left commercial companies—many of whom play an important part in running public services—exposed to liability for homicide when a public body doing the same work would not be.

I must express a great debt of gratitude to Oxford University Press, and in particular to its Law Editors, for their extraordinary patience in waiting for the delivery of the manuscript for this book, a wait that included five years whist I was at the Law Commission (although I hope that experience has improved my work). I am also very grateful to the Law School, King's College London, for granting me a term of sabbatical leave in the Autumn of 2011, without which I could not possibly have finished the work.

New Year's Day, 2012.

Acknowledgements

I am grateful to the Sweet & Maxwell (respecting 1 below), to Hart Publishing (respecting 2 and 4 below), to Ashgate (respecting 3 below), and to LexisNexis (respecting 5 below), for permission to reprint, in whole or in part, the following articles:

1. 'Transferred Malice and the Remoteness of Unexpected Outcomes from Intentions' [2006] *Criminal Law Review* 383 [Chapter 7].

2. (With David Hughes) 'Joint Criminal Ventures and Murder: The Prospects for Law Reform' (2009) 20 *King's Law Journal* 379 [Chapter 6].

3. 'Homicide and the Changing Character of Legal Thought' in Chris Clarkson and Sally Cunningham (eds), *Criminal Liability for Non-Aggressive Death* (Farnham: Ashgate, 2007) [Chapter 2].

4. 'The Changing Face of the Law of Homicide' in Jeremy Horder (ed), *Homicide Law in Comparative Perspective* (Oxford: Hart Publishing, 2007) [Chapter 3].

5. 'The Criminal Liability of Organisations for Manslaughter and other Serious Offences' in Simon Hetherington (ed), *Halsbury's Laws of England: Centenary Essays 2007* (London: LexisNexis, 2007).

Contents

III. DEFENCES TO MURDER

Table of Cases

Table of Legislation

PART I

HOMICIDE LAW REFORM AND LAW REFORMERS: THE ENGLISH EXPERIENCE

1

Safe in Whose Hands? Judges, Experts, and Public Opinion in the Homicide Reform Process

I. Introduction and Overview

Murder and manslaughter are manifestations of the ultimate violation. They are examples of what I will call 'violative' crimes, because they involve the violation of a person him or herself, and not merely (and not in every instance) the violation of that person's rights. Indeed, as crimes, they have been described not just as amongst the most serious violations but as nothing short of 'horrific'.[1] That is one consideration lying behind an argument, yet to be fully explored, that reform of the nature and scope of these crimes should not be left solely in the hands of one or more of the ruling elites in England and Wales,[2] solely in the hands of experts, or solely in the hands of any others—such as newspaper editors or pressure groups—liable to suffer, however understandably, from an inflated sense of self-importance in virtue of their position when seeking to influence or determine the law reform process. Where reform of homicide (or of other violative crimes) is concerned, the reform process should not be conceived of as little more than an opportunity for one or more such groups to seek to stamp their own authority decisively on the direction of travel. The process should not even be seen (somewhat less ambitiously), *merely* as an opportunity for interested groups to try to promote or secure their 'single issue', although there must always be room for this. We should have greater ambitions for reform of violative crime. The contributions of all legal

---

[1] Stanton-Ife (2010). In Stanton-Ife's words, 'One should not conceive of the victims of crime in all *mala in se* offences as simply those whose interests have been violated. Victims of horrific crimes have been violated themselves' (*ibid*, at 148–9 and 162). In Ch 5, I will explain why I prefer to speak of homicide as violative, not as horrific.

[2] By 'ruling elites' I mean, first, judges, who have power to change the law but who lack a democratic mandate when they do so (which is not to say that powers are politically illegitimate, given the limited scope that they have); but the notion of ruling elite needs to be understood more capaciously. It must be understood to cover others without a democratic mandate, such as the House of Lords, civil servants, or Parliamentary Counsel, whose functions are politically crucial to the exercise of power by the House of Commons when it changes the law. If the idea of a 'ruling elite' also conjures an image of an educationally and socially privileged group, that image would not be out of place (it applies to legal experts too), although it plays no part in the argument here.

or other experts, and of other interested parties, together with the contribution of Government in the period leading up to any change in the law, should be understood by all as in an important sense greater than the sum of the parts. The contributions of more or less specialized stakeholders should be seen as just one part of the way in which an ongoing dialogue is maintained with the citizenry, whose views should be central to the law reform process, in a (never-ending) quest to give the law of homicide greater moral and political legitimacy.

Antony Duff has argued that the criminal law—and hence, I suggest, its reform—is 'the proper concern of all citizens in virtue of their shared membership of the polity'.[3] Accordingly, the question should be not whether, but how best, to turn that 'proper concern' into a meaningful contribution to reform of the law of homicide. Yet, as we will see, the history of law reform efforts in England and Wales is one in which the citizenry, as such, has been almost always excluded from its processes. In itself, it is not surprising to find that citizens as such are the dispossessed class in the law reform process. The idea that citizens might have a role to play as participants, and not merely—at best—as an audience, in the law reform process, is one that has seemed threatening to some. It may seem threatening either to the elite status of certain groups in the law reform process (judges being the most obvious example, but civil servants can be included), or to the privileged status as experts of other groups (legal scholars or practitioners being the most obvious examples, but some groups representing victims could be included). Yet, the threat largely dissipates if members of such groups come to see themselves not as those with ruling or privileged status, but simply as people with something valuable and distinctive 'to bring to the table' in the search for a morally and politically legitimate criminal law. That is a search properly conducted only with citizens at the table, rather than without them.

In this chapter, my main focus will be on how, over nearly 200 years, judges and more recently scholarly legal experts have benefited from or sought—in the case of the latter, largely unsuccessfully—a privileged or elite position in the process of homicide law reform at the expense of the public at large. By contrast, as we will then see, ministers and civil servants have recently taken more seriously Parliament's role as the people's representative in the reform process. They are committed to 'public' consultation,[4] and have turned decisively away from reliance on the judiciary as the principal source of guidance on homicide law reform. However, the absence of this old conservative restraint has been replaced by poor use, or even misuse, of a democratically elected Government's freedom to legislate in the national interest. Public opinion—properly and professionally researched public opinion—on homicide law reform remains regarded as largely irrelevant to the legislative process. It is almost never subject to investigation—a position remarkable not least for being the one thing on which judges, criminal law scholars, and Governments can usually agree. Further, Governments, along with the law reform bodies that advise them, have become prone to the (sometimes almost

---

[3] Duff (2010), at 88–9. See further Duff and Marshall (1998).
[4] <www.bis.gov.uk/policies/bre/consultation-guidance>.

cynical) manipulation of the views of interest or pressure groups and other stake-holders,[5] in order to shore up a preferred view with the appearance of broad or influential support. This situation needs to change.

To make the change, significant but hardly earth-shattering process reforms are required, when reform of violative crimes such as homicide is in issue. First, the Government must regard as obligatory an investment in properly con-ducted public opinion research on the agenda for (homicide) law reform, as well as on any potential changes that may emerge from deliberation on that agenda.[6] Secondly, it must then accept a heavy burden of justification if, having commis-sioned the research, it wishes to depart from the results. Nothing less than that should be regarded as satisfying what Duff refers to as the 'proper concern' with the criminal law of citizens themselves, as those in whose name the Government purports to act.[7] Only thus can we move beyond the idea that fully 'public' consultation can consist in little more than taking soundings from a coterie of interest groups and factions ('stakeholders') who may claim to, but cannot truly, represent public opinion. Finally, Governments should commit themselves to building into wide-ranging legislative reform of homicide (or of other violative crimes) a procedure for long-term periodic review of the substance of that reform, and not just of the medium-term effectiveness of its implementation. In short, the merits of morally controversial legal reforms should be made automatically subject to review (roughly) every fifteen to twenty years. It is not sufficient to know, as a matter of practical politics when passing legislation, that at some future point a Government probably will (although it may not) be pressured into re-considering the issues.

Those who have fought hard to establish, say, the legality of suicide or abortion, or who long campaigned for a defence of excessive defence, may fiercely resist such a proposal. However, the proposal is at the heart of a vision of governance in which the search for truth in the outcome of practical reasoning, when appropriately embodied in law, is not satisfactorily understood as a contest in which some viewpoints 'win' at the expense of others, following which the relevant legislative field of battle is more or less permanently cleared. On the contrary, good govern-ance requires a commitment not simply to looking for 'definitive' answers to controversial legal questions, but also to the good of friendship with members of the polity,[8] to the good of respect and concern (in Dworkin's sense[9]) for all citizens, in conducting the search for those answers. In this context, I believe that to accept this entails two commitments. There must be a refusal to regard the legal scope and

---

[5] A status to which judges and scholars have now—in the eyes of Government—been reduced.

[6] Something that it already does, in relation to sentencing: see section V.1. below. It should scarcely need saying that I do not suppose that conducting worthwhile and productive research into public opinion is an easy matter. For some useful recent reflections on the issue, see HomRag (2011); Mitchell and Roberts (2012).

[7] I will not make a specific case for the burden of justification being heavy, as it seems to me to come automatically with a commitment in good faith to investigate public opinion in the first place.

[8] In John Finnis' extended sense of that term: Finnis (2007).

[9] Dworkin (1977), at 272.

substance of violative crimes such as homicide as ever permanently settled. There must also be, in consequence, a determination to afford citizens who disagree in principle with the morally controversial elements of the scope and substance an opportunity periodically to seek changes to them. As Sellers puts the point (focusing on political or legal decision-making more broadly):

Decent humility requires that we defer to a reasonable system for resolving conflicting perceptions of moral truth, even when we are unconvinced by the results. People should and will recognize that they may be wrong. The great value of public deliberation about ultimate truths is that it helps us to correct our own moral mistakes [even though] a good republican technique goes further and enables us to defer when we ought to, without admitting mistakes, if we are not convinced. . . . The point is that people who are interested in finding truth will recognize that their own perceptions and reasoning are not always accurate, and be willing to co-operate to improve them.[10]

II. The Ruling Elite and Criminal Law Reform: The Judiciary in Control

Homicide law reform involves tackling complex substantive and procedural legal matters. Consequently, as former Prime Minister William Pitt once insisted, it might be argued that reforms are best 'fully weighed and settled by those learned and able men who filled the highest station in the Law Department',[11] namely judges. This late eighteenth-century argument continued to make its influence felt throughout the nineteenth century and beyond.[12] In the early years of nineteenth century, Smith has observed that the Law Officers, amongst others, all expressed the firm opinion that 'the collective wisdom of the twelve [puisne] judges . . . approximat[ed] to the strongest evidence of the appropriate view to be taken on penal questions'.[13] Smith goes on to say:

Overall, it might be concluded that the judiciary perceived itself, and was viewed by many others of high authority, as the pivotal, referential point for changes in the criminal law, whether through a Parliamentary or common law route.[14]

However, before exploring this view, in the context of this chapter's argument as a whole, we should briefly take note of an early effort to set criminal law reform on a different course—a course not taken as seriously again for over 150 years.

---

[10] Sellers (1991), at 276.

[11] *Parl Hist* (1786–88) 26, 1058, cited by Smith (1998), at 62–3. At 63 fn 26, Smith also cites Lord Ellenborough's view it is judges who are the 'persons with whom alterations to the conduct of criminal justice ought to originate'.

[12] An early but important historical treatment can be found in Radzinowicz (1948). For excellent modern historical analysis, on which I rely for much of the historical detail in the following argument, see Smith (1998); also, Hostettler (1995); Farmer (2000).

[13] Smith (1998), at 62.

[14] *Ibid*, at 63. See Farmer (2000).

1. Radical beginnings: The 1819 'Committee of Inquiry in the Criminal Laws'

Liberal-progressive restrictions on the death penalty became a feature of Enlightenment Criminal Codes in Europe at the end of the eighteenth and beginning of the nineteenth century.[15] In England, similar changes were brought about by legislation in the early nineteenth century,[16] sometimes following agitation by 'men of letters'[17] or by what we would now call pressure or interest groups, such as the pithily named Society for Diffusing Information on Punishment by Death.[18] In late eighteenth- and early nineteenth-century England, there were already many critics of common law development-led criminal law reform. Jeremy Bentham, of course, sought to counter the idea that the judge-made common law was largely popular sentiment writ large, by associating the perpetuation of such law with judicial self-interest:[19]

They [the judges] love the source of their power, of their reputation, of their fortune: they love unwritten law for the same reason that the Egyptian priest loved hieroglyphics, for the same reason that priests of all religions have loved their peculiar dogmas and mysteries.[20]

So far as the criminal law in particular was concerned, for Bentham, the role of judges in reform had led to, 'instead of compliance and obedience, the evil of transgression, mixed with the evil of punishment . . . and in the hands of the judge, power everywhere arbitrary, with the semblance of a set of rules to serve as a screen to it'.[21] He was supported in this line of attack by other commentators. Some even espoused the heresy that senior judges might not be competent in matters of criminal law reform. As early as 1813, Sir Samuel Romilly opined that he knew no reason why, in matters of criminal law reform, 'the authority of the Lord Chief Justice should be singled out as superior to every other: he did not try so many criminal cases as other judges'.[22] Such heretical opinions briefly made political headway in the early nineteenth century, with the appointment of one of the earliest proper criminal law reform bodies ever set up in England. This body was perhaps the first (and until the beginning of the twenty-first century, the last) to seek to base its conclusions on a genuine attempt to investigate public opinion on a controversial legal question: in this instance, on the reach of the death penalty.[23]

---

[15] As in Tuscany (1786), Austria (1787), France (1791; 1810), and Bavaria (1813), on all of which see Farmer (2000), at 399–400.

[16] See *Ibid*, at 406–7.

[17] An early example being Granville Sharp (1773).

[18] An organization founded by B Montague, a barrister, who corresponded with Sir Samuel Romilly about criminal law reform, and supported Romilly's efforts to restrict the applicability of the death penalty. See further, Eastwood (1994).

[19] An association that, as we will see in section III.4., parallels that made between legal experts and their values by Karl Mannheim early in the 20th century.

[20] Bentham, in Bowring (1838–43), at 206, cited by Smith (1998), at 51.

[21] Cited by Schofield and Harris (1998), at 20.

[22] *Parl Debs* (1813) 25, 385, cited by Smith (1998), at 62.

[23] See the discussion in Smith (1998), at 62–4. There is a very full discussion in Radzinowicz (1948), at 526–66, on which the following summary is based.

The (ultimately successful) 1819 Select Committee on Criminal Laws[24] was a Committee set up, in spite of Government opposition, as part of a deliberate attempt to distance the law reform process from the judiciary.[25] The Committee included no judges and took no evidence from them, but went on to recommend the abolition of numerous capital felonies, and a consolidation of the law of forgery. The Committee's recommendations (in fact, with the subsequent help of the judiciary) were carried through as part of Robert Peel's reforms some years later.[26] Most importantly, the Committee was set up against a background of widespread dissatisfaction in many quarters with the operation of the death penalty. It was widely believed that, at this time, the possibility that the death penalty might be applied in over 200 criminal statutes led to an unwillingness to prosecute in anything other than the worst cases (especially when theft and related offences were in issue), with the result, ironically, that crime could often be committed with effective impunity.[27] The Corporation of London itself had petitioned Parliament to consider reform of the criminal law for just these reasons, with some 12,000 people putting their names to petitions to that effect by the summer of 1819.[28] In consequence, the 1819 Committee was established by Parliament. As one MP explained the decision:

If we look, Sir, to the motives which led to this great and important decision, we must in the first place, ascribe it to the previous verdict of a tribunal, to which even the omnipotence of Parliament ought to bow; I mean the verdict of the public opinion, which has loudly and unequivocally pronounced upon the penal code, as it stands in the Statute Book, a sentence of indignant condemnation.[29]

This view accorded with many others in that period, with one commentator suggesting (rather optimistically, as things turned out) that, 'the deference formerly paid to custom and authority is every day diminishing and the public has now acquired a new confidence in its own judgment'.[30] The motion to establish a Committee of Enquiry was passed by a majority of nineteen, against the Government.

---

[24] Select Committee (1819).

[25] See the discussion in Smith (1998), at 62–4.

[26] *Parl Debs* (1827) 17, 592, and 1261, cited by Smith (1998), at 64. Peel did not himself favour reform, but fearing that backbench pressure would bring it about anyway, he introduced his own reforms. In so doing he made the Home Office (which in 1782 had employed a total of 12 people) a much more influential body in criminal law reform: see Eastwood (1994), at 197.

[27] Radzinowicz (1948), at 526. At this time, a thief could in theory be hanged for stealing five shillings in a shop (as well as for a raft of other relatively trivial offences), and yet it was estimated that the number of people committed for trial had more than doubled between 1812 and 1818, from 6,576 (4,605 in 1805) to 13,932. Naturally, these beliefs were articulated in part to suit the agenda of those expressing them rather than because they necessarily bore any relationship to the truth (although some evidence was produced for the thesis: see Radzinowicz (1948), at 537–8). As some contemporary commentators recognized, the transition from war to peace, and hence the sudden presence in England of 300,000–400,000 demobilized men had its own impact on the crime rate at this time.

[28] Radzinowicz (1948), at 527.

[29] *Parl Debs* (1819), Vol 39 HC, May 8, cols 903–06, cited by Radzinowicz (1948), at 528.

[30] John Miller (writing in 1812), at 195, cited by Smith (1998), at 65 fn 40.

The remit of the Committee was to consider whether it was necessary or effective to have capital punishment available, 'in most cases of offences unattended with violence'.[31] Although the Committee's reasoning and conclusions are not central to the theme being developed here, the procedure that it adopted to reach its conclusions is very significant. Foregoing the easy option of simply consulting the great and the good, the Committee decided to proceed by an investigation of public opinion. Taking the view that this could not be discovered, 'from the state of sentiments of isolated individuals chosen at random and brought before the Committee by accident or coincidence',[32] the witnesses were carefully selected from different social classes and professions. Sixty-one people gave evidence, of whom Radzinowicz says most were, 'shopkeepers and tradesmen, merchants and manufacturers, insurance brokers and brokers to merchants, and bankers'.[33] The Committee also attempted to be rigorous in the way that it sought information from these witnesses. So, it did not ask for their opinion on very general questions about criminal justice, but instead asked for facts based on personal experience, and for an opinion of whether the witness thought that their views would be shared by others in their social or professional group.[34] The Committee also examined witnesses who worked in the criminal justice system, including magistrates, clerks to magistrates, a solicitor, two prison chaplains, and two gaol keepers.[35] For the Committee, this evidence was more important than anything that might be gained by consulting the judiciary because, it said:

Of the cases which never appear [in court], and of the causes which prevent their appearance, [the judges] can know nothing. Of the motives which influence the testimony of witnesses, they can form but a hasty and inadequate estimate. Even in the grounds of verdicts, they may often be deceived.[36]

Of the evidence that the Committee did gather, Radzinowicz remarked, 'It is to be doubted whether any other country possesses equally well-arranged returns for so early a period'.[37] This was, though, by no means a universal view. In an article following the publication of the Report,[38] John Miller, of Lincoln's Inn, suggested that the witnesses had been selected because they could be expected to support reform (unlike the judges), that they were too few in number for firm conclusions to be drawn, and that they were in any event not representative of their social class. In that regard, it is important to note that the liberal-progressive thrust of the Committee's conclusions, against which Miller was arguing by attacking its methodology, was to become a powerful factor in some later attempts to reform the law of homicide through codification, both in the nineteenth century and (more

---

[31] Select Committee (1819).   [32] Radzinowicz (1948), at 542.   [33] *Ibid.*

[34] *Ibid.* Radzinowicz cites two conjoined questions as being asked of the witnesses: 'Have you made any observation on the effect of capital punishments for a certain class of offenders? Have you heard that opinion repeatedly expressed?' Lest this be thought simply crude and antiquated as a research tool, it is still employed as a method of investigation by, for example, bodies investigating the extent of 'hidden' or unreported crime, such as bribery.

[35] Amongst other things, the chaplains and the gaol keepers were asked about the reaction of condemned prisoners to the death penalty.

[36] Cited by Radzinowicz (1948), at 546.   [37] *Ibid*, at 544.   [38] Miller (1820–21).

assertively) in the twentieth century. Whether or not Miller's criticisms hit the mark, the importance of the procedure adopted by the Committee is that it has proved to be in some respects unique, for a criminal law reform body. A criminal law reform body freed from judicial domination made an attempt—albeit quite crude—to investigate popular opinion in a broadly social scientific way, and then to make the conclusions it drew from that investigation the basis for its recommendations. Having said that, those the Committee consulted were almost all people who would today be consulted through professional interest groups that represent them, such as the Federation of Small Businesses or the Association of British Insurers. So, this exercise was really one of an 'interest group' kind (considered in section IV below), rather than a genuinely 'public' consultation, as the Committee itself had emphasized.[39]

It is also important to bear in mind the context in which the 1819 Committee was set up, why it felt free to adopt the procedures it did, and why it was in some measure successful in spite of, rather than because of, its procedural radicalism. At the time of the 1819 Committee, direct official engagement with the public on a controversial matter such as the death penalty must have seemed a positively attractive way forwards to the liberal-minded movers behind it[40] (a position that had been decisively reversed a century later[41]). This was because there was then a strong body of support for liberal-progressive thinking about criminal law reform, both inside and outside the House of Commons,[42] that—as many criminal law scholars would have us believe—has now more or less completely evaporated. In that respect, there is a considerable irony about the consistency in approach to the value of public opinion of those who then saw, and now currently see, themselves as swimming against the tide. Consider first, for example, following the work of the 1819 Committee, Sir Robert Peel's dismissal of public opinion as incapable of amounting to a 'liberal' outlook or viewpoint, as compared with the Government's own (more conservative) policy:

Do you think that the tone of England—of that great compound of folly, weakness, prejudice, wrong feeling, right feeling, obstinacy and newspaper paragraphs, which is called public opinion—is more liberal, to use an odious but intelligible phrase—than the policy of the Government?[43]

To anyone who has followed modern debates about the direction of criminal justice policy, especially as it relates to the treatment of homicide (and child sex) offences, Peel's assessment of the demerit of public opinion, as the basis for Government action, will sound all-too familiar. It is reflected, for example, in John Spencer's recently expressed view that:

---

[39] See text at n 32 above.

[40] Such as Sir Samuel Romilly and Sir James Mackintosh.

[41] See the discussion of the fate of Labour Government's post-war abolitionist efforts in Ch 8 below.

[42] In the latter case, a dramatic change from only ten years before: Radzinowicz (1948), at 541.

[43] Letter to John Wilson Croker, cited by Radzinowicz (1948), at 562. As noted earlier (n 26), Peel himself undertook to introduce reform, taking the initiative away from the back benches.

Legislating about criminal justice in the hope of pleasing public opinion as reflected in the popular press is a dangerous and foolish game to play, because on criminal justice matters, public opinion—as misled by the popular press—is seriously misinformed.[44]

No doubt, the point Spencer makes about the role of the popular press is a sound one. Even so, one wonders if he—or other modern liberals—would be so quick to dismiss public opinion as 'seriously misinformed' if that opinion in fact supported a more liberal direction for criminal justice policy, as it had in Peel's day (which was, of course, why Peel was equally anxious to dismiss it). As we will see later, that liberal-minded modern Governments, civil servants, and law reformers, have almost always shared a distrust of public opinion is evident in the fact that the reform processes they developed, from the mid-twentieth century onwards, were ones largely immune from the 'wrong kind' of lay influence.

This radical early blossoming of what, in time, might have become the establishment of an independent criminal law reform body committed to public engagement, quickly withered on the vine. Why was that? As Smith reminds us, it is important to keep in mind the close connections between the (small) legal and political worlds when analysing the role of the judiciary in the nineteenth century.[45] Until 1830, the King's Bench was comprised of the Lord Chief Justice and just three or four puisne judges.[46] They could be expected to have close links with the executive, and open political allegiances. The links and allegiances came about in part through the fact that a considerable number of judges would have previously served as Solicitor-General or as Attorney-General before being elevated to the bench. The Lord Chancellor who was responsible for their appointment had himself, of course, at that time a highly significant political role.[47] The participation of the Lord Chancellor and the Lord Chief Justice in House of Lords debates was throughout that time regarded as a normal part of constitutional government,[48] and they were not the only ones with an unquestioned dual legal-political role.[49] Judges themselves were at one time entitled to sit in the House of Commons, the last judge so eligible—although he did not avail himself of the privilege—being Sir George Jessel (1824–1883), who had also served as Solicitor-General and went on to be Master of the Rolls. It should not be a surprise to find that judicial control of criminal law reform rapidly reasserted itself during the course of the nineteenth century. As barrister Anthony Hammond suggested of the judiciary (in Benthamite spirit) in 1829:

A body of men are little disposed or qualified to question a system, in the principles of which they have been educated, and when regarded as their peculiar patrimony. . . . [50]

44 Spencer (2008a), at 12.   45 Smith (1998), ch 2.
46 *Ibid*, at 51.   47 *Ibid*, at 51–2.   48 *Ibid*, at 61.
49 The Recorder of London was also a Member of Parliament, at the time of the 1872–74 Homicide Bill: Smith (1998), at 146. Other high-profile recorders were also Members of Parliament at that time. It still remains possible to sit part-time as a Recorder whilst being a Member of Parliament.
50 Hammond (1829), preface ix, cited by Smith (1998), at 82. See further the later views of Andrew Amos, who unflatteringly dismissed the perceived need to take account of the views of the judiciary as akin to the Roman practice of using the responses of chickens, 'whether the sacred chickens peevishly

2. The common law triumphant? The 1878–79 Code

The most significant product of judicial control of criminal law reform was the 1878–79 Draft Code.[51] The background to the introduction of the Code to Parliament is of some relevance in the present context. James Stephen (not yet having been appointed a judge) had himself, not long prior to this, drafted what is known as the Homicide Bill 1872–74, in conjunction with his cousin, Russell Gurney, MP, the Recorder of London. When the Bill was considered in 1874, the (lay) members of the Select Committee rejected it, under pressure from the Lord Chief Justice, Lord Cockburn, who claimed he did not favour partial codification, and from Blackburn J, who preferred the elasticity of the common law to codification. The failure of the Bill can be regarded as illustrative of the pivotal role that the higher judiciary played at that time in determining the prospects for criminal law reform.[52] It was still the case, by the end of the nineteenth century, that too many in the ruling elite—like Blackburn J—felt more at ease with the common law. As Sir Leon Radzinowicz put it:

As Codes go, [the Stephen Code] was good and worth the trouble of re-amending and revising; but its chances had been wrecked by the deeply rooted hostility against codification *per se* and its threat to the common law ... which is much more precious than the shapely codes which the seekers after a legal paradise aspired to create.[53]

The origins of the 1878–79 Code lie with Stephen writing in early 1877 to the Attorney-General, Sir John Holker, suggesting that his (Stephen's) *Digest* be taken as the basis for a Draft Code. Holker secured the agreement of the Lord Chancellor, Lord Cairns, to the project, and Stephen produced a Bill by May 1878. To this point, the procedure had largely followed that of the 1872–74 Homicide Bill, but with a crucial difference. The positive involvement of the Attorney-General and the Lord Chancellor meant that the initiative had greater backing from the ruling elite than the initiative that led to the 1872–74 Homicide Bill. Indeed, the 1878–79 Code initiative was also supported by the Home Secretary, RA Cross, although he pointedly added that the Bill would not be passed in a single session of Parliament unless members:

practically forego their rights of discussion; and this they will not do without some guarantee that the Bill has already been accepted by the *leading members of the profession* ... and is backed by all the strength of the Government.[54]

Accordingly, following the Bill's second reading, it was not immediately taken further but instead made the subject of a Royal Commission composed entirely of serving judges—Lord Blackburn (Chairman), Lush LJ, and Barrie J (later

---

tossed aside with their beaks the food offered to them ... or gratefully took it without sticking it in their gizzards': Amos (1856), at xx, cited by Smith (1998), at 138.

[51] For detailed discussion, see Smith (1998), at 146–9, and Hostettler (1995), at 170–4.
[52] See generally, Farmer (2000).
[53] Radzinowicz (1957), at 21.
[54] Cited by Hostettler (1995), at 171 (my emphasis).

omitted)—alongside Stephen himself, who was not long thereafter to be elevated to the bench. Not insignificantly, this course was adopted in part because it appears that the Statute Law Consolidation Committee (amongst others) did not believe that Stephen by himself had the status and authority to be given a 'large order' for consolidation or codification.[55] Even so, in a development that has taken on increasing significance in modern times, the Attorney-General noted in support of the Bill that it had been favourably received by the press (and in particular by the *Law Times*[56]). Of the composition of the Royal Commission, *Punch* remarked approvingly that the Code was to be considered by:

Minos, Aeachus and Rhadamanthus, in the persons of Justices Blackburn and Lush and Sir James Stephen himself, its parent . . . as competent a three as England can supply. . . .[57]

However, others were not so impressed with the membership of the Commission. The Trades Union Congress, for example, complained that the membership was too small and too narrowly drawn, and some MPs thought that it ought not to have been confined to lawyers.[58] In fairness to the Commission, it did not rely wholly on the learning of its own members, and consulted widely amongst practitioners (although it failed to publish the results of that consultation).[59] However, complaints of the sort just mentioned (a lack of 'inclusiveness' in membership or in consultative procedures) were beginning to undermine the legitimacy of a reform body that sought to rest the authority of its conclusions solely on the high status of its members.

   Sure enough, although the Attorney-General spoke strongly in favour of the Bill in the House of Commons in April 1879, there was opposition because (amongst other things) even some of its supporters accepted that the House should not, in the words of Farrer Herschell, 'abdicate its functions by accepting [changes] on trust from a Commission composed of men, no matter how experienced and able'.[60] Even so, this view was opposed in the *Law Times*, which wrote in favour of judicial control of the process, expressing its disapproval that, 'so clear and logical a Bill had to run the risk of being marred by the tinkering of amateur lawyers'.[61] This view was predictably shared by Sir James Stephen, who complained:

As to the Code becoming law, Parliament is an ass made up of clever fellows who empty their talents merrily in ignoble squabbles, and pretty successful attempts to fall to the level of the constituencies which they properly despise.[62]

The Bill did, in fact, obtain a second reading. This was not least because it was now claimed that codification was widely supported by working class people, Sir James

[55] See the discussion in Hostettler (1995), at 173–4.
[56] Vol 159, col 332 (April 1884).
[57] (20 July 1878), at 15. In Greek mythology, Minos, Aeachus, and Rhadamanthus were judges in the underworld.
[58] Hostettler (1995), at 179.
[59] *Ibid*, at 180.
[60] *Hansard* (1879) vol 245, col 310.
[61] (1878) vol 65, at 116, cited by Hostettler (1995), at 190–1.
[62] Letter to Lord Lytton, 29 August 1879, cited by Hostettler (1995), at 189.

Stephen having in the past spoken at length about the virtues of codification at a meeting of the Trades Union Congress ('TUC') (who had good reason to dislike judge-made common law).[63] Indeed, the Bill was set fair to be one of the major pieces of legislation in the 1880 session. However, it fell when Disraeli's Government lost the election in April that year, and there was subsequently said to be no time to re-introduce it.

What was the tenor of the intended codification of the law of homicide, in particular, embodied in the efforts of would-be codifiers during the nineteenth century? This is not the place for a minute examination of the differences between the various codes.[64] For present purposes, we can glean a certain amount from what Stephen himself said about the law as stated in his *Digest of the Criminal Law*,[65] which was intended as a statement of the existing law, and the draft proposed by the Criminal Commission of 1878–79 which, with some important exceptions, closely followed the *Digest*.[66] Nowhere evident here is the kind of radical Benthamite restructuring and utilitarian regeneration of legal principle sometimes associated almost by definition with 'codification'. On the contrary, apart from his criticism of the breadth of 'felony-murder' as stated by Coke,[67] Stephen's Code, like the work of the Criminal Law Commissioners (1833–49), was, to use the words of the latter in describing their own code, largely, 'limited to the reduction and consolidation of the existing Law of England, as well written as unwritten, concerning crimes'.[68] So, for example, under the 1878–79 Code, murder was to encompass, amongst other things:

(a) killing, where D meant to cause death;

(b) killing, where D meant to cause a bodily injury known to him or her to be likely to cause death, and was reckless whether death ensued;

(c) killing, in the intentional furtherance of an unlawful purpose knowing—or where D ought to know—that the act is likely to cause death;

(d) killing with intent to inflict grievous harm in order to facilitate (a certain range of) offences;

(e) killing as a result of administering a stupefying substance to facilitate (a certain range of) offences; and

(f) killing by intentionally stopping the breathing of another person to facilitate the commission of (a certain range of) offences.[69]

---

[63] *Hansard* (1879) vol 245, col 1751. On Stephen's talk to the TUC, see Hostettler (1995), at 165–70.

[64] See Cross (1978); Farmer (2000), at 404.

[65] Stephen (1887).

[66] Stephen (1883), vol 1, at 79–87.

[67] *Ibid*, at 79–80.

[68] Criminal Law Commissioners (1839), at v–vi, cited by Farmer (2000), at 408. On Stephen's love for the common law, see Horder (2002b).

[69] The offences in question were piracy and piracy-related offences, escape or rescue from prison or lawful custody, resisting lawful apprehension, murder, rape forcible abduction, robbery, burglary, and arson.

This, by modern standards, cumbersome definition was described by Stephen as no more than an effort, 'to give the equivalent of [malice aforethought at common law] by a statement of the various states of mind which have been held, by the various authorities referred to, to constitute it'.[70]

More significant, though, than the far-from-radical detail, is the way in which Stephen understood his Code's standing and authority, when put together with what he says about the punishment for murder. In part, its authority is to be derived from its morally conservative nature, in keeping with broader public sentiment as he idealized it:

I think, in short, that s.174 [defining murder] reproduces in plain language that part of the existing law which would be in harmony with the common standard of moral feeling: it describes in perfectly unambiguous language all the worst and most dangerous cases of homicide.[71]

Victorian judges claimed authority over the direction of criminal law reform. However, the inherent conservatism of much of their reform programme provided a crucial counter-balance to the unilateral introduction (untested through the democratic process) of any element of liberal-progressive thinking that they wanted, such as restriction of the felony murder rule. It enabled judges such as Stephen to maintain the plausibility of their claim that the reforms as a whole were in keeping with, 'the common standard of moral feeling', even though they feared and detested (in equal measure) the actual influence of public opinion on the criminal law reform and sentencing.[72]

3. The legacy of the era of judicial control

It now seems quite obvious that wholly judicial determination of the agenda and direction of criminal law reform is far too redolent of the *ancien régime* to have any remaining legitimacy, however wise and skilled in the interpretation and application of law judges may be. Indeed, the late twentieth and early twenty-first centuries saw the role of judges—or, more accurately, separate judicial group-ings[73]—reduced from the lofty one endorsed by Pitt,[74] to one little more elevated than that of a stakeholder jostling for attention alongside other influence-seekers in the law reform process. However, the era of judicial control left an unfortunate legacy. First, in seeking to keep criminal law reform under its control, the judiciary failed to use its great influence to secure a statutory basis for a standing law reform commission of some kind, one with the legal authority to pursue its recommendations with some prospect of success through the parliamentary

---

[70] Stephen (1883), vol 1, at 82–3.

[71] *Ibid*, at 84.

[72] For just one example of the low esteem in which Stephen held public opinion, see passage cited at n 62 above. We will encounter another example in due course.

[73] Such as HM Circuit Judges, the Rose Committee, the permanent judges of the Central Criminal Court, and ad hoc committees of senior judges, amongst others.

[74] See text at n 11 above.

process.[75] This ultimately led to a lengthy and damaging period of stagnation in relation to codification in the early twentieth century. So far as the substantive criminal law is concerned, following the failure of Stephen's 1878–79 Homicide Bill, in the view of one commentator:

The legal profession, having exhausted much of its zeal in the reforms of the nineteenth century, were by and large content to lapse into another of its periods of complacency and self-congratulation. . . . [76]

A law reform body of a serious and substantial kind was not to be established until 1934, when Lord Sankey, then Lord Chancellor, set up the Law Revision Committee. Although its membership was drawn from both the judiciary and from academe, there were five judges (including the Master of the Rolls), six practitioners, and only two academic lawyers.[77] This pattern to membership of such committees was followed when the Criminal Law Revision Committee (CLRC) was set up in 1959, half of its members being drawn from the judiciary, but including three academics.

There was, secondly, a further negative aspect to the legacy of the long period in which senior judges held sway over the movement for reform, one of equal significance in the present context. As part of the ruling elite, senior judges could take for granted direct access to and (some) influence over legislators. In that way, they could expect that their views might, if they had any effect at all, directly shape the use of power by the legislature. At no point was it ever contemplated by a largely patrician judiciary that the legitimacy of their influence should depend on lay or popular input. There was, for example, no room created for lay membership of the CLRC (just as there has never been room for lay membership of the Law Commission). No doubt, this was due to the deep-rooted suspicion, even hostility, of judges to the involvement of lay people in the law reform process. Yet, some early twentieth-century writers were already beginning to doubt whether the legitimacy of criminal law reform, especially in relation to sentencing, could be sustained without adequate account having been taken of lay opinion. Ewing, for example, cautioned that if sentencers became too remote from public opinion in their understanding of the just measure of pain, 'the moral judgments of those who represent the State . . . will cease to be taken seriously'.[78] Roscoe Pound likewise counselled against creating a 'permanent gulf between legal and popular thought',[79] and Sharp and Otto introduced their empirical studies by

---

[75] The Criminal Law Commissioners (1839) had proposed incorporating into a criminal code a special power to make further amendments: Farmer (2000), at 407.

[76] Farrar (1974), at 9. In fact, this is something of an exaggeration. Influential members of the legal profession were active in securing some important legislative changes to the law of homicide in the early twentieth century: see Ch 8 below. However, codification remained off the agenda in the first half of the twentieth century.

[77] The Committee sat until 1939, and was eventually replaced by the Law Reform Committee in 1952, a Committee criticized in some quarters for lack of lay membership and for a more general failure to consult or to try to communicate with the public.

[78] Ewing (1929), at 95.

[79] Pound (1907), at 611.

emphasizing that 'popular attitudes towards retribution as a ground of punishment by the state . . . is a matter about which the moralist and student of political and social life need definite knowledge'.[80] Further, as Farrar rightly points out,[81] there have been no inhibitions about involving non-lawyers in criminal law reform when Royal Commissions have investigated even highly technical areas of criminal procedure. It has not been thought that the elite political status such bodies were assumed to need, to establish their authority, entails, for example, a legally qualified chair.[82] It was just such a Commission, of course, that—chaired by a civil servant[83]—began the modern process of homicide law reform, and ushered in a new era of debate about its nature and scope.[84] We consider the reforms and recommendations of the Royal Commission on Capital Punishment in Chapter 8 below.

Turning to the possibility of a much broader input from the public into law reform, we have already come across Stephen's contempt for the opinions of lay people in general on criminal law reform.[85] In this context, perhaps equally telling were his views on whether the jury should be the body (as opposed to the trial judge) left to decide whether the facts of a murder case were such as to warrant commuting the death sentence:

I would on no account leave to the jury either the question whether the circumstances of mitigation existed . . . or the question whether the sentence should be mitigated. There is no subject on which the impression of a knot of unknown and irresponsible persons, who have to decide at a moment's notice without reflection, is less to be trusted than the question whether or not the punishment of death should be inflicted in a given case.[86]

There is a considerable irony here. When the Royal Commission on Capital Punishment reported some seventy years later, jury involvement in the question whether the death penalty should be passed became the centrepiece of one set of its recommendations.[87] In effect, the Royal Commission proposed a case-by-case working relationship between lay jury and professional judge. The latter would be freed to pass a sentence other than the death penalty in murder cases, if the former first indicated that in their view this was an appropriate course in the light of mitigating circumstances. This radical approach was rejected by the Government of the day, and is now as far away as ever. The focus in point of reform at that time, as now, came to be on doctrinal changes to the substantive law of homicide (fault; partial defences; lesser offences), which juries must then follow as directed by the trial judge. Sentencing issues remained outside the jury's remit. What has emerged to replace judicial control is now a system in which interest groups, factions, or 'stakeholders' (including, in their new guise, various judicial groups[88]) compete for

---

[80] Sharp and Otto (1909), at 341.   [81] Farrar (1974), at 13.

[82] The Royal Commission on Quarter Sessions and Assizes had a lay chairman, in Lord Beeching.

[83] Sir Ernest Gowers.   [84] Royal Commission on Capital Punishment (1953).

[85] See text at n 62 above.   [86] Stephen (1883), vol 1, at 86.

[87] Royal Commission on Capital Punishment (1953), at para 15.

[88] More research is needed on the roles, relationship between, and influence of these more or less formal groups, such as the Rose Committee, the Criminal sub-Committee of HM Council of

the very same kind of direct influence over legislators in relation to homicide law reform that senior judges a century or more before enjoyed as a matter of course. In very broad terms, one such 'faction' is constituted by criminal law scholars (and reform-minded practitioners), and it is to their efforts to gain direct influence over legislators—irrespective of popular backing—that I now turn.

III. 'Seekers after Legal Paradise':[89] Scholars and the Utopian World of Law-craft

If that part of the ruling elite most familiar with the criminal law, the judges, no longer possess the moral legitimacy necessary to take sole charge of the direction of homicide law reform, what about leaving it to a wider group of experts in a broader sense? Discussion of this possibility has been a persistent theme in the history of efforts to reform the law in general (not only the law of homicide). As we will see, it still exercises a strong hold over some, in virtue of widespread tendency to see a unique—and uniquely virtuous—blend of *sophia*, *epistēmē*, and *techne*[90] in the input of scholars and practitioners (along with judges in their role as experts rather than as members of the ruling elite). Historically, there has always been uncertainty about the legitimacy of scholars and other experts in leading law reform efforts. On the one hand, in 1846 a Commons Select Committee Report bemoaned the low status of:

That important class of writers and thinkers . . . disengaged from the turmoil and labour of its daily technical duties [who] have, with disposition and capacity, leisure also, and opportunity to keep the profession up to the intellectual height, to which it should be its proudest boast to aspire.[91]

Taking up this theme, Benthamite John Austin,[92] not satisfied with having been appointed a Criminal Law Commissioner in 1833 to draft a criminal code, longed for the 'disengagement', from the world of law in practice, that he believed was essential to radical reform:

If they would give me two hundred a year for two years, I would shut myself in a garret and, at the end of that time I would produce a complete map of the whole field of Crime, and a draft of a Criminal Code. *Then* let them appoint a Commission to pull it to pieces.[93]

Austin resigned from the Commission after three years, in 1836.

Circuit Judges, Senior Judicial Working Parties, the Permanent Judges of the Central Criminal Court, and others.

[89] See Radzinowicz (1957), at 21.
[90] Respectively, wisdom, knowledge in practical reasoning, and technical craft 'know-how'.
[91] *Parl Reports* (1846) 10, xxxiv, cited by Smith (1998), at 362.
[92] See Lobban (2000).
[93] Austin (1879), Preface, at 11, cited by Smith (1998), at 128. Stephen's asking price for doing the same work years later was not so cheap. In 1877, he was offered 1,200 guineas, asked for (and was given) £1,500, and was paid a further £1,500 for his work on the 1878 Codification Commission: Hostettler (1995), at 170–1.

On the other hand, there persisted a widespread opinion that the development of reform proposals was not to be achieved, in Fifoot's words, 'in sedate seclusion by those who scanned the battle from afar', but instead, 'more strenuously by those who lived in the thick of it and who knew by close and grim experience what legal conflict really meant'.[94] It is not, though, the practical disengagement of scholars from the world of legal practice that ought to have concerned Fifoot about the law reform process. Had Austin, for example, not thought himself so superior to his fellow Commissioners, he could have remedied such a defect simply by sticking to the task of working alongside practitioners. Fifoot should have been more concerned with the legitimacy of scholars seeking to incorporate their liberal-progressive agenda into homicide law reform, without any public discussion or mandate.[95]

1. The shadow cast by Macaulay's Code

By the middle of the nineteenth century an 'academic–expert model' for law reform had already scored one spectacular success, in the shape of Macaulay's Indian Penal Code,[96] a success that may well have overshadowed as well as inspired subsequent attempts to achieve the same result using the same model. Working almost single-handed (putting aside the nominal involvement of his fellow Law Commissioners[97]), Macaulay[98] managed to produce a Criminal Code commonly acknowledged to be a model of clarity of expression,[99] a code that self-consciously departed from what Macaulay derided as the 'fashion ... to darken by gibberish, by tautology, by circumlocution, that meaning that ought to be transparent as words can make it'.[100] In that respect, at least, it is clear that Macaulay's definition of murder is far superior to that contained in either Stephen's *Digest*, or in his Code.[101] However, Macaulay's laudable attempt to de-mystify the language of the law also embodied a contentious determination to re-write the substantive rule of the criminal law in a liberal-progressive direction.

Macaulay's definition of murder is a good example of this.[102] Smith notes that, as part of a supposed 'linguistic modernism' in Macaulay's Code, '[a]s a matter of fundamental policy, the Code declared its firm stance against the English law of constructive liability, most particularly the felony-murder rule ... '.[103] Clauses 294–5 of the Code provided a model under which murder was a variant of the

---

[94] Fifoot (1959), at 23, cited by Smith (1998), at 364.
[95] On the progressive cast to intellectuals' contributions to thinking about law reform in the nineteenth century, see Smith (1998), at 141–2.
[96] Smith (1991), at 145. The Code became law in India in 1860.
[97] See Leader-Elliot (2010).
[98] A colonial administrator as well as historian and poet.
[99] For an outstanding discussion of Macaulay's work, see Chan *et al* (2011).
[100] Council Minute (11 May 1835), at 148, cited by Smith (1998), at 140 fn 89.
[101] On which, see text at n 69 above.
[102] The following description of the Model is taken from Morgan (2011), at 66.
[103] Smith (1998), at 141. We will encounter later more modern examples where substantive policy changes have been presented as merely 'technical' drafting changes, thus keeping them within the realm of the experts.

generic offence of 'culpable homicide' (a model employed, as Macaulay was aware, under the 1810 *Code Pénale* in France). 'Voluntary culpable homicide' was committed where the accused intended to kill or knew that death was likely (variations on forms of fault common in mainland European jurisdictions: *dolus directus* and *dolus indirectus*). Voluntary culpable homicide was murder unless it was committed under the terms of one of three special exceptions: provocation, consent, or excessive private defence (again, exceptions following a model such as that to be found in the German criminal code). Much clearer and simpler though Macaulay's approach might have been, the protective covering over its highly liberal-progressive character, provided by the claim that it is linguistic and doctrinal simplification that is intended, is nothing more than a fig leaf. Macaulay's definition of murder introduces the 'correspondence principle'—hitherto unknown to English law—to the law of murder:[104] D was not to be convicted of murder unless he or she intended to cause death or least knew that death was likely to occur. So, as Morgan points out in his discussion of Macaulay's Code,[105] where (for example) D subjected V to invasive surgery without anaesthetic for the pleasure of torturing him or her, but accidently killed V in so doing, under the liberal-progressive view embodied in Macaulay's Code, that would not be murder. The living embodiment of John Austin's law reform pipe-dream,[106] unaccountable to the public in his decision to pursue a liberal-progressive agenda in the name of linguistic simplification, it is small wonder that Macaulay's newly minted correspondence principle to govern the scope of murder was so radically modified in the Indian Penal Code itself.[107] Rejecting the correspondence principle, the Code extended the scope of murder beyond the limits set by Macaulay, to include:

300. Murder.—Except in the cases hereinafter excepted, culpable homicide is murder...

3rdly.-If it is done with the intention of causing bodily injury to any person and the bodily injury intended to be inflicted is sufficient in the ordinary course of nature to cause death, or-

4thly.-If the person committing the act knows that it is so imminently dangerous that it must, in all probability, cause death, or such bodily injury as is likely to cause death, and commits such act without any excuse for incurring the risk of causing death or such injury as aforesaid.

The liberal-progressive character of Macaulay's murder provisions was, though, successfully enhanced by the proposed 'consent defence',[108] which made its way into exception (5) in section 300 of the Indian Penal Code. This was another change without precedent in English law, which had struggled for more than two

---

[104] The more common, subjectivist, version of the 'correspondence principle' requires an element of subjective fault (usually intention or recklessness) to correspond to all the 'external' elements of the offence: see Ashworth (1993).

[105] Morgan (2011), at 66.

[106] See text cited at n 93 above.

[107] The modifications came about when the draft passed through the hands of the judges of the Calcutta Supreme Court, of which Sir Barnes Peacock was the first Chief Justice.

[108] That was a partial defence, leading to a much more lenient maximum sentence, as under s 216 of the 1871 German Penal Code.

hundred years to civilize society by asserting the authority of the law of murder where consent to the risk of killing—if not to killing itself—was in issue in fatal duelling cases.[109] Predictably enough, exception (5) gave rise to a series of cases that brought into question the law of murder's claim to have a civilized scope and application. Exception (5) naturally applied to an almost unrestricted range of allegedly consensual 'mercy' killings and assisted suicides; but the courts felt obliged to go further. They held that if V consented to be castrated, and the operation accidentally killed him, that was also not murder.[110] They also found that if V consented to be killed in order to drive the devil out of her, that was also only culpable homicide not amounting to murder.[111]

In the modern era, the unique success of Macaulay's Code, when compared with the frustrations experienced by Austin, has cast a long shadow. It has given rise to a number of recurring themes or assumptions in scholarly or expert debates about criminal law reform. Three important themes or assumptions are that:

(a) reform is best left in the hands of independent or 'free-floating' scholars and experts whose (liberal-progressive) principles are better suited to infuse the content of the law than merely pragmatic or compromise solutions that seek to accommodate a range of interests;

(b) scholars and experts must be involved in any law reform process because of their technical or 'craft' skills in fashioning the right kind of legislation; and

(c) technical or craft skills extend to a proper understanding of so-called 'juristic principles' or 'basic rules' whose status as such is a matter determined by experts rather than by law-makers.

So far as (b) and (c) are concerned, for example, it is common to find some scholars denigrating Government-inspired criminal law reform as, 'mere politicking rather than deliberate *craftsmanship*',[112] in that '[s]tatutes, which are generally drafted by Government officials, often neglect juristic principles',[113] being 'inartistically drawn'.[114] The image conjured by such legal scholars is of a world in which criminal law reform is and should be a matter of artisan or guild craftwork, unsullied by mere 'politicking', and instead fashioned in accordance with a set of ends determined (to use Glanville Williams' words) by 'open Government using the best brains of the legal profession [shaped by] reasoned consideration and

---

[109] See Horder (1992d). Exception (5) to s 300 of the Indian Penal Code read as follows: 'culpable homicide is not murder when the person whose death is caused, being above the age of eighteen years, suffers death or takes the "risk" of death with his own consent'.

[110] *The Queen v Baboolun Hijrah* (1866) 5 WR (Cr) 7.

[111] (Unreported) Cr.R.C. No. 646 of 1925, discussed in *Re Kanaga Kosavan Alias v Unknown* (1931) 60 MLJ 616.

[112] Robinson, Cahill, and Mohammed (2000), at 64 (my emphasis).

[113] Williams (1983), at 18. See further Spencer (2008a), at 595 (my emphasis): 'When blunders take the form of overlooking *basic rules*, the explanation can only be that those who prepare the legislation . . . lack a basic knowledge of the underlying law, and do not trouble to consult with those who have the knowledge they do not.'

[114] Williams (1983), at 17.

consensual amendment'.[115] This technocratic image of law reform was perhaps popularized, in the world of the 1950s and 1960s in which the twentieth century founders of criminal law scholarship came to prominence, by the influence of mid-twentieth century proponents of Government through expert-led social and economic planning.[116] Leading criminal law scholars of that time perhaps saw themselves as akin to their scientific colleagues, about whom Prime Minister Harold Wilson said that they constituted:

a reservoir of unused and underused talent, of skill and craftsmanship, of inventiveness, and ingenuity, of administrative ability and scientific creativeness which if mobilised will, within a measurable period of time enable us to become—not the workshop of the world; that is no longer our role—but the pilot plant, the tool room of the world. Our scientists are among the finest in the world. The tragedy is we don't produce enough of them, and those we do produce we do not use intelligently. . . .[117]

Imagining oneself as such as an underused expert resource may easily, though, turn into the promotion of what Williams' contemporary, Lord Scarman, criticized as the idea that there is a 'cosy little world of lawyer's law in which learned men may frolic without raising controversial issues'.[118] Moreover, a sleight of hand is involved in such a move.

2. Unmasking the 'technocrats'

The association of scholarly input with 'craftsmanship' or 'technical [criticisms] related to . . . drafting',[119] portrays the scholar as akin to (albeit practicing a different craft from) a legislative drafter endowed with 'the particular mental skills which as a group they [drafters] have, the first of which is an astonishing ability to see their way through linguistic mazes in which normal mortals are likely to get lost'.[120] In that respect, no one puffed up the importance of the drafter's craft more than the so-called 'father' of Parliamentary draftsmanship, Lord Thring, who said, relying on Austin:

Mr Austin, no mean authority, writes in his work on Jurisprudence, 'I will venture to affirm that what is commonly called the *technical* part of legislation is incomparably more difficult than what may be called the *ethical*. In other words, it is far easier to conceive justly what would be useful law, than so to construct that same law that it may accomplish the design of the law giver.'[121]

Yet, what we must bear in mind is that the technical skill of the drafter cannot be equated to what is portrayed as the 'craft' of the scholar, in the passages from

---

[115] *Ibid*, at 18.
[116] See Sampson (1962), at 248 and 454.
[117] Harold Wilson, Speech at National Press Club, Washington, 1 April 1963, in Wilson (1964), at 215–16.
[118] Scarman (1968), at 25, cited by Wells (1980), at 689.
[119] Spencer (2008a), at 590.
[120] *Ibid*, at 596, speaking of the art of the drafter.
[121] Lord Thring (1902), introduction (his emphasis).

scholarly writing just cited. Those who draft legislation do so in order to implement policy decided on by others, *not* to implement their own policies: so a drafter may say, 'if you are going to do this (stupid) thing, at least do not do it in this (stupid) way'. Scholarly experts, by way of contrast, are prone to elide the distinction between what Lord Thring called the 'technical' and the 'ethical' part of law-making, when they speak approvingly of legislative drafting only when it embodies (liberal-progressive) 'juristic principles' and supposedly 'basic rules'[122] of criminal liability.[123] That, largely unacknowledged, merging of the technical and the moral or political brings us to (a) above[124]—the idea that law reform is best guided by the (liberal-progressive) principles of criminal liability expounded by scholars.

So far as (a) is concerned, many scholarly legal experts believe either that the criminal law possesses, 'features or characteristics that *most theorists* regard as crucial if impositions of criminal liability are to satisfy *our* principles of justice',[125] or that if the criminal law does not actually possess these (liberal-progressive) features or characteristics in practice, it should be deemed to do so.[126] This means that, when seeking to reform the law, other groups with an interest in law reform should consult, or perhaps ideally defer to, such experts on the nature of these features or characteristics.[127] In the homicide context, Spencer, for example, has argued on the following lines:

> That the present law of murder is unsatisfactory most *commentators* would agree. In a nutshell, the basic offence is too broad and the available defences are too narrow, and the resulting injustices are much exacerbated by the fact that it carries a life sentence.[128]

Very plain here is the association between a cadre of expert commentators on homicide law, and the determination to infuse the law with liberal-progressive principles. One such principle commanding widespread scholarly assent is that murder should be confined, in point of fault element, to instances in which

---

[122] Spencer's phrase: see Spencer (2008a), at 595, speaking of the presumption of fault principle. The 'basic-ness' of this example of Spencer's basic rules may in fact be questioned. As he must be well aware, the presumption of fault principle is very far from being 'basic', if the practice of the courts is anything to go by, because the courts have never made it clear when it does and does not apply: see Horder (2002b).

[123] For an example where substantive criticism of a Government restriction on the scope of a sexual offence, by confining it to those acting 'for the purpose of obtaining sexual gratification', is presented as nothing more than supposedly 'technical' criticism of drafting, see Spencer (2008a), at 590–1. Spencer effectively merges a technical critique of the (stupid) way in which legislation is drafted with a substantive critique—with which, as it happens, I agree—of the relevant (stupid) legal provision.

[124] See text following n 111 above.

[125] Husak (2008), at 34 (my emphasis).

[126] Ashworth, for example, speaks of the 'rhetoric' of English law, in relation to its (liberal-progressive) commitment to what Spencer regards as 'basic' rules (see n 122 above) of criminal liability or culpability: Ashworth (2000), at 228. Ashworth has the better of it here, because the criminal law's commitment to, for example, the presumption of fault has indeed largely been rhetorical, but in a way that does not matter. What matters is the maintenance of the liberal-progressive *image* of English criminal law, which scholars are meant to be especially well-placed to explain.

[127] See, eg, Spencer (2008a), at 600–1.

[128] Spencer (2008b), at 5 (my emphasis).

D intentionally killed V.[129] Having initially consulted on the adoption of such a narrow fault element for first degree murder,[130] the Law Commission found consultees divided on the issue[131] and hence recommended a marginally broader fault element:

We recommend that first degree murder should encompass:

(1) Intentional killings, and

(2) Killings with the intent to do serious injury where the killer was aware that his or her conduct involved a serious risk of causing death.[132]

It is rightly considered to be one of the primary tasks of a Law Commission to seek to secure the widest measure of agreement, and of willingness to compromise, amongst consultees. However, for some expert or scholarly commentators, it seems that the move to the broader definition of the fault element for murder was an example of preferring mere 'pragmatism' over principle. Ashworth has suggested that:

The most significant change from the consultation paper is the widening of the ambit of murder 1: given the strong arguments of principle adduced in the consultation paper for restricting murder 1 to cases of an intent to kill, the change is introduced on the basis that it creates 'a greater measure of consensus'. Of course there are arguments of principle in favour of both the narrow and the broader scope of murder 1, but it was clearly pragmatism that brought about change.[133]

What is left unclear by this criticism is why an official law reform body seeking to make the most of a consultation exercise in what is, as Ashworth rightly says,[134] a highly politically charged area, should stand firm in resisting 'pragmatic' considerations when shaping its recommendations. Ashworth does not himself put forward a definition of what is 'pragmatic' as opposed to 'principled', but in the context of this discussion, an understanding of both is essential.

I will, speaking loosely, take arguments or statements of 'principle' to be arguments or statements about what ought (morally) to be done, either as a matter of individual or group conduct, or—more significantly in this context—in connection with political and legal governance and change. Naturally, arguments or statements of principle in this sense can be 'moral' even if they are observed only by a minority. Thus, when Husak and Spencer speak of the liberal-progressive principles widely accepted respectively by 'theorists' or 'commentators', they are articulating a set of moral principles espoused and advocated by a relatively distinct but loosely associated minority, although of course these principles may be accepted or championed by others outside that particular minority group. In that regard, though, a distinguishing feature of theorists or commentators is that they do not see

---

[129] Putting aside, for the purposes of the present discussion, issues about the meaning of 'intention', or defences to murder.

[130] Law Commission (2005).   [131] Law Commission (2006), at paras 2.53–2.54.

[132] *Ibid*, at paras 2.50–2.69.   [133] Ashworth (2007), at 343.

[134] *Ibid*, at 342.

themselves as in quite the same 'boat' as other groups with a shared moral or principled outlook on homicide law reform. As we will see in more detail below, theorists or commentators do not believe that they should be treated as mere stakeholders, such as victims' family representatives or more narrowly focused groups such as Dignity in Dying, Victim Support, or the Lawyers' Christian Fellowship.[135] The expert status of theorists or commentators means that when making any change to the criminal justice system the Government must, according to Spencer, '*In particular*... be prepared to talk to the judges, who run the system and will have to implement the changes, and to academics working in the area, who spend their lives thinking and writing about it.'[136] So, the claim more generally seems to be that scholars have a special claim to the ear of Government on matters of 'juristic principles' (subject to any input from the judges, who will be running the system in accordance with those principles); but how secure is such a claim?

3. Legal scholars: high priests of principle, or mere liberal-progressive stakeholders?

There is, of course, such a thing as legal expertise;[137] and something has gone wrong with the law reform process if experts in an area of law are never consulted on what it would be right to do if that area of law is to be reformed. Such a failure to consult experts will be particularly remiss if a proposed change makes assumptions about empirical evidence that may not be justified, or if it fails to attend to (say) a history of the failure of similar reforms.[138] Furthermore, there may be nothing very wrong with (indeed, there may be much to be said in favour of) liberal-progressive principles as a guide when changing the law.[139] These two things— becoming a legal expert and espousing liberal-progressive principles—should not, though, be run together such that to take expert advice on (homicide) law reform will entail accepting such principles. Commendably, Spencer recognizes this when, comparing the English law of homicide unfavourably with French homicide law, he concludes:

[I]n France, the penalty for murder is effectively in the discretion of the court at trial. . . . [I]n French law, the equivalent of murder has always been defined in such a way as to limit it to killings that are intended. . . . In all of these respects, the French law of murder conforms to the shape that *liberal reformers* in this country have usually advocated for the law of murder

---

[135] Alongside theorists and scholars, with their particular 'take' on liberal-progressive legal principles, other groups consulted by the Law Commission in its work on murder included, for example, 'Care Not Killing Alliance', 'Dignity in Dying', 'Rights of Women', and the 'Lawyers' Christian Fellowship', amongst others: see Law Commission (2006), app G.

[136] Spencer (2008a), at 600 (my emphasis).

[137] See Harris (1979), at 46, discussed in Horder (2006), at 80.

[138] See, eg, the excellent analysis by Zimring of the deficiencies of the legislative process leading up to the passing of the 'three strikes and you are out' law in California: Zimring (1996–97).

[139] See, eg, Horder (2004), chs 4–6.

here. That all this can be so in a country which faces similar social problems to our own . . . seems to me to give our liberal reformers a simple message: *bon courage*.[140]

As Spencer does here, legal experts should support the parts of their argument for change that rest on moral or political views as such, rather than wrapping them up as part of a purely casuistic or technical case for change. Why? Legal experts are best understood as just one set of stakeholders in the legal reform process amongst many. They provide a particular kind of input which others may not be able to replicate, but others—such as Victim Support, or victims' family groups—provide just as valuable an input (with a scope that may in principle be just as wide) on the same footing. In part, though, the role of the scholarly expert may be more modest in the case of homicide law reform because there is not as much need (although there is some) for technical skills or 'law-craft' as in other areas of law. As Ashworth himself remarks:

Reform of the criminal law is unavoidably political, and reform of homicide law is essentially political. There is no reason why lawyers should try to keep the cards close to their chests, and every reason to encourage public debate.[141]

This perfectly correct observation destabilizes the position of scholars accustomed to treating liberal-progressive principles as integral to the expert dimension of their craft that Government (they claim) ignores at its peril. Ashworth's observation rightly reduces scholars, along with judges, to the same level as other interest groups or stakeholders with a legitimate interest in homicide law reform, whether what is at stake is scholars' expertise or their moral and political opinions. It is at this level, along with every other stakeholder, where they belong, because public debate on law reform—especially law reform bearing on violative crime—should not take place only on in relation to a political and legal agenda set by experts.

Scholarly experts will naturally have strong views on the issues thrown up by homicide law reform; and the enduring value of free speech and independence in conducting university research demands that scholars remain free to develop those views in whatever ways they believe to be intellectually profitable. However, by presenting their moral or political arguments as if they were purely casuistic or technical, such would-be reformers may wrongly be seeking to establish or maintain a measure of expert authority over what ought to count as a good or decisive argument in this context.[142] In legal-theoretical terms, they may be seeking to persuade others to follow their advice in the form of a 'protected' reason, a reason not only to follow the advice but also to disregard advice to the contrary.[143] In some contexts in which experts give advice, there can be good reasons to persuade people to accept authority in this form. An example might be where a doctor seeks to persuade a patient who is a recovering alcoholic henceforth not only to accept the doctor's view that drinking alcohol is harmful and should be avoided,

---

[140] Spencer (2007), at 50 (my emphasis on 'liberal reformers').
[141] Ashworth (2007), at 342.
[142] On the nature of expert authority, see Raz (1979), at 21–2.
[143] For an explanation of protected reasons, see *Ibid*, at 16–19.

but also to disregard any arguments the patient might hear to the contrary that drinking some kinds of alcohol can be good for you. In practice, legal experts may seek to establish this kind of authority over others. So, civil servants, advised by Parliamentary Counsel,[144] may on occasion urge the Government not only to avoid the use of a particular form of wording in a new statute designed to achieve some desired end, but also to refuse to pay heed to attempts to persuade the Government of the virtues of that wording. In this context there is, though, something suspicious about such appeals to treat reasons to legislate, or to draft legislation in a certain way, as protected reasons, especially when it comes to the evaluation of moral and political arguments. When the latter are at stake, legal experts should not be seeking to persuade others rightly involved in that process to accept their authority in the sense just described, even if those others have only a poor or ill-founded grasp of the applicable moral or political arguments. As Herschovitz puts it:

It is harder to pick out experts in moral and political matters than it is in medical or musical matters. Indeed, some argue that there are no moral experts. . . . We are equals, and respecting this requires that we participate as equals in the decision-making process that orders much of our moral universe. Not only does democracy allow us to participate as equals, but it reinforces that status.[145]

Even if someone ('E') is said to be in some sense an expert on the moral and political considerations applicable in a particular context, it is wrong for E to seek to persuade others to regard E as an authority on those arguments, such that those others now believe that they have a reason not merely to follow E's advice but, crucially, *also* to disregard contrary advice that may be offered to them. That is not an appropriate way to exploit moral or political expertise, because it is an interference with 'republican' freedom, with the freedom (discussed further below) of *all* to seek truth and justice so that these may guide individuals and the state in their actions.[146]

4. Can scholarly work on homicide law reform bridge the 'legitimacy gap'?

During the second half of the twentieth century, liberal-progressive criminal law scholars began more consistently to attain positions of potential influence in the world of law and legal policy-making, both in England[147] and the

---

[144] For the expert basis of Parliamentary Counsel, in this respect, see the inimitable words of John Spencer (2008a), at 596, cited in the text at n 120 above.

[145] Hershovitz (2003), at 214.

[146] See Sellers (1991), at 273. See further the excellent discussion in Hershovitz (2003).

[147] JWC Turner had become the editor of *Russell on Crime*; Glanville Williams was a member of the Criminal Law Revision Committee from 1959–80; Sir John Smith, also a member of the Criminal Law Revision Committee, was a member of the Law Commission's codification team and knighted for services to law reform.

USA.[148] Indeed, Zimring goes so far as to argue that for a considerable post-war period, the Federal Government operated what he calls a 'hands-off' policy towards the administration of criminal justice, in deference to the experts at that time influential in directing it.[149] Yet, so far as the substantive criminal law is concerned, scholars in a position to influence public policy were never really subjected to a sociological investigation into the grounds of their knowledge.[150] They were thus free to remain comfortable in the illusion that the reforms they envisaged must inevitably be the product of, 'reasoned consideration and consensual amendment', using the 'best brains of the legal profession.[151] Yet, not long before this time, Karl Mannheim, the father of sociology of knowledge, had been developing, 'a scepticism towards knowledge-monopolising experts of all kinds . . .'.[152] For Mannheim:

[E]very historical, ideological, sociological piece of knowledge (even should it prove to be Absolute Truth itself) is clearly rooted in and carried by the desire for power and recognition of particular social groups who want to make their interpretation of the world the universal one.[153]

One can reject the crude relativism in this argument, whilst still taking note of the tendency of criminal law reform-minded scholars to rely (as judges a century before had done, in relation to common law values) on a supposed consensus behind their arguments, or on the universal appeal those arguments are imagined to have. Peter Glazebrook, for example, has sought to keep some aspects of homicide law reform above politics, by appealing not so much to Mannheim's 'Absolute Truth', but to a supposed universal consensus.[154] Speaking of the need for a 'lesser evils' defence, he suggests that one should be created to cover, amongst other things (a) obtaining an abortifacient to avert a threat of committing suicide, and (b) giving drugs which it is known will hasten death in order to keep a terminally ill patient free from pain.[155] Of these defences, he says, 'is there, one may ask, a single one of these decisions that is not eminently sensible, and does not represent a clear moral consensus in our society?'[156] He adds rhetorically:

[C]an it really be doubted that in England and Wales it is lawful to do *whatever* is known (and not criminal to do *whatever* is believed) to be necessary and is, in all the circumstances, reasonable . . . to avoid any injury (whether unlawful or not), or any pain or suffering (whether caused unlawfully or not); or . . . to discipline a child who is in one's care. . . . And

---

[148] I have in mind the issuing of the scholar–expert inspired Model Penal Code: see Dubber (2000–01). See further Zimring (1996–97) for some examples of important scholarly influence on criminal law and policy in the post-war USA.

[149] Zimring (1996–97), at 254.

[150] In his work on Karl Mannheim's seminal discussion of the sociology of knowledge, Wirth (1936) says of intellectuals, at xxxi, 'The composition of this group, their social derivation and the method by which they are recruited, their organisation, their class affiliation, the rewards and prestige they receive, their participation in other areas of social life, constitute some of the more crucial questions to which the sociology of knowledge seeks answers.'

[151] Williams (1983), at 18.　　　[152] Englund (2002), at 281.

[153] Mannheim (1928), at 196–7.　　　[154] Glazebrook (1996).

[155] *Ibid*, at 205–6.　　　[156] *Ibid*, at 206.

if it cannot reasonably be doubted, ought not these eminently rational propositions to find a place in *any* codification of general defences...?[157]

I do not believe that this kind of justification for homicide reform should now pass muster. It cannot stand alongside what Ashworth rightly calls the 'unavoidably political' nature of the process governing homicide law reform.[158] What Glaze-brook presents as that which 'cannot reasonably be doubted', and as 'eminently sensible [or]...rational', is for many, highly controversial. For example, can it really 'not reasonably be doubted' that the use of lethal force should fall outside the scope of the criminal law merely because it is wrongly believed—however contemptibly inadequate the grounds—to be necessary? Appeals by scholars to what they claim to be 'eminently rational' (in a seemingly questionable sense of 'beyond argument') will inevitably fail in the modern world. As we shall see, Glazebrook would have done better to focus on what he calls the 'clear moral consensus' about the examples he discusses, but with the benefit of professionally researched evidence for this consensus, rather than assertion, to support his claim.

5. Scholars as educators in the public domain: letting go of judicial coat-tails

This brings me back to the nature of 'pragmatism' in Ashworth's argument about homicide law reform.[159] There is a more or less explicit assumption made by all the groups bound by shared principles—including liberal-progressive scholars—seeking an input into law reform. This is, when it comes to political and legal change, that:

(a) unless one group's claim is given privileged or protected status, the only alternative is,

(b) marriages of pure convenience or accommodations between the rival claims of such groups.

This line of thought, in relation to reaching moral as well as legal judgement, has a long intellectual history, dating back at least as far as JS Mill, who argued in his famous essay, 'On Liberty':

Truth in the great practical concerns of life, is so much a question of the reconciling and combining of opposites that very few have minds have sufficiently capacious and impartial to make the adjustment with an approach to correctness, and it has to be made by the rough process of a struggle between combatants fighting under hostile banners.[160]

So far as (a), privileged status, is concerned, here is a reason why legal experts tend to perceive, and jealously to guard, their liberal-progressive moral and political principles as in the domain of *Recht*, only fully accessible through expert opinion. It has to do with the strong association this standpoint has with what some take to

---

[157] *Ibid*, at 206–7. [158] See text at n 141 above.
[159] See text at n 133 above. [160] Mill (1859), ch 2, at para 36.

be the constitutional role of judges. In many liberal-progressive societies, higher court judges adhere to what John Rawls called 'certain fundamental intuitive ideas viewed as latent in the public political culture of a democratic society'.[161] In virtue of that adherence, it becomes part of the function of judges, and by extension part of the function of legal experts who teach, advise, or appear before them, to act as guardians of these 'fundamental intuitive ideas': a moral and legal code understood to be in some sense beyond mere politics. As Raz puts it:

> The courts are, or at least they should be, above the rough-and-tumble of everyday political pressures. They should be relatively immune to passing fashions. In constitutional matters they may succeed in representing a lasting consensus, even at times when prevailing trends disguise its existence from the majority of the public, and even in the face of a government whose reforming zeal blinds it to the need to preserve the fabric of the political culture.[162]

Whatever the merits of such a claim in constitutional law,[163] I hope that I have given sufficient reasons for thinking that, as a model for law reform, it lacks adequate legitimacy, whether it is judges or scholars who are accorded the privileged status of representing 'a lasting consensus'. When evaluating law reform proposals, it is wrong to suggest that judges and scholars are unaffected by (to use Raz's phrase) 'passing fashions', and it is insulting to politicians, civil servants, and the public to suggest that they cannot rise above such fashions, blind zeal, the rough-and-tumble of politics, and so on.[164]

So far as (b) above is concerned, if would-be law reformers can aspire to no better than marriages of convenience between rival groups and their viewpoints, the best that can be hoped for law reform is that it will be the product of a kind of inclusive, interest-group pluralism, in which the views of as wide as range as possible of groups or stakeholders are accommodated. On that assumption—an assumption that, I suggest, underlies Ashworth's critique of the Law Commission recommendations on the fault element for first degree murder—pragmatism turns out to be little more than, 'taking the line of least resistance'. Pragmatism is presented as seeking to please the greatest number of people or groups to some extent, even if that means pleasing no individual or group completely. As a characterization of decision-making by the Law Commission, or by the Government when it decides on change, in the light of consultation, this understanding of pragmatism has some truth to it. However, to concentrate solely on the element of truth in that impoverished understanding of pragmatism is to overlook a richer and more important sense of 'pragmatism' in which interest-group pluralism is seen as part of a wider project of engaging the public in the search for a just law of homicide (considered below).

---

[161] Rawls (1987), at 6.   [162] Raz (1986), at 260.   [163] For criticism, see Waldron (1993).
[164] Further, who is to know which of these proposals has been mis-labelled and will in fact become part of a 'lasting consensus'? The movement to abolish the death penalty would unquestionably have been regarded by senior judges as no more than a passing liberal fashion 50 years ago: see Bailey (2000). Now, senior judges would almost all regard the death penalty's unconstitutionality as part of our 'lasting consensus'. The difference between 'passing fashion' and 'lasting consensus' is itself a matter of moral and political disagreement.

I conclude, then, that homicide law reform is not best left in the hands of scholarly experts, any more than it is best left to judges. However, a final point about the role of experts raised by Mannheim's work is worth dwelling on. Mannheim's bleak-sounding description of claims to knowledge as a kind of Nietzschean 'will to power' is not, when understood in context, in fact just an example of the kind of implausible non-cognitivism popular among some philosophers at that time in England.[165] For Mannheim, the importance of exposing epistemological weaknesses in the claims to authority of 'knowledge-monopolising experts' was in fact to encourage them to turn away from power-seeking for themselves. Instead, under his theory, experts would turn towards the liberation (through education) of the capacity in every citizen to aspire to knowledge and critical self-consciousness him or herself, and hence gain greater control over his or her destiny. So, ironically, a crucial role in Mannheim's thinking *was* to be played by the educated elite, his (in)famous 'free-floating intelligensia'.[166] Liberated in the formulation of ideas from the influence of class such intellectuals could 'achieve transformative social actions as an expression of their emancipation from the constraints of ideology'.[167] Such 'transformative actions' would not come about, though, through intellectuals' domination of the legal and political process. Instead, the role of the intelligensia was, through education of fellow citizens, to keep an ever widening and more demanding process of democratization in step with the ever more complex and publicly inaccessible process of understanding advances in natural and social (including legal) science.[168]

We can think of this role for scholars as one in which they seek to bridge or narrow what can be called the 'legitimacy gap'. As we have already seen, some sentencing theorists in Mannheim's time were well aware of this gap, arguing for example that, if the sentencing process became too remote from the viewpoint of ordinary citizens, 'the moral judgments of those who represent the State... will cease to be taken seriously'.[169] In that respect, on Mannheim's view, the role of the intelligentsia was to shift the focus of education away from the transmission of the ideals of elite culture, to the creation of a generation of citizens from all classes with sufficient social awareness to make and act on informed political judgements themselves.[170] Mannheim's own interest in developing this role for the intelligentsia in bridging the legitimacy gap concerned teaching,[171] but one may also seek to draw out some implications for legal research. Scholarly legal experts come closest to bridging the legitimacy gap between, on the one hand, an enfranchised but inadequately (or wrongly) informed populace, and on the other hand, themselves, Government, and the ruling elite, when they subject law reform options to methodologically sound empirical testing in the public domain. This is in part because, as part of that testing, it will be essential to inform participating members

---

[165] See, eg, Stevenson (1944). See further the discussion of intuitions in section V.2. below.

[166] 'Intellectual activity is not carried on exclusively by a socially rigidly defined social class, such as a priesthood, but rather by a social stratum which is to a large degree unattached to any social class and which is recruited from an increasingly inclusive area of social life': Mannheim (1936), at 139.

[167] Kettler and Meja (1993), at 9.   [168] Kettler, Volker, and Stehr (1984), at 20.

[169] Ewing (1929), at 95.   [170] See generally, Loader and Kettler (2002).

[171] Mannheim (1951); Loader and Kettler (2002).

of the public of the applicable rules, so that they can critically engage with the reform proposals they have been asked to evaluate.[172] That is, of course, to take nothing away from the importance of the work done by legal scholars in generating and debating ideas for their own sake; but in engaging in that work, legal scholars have too often confused two perspectives on scholarship rightly distinguished by Waldron, in discussing political philosophy and political philosophers.

On the one hand, a scholar can be passionate partisan of a particular theory, albeit remaining (in a Cartesian spirit) open to his or her own self-criticism.[173] On the other hand, scholars, as a community, must accept the limits to as well as the possibilities of the market-place of ideas in which they make their contribution. That means accepting that, as Waldron puts it, 'it is wrong to expect any particular theory, no matter how attractive or well-argued, to survive the process of debate unscathed'.[174] In the world of law reform, especially the reform of violative crime, that means being honest about the moral and political values informing one's proposals, and hence accepting that the proper working of the democratic process *itself* entails that those values cannot and should not gain acceptance simply because scholars earnestly and passionately believe them to be true values.

IV. Officialdom, Interest Group Pluralism, and the Myth of Public Consultation

1. The Law Commission in the shadow of the CLLPU

If neither judges nor legal experts should by themselves be expected to take the leading role in homicide law reform, then who should? One option is to establish a body of civil servants who can develop an expertise in that role yet remain directly accountable to Government ministers. Another option is to establish an official or quasi-official body more independent of Government, perhaps comprised of an array of judges, experts, practitioners, and others (as seems appropriate), that reports to the civil service or directly to ministers. So far as the criminal law is concerned, in post-war England and Wales we have come to have both, in the shape of the Criminal Law and Legal Policy Unit ('CLLPU') within the Ministry of Justice's Justice Policy group, and the Law Commission for England and Wales. It may seem strange to be discussing a shadowy Unit within a Government department alongside the much-discussed role of the Law Commission in law reform. Surely, it might be said, civil servants are there to give confidential advice to but ultimately to do ministers' bidding, whereas the role of the Law Commission—albeit paid for by Government—is to debate proposals publicly, being free to reach its conclusions independent of ministerial thinking? That picture over-simplifies matters. In any event, it is what links the two bodies together, a shared

---

[172] See Roberts (1992); Mitchell and Roberts (2011).
[173] Waldron (1993), at 31.   [174] *Ibid.*

foundation stone of their legitimacy, that concerns me in this context: the duty to consult publicly.

For much of the post-war period, criminal law reform was looked after by Home Office Unit C4, which also had within its remit criminal injuries compensation, criminal procedure, criminal evidence, and (latterly) victims' rights. Following Labour's election victory in 1997, the Unit has undergone two transformations. In 1997, following a senior management review, the Sentencing and Offences Unit was created, to combine the functions of two formerly separate Units, dealing with both criminal law reform and sentencing. Sentencing was split off from the new Unit's set of responsibilities in 2002. The Unit then became the Criminal Law Policy Unit, as part of the formation of two separate directorates covering correctional services and criminal justice (sentencing went with correctional services, criminal law reform staying with criminal justice). Criminal evidence and procedure was also removed from the remit of what had been Unit C4, being taken by the Office for Criminal Justice Reform (and within that, the Better Trials Unit). In terms of numbers of civil servants working on reform of the substantive criminal law, these grew from around twelve in the 1980s, to about fifteen in the 1990s, to about twenty-five (not all working full-time) in 2002. The Criminal Law Policy Unit—now the CLLPU—is divided into teams looking at different areas of the substantive criminal law. The work of the Unit is commonly divided into what might be called major projects, such as the Murder Review of 2005–06, that involved several people working full-time; smaller projects likely to generate clauses in larger Bills; implementation projects; EU work related to criminal projects; and some other ongoing projects.[175]

This brief history is a familiar Weberian one within bureaucratic organizations, of increasing specialization through concentration on particular areas of work. The CLLPU is not merely playing a key strategic role in criminal law reform (as a fringe member of the ruling elite[176]) but can claim—through its increased specialization over time—to have achieved expert status in the performance of that role. In that regard, of course, the Head of the CLLPU has direct access to ministers, the kind of access craved by criminal law scholars, and enjoyed by judges until the latter part of the twentieth century. Hence, the CLLPU's Head's advice is more likely that of, say, the Law Commission, to be taken not only as correct but as a 'protected reason' in the sense described above.[177] That is to say, much of his or her advice will probably be taken by the relevant minister as authoritative, 'as both a reason for action and an exclusionary reason for disregarding conflicting reasons'.[178] When the CLLPU's advice also wholly or largely reflects the views of the Law Commission on the same subject, then the case for taking it as authoritative is

---

[175] What is now the CLLPU should certainly have attracted more scholarly interest from criminal lawyers, but for some reason that has not been so.

[176] See n 2 above.

[177] Text at n 143 above.

[178] Raz (1979), at 21. Anyone who has ever watched a minister at the dispatch box fending off objections from other Members of the House by sticking faithfully to the arguments in his or her script will be familiar with this phenomenon.

enhanced. However, given the unique strategic position that it occupies, the authority of the CLLPU's advice is far from undermined if it contradicts the Law Commission's own views. Accordingly, not too much should be made of the Law Commission's vaunted claim to independence of Government, in reaching the recommendations it advises Government to accept.[179] The increasingly expert status of the CLLPU in relation to criminal law by its nature confers on the Unit's work an important degree of independence from the dictates of mere (ministerial) opinion. It is true that ministers can demand that certain specific policy objectives be pursued by the CLLPU, irrespective of what the CLLPU (or others) make of those objectives. However, that is not likely to happen, if it happens at all, before the CLLPU has already made substantial initial progress, in much the same way that the Law Commission does, on shaping policy objectives when looking into complex as well as controversial legal issues.

Whatever one's view about the relative significance of the CLLPU and the Law Commission, more significant is something that binds both the CLLPU and the Law Commission together, so far as the authority of their work is concerned. Society's increasing dependence on the expertise that comes with specialization in powerful bureaucracies can lead to alienation of the very (non-expert) citizens those organizations are there to serve,[180] widening the legitimacy gap referred to above.[181] It is reasonable to think that narrowing that gap is a particularly important concern when reform of violative crimes is being undertaken. What that means for both the CLLPU and the Law Commission, as official (bureaucratic) expert organizations, is that they must seek to differentiate, in one crucial respect, the way they reach judgement on the direction of law reform, from the way that judges or scholars reach the same judgements. Both bodies are now bound in practice to consult openly and in good faith on possible reforms, and to explain how and why any ultimate recommendations arise or depart from that consultation process. Both bodies—along with Government—are now in effect bound to accept that, in Mannheim's words, '[d]emocracy cannot exist unless *all* its institutions are thoroughly oriented to democratic ends'.[182] The consultation process—rather than claims to expertise or independence—is what is meant to put Mannheim's insight into practice, and ministers must by and large respect that, however strong their personal view on particular issues. Yet, how 'thoroughly oriented' (to use Mannheim's phrase) towards democratic ends are the consultation processes in which both of these bodies engage, processes the legitimacy of which lends a vital element of authority to their advice?

---

[179] Contrary to appearances, that is not to belittle the contribution of the Law Commission to law reform. The Commission does much of the 'heavy-lifting' in relation to the development of the template for reform in areas Government requests it to look into, work that it would be beyond the capacity of the CLLPU to do. The Commission thus often finds itself in a position to further its preferred agenda, in so far as it has one, simply because the CLLPU will not have the time and resources to go back (and re-write), rather than taking that agenda forward.

[180] See, more generally, on specialization, Baurmann (2002), at 13–15.

[181] On which, see text following n 168 above.

[182] Mannheim (1951), at 173 (my emphasis).

2. Keeping it in the family: the CLRC and 'public' consultation

It is instructive to begin answering this question with the work on homicide of the first semi-official body set up in the post-war period to look at reform of the criminal law, the Criminal Law Revision Committee, and how its recommendations were adapted by the Law Commission as part of its codification project. When working on its Fourteenth Report,[183] the CLRC did so with an impressively broad mandate under its terms of reference, 'to review the law relating to, and the penalties for, offences against the person, including homicide...'.[184] The Committee said that its aim was not to turn the common law into a code as such, but 'to lay a foundation of law which at some later date can either be brought into a code or used to make a code'.[185] This turned out to be a way of saying that substantial elements of the law were now to be re-written in such a way as to follow a more liberal-progressive agenda (in that respect, building on the reforms in the Homicide Act 1957), and carrying on the pattern set by Macaulay a century before.[186] However, before defending that claim in detail, we should note the important (albeit very limited) precedent set, in relation to consultation, by the CLRC in its approach to reform of the general criminal law.

By 1959, warring 'special interest' pressure groups had already become an important feature of the landscape confronted by officials exploring changes to homicide-related criminal law.[187] For example, just prior to the passing of the Road Traffic Act 1930,[188] the Pedestrian Association was set up in 1929[189] (in response to a report issued by the Royal Commission on Transport),[190] specifically to lobby the Government on behalf of pedestrians.[191] Predictably, the Pedestrian Association was opposed on many issues, such as the need for speed limits, by the Automobile Association (founded in 1905) and the Royal Automobile Club (founded in 1897). Significant amongst the Pedestrian Association's claims were that it had been formed, 'for the defence of public rights, especially of pedestrians'.[192] The Association saw itself, thus, as a special interest group engaging in a rights-based conflict with other rival groups representing different interests, in the struggle for influence over law reform. Indeed, the incoming Government of Ramsey MacDonald acknowledged as much in 1929, by giving the organization official recognition as a representative of pedestrian opinion, and established regular

---

[183] CLRC (1980).   [184] *Ibid*, at para 1.
[185] *Ibid*, at para 4.   [186] See Smith (1998), at 329–31.
[187] In some shape or form, of course, pressure or special interests groups have long been influential in law reform: see, eg, text at n 18 above. As we will see, it is their acknowledged status as 'stakeholders' who should always be consulted in relation to reform in certain areas that is a more modern development.
[188] By virtue of the 1930 Act, speed limits were abolished, but offences of reckless, dangerous, and careless driving were introduced as a 'replacement' of sorts for the abolition of these limits.
[189] AL Goodhart was its President from 1950 to 1962, almost immediately following his 20-year stint as Professor of Jurisprudence at Oxford.
[190] Royal Commission on Transport (1928–30).
[191] Pedestrians formed half of the roughly 7,300 annual deaths on Britain's roads at that time.
[192] See the brief history at <www.livingstreets.org.uk/about/our-history/>.

links for the organization with the Ministry of Transport.[193] That kind of pattern for purported engagement with the public—fostering links with lay pressure groups, whose support could then provide legitimacy for law reform proposals— was soon to become the standard pattern for official consultative bodies, when what was in issue was the general law of homicide.

In its turn, the CLRC also embraced a consultative approach of an interest group kind, but a rudimentary one (and by invitation only).[194] It received evidence from some lay and legal pressure groups, such as the Voluntary Euthanasia Society[195] (founded in 1935) and Women for Life (a pro-life organization), and also from expert groups such as the Royal College of Psychiatrists.[196] In one way, this constituted a major contrast to the far more elitist manner in which so many law reform proposals had been drawn up in the past. Even so, as a consulta- tion exercise, this was little more than a conversation between friends;[197] and the CLRC was criticized at the time for having done too little to make it clear how, if at all, it had been influenced by the evidence it received. Wells remarked at the time:

[The CLRC] gives the overriding impression that, by issuing a Working Paper and receiving comments thereon, it has successfully confronted the problem. Thereafter, it can select which comments are to be taken as valuable without much more. Of course, the Report is not all assertion and no argument. But far too much is.[198]

Ironically, as Wells indicates, the subject on which the CLRC had invited evidence from rival lay organizations—euthanasia—was the one key area in which the CLRC found itself unable or unwilling to enter into any kind of controversy. In its 'disarmingly coy',[199] conclusion on this issue the CLRC said, 'we were reminded that we were dealing with a fundamental ethical problem and that as lawyers we had no special qualifications or experience for solving it'.[200] This claim misses what should have been the whole point of the consultation with the pro- choice and pro-life groups invited to give evidence, namely that they could provide (albeit on a partisan basis) some knowledge and experience on which the CLRC could then rely in reaching a conclusion. The claim also assumes—perhaps, pre- dictably—that the determination of such a matter is something purely for 'experts', but just a different set of experts (whoever they might be). More significantly for present purposes, there is no reference to the fact that, at that time, roughly 70 per cent of the population believed in legalizing euthanasia in some (restricted)

---

[193] See *ibid*. Amongst the Association's successes were the introduction of pedestrian crossings and driving tests, and of an obligation to build pavements.

[194] CLRC (1980), at para 2.

[195] As it was then known. It is now Dignity in Dying.

[196] In addition to receiving comments from the more usual suspects, such as the Senate of the Inns of Court and the Bar, the Police Federation, and the Association of Chief Police Officers.

[197] It is worth reminding ourselves that Glanville Williams, as well as having been a long-standing member of the CLRC, had also publicly supported and been Vice-President of the Euthanasia Society (as it was then known) at a time when the Society was trying to broaden its popular support as well as to influence legal change.

[198] Wells (1980), at 689.   [199] *Ibid*, at 681.   [200] CLRC (1980), at para 23.

form.[201] By contrast, at crucial junctures, the CLRC places reliance on what it takes 'public opinion' to be, gleaned from the evidence given by the very limited range of interest groups who gave evidence. Yet, the CLRC neither conducts any empirical research into public opinion, nor cites any existing research of this kind, nor recommends that the Government do either of these things before legislating. What is assumed on flimsy evidence to be the public's opinion is invoked in a quite cynical way, only when it suits the CLRC to refer to it, in search of a justification for its own view. An example crying out for some basic research into public opinion arises from the CLRC's rejection of the Law Commission's former view that the offence of murder should be abolished.[202] The explanation, at the outset of the CLRC's discussion of murder, is that:

As far as we have been able to judge from the memoranda submitted to us the public generally wants murder to be retained as a separate offence. If we were to propose the abolition of the separate crime of murder...many people would certainly find it hard to appreciate that the proposal was not meant to weaken the law and would be likely to think that law no longer regarded the intentional taking of another's life as being especially grave.[203]

There is a pointed contrast between the way in which these two points in favour of murder's retention is made. The first appears—on the surface at least—to grant the public the intelligence to understand what, morally speaking, is desirable by way of structure in the law of homicide. By way of contrast, the second is the classic 'counsel of despair' respecting public opinion: as the public will misunderstand ('desirable') proposal A as having ('undesirable') consequence B, ('desirable') proposal A, the more liberal-progressive proposal to abolish murder, cannot be recommended. Had the CLRC bothered to look into the matter, it would have found that properly conducted public opinion polls on murder had in fact been commissioned at regular intervals from at least some thirty years before that supported its position on the retention of the murder category. In 1948, one poll investigated the public's views on whether degrees of murder should be introduced, to confine the use of the death penalty to the 'worst' cases.[204] The results at that time were discouraging for would-abolitionists: only 7 per cent of those polled preferred this course, as opposed to 69 per cent who favoured retention of the death penalty (as much on a just deserts as on a deterrence basis) in all murder cases.[205]

[201] Of course, polling can be a simplistic and misleading measure when complex issues such as euthanasia are being discussed: see, eg, <www.carenotkilling.org.uk>. My point is about the CLRC's methodology.

[202] A view only now maintained by a few unrepentant and uncompromising consequentialists unwilling to acknowledge the deep significance of the intrinsic value of preserving (in both morality and law) certain labels, such as 'murder': see, eg, Morris and Blom-Cooper (2011). Even in his Preface to this work, the Lord Chief Justice cannot find it in himself to agree even to some extent with the conclusion so forcefully argued for by the authors.

[203] CLRC (1980), at 15.

[204] Mass-Observation Archive, File No. 2996, Capital Punishment Survey 9, cited by Bailey (2000), at 337.

[205] Modern polls tend to show dwindling, although still very substantial (around 50 per cent), support for the death penalty for all murders, and around 60–70 per cent of those polled supporting

However, what the poll did show was rock-solid implicit support for the crime of murder itself, howsoever defined. In the aftermath of the abolition of the death penalty for murder in 1965, polls continued to show strong support at the same level during the 1970s for the death penalty for murder, and (more importantly, in this context) by implication strong support for the separate crime of murder at the time of the CLRC's Report.

3. The view from nowhere: the CLRC's recommendations for homicide

Significantly, the views of the public are far less evident in relation to the CLRC's case for many of its recommendations for reform of homicide that *were* liberal-progressive in character. That is not surprising, especially in the light of legal developments elsewhere. Only four years prior to the CLRC's Report, in 1976, the US Supreme Court had reinstated the death penalty after a ten-year moratorium.[206] The main plank of the Court's justification, at a time of rising support for the death penalty (following historically low levels of support in 1960s America), was that strong majority support amongst the general public for that penalty showed that it could not be cruel and unusual. Putting aside the issue of the death penalty itself, and the sometimes questionable logic employed in the majority opinion, the case sent to the world the clearest possible warning that if liberal-progressive principles were to infuse the law of homicide, public opinion on such issues would have to be ignored.[207] There are, of course, many important arguments against unvarnished opinion poll-led policy formation,[208] but there are much more sophisticated ways of discerning lay opinion than through crude opinion polling.[209] More importantly, what justification was there for the CLRC (as a public body) to make no effort whatsoever to gauge public opinion, before pressing ahead with its main recommendations? Reviewing the work of the Law Commission in the 1970s, Farrar suggested that:

Commissioners, by analogy with Burke's conception of the role of a Member of Parliament, should give great weight to public opinion but ultimately should not sacrifice their 'unbiased opinion ... mature judgement ... and enlightened conscience' to it.[210]

Whatever one's view on this particular issue (addressed in the final section), implicit in it is a recognition that would-be law reformers on official bodies should at least try to discern what public opinion is on key issues. If they do not, they cannot avoid the accusation that they are treating their task in seeking an improved basis for law

---

the death penalty for some murders or murderers, such as murders of children, police officers, and serial killers: see <http://UKpollingreport.co.uk>.

[206] *Gregg v Georgia* (428 US 153, 1976).

[207] Which was precisely what liberal-progressive critics of the decision in *Gregg v Georgia* proposed to do: see, eg, Finckenauer (1988).

[208] See, in this respect, on *Gregg v Georgia*, Finckenauer (1988).

[209] See, in the homicide context, eg, Mitchell (1998); Mitchell (2000); Almond (2009).

[210] Farrar (1974), at 71.

reform as if it were indeed within Lord Scarman's 'cosy little world of lawyer's law in which learned men may frolic without raising controversial issues'.[211]

So, what were the liberal-progressive proposals for homicide reform treated in the way that Scarman feared by the CLRC? An example involves the case where death had been caused by an act involving recklessness as to the causing of serious harm, but not death.[212] The CLRC recommended removal of such cases from the scope of murder.[213] This recommendation was not justified by reference to the outcome of consultation. Instead, reference is made only to the CLRC's own opinion (twice) in the justifying paragraph.[214] In the CLRC's opinion, prominent amongst the reasons for its recommendation was the now very familiar subjectivist mantra that criminal liability should depend on 'intention or recklessness in relation to any [prohibited] result'.[215] This—the 'correspondence principle'—is, of course, a principle of scholarly invention that has never been, is not, and almost certainly never will be a legal principle governing the law of homicide in this, or in all probability in any other, legal system world-wide.[216] Why, then, should that principle have been introduced as a basis for recommending key changes to the law of homicide, without at least a recommendation that some rigorous investigation of its appeal to the public be undertaken by Government? As we now know, it is—and always has been—simply false to say that the public is incapable of understanding what is at stake in the scholarly debates relevant to the matter. As Robinson and Kurzban put it:

[C]ontrary to common wisdom, available evidence suggests that human intuitions of justice about core wrongdoing [including]...the relative seriousness of wrongdoing—are deep, predictable, and widely shared. While there are disagreements about the relative blameworthiness of wrongdoing outside the core, the core wrongs themselves...are the subject of nuanced and specific intuitions that cut across demographics.[217]

The CLRC did seek to justify its proposed restriction of the law of murder by reference to the consultation exercise, even if not by reference to public opinion. Putting aside cases of intention to kill, murder was to be restricted along 'Macaulay lines'[218] to cases in which D had intended serious injury, knowing that there was a risk of causing death.[219] This was apparently the view of the majority of those who commented on the proposals although some legal specialists apart, the only such commentators specifically mentioned are the Police Federation. However, the CLRC also acknowledged what they thought might turn out to be a weakness

---

[211] See text at n 118 above.
[212] The inclusion of such cases within murder had been re-affirmed in *DPP v Hyam* [1975] AC 55.
[213] CLRC (1980), at paras 20–1.
[214] *Ibid*, at para 20.
[215] Law Commission (1978), at para 89; CLRC (1980), at para 21.
[216] See the discussion in Horder (1997a).
[217] Robinson and Kurzban (2007), at 1892.
[218] See text at n 103 above. The CLRC does not refer to Macaulay in its reasoning.
[219] CLRC (1980), at para 28. This is the Law Commission's current position only in relation to first degree murder: see Law Commission (2006).

in such a restriction.[220] They alluded to public fears about terrorist actions taking the form of leaving bombs and giving warnings as to when they would explode, when despite the warnings the bombs did explode and kill. In such cases, there was as such no intention to cause death or even serious injury, but given the indifference to life involved why should such cases be treated as manslaughter only?[221] Holding its nose, the CLRC said that although it could not itself recommend it, Parliament might well have a different opinion, and adopt a wider definition of murder capable of covering such cases (as, broadly speaking, under Stephen's Code[222]). Under this wider definition, it would be murder to cause death through an act intended to cause fear of death or serious injury, and known to involve a risk of causing death.[223] Sharing the same liberal-progressive agenda as the CLRC, the Law Commission's subsequent Code team simply dropped this possible extension, without feeling the need for any further consultation on the issue. It said tersely, 'We do not regard it as a satisfactory provision'.[224] The team did not say who, apart from themselves, found it unsatisfactory, or why it was unsatisfactory.

More surprising was the CLRC's recommendation—without reference to its consultation exercise—that it should be manslaughter and not murder, 'where a defendant kills in a situation in which it is reasonable for some force to be used in self-defence but he uses excessive force'.[225] By way of contrast with the current law,[226] a manslaughter verdict was to be appropriate so long as D 'honestly believed that the force he used was reasonable in the circumstances',[227] even if that belief was attributable wholly to voluntary intoxication, and (in theory) even if the force used was grossly excessive.[228] Construed literally, this would have meant that almost any violent drunk who grossly overreacted by intentionally killing, in order to avoid the most minor unlawful push or shove, should be acquitted of murder.[229] What is striking is not so much the unattractiveness of such extreme subjectivism,[230] but the fact that it is justified solely by reference to the CLRC's own views, rather than to views of any of their consultees (still less, those of the public).[231]

---

[220] CLRC (1980), at paras 30–1.

[221] The issue has taxed many commentators, and was considered again in the Law Commission's more recent examination of the law of homicide: see Law Commission (2005); Pedain (2003).

[222] See text following n 69 above.

[223] The Law Commission's most recent recommendation is that such cases should be regarded as second degree murder: see Law Commission (2006).

[224] Law Commission (1989), at para 14.5.

[225] CLRC (1980), at para 288.

[226] Coroners and Justice Act 2009 ('the 2009 Act'), s 55(3).

[227] CLRC (1980), at para 288.

[228] *Ibid*, at para 277.

[229] One would have to go back to the quasi-justificatory approach of the eighteenth century to find a basis for reducing murder to manslaughter so generous to a display of grossly excessive violence in response to a minor threat or assault: see Horder (1992a), ch 2.

[230] The recommendation fails even to distinguish between mistakes as to the facts and mistakes on matters of evaluation, such as whether force is within the bounds of reasonableness.

[231] There is a marked contrast, thus, between the CLRC's recommendation and the Law Commission's recommendation in relation to the same issue, subsequently adopted in modified form in the 2009 Act, s 55(3). The latter was extensively discussed with those likely to affected by it: abused

Emboldened by the possibilities opened up by the absence of a need for much in the way of public accountability, the CLRC's proposed reforms for manslaughter took the liberal-progressive agenda even further. Manslaughter was to be confined to causing death with intent to do serious injury, or causing death being reckless as to whether death or serious injury was caused.[232] As the CLRC indicated, this recommendation would have required (at the very least) radical restriction of the offence of causing death by reckless driving, introduced only eight years previously after many years of campaigning and of genuine consultation with interest groups.[233] The recommendation would also have seen the end not only of manslaughter by unlawful and dangerous act, but also of gross negligence manslaughter.[234] The justification for this dramatic pruning of the law of manslaughter was that, at least in the case of manslaughter by unlawful and dangerous act, '[i]n our opinion, [it] should not be treated as manslaughter because the offender's fault falls far too short of the unlucky result'.[235] Characteristic of the CLRC's reliance on its own opinion is not only that it was formed without regard to public opinion at all, but that the CLRC does not say who from amongst their own consultees, if any, assented to their opinion. In fact, we are told only that it was opposed by the Senate of the Inns of Court and the Bar, and by the Prosecuting Solicitors' Society of England and Wales.[236] This is significant, in that, had the CLRC conducted or recommended research into public attitudes on the culpability issues in homicide cases, it might have found that those attitudes are inimical to the crude subjectivism of the CLRC. In broad terms, as Robinson and Darley put it, speaking of successful and unsuccessful attempts and of endangerment:

[T]he subjects [lay questionnaire respondents] as a group are objectivist as to grading, but subjectivist as to minimum requirements. If their subjectivist minimum requirements are met, they shift to their objectivist view to determine how much liability to impose.[237]

This strongly suggests (even if it does not prove) that if, in the eyes of the jury, the fault element passes a minimum threshold in unlawful act or gross negligence cases, then the fact that death has been caused *is* a reason to hold D criminally liable for causing that death, and is not just a matter of bad luck as the CLRC asserts. It suggests, in other words, that the correspondence principle is a principle alien to

---

women who kill their abusers, and (armed) police officers who overreact in seeking to prevent violent crime: Law Commission (2006), pt 5.

[232] CLRC (1980), at para 131.

[233] Road Traffic Act 1972, s 1. See CLRC (1980), at para 131. The offence, as originally enacted in 1972 extended to causing death by 'dangerous' driving, an extension removed by the Criminal Law Act 1977, s 50.

[234] Making, for example, the conviction of a company for manslaughter even more difficult than it was already; but corporate manslaughter was well beyond the CLRC's restricted field of vision.

[235] CLRC (1980), at para 56. Indeed, the CLRC would have gone still further, and abolished causing death through an intention to cause serious injury as a homicide offence, believing that, 'it may be that at some future date such a radical change from the present law will be acceptable': CLRC (1980), at para 55.

[236] CLRC (1980), at 57.

[237] Robinson and Darley (1998), at 430.

ordinary moral judgement in homicide cases.[238] The nuanced approach reflected by properly research public opinion was evident in a later study conducted by Robinson and others[239] in which, whilst those surveyed rejected the common view in the USA that an accidental killing in the course of a felony is murder, they nonetheless supported a conviction for manslaughter.[240] One study has shown that this kind of approach is also taken by the public in England towards, for example, drunk drivers who kill.[241] In such cases, latent knowledge of the risks of drinking and driving was regarded by those interviewed as being sufficient to justify conviction for manslaughter (not just for a road traffic offence), even in the absence of 'front of the mind' advertence to a risk.[242]

Lay people are not the wild-eyed retributivists that it suits many liberal-progressive scholars or would-be law reformers to regard them as being;[243] but neither are they wedded to the extreme subjectivism preferred by many such scholars or would-be law reformers. Naturally, the simple fact that lay opinion on culpability and harm in homicide cases rejects the full-blooded subjectivist version of the correspondence principle (supposing that it does reject it) cannot by itself *entail* that the principle should be rejected in law. My point here is that the CLRC failed in its duty, as a public body, by failing to investigate public opinion or by failing to recommend that Government undertake such an investigation. By undertaking or recommending such investigation, the CLRC could have sought to avoid the reliance on self-validating assertions concerning the correctness of liberal-progressive principles that underpin the bulk of its recommendations. In effect, the CLRC did more to widen the legitimacy gap than it did to improve the law of homicide.

4. *Plus ça change*: the failed codification project

Having said all that, we should acknowledge that the procedure adopted by the CLRC owes at least something to the developing idea that interest group pluralism is a way to manage the growing expectation that public opinion will feature in deliberations about the law reform process. However, in the development of the draft criminal code, in the light of the CLRC's recommendations, the Law

---

[238] Mitchell (2000) squeezed a droplet of support for the correspondence principle from his re-examination of a survey of public opinion on the law of homicide, but as only seven interviewees expressed a view, in his own words (at 820), 'it would be foolish to draw any clear conclusions'.

[239] Robinson *et al* (2010).

[240] *Ibid*, at 1978. The same study showed support for negligence-based liability, whilst rejecting purely strict liability.

[241] See Mitchell (2000), at 819.

[242] Mitchell (2000) interprets the interviewees' responses in a different way, as indicative of subjective 'pre-meditation' when drinking, and thus as support for a subjectivist approach to liability (at 819). However, that interpretation is, with respect, far-fetched. It fails to distinguish between the killer who drinks to excess in order, for example, to give himself the courage to drive in a manner posing a danger of death, and someone who drinks to excess without thinking of the possible consequences, or in the belief that he or she is safe to drive. In any event, no self-respecting subjectivist treats latent knowledge as on a par with patent knowledge.

[243] See, eg, Finckenauer (1988); Spencer (2008a), and text at n 308 below.

Commission did nothing over the next ten years to build further on this beginning. When the Law Commission was established in 1965, it was committed to move towards codification of the (criminal) law.[244] However, it is important to keep in mind that the criminal law codification project did not initially have the direct Government backing that the CLRC enjoyed in working on its Fourteenth Report. Instead, the project has its origins in an initiative of the (then) Society of Public Teachers of Law, which put forward the idea that a group of its own members should make codification proposals to the Law Commission.[245] Consequently, the most important work done towards this end was that of a sub-group from the Society, chosen by the Law Commission in 1981. It was this group that produced the renowned criminal code of 1989. As the Commission rightly said of the group, it brought to the codification project 'unrivalled knowledge . . . and the determination and industry which was essential to complete it'.[246]

By way of contrast with Commission itself, this sub-group was entirely comprised of academic lawyers.[247] Consequently, it bears the hallmarks of academic–expert development of law reform policy noted above:[248] an absence of consultation with the public, and an absence of any attempt to gauge, or to engage, public opinion on matters of form or substance, coupled with the development or endorsement of an almost entirely liberal-progressive agenda. Yet, formally at least, there was to be no reform agenda, on matters of substance. The code was seemingly to be more concerned with the existing law than with reformed law. The team said:

Codification does not necessitate reconsideration of the relevant law with a view to reform: it may entail no more than a restatement of existing principles. A substantial part of the draft Criminal Code Bill appended to the team's Report limits itself to such a restatement, with relatively minor changes intended to deal with inconsistencies, gaps and anomalies in the present law.[249]

No doubt, the code team was fully aware that, without Government backing to develop a substantive reform agenda (of the sort the CLRC enjoyed), the team would have stood accused of arrogating to itself the power to shape and determine the conditions under which ordinary citizens stood to be condemned as criminals and punished accordingly.

It seems strange, then, that the team's strategy was to deliberate and decide largely on its own what the substantive law should be, and then leave the matter of consultation with and persuasion of the public until later.[250] It was only to be

---

[244] For detailed discussion, see Farrar (1974), ch 3.
[245] See Law Commission (1980–81), at para 1.6.
[246] Law Commission (1989), at para 1.17.
[247] Professors JC Smith, Edward Griew, and Ian Dennis.
[248] See sections III.1. and III.2. above.
[249] Law Commission (1985), at para 16.
[250] The Commission had received comments on the code from some individuals and organizations, but almost entirely persons or bodies in or connected with the law and the legal profession. There was no attempt, in consultation, systematically to employ the slightly broader interest group-based approach favoured, at least to some extent, by the CLRC, still less any kind of survey of public opinion.

following the completion of the work of codification that the team would, through Law Commission channels:

submit the issue of codification in the law of England and Wales to a wider audience... to stimulate discussion... [and inform] the profession and the public how a code might embody the general principles of the substantive criminal law.[251]

Little seems to have changed, in terms of academic–expert reform methodology, in the century since Austin thought the best way to proceed was to shut himself in his garret and 'produce a complete map of the whole field of Crime, and a draft of a Criminal Code. *Then* let them appoint a Commission to pull it to pieces.'[252] Having said that, such a methodology would have been more acceptable, had it been true that the code was simple a means by which to 'embody the general principles of the substantive criminal law' (to use the words at the end of the passage just cited). However, as we saw earlier, an academic–expert model of law reform commonly involves using the rhetoric of specialized scholarly 'crafts-manship' to justify what is in fact often highly controversial substantive reform.[253] In the case of homicide, such reform typically involves the furtherance of liberal-progressive thinking.

For example, when it came to deciding on what should be included by way of substantive law (including homicide) in the code, having said that, 'our primary purpose has been... that of re-stating the law',[254] the code team later went on to say:

Most important of all, we thought it right to incorporate into the code recommendations for the reform of the law made by public bodies—the Law Commission, the Criminal Law Revision Committee.... When such expert and responsible agencies have closely scrutinised the law, found it to be defective and recommended reforms, it would be entirely wrong to propose the perpetuation of the existing law.[255]

Yet, as we have seen, the CLRC's recommendations for reform of the offences against the person, not least homicide, involved about as radical a departure from the existing law, in a wholly liberal-progressive direction, as has ever been suggested by any English reform body (putting aside the exceptional case of Macaulay's Code), before or since. The idea that it could be claimed that a code incorporating those reforms remained true to the 'primary purpose'[256] of merely re-stating the law is illusory; but it was, of course, an important illusion to sustain, given that the code team had no public mandate to take the law in a liberal-progressive direction (or, indeed, in any reformed direction at all). Consequently, as de Búrca and Gardner argue:

---

[251] Law Commission (1985), at paras 13 and 25.
[252] See text at n 93 above.
[253] See section III.1. and III.2. above.
[254] Law Commission (1985), at para 1.10.
[255] *Ibid*, at para 1.14.
[256] *Ibid*, at paras 3.31–3.34.

[The] exceptions [permitting the Commission to change the substantive law] are in fact highly elastic and allow a 'need' for reform to be identified at will. Other changes are made without attempting to fit them within these grounds at all.... All in all, one is driven to conclude that the approach to the question of reform is a highly selective one, governed by some agenda which is never disclosed.[257]

In that respect, in failing to test the CLRC's subjectivist heresies at the bar of public opinion, the Commission passed up a great opportunity to forge a real bond between the state and its citizens, in the way that their relationship is expressed through a criminal code. As the Commission had itself acknowledged:

[S]ince the criminal law is arguably the most direct expression of the relationship between a State and its citizens, it is right as a matter of constitutional principle that the relationship should be clearly stated in a criminal code *the terms of which have been deliberated upon by a democratically elected legislature.*[258]

Yet, without proper investigation of how citizens understand the expression of that relationship, by those whose responsibility it is to advise on the best basis for public debate—such as the Law Commission and the code team—how can this constitutional principle ever be given proper effect? Before the revised Code was published in 1989,[259] great effort had been made to subject it to searching examination by circuit 'scrutiny groups' comprised largely of judges and practitioners who considered on the Law Commission's behalf discrete areas of law.[260] But what this closed and limited form of 'consultation' shows, more than anything, is only how the role of the judiciary in criminal law reform had changed over a century. Judges were by now, and have remained, reduced to the role of 'stakeholder', on whom reforms devised by others are tried out, rather than being regarded as taking primary responsibility for criminal law reform (or the lack of it).

5. Promoting subjectivism: phoney invocations of rule-of-law principles

Before moving on, we should note that a new argument began at this point to find favour with liberal-progressive thinkers, in relation to codification. This is the argument that the rule of law would be compromised by a code that was not only unclear, but also 'unfair', in that it failed to accord with a consistent set of (liberal-progressive) principles.[261] On the face of it, this argument is apt to gain more traction, in point of legitimacy, than an argument that only the scholar–expert's craft knowledge can reveal the appropriate principles of criminalization. This is because it is an argument that seeks to promote one public good (codification) in the name of another (the rule of law). However, in responding to the publication of the code, de Búrca and Gardner argued powerfully that, in the name of removing 'inconsistencies' that might undermine the rule-of-law credentials of the code, a subjectivism quite alien to the existing law the code was meant

---

[257] De Búrca and Gardner (1990), at 564.
[258] Law Commission (1989), vol 1, at para 2.2 (my emphasis).
[259] *Ibid*, vol 1.   [260] *Ibid*, vol 1, app E.   [261] *Ibid*, vol 1, at para 2.2.

largely to embody was allowed to run riot through its provisions.[262] Respecting the codification project, the Commission claimed that:

[I]f the law is not perceived by triers of fact to be clear and fair, there is a risk that they will return incorrect or perverse verdicts through misunderstanding or a deliberate disregard of what they are advised the law is.[263]

There is a considerable degree of hyperbole about this passage in that (few will need reminding) almost all 'triers of fact' are magistrates, who are hardly likely to disregard the law intentionally although they may very occasionally misunderstand it. Putting that on one side, I scarcely need to labour the point that in this passage the Commission mixes up a pure 'rule-of-law' point (complex or unclear law may be misunderstood or disregarded, whatever its content) with a point about the law's substantive merits or fairness. Apparently, if we value the rule of law, we must either swallow the CLRC's radically subjectivist agenda, as embodied in the code, together with the improvements in clarity and certainty that come with the way that the agenda is expressed, or refuse to take our codificatory medicine at all. Through this argument, the values of the rule of law and of liberal-progressive law reform come to be unified. Yet, even if it is true that the law will only be respected if it is 'fair', as well as if it is clear and certain, why should anyone have to take for granted that the CLRC's vision of fairness should be the one with (at least) possessory title within the code? The Commission had no real justification for relying on the claim that triers of fact might not regard the existing law as fair, and on the implicit claim that triers of fact would regard the CLRC's reform agenda as fairer, without proper research into those very questions.

6. New steps in a familiar dance: the Law Commission's work on murder

To what extent had things changed by the time that the Law Commission reviewed key aspects of the law of homicide in the mid-2000s?[264] The substantive recommendations made by the Commission, some of which found their way into legislation, are analysed in detail elsewhere in this book.[265] In this context, what is more important is the relationship between substance and (consultative) procedure. The Commission's starting-point, where substance was concerned, was to avoid the radicalism of the CLRC and the code team, by putting out what was essentially old wine in new bottles. To be sure, a more liberal-progressive definition of 'first degree' murder was recommended, one that accorded with the correspondence principle. It incorporated intentional killings and killings where the intention was to do serious injury with an awareness of a serious risk of causing death.[266]

---

[262] De Búrca and Gardner (1990), at 564–6. At 566 fn 50, they refer to the code team's 'religious adherence' to subjectivity.

[263] Law Commission (1989), vol 1, at para 2.5.

[264] I will not distinguish in a formal way between Law Commission (2004) and Law Commission (2006) in the analysis that follows.

[265] See Ch 3 below (offences) and Ch 8 below (partial defences).

[266] Law Commission (2006), at para 1.67.

However, the introduction of the 'second degree' murder category allowed the Commission to retain as a species of murder killing with the intention to do serious injury,[267] the species that, in spite of its long common law history, had been rejected by the liberal-progressive CLRC and consequently by the code team. The creation of this new category of murder also allowed the Commission to introduce a new species of murder (rejected by the code team) loosely based on that which found its way into Stephen's definition:[268] killing where the offender intended to cause some injury, or a fear or risk of injury, being aware of a serious risk of causing death.[269] Whatever one makes of its individual merits, the creation of this species of murder might be presented as a kind of 'counter-balance' to the recommendation for a definition of first degree murder reduced in scope from the definition of murder at common law. Understood in this way, it would be harder to say of the package of reforms, as a whole, either that they bore a distinctively liberal-progressive stamp or, on the contrary, that they were a mere re-statement of a common law definition of murder, and of defences to it,[270] that seemed to satisfy so few people. This understanding is reinforced (a) by the Commission's recommendation for little change to the (distinctly non-subjectivist) law of manslaughter;[271] (b) by its adherence to objective standards by which to judge mentally competent persons pleading duress or provocation,[272] whilst at the same time recommending broadening the provocation defence and permitting duress to be a defence to murder; and (c) by its refusal to wade into the argument that some euthanasia cases might be treated as second degree murder or manslaughter.[273] Brian Hogan once said of Law Commission work, 'I envisaged it as an architect of a new law, not a jobbing builder to the old',[274] a preference (one might say) for Macaulay's Code ahead of Stephen's. However, so far as reform of the central tenets of law of homicide in England and Wales are concerned, there is little evidence that taking a revolutionary stance as one's starting-point stands any better chance of success than starting with evolutionary change, whoever is the driving force behind the proposals.

The other side to this re-packaging of what was by and large the status quo was a much greater degree of interest group-centred consultation than was ever

---

[267] Law Commission (2006), at para 1.67.

[268] See text following n 67 above.

[269] Law Commission (2006), at para 1.67.

[270] It would be fair to point out that the Commission recommended (Law Commission, 2006), and the Government subsequently created, a new defence of what might be called 'excessive defence' (see Ch 8). However, that recommendation in a way did little more than restore to the law a partial defence that had become lost in the re-conceptualization of the provocation defence in the late nineteenth and early twentieth centuries: see Ch 8 below.

[271] Law Commission (2006), at para 1.67.

[272] *Ibid*, at paras 9.17 and 9.21.

[273] *Ibid*, at para 9.25. The Commission recommended that a separate consultation be undertaken, in relation to 'mercy' killing. No doubt, many commentators will judge that response to be weak-kneed. However, it should not be forgotten that, at the same time as the Law Commission's consultation and Report, a Bill sponsored by Lord Joffe was going through Parliament to give, under restricted circumstances, a right to doctors to terminate the life of a terminally ill person. It would have made little sense for the Law Commission to seek to go over that ground at the same time.

[274] See his comment on Law Commission (1989), in Hogan (1978), cited by Wells (1980), at 689.

contemplated or undertaken by the CLRC or the code team. Aside from twenty-eight individuals (some, former scholars or practitioners in any event), responding to or participating in the Law Commission's work were forty-six academics, four Government departments and public bodies (excluding the Ministry of Justice), thirty-one judges, eighteen non-governmental organizations, seventeen practitioners, sixteen professional organizations (including judicial groups), and four religious groups, together representing thousands of people.[275] Welcome though this step-change in the breadth and depth of interest group consultation was, it would nonetheless be both misleading and unrewarding to speculate on how representative of conflicting public opinions it could hope to be. This is because, subject to what will be said below about the Law Commission's consultation, even much more extensive modern consultations do not seek to discover public opinion, as such. Instead, the function of such consultations is, in a small way, to gain expert input on particular features of the law;[276] but it is also, in a much larger way, to put together a sufficiently persuasive or powerful 'faction' in favour of a recommendation, to increase its political legitimacy. So, for example, in the Law Commission's final report, we can see the importance to the Commission of highlighting the (ever-changing) range of interest groups favouring or rejecting the initial proposals on which it consulted, even as it in fairness seeks to explain why other groups took a different view.[277] This kind of approach is encouraged by the (not untypical) way in which the Law Commission's terms of reference were set up. In July 2005, the Government had asked the Law Commission to review key aspects of the law of murder, such that:

The process used will be open, inclusive and evidence-based and will involve:

(a) A review structure that will look to include key stakeholders;

(b) Consultation with the public, criminal justice practitioners, academics, those who work with victims' families, parliamentarians [and] faith groups. . . . [278]

There is no mention here of pro-active, rigorous, professional investigation of public opinion (and in any event no resources were made available to conduct it), and the 'public' contribution to the consultation turned out to be a paltry twenty-eight responses from individuals. The clear intention is that an 'open, inclusive, and evidence-based' process is one mainly concerned with gathering the arguments of potentially 'noisy' or influential interest and lobby groups, whose exclusion from the process might undermine its legitimacy, even if their inclusion in it did not result in the accommodation of their views. The design of the process constitutes an attempt to bridge the legitimacy gap between a professional, expert body, and the public, on an issue—the reform of a violative crime—of fundamental importance in the relationship between the state and its citizens. However, it is hard

---

[275] Law Commission (2006), at app G.
[276] Such as, for example, the input of the Royal College of Psychiatrists on the diminished responsibility defence: Law Commission (2006), at paras 5.89–5.90.
[277] See, eg, *ibid*, at paras 2.2, 2.37, 2.53–2.54, 2.76, 2.100, 2.126–2.127.
[278] *Ibid*, at para 1.1.

to see how the process is capable of bridging that gap. It is almost too obvious to be worth mentioning that special interest and lobby groups do not necessarily represent the public as a whole, and in almost all cases do not purport to do so. At best, they may contribute insights not otherwise available to those charged with drawing up reform proposals; at worst, their participation may owe more to political influence, political correctness or successful self-publicity than to the potential for meaningful contribution.

7. Betraying the ideal of public consultation in good faith

The Ministry of Justice, responsible for the decision to take forward, modify, or abandon Law Commission proposals, is naturally in a much better position than the law reform bodies acting under its aegis to engage in proper public consultation on law reform proposals; but in practice it does not do so. For the most part, it merely wastes resources repeating the consultation exercise with largely the same interest groups initially consulted. So, the Government's own consultation on the Law Commission's recommendations predictably yielded an even poorer crop of responses: twenty-seven from individuals, eighteen from scholars, six from professional organizations, two from legal practitioners, one from a psychiatrist, and one from a Law Lord.[279] This is an incalculable waste of the Ministry's enormous institutional and financial potential to reach beyond the limited ambition of 'rounding up the usual (consultation) suspects'. An interest group model of consultation, perhaps both innovative and sufficient in itself in Ramsey Mac-Donald's time in relation to reform of road traffic law,[280] is in urgent need of supplementation in a modern democracy.

In an important break with the interest group model of consultation, in 2003–04, the Law Commission was given a special grant by the Home Office to commission a professionally conducted investigation of public opinion, in the form of structured questions posed to a representative group of lay people about (inter alia) the provocation defence.[281] The investigation revealed strong public support for a provocation defence that went beyond an over-reaction to a threat of serious violence, to encompass other forms of very grave provocation. One example considered by the representative group concerned a woman who had just witnessed the attempted rape of her daughter and was then subjected to racial abuse, following which she chased after the escaping perpetrators and stabbed one of them to death.[282] 70 per cent of the representative group thought that she should receive a sentence of, at worst, five years' imprisonment, and more than 40 per cent thought that she should receive only a non-custodial penalty. The fact that there was such strong public (not merely expert or interest group) support for leniency in this kind of case was subsequently openly acknowledged by the Government to have been crucial to its decision to retain a provocation defence with a basis going

---

[279] Ministry of Justice (2009), at para 10. [280] See text at n 193 above.
[281] Law Commission (2004), app C.
[282] See the discussion of this example in Law Commission (2006), at paras 5.74–5.76.

beyond an over-reaction to a threat of serious violence.[283] Yet, the Ministry of Justice failed to follow through this important initiative. The Law Commission was given no further grant to gauge the public's opinion of the proposed distinction between (and the ingredients of) first and second degree murder, when it reconsidered the issues in 2005–06, although it was able to take the benefit of some other empirical work being done at the time on defences to murder, and on infanticide and diminished responsibility.[284]

Having received the Report, the Ministry of Justice itself then took no further steps to commission professional and impartial investigation of public opinion, even in relation to changes it was minded to take forwards. The nadir, in this respect, came in January 2007, when the Ministry of Justice had received the Law Commission's final report on homicide. The Ministry then held a small number of 'public' consultations, at one of which, the only London-based consultation seminar on complicity in murder, it mustered only eleven consultees, all bar one of whom was already working in a law-related public service of some kind, such as the Crown Prosecution Service, the Association of Chief Police Officers, the Home Office, and the Attorney-General's office. If not quite the apotheosis of absurdity, this makes a travesty of the notion of a properly consultative law reform process in relation to violative crime.[285] Consider, by way of contrast, the effort invested by the Home Office in its consultation on what became its key strategy document for seeking an end to violence against women and girls.[286] It issued paper surveys to which it received 2,400 responses, with a further 5,156 surveys completed online. It received 1,007 emails and 76 written responses. Even more significantly, almost 700 professionals were dispatched to attend no less than nine regional events on the subject, and a staggering twenty-four focus groups spoke to over 300 survivors of violence.[287] No one could possibly doubt the importance of and the need for this kind of deep and widespread consultation on such an important issue; but can it really be argued that reform of the law of homicide, and in particular the public's view of reform, is of such minor importance that investigating it was rightly granted, in comparison, so little in terms of resources and commitment? What we got instead was a Ministry of Justice proving itself all-too adept at employing the interest group model of consultation in the 'factional' way referred to above,[288] when seeking to legitimate new proposals superimposed on the Law Commission recommendations.

Under section 55(6)(c) of the 2009 Act, words or conduct constituting infidelity must be disregarded by the jury when considering a provocation plea, a provision

[283] See Ministry of Justice (2008), at para 33. How important this was can be judged by the fact that the Ministry had been minded to take the view that, '[mitigation] would be an excessively lenient response to behaviour which society does not consider, or no longer considers, acceptable' (at para 31).

[284] Law Commission (2006), apps C and D.

[285] There should at least have been an effort to ensure that amongst those attending—or providing written evidence—were groups in favour of change, such as London Against Injustice, or INNOCENT, and those against it, such as Baroness Newlove.

[286] Home Office (2009).

[287] The National Children's Bureau also ran focus groups with over 150 younger people.

[288] See text following n 276 above.

considered in more depth in Chapter 8. Putting the merits of this provision on one side for now, it is interesting to note the way in which the Government sought to legitimate the provision in terms of the consultative process. The Government explicitly mentions as 'strong' supporters of the provision, Justice for Women, Welsh Women's Aid, Women's Aid (England), Broken Rainbow, the Women's Aid Federation (Northern Ireland), along with the Committee for the Administration of Justice (Northern Ireland), the Probation Board (Northern Ireland), Victim Support (England),[289] and Victim Support (Northern Ireland).[290] Unmentioned others are also said to have supported the provision. What should one make of the consultative response? Rare, indeed, must have been the occasions when the Government has felt the need explicitly to rely on the views of four groups from Northern Ireland, out of nine groups mentioned in total, in order to justify a major change to the law of homicide driven by problems arising in the law of England and Wales, predominantly consulted on in England and Wales,[291] and now governing England and Wales.[292] In a context in which the Government had clearly already decided what it wanted to do prior to the consultation, what really mattered was simply to have been supported by those groups, whether or not they were representative of public opinion, or even of legal opinion. So far as the arguments of opponents of the provision are concerned, the Ministry of Justice notes that, 'there was significant concern about the exclusion from a number of respondents',[293] including concern amongst women's groups.[294] However, the Ministry gives us no basis on which to assess the weight of the objections.

Naturally, an adequate response to consultation is not exemplified by the mere counting of responses for and against.[295] However, in this instance, the Government appears to be exploiting an interest group consultative model for the purpose of delivering an unstated message: to oppose this provision is (putting aside the views of a few malcontents 'letting the side down') to be against women's interests. So, the Government could say, 'who out there now dares to confirm that they are against women's interests, by opposing our provision?' As things turned out, very few dared. It hardly needs saying that to oppose the provision is not necessarily to be against women's interests as such;[296] but to dwell on this would, in this context, be to miss the point. The point is that a consultation process should not be used to manipulate what emerge as more or less factionalized groups in favour or against certain changes, because doing so will lend some credibility to what it has already

---

[289] It should be noted that Victim Support is opposed to the doctrine of provocation in almost any form, and was thus bound to support the exclusion in any event.

[290] Ministry of Justice (2009), at para 47.

[291] The Law Commission is, of course, the Law Commission for England and Wales. Northern Ireland has only had a Law Commission of its own since 2007.

[292] Albeit applicable to Northern Ireland as well.

[293] Ministry of Justice (2009), at para 48.

[294] *Ibid*, at para 48.

[295] As the Government's *Code of Practice on Consultation* (DBIS 2008) emphasizes at para 6.1: 'Analyzing consultation responses is primarily a qualitative rather than a quantitative exercise.'

[296] The very fact that some women's groups opposed the introduction of the provision is evidence for that.

been decided it is politically expedient or desirable to do. To do this not only insults the groups in favour of as well as against the provision, but also further corrupts the interest group model of consultation, hence undermining what remaining credibility it has as the main means by which it is sought to bridge the legitimacy gap.[297] It cannot be sufficiently emphasized that this is not, in itself, a substantive criticism of section 55(6)(c).[298] The issue is one about open, fair, and properly modernized law reform processes. A Government acting in good faith would have supplemented interest group-based consultation on section 55(6)(c) with research into, for example, the views of a proper cross-section of women (and men) on the infidelity exclusion. It would, in other words, have sought to test the provision at the bar of public opinion, before reaching judgement.

It is ironic, thus, that the biggest challenge not only to section 55(6)(c) but to the Government's reform programme as a whole, came not from the results of the consultation process, but from the ruling elite. The House of Lords sought to scupper the section of the Coroners and Justice Bill dealing with defences to murder. It threatened to exercise its coercive power to deal a death blow to proposed legislation, by pressing an amendment at the last moment. Although adapted from the French Penal Code, the amendment effectively revived in an improved form an older recommendation for reform put forward by the Royal Commission on Capital Punishment 1953:[299]

Murder: extenuating circumstances:

(1) In a trial for murder the trial judge may in the course of his summing up direct the jury that if they are satisfied that the defendant is guilty of murder, but are of the opinion that there were extenuating circumstances, they may on returning their verdict add a rider to that effect.

(2) The judge may not give such a direction unless there is evidence on which a reasonable jury might so find.

(3) Where the jury has so found, the judge shall not be obliged to pass a sentence of life imprisonment but may pass such other sentence as he considers appropriate having regard to any extenuating circumstances found by the jury.

(4) If the judge passes a sentence other than a sentence of life imprisonment, he shall be obliged to state his reasons.

(5) If it appears to the Attorney General that the sentence so passed is unduly lenient he may refer it to the Court of Appeal under section 36 of the Criminal Justice Act 1988 (c. 33) (reviews of sentencing).

The amendment was strongly supported in the Lords, with its advocates confident that it would be backed by the public, or at least by the majority of juries.[300] However, setting aside the merits of the amendment, what its supporters fail to explain is why the Government should accept such an amendment, when two sets

---

[297] See text following n 168 above.
[298] For further discussion of that section, see Ch 8 below.
[299] Discussed in greater detail in Ch 8 below. The amendment was pressed by Lord Lloyd, but drafted by Professor Spencer QC, Cambridge University.
[300] See <www.publications.parliament.uk/pa/ld200809/ldhansrd/text/91026-0007.htm>.

of consultations with the public had already been conducted in relation to the provisions that the amendment would replace. Acceptance of the amendment would have amounted to nothing less than a betrayal of the individuals and groups representing thousands of people who supported some or all of the Government's proposals for reform, whatever the defects of the consultative process in which they were involved. The efforts of the House of Lords were efforts to re-assert a homicide law reform model determined by a ruling elite. Those efforts, on the part of an elite that was supreme primarily in its confidence that its opinion was both correct and (without a shred of evidence to back this) supported by the public, were rightly spurned by the Government. The proper course would have been, at a much earlier stage, to insist that the Government conduct research into the public's views about its own proposals, as well as about the 'extenuating circumstances' model. The latter has much to recommend it as a matter of substance, and further support will be provided for it in Chapter 8. However, the House of Lords, like the Government, simply failed to see the potential for such research to bridge the legitimacy gap. Like the Government in relation to section 55(6)(c), the House of lords simply preferred to try to ensure its own view made its way into legislation, by ignoring that gap.

V. Opening Pandora's Box? Homicide Law and Public Opinion

1. In search of a role for the public: from stakeholders to opinion formers

We have already encountered a range of attitudes towards public opinion amongst would-be law reformers. The 1819 Committee of Inquiry on Criminal Laws that led to the abolition of a number of capital felonies was one of the few bodies to have made an enquiry into the views of ordinary people central to its deliberations.[301] However, those consulted were really people whose views would today be 'bureaucratized', meaning that their views would become subject to representation by a professional interest group of some kind. So, the 1819 consultation was (on the Committee's own admission[302]) not a truly public consultation after all. Further, the purity of the Committee's motives for involving the consultees in question is coloured by the fact that there was already a favourable wind blowing in the direction of the reforms eventually agreed on. For the most part, nineteenth-century judges seem to have taken one or both of two, complementary views. On one view, the common law was already the embodiment of community values, and for that reason should not be subject to radical—still less, politically driven—reform.[303] On the other view, the public at large were regarded as too ignorant or prejudiced to be involved in the process of criminal law reform.[304]

---

[301] Albeit only those in some profession that meant they might be victims of the crime in question.
[302] See text at n 32 above.
[303] See Horder (2002b).
[304] See sections II.1. and II.3. above.

In the twentieth century, with the bureaucratization of the criminal law reform process (and, increasingly, with the rise and bureaucratization of voluntary, special interest, and pressure groups, along with trade associations), came the rise of interest group-led consultation from the 1930s onwards. This form of consultation assumes that lay people have something to contribute to the law reform process. However, that contribution does not come through input in the form of 'public opinion', howsoever investigated. It is legitimated only when it comes in the form of expert, special interest or (in the case of victims' family groups) experience-based knowledge. Lay input, then, although clearly value-laden, is fully legitimate only when it is a mirror of law reform bureaucracy itself, in that it contributes (in Weberian terms) to the element of the '*zweckrationell*'[305] in law reform: in Weber's words, 'mak[ing] possible a particularly high degree of calculability of results for the heads of organisation and for those acting in relation to it'.[306] In this bureaucratized process, the paradigm case of the consultee is the 'stakeholder', someone—normally a group—who already has some kind of interest in the process (whether or not vested) in virtue of their expertise, knowledge, or experience, or in virtue of their strategic importance within the criminal justice system: as in the case of judges or practitioners. In theory, as Weber indicates, the aim is to ensure that those with authority to effect change to the criminal law do so on the basis of as full as possible an understanding of the likely consequences of change.[307]

In this process, scholars, as mere stakeholders, now find themselves dealt with by law reform authorities such as the Ministry of Justice (if not by the Law Commission, which is ultimately itself a kind of stakeholder) on the same level as victims' family groups and others who bring 'only' experience-based knowledge rather than research-based or pedagogic knowledge to the table. How much this rankles is quite plain amongst those scholars prepared (most admirably) to be honest about what they really think about lay input. For example, in his discussion of the double jeopardy rule, Paul Roberts has made this argument concerning the possible influence of victims' family groups on law reform (including their possible influence on the rules governing re-trial for homicide[308]):

For the purposes of designing and implementing a system of criminal justice, it is best that the opinions of those stricken by fear or grief should defer to the deliberations of more sober and reflective citizens, who can take proper account of the experiences of victimisation alongside the full range of other pertinent considerations . . . any narrower or more truncated approach soon exhausts itself in ignorance, prejudice or dogmatic assertion.[309]

---

[305] 'Goal-rationality', as opposed to the '*wertrationell*', value-rationality.

[306] Weber (1947), at 337.

[307] However, as we have seen, this process has a weakness. It is open to corruption, through the selective use by the Government of the input of particular interest groups who support the Government's position.

[308] Roberts refers to Stephen Lawrence, whose killers could not, at the relevant time, face a re-trial for murder, as the 'poster-boy for the double-jeopardy rule's opponents': Paul Roberts (2002), at 205.

[309] *Ibid*, at 216.

In this passage we are being invited to welcome the input into the reform process of 'sober and reflective citizens' who are privy to knowledge of 'the full range of . . . pertinent considerations': in other words, experts such as himself. We are simultaneously invited to discount the input of those motivated by personal loss to seek reform, because they should be deferring to the experts. Roberts acknowledges that this approach may seem arrogant in that it is, as he puts it, 'to lecture grieving or frightened crime victims about freedom, democracy and justice'.[310] However, he says in response, the approach is only arrogant 'if human anguish is to be the arbiter of reason'.[311]

What remains absent from his account is any evidence indicating that the views of victims of crime, or organizations representing them, are indeed little more than the anguished lashing out of those 'stricken by fear or grief'. For example, most homicide-related organizations focused on victims are charities, whose primary function is to provide support for the bereaved.[312] Such groups have, in effect, become part of the voluntary arm of the welfare state.[313] Of those groups that have clear policies on homicide law reform, it would be a complete mis-characterization to describe those policies as nothing more than 'ignorance, prejudice or dogmatic assertion'.[314] Victim Support, for example, in its comment on what was then the Coroners and Justice Bill 2009, called for two reforms:

The creation of a national support service for people attending inquests (to mirror the services Victim Support already runs for witnesses attending criminal courts) with the resources to back it.

Clarity on the reform of the defences to murder, including a definition of a 'recognised medical condition' and why sexual infidelity is singled out as not being a ground for provocation.[315]

These are perfectly reasonable views that might well be shared by some of the experts Roberts believes to be engaged in the reform process at a supposedly superior level of reasoning. To be sure, victims and victims' family groups are reasoning from a distinctive point of view; but that is true of many contributors to the law reform process, including liberal-progressives.

In truth, like many liberal-progressive scholars, Roberts simply fears the opening of Pandora's box. The thinking is that if populist opinion is allowed to play a central role in law reform, liberal-progressive values stand to be washed away in a tide of repression fuelled by visceral hatred of (in this context) unjustified killers. Even if this were genuinely a worry in England and Wales, the answer would not be to allow liberal-progressive experts to ram their principles down the public's throat, on the grounds that the latter should be deferring to the former; such an approach can serve only to widen the legitimacy gap. Fortunately, the spectre of repression through the law of homicide, if the public is allowed a say in its development, is

---

[310] *Ibid*, at 216.   [311] *Ibid*.
[312] As is the case, for example, with Support After Murder and Manslaughter, or Mothers Against Murder and Aggression.
[313] For a wide-ranging discussion, see Rock (1998).
[314] Paul Roberts (2002), at 216.   [315] Victim Support (2009).

only apparent, not real. There are now a number of studies which show that, when their views are sought through professionally conducted surveys, representative sections of the public in fact turn out to hold not only (as we have seen) nuanced but also, ironically, quite liberal-progressive views about criminal law and punishment. So, for example, an authoritative survey has shown support for a relatively wide defence of provocation,[316] for the humane treatment of the mentally disordered, and for lenient punishment of those who perform genuinely consensual 'mercy' killings.[317] Another important survey has shown low levels of public support for 'whole life' or thirty-year-minimum sentences, even in cases where such sentences ought to be the starting-point for sentencing under the current law.[318] Naturally, we need to take care that, for example, a left-liberal (or, alternatively, a right wing 'law-and-order') bias is not built into to the way that questions are asked of the public, such that the answers generated are more likely to reflect the wishful thinking of the researchers; but that is a topic for another occasion.

The survey on sentencing for murder is an especially significant one. In recent years, it has become accepted by legislatures, courts, and by some scholars, that sentencing practices and policies must not become radically detached from properly researched and representative public opinion.[319] Both the legislature and courts now generally distance themselves from the Court of Appeal's former view that 'the main duty of the courts is to *lead* public opinion',[320] a duty the courts fail to discharge in any event, because there is no evidence that public opinion is affected by judicial sentencing practices.[321] Many scholars, though, have been slow to accept the important role of public opinion in the post *Gregg v Georgia*[322] era, because they have preferred to focus on what is in fact an unrepresentative example: capital punishment. Notoriously, the modern legislature has proved resistant to strong public opinion favouring the re-introduction of the death penalty; but whether or not it has been right to do so is a distraction from the state's evolving attitude towards the role of public opinion in shaping sentencing practices more generally. Here, the detailed professional exploration of public opinion has flourished,[323] and it became important to the work of what is now the Sentencing Council. This development owes much to the changing public understanding of what gives legitimacy to criminal justice institutions, including those charged with reform. The public is now more likely to see any legitimacy gap as narrowed only little (or not at all) by the intellectual or practical authority of those charged with the business of devising reforms. Instead, the public sees that gap as narrowed in large part by the extent to which criminal justice institutions make efforts to keep

---

[316] See text at n 281 above.
[317] Mitchell (2000), at 815 and 820; Mitchell and Roberts (2012).
[318] Mitchell and Roberts (2011), at 460.
[319] See, eg, Home Office (2001); Morgan (2002), at 215.
[320] *Sargeant* (1974) 60 Cr App R 74.
[321] See generally, Roberts (1988).
[322] 428 US 153, 1976. See text at n 206 above.
[323] Russell and Morgan (2001); Clarke, Moran-Ellis, and Sleney (2002).

their work in touch with public opinion.[324] Far from regarding this development as a fundamental threat to its authority, or to the integrity and fairness of the criminal justice system, the Sentencing Council has embraced that change, unlike its counterparts working on the substantive criminal law.[325] The Council says of its approach, 'the Council will engage with the public on sentencing, offer information and encourage debate. It will focus on three areas of work; sentencing guidelines, research and analysis and public confidence.'[326] My suggestion is that in the case of the substantive criminal law, the CLLPU and its ministers should follow suit. They should not develop rules and principles for reform without ensuring that those reforms have a firm foundation in properly researched and representative public opinion.

In expressing the point thus, I am not claiming that law reformers are *bound* to shape the law in accordance with the results of such research, come what may. As Edmund Burke put the matter, 'Your representative owes you, not his industry only, but his judgement; and he betrays you instead of serving you, if he sacrifices it to your opinion.'[327] However, in seeking to make the best use of public opinion to assist the legislature, there is another analogy to be drawn with the use of public opinion in relation to sentencing. If the effort to make sentencing principles more reflective of public opinion is to remain fair, the public needs to be educated about the context in which those principles have emerged, so that there are no misunderstandings on their part about the reasons for guilty plea discounts, discretionary early release, and so on.[328] A similar, 'educative' part should be involved when the public are asked about the law of homicide, in the form of a description of the existing rules, and the reasons for them, as a backdrop for opinion-formation. The ideal, then, is of an attempt in good faith to shape the law broadly (if not in every detail) in accordance with properly *informed* public opinion, within a context in which the law must not be allowed to become arbitrary, procedurally discriminatory or too difficult or costly to administer. This is what, in this context, it can mean to deliver on Mannheim's vision for the reduction of the legitimacy gap, in a society in which no one—not even the greatest legal expert—is believed to have privileged access to the truth and an unaccountable right to exercise authority over legal reform.[329] Making representative public opinion the firm foundation for reform of the substantive law also means that ministers and civil servants should not be regarded as completely free, having duly considered such opinion, to ignore it completely and do exactly as they choose in the name of 'fairness' or of some other process value.[330] Criminal lawyers, and homicide law reformers in particular, are yet to learn these lessons, and it is time to examine why they must do so.

---

[324] I owe these points to Julian Roberts, Worcester College, Oxford.

[325] See now: <http://sentencingcouncil.judiciary.gov.uk/facts/research-and-analysis-publications.htm>. The Council says that it intends, 'to play a greater part in promoting understanding of, and *increasing public confidence* in, sentencing and the criminal justice system' (Council's emphasis).

[326] <http://sentencingcouncil.judiciary.gov.uk/about/our-work.htm>.

[327] Burke (1854), at 130.

[328] Julian Roberts (2002), at 31–2. See further the statement by the Sentencing Council, n 325 above.

[329] See text at n 152 above.

[330] That he opens the way for this kind of possibility is the weakness in Farrar's assessment of the way in which criminal law reformers should go about their business: see text at n 210 above.

2. Law reform and citizenship

Let us return to Duff's suggestion that criminal law 'is the proper concern of all citizens in virtue of their shared membership of the polity'.[331] What does this mean for the law reform process? Duff and Marshall argue that the central concern properly regarded as a matter for the public is the nature of wrongdoing—wrongdoing to be regarded as criminal.[332] So, for example, whether liability for homicide should be imposed when death has been caused by (gross) negligence, rather than intentionally or recklessly, is a proper concern of the public, because it is a matter bearing on the limits of criminal wrongdoing. However, a concern with wrongdoing, as such, cannot exhaust the matters on which the citizenry should be engaged as members of the polity. Any matter of moral or political principle that does not depend solely on empirical evidence, or on expert judgement, to understand and argue about its relevance or weight, falls in this sense within the proper sphere of citizen engagement. So, for example, falling within that sphere are questions about fair labelling, about whether undoubtedly criminal wrongdoing, such as a killing under provocation, or brought about by recklessness or gross negligence, should be regarded as murder (or as first or second degree murder), manslaughter, or as some other form of unlawful homicide.[333] By contrast, the question whether the Attorney-General's consent should be required for a prosecution for homicide (as opposed to, say, the consent of the Director of Public Prosecutions), when the death has occurred more than three years after the initial injury,[334] is largely an expert matter that need not be regarded as of concern to the public. In that respect, it should scarcely need saying that because there can be no proper governance without adequate mutual trust and respect between Government and citizens, it is not wrong that Government itself seeks to determine which matters are the ones that are the proper concern of citizens. This is not wrong, so long as Government performs the task in good faith and with the commitment to take properly into account the views of citizens on the matters it knows or believes are their concern.

What gives moral as well as political weight to that commitment is the fact that, as we have seen,[335] evidence shows that in many Western democracies (and beyond), citizens' views on the nature of crime and the appropriateness of punishment(s) are not generally outlandish or cruel. The urge to give full vent to hatred and disgust at violative crime, when devising laws and punishments for such offences, is always liable to be moderated and tempered in representative samples of citizens by a nuanced and humane set of moral considerations. This is because those citizens will be part of or from societies where the institutionalization of such considerations are stable and valued social and political achievements with which

---

[331] Duff (2010), at 88–9. See text at n 3 above.

[332] Duff and Marshall (1998).

[333] For example, Mitchell's investigation revealed some public support for the view that killing attributable to drink driving was trivialized by its current label, and should be regarded as murder or manslaughter: Mitchell (2000), at 819.

[334] Law Reform (Year and a Day Rule) Act 1996, s 2.

[335] See Robinson and Kurzban (2007), at 1892–3.

citizens identify.[336] It follows that public opinion on the shape that crime and punishment should take cannot be dismissed on the grounds that intuitions lack justificatory import. Scheffler argues that 'it is difficult . . . to see how there could be *any* plausible conception of ethical justification that did not assign a substantial role of some kind to ethical beliefs and intuitions'.[337] Does that mean that it is ultimately some kind of moral relativism that underpins the view that, in the absence of moral truth, the best vantage point for progress is to track what researchers can discover about public opinion?[338] After all, as Simons argues,[339] social practices and lay intuitions can be open to moral critique, and law may for that reason legitimately lead public opinion on occasions. Two remarks should be made about that argument. First, as Scheffler himself remarks, in societies that are already well-ordered morally and politically, that moral critique is itself 'likely to be rooted in values or principles that have a high degree of social acceptance'.[340] The character of almost all moral arguments is shaped by, and draws on for its force, variations on familiar examples that are an intrinsic part of a 'common evaluative culture'.[341] As Robinson and Kurzban put it:

The greatest success in shaping the perceived wrongfulness of particular conduct may not be to fight people's intuitions of justice but rather to try to harness them, by providing information or arguments that strengthen (or weaken) the analogy between the target conduct and the core wrongdoing on which people have strong intuitions.[342]

An example might be a change in the law of gross negligence manslaughter, to make the test sensitive to D's capacities.[343] There may be some arguments for having a test of 'negligence' that judges everyone by reference to the standards that would be observed by an adult with normally developed capacities to appreciate risk, take adequate precautions, and so on.[344] However, an argument to the contrary, that the test should account for disabilities such as blindness, or impaired mental states such as very low intelligence, is not simply one more example of a 'subjectivist' argument, to be ranked alongside other such arguments for the correspondence principle, for the irrelevance of harm to criminal liability, and the like. This is because the argument for a capacity-sensitive negligence test appeals to values of non-discrimination and equal concern that are integral to the very moral fabric from which rules of (criminal) liability are fashioned.

Secondly, in response to Simons, it can be argued that properly researched enquiries into public opinion, into the moral judgements held by the public, can help us discover not merely common shared intuitions but also the true structure of the moral domain, the domain underpinning the law of violative crime. As the moral realist Sabina Lovibond puts it:

---

[336] See Scheffler (1992), at 137. [337] *Ibid*, at 144 (my emphasis).
[338] For such a view, arguing that reliance on public opinion reflects deep-seated relativism, see Simons (2001), at 640.
[339] *Ibid*. [340] Scheffler (1992), at 143.
[341] Lovibond (2002), at 43. [342] Robinson and Kurzban (2007), at 1893.
[343] See Simester (2000); Law Commission (2006), at para 3.60.
[344] See, eg, *Elliot v C (a minor)* [1983] 2 All ER 1005.

[W]e can think of particular moral judgments—when they are true rather than false—not just as bringing us into harmony with a certain consensus of feeling or opinion, but as disclosing to us the 'layout' of a certain domain of reality, namely the moral domain.[345]

Suppose, though, that confidence about the widely shared character of moral judgements on which rules of liability for homicide are based is misplaced. Suppose that there are in fact deep differences between more or less equally divided sections of society, each of which adheres to a set of irreconcilable liability principles concerning, say, the scope for a full or partial defence of euthanasia or the place of liability for negligence in homicide. In such circumstances, there would still be an obligation on Governments to find out the extent and nature of that disagreement through research into public opinion, something they now conspicuously fail to do. That enquiry would, in turn, generate a further obligation to explain why a Government finds the arguments of one side convincing, whilst remaining prepared to acknowledge that it (the Government) may be mistaken about its convictions. That is, of course, no more than Governments currently do, when publishing reports and responses to consultation, as the Government did before it reformed the law of murder through the 2009 Act.[346] However, there is a final obligation arising from the need to legislate in conditions of disagreement, an obligation that Governments typically fail to discharge either at all, or in a systematic way open to public scrutiny, when reforming the law of violative crime. This is the obligation to recognize that, whatever the strengths of one's convictions, given that one may turn out to be wrong, built-in trial periods for or periodic review of legislation, together with rigorous post-legislative scrutiny, are essential to a fully democratic process of law reform.[347] They are no less than what is owed to fellow citizens who disagree on matters of high principle. The need for such scrutiny has been accepted by Government, in a limited form.[348] The Government said:

It would also be helpful if reviews normally considered only Acts which have received Royal Assent at least 3 to 5 years earlier: this would allow for a 'cooling-off' period from the parliamentary passage of the bill itself, as well as providing sufficient time, in most cases, for the implementation of the Act to be assessed.[349]

The reference to a need for a 'cooling-off' period here is an illustration of what Perry has called a 'Burkean' approach to the stability of law over time.[350] On a Burkean

---

[345] Lovibond (2002), at 45.

[346] See Ministry of Justice (2008); Ministry of Justice (2009).

[347] The Law Commission has supported the view that it is better to have rigorous post-legislative scrutiny of a small number of major pieces of legislation, than perfunctory scrutiny of all legislation. There are precedents for legislative experimentation, a relevant one in this context being the temporary suspension of the death penalty for five years by the Murder (Abolition of the Death Penalty) Act 1965.

[348] Office of the Leader of the House of Commons (2008).

[349] *Ibid*, at para 7.

[350] Perry (1987), at 221. Perry applies the approach in the context of an analysis of the common law doctrines of precedent, so I am extending it by analogy here to the activity of the legislature. As Perry indicates, the Burkean approach has nothing to do with the actual views and philosophy of Edmund Burke. As he puts it (at 221), the approach is so named 'simply to convey the idea of a presumption of some sort in favour of previously accepted practices'. Perry draws a distinction between 'weak' and

approach, the legislature initially takes a decision, on the balance of applicable first-order reasons, to embody a particular policy in legislation. As a body that takes seriously its obligation to provide authoritative and reliable guidance, the legislature does not normally (other things being equal) then replace that legislation solely because it has changed its mind on how the balance of reasons tips. But neither does a responsible legislature close its mind to the possibility of change, if there is a sufficiently strong reason for it.

More significantly, in the present context, in the passage cited above[351] the Government indicated that its view is that, over a three- to five-year period, there should an investigation of the 'implementation' of legislation. It is quite clear that falling outside the scope of such an investigation will be any re-consideration of the policy debates that lay behind the passing of any Act selected for post-legislative scrutiny.[352] The exclusion of an *automatic* re-consideration, even over a longer period of, say, ten to fifteen years (in relation to specific Acts), is an unwelcome development. First, it gives undue weight to the need for long-term finality in authoritative decision-making bearing on highly controversial issues. In practice, as we will see in Chapter 2, it is quite evident that Governments quite commonly *do* experiment, even in the short-to-medium term, with different formulae to define homicide-related offences, and hence to deter life-threatening conduct.[353] Secondly, excluding the re-running of policy arguments from the scope of medium-to-long term review of legislation governing violative crime risks creating a class of 'perpetual winners' and 'doomed losers' on policy issues of great personal as well as political significance to many people.[354] Parliament should have the courage to build in provision for long-term review of legislation governing violative crime, even if that means having to re-run arguments about (say) abortion, euthanasia, the ending of life-support, assisted suicide, and so on, that it would rather not confront. That would, after all, only systematize what is already in some areas—such as the death penalty or voluntary euthanasia—the practice, in the sense that supporters and opponents of these possible dimensions to the law of homicide have for many years periodically, but in a haphazard manner, been given the opportunity to re-run (in different forms) debates for and against.

What the practice shows is that the legislature does in fact, and should systematically, embrace a philosophically 'pragmatic' approach to the possibility of legislative change. This is a richer form of pragmatism than the form the Law Commission is commonly accused of embracing, that I identified as a possible meaning of that term earlier in the chapter.[355] By a 'pragmatic' approach I mean philosophical pragmatism, a pragmatism that regards the process of moral and political argumentation as partly experimental, as always subject to improvement, revision, and even

---

'strong' versions of the Burkean theory, but that distinction is questionable and I will not employ it here.

[351] See text at n 349.
[352] Office of the Leader of the House of Commons (2008), at para 8.
[353] See the discussion of road traffic law in Ch 2.
[354] Especially when the 'winners' succeed in gaining constitutional protection for their policy gain, on the basis, inter alia, of its universalizability. On the evils of such a system, see Waldron (1993).
[355] See text at n 133 above.

falsification in the light of experience and further argument.[356] In that regard, there is a strong analogy between the process of law reform, and the process of seeking true moral judgement. We could treat reaching a moral judgement as being in principle like the acceptance of a mathematical truth. On that view, one simply comes to see (or not, as the case may be) that some proposition has moral validity, at which point one is then in a position simply to discount the views of those who deny its validity (or one continues patiently to explain why they are wrong);[357] but that analogy has too little appeal in a largely multi-faith or secular society. It fails to account for the fact that moral thought is characterized by large-scale disagreement, whereas mathematical theorizing is characterized by very widespread agreement, over fundamental propositions.[358] The search for moral truth, then, may turn out to involve a very different kind of exercise.

Most people—and Governments—may very well begin with an intuition that something is a 'violative' crime, but what may seem intuitively obvious may also in some circumstances come to be discredited as such. Consequently, we must be prepared to have our intuitions confirmed, revised, or confounded in the light of our encounter with reasoned argument, thought experiments, experiences, and so on.[359] As Cheryl Misak argues:

I might come to see an act in a different light or from a different perspective.... That is, because experience is a matter of interpretation, not only can (and should) we expose ourselves and others to new experiences, but we can also arrive at better interpretations.... Through critical reflection, exposing oneself to more experiences and perspectives, one's background beliefs can be improved and one's judgments revised.... '[360]

In that respect, as Misak argues, when it comes to moral enquiry, we are—and should—all be involved. As she rightly suggests, when it comes to the standards to be observed in that enquiry, 'this does not mean only, or even mainly, "experts" who sit on ethics boards in hospitals and the like and those... who engage in particular issues'.[361] No one should be left out. As we have seen, many in the ruling elite and amongst legal scholars and practitioners see criminal law reform in much the same way as 'old school' doctors and surgeons saw medicine and medical ethics: as a matter primarily for the professions rather than the public. Most would probably agree with Bagaric and Edney's view of sentencing that:

Seeking public views on sentencing is analogous to doctors basing treatment decisions on what the community thinks is appropriate or engineers building cars, not in accordance with the rules of physics, but on the basis of what lay members of the community 'reckon' seems about right.[362]

---

[356] On the work of CS Peirce, in this respect, see Misak (1997).
[357] It could be argued that such a view of moral judgement guides Glazebrook's appeal for certain 'eminently rational' reforms of the law of homicide to be made: see text at n 157 above.
[358] See Misak (1997), at 210 and 214.
[359] See, eg, the discussion of 'public reason' in Cumper and Lewis (2011).
[360] Misak (1997), at 212.
[361] *Ibid*, at 214.
[362] Bagaric and Edney (2004), at 129. I am grateful to Julian Roberts, Worcester College Oxford, for bringing this passage to my attention.

As should by now be evident, such views seek to ensure that moral and political value judgements remain the prerogative of experts or of those in authority, leaving public opinion (however carefully investigated) out of the picture; that is wrong. The equally significant point now being made, though, is that, in some circumstances, people may also be 'left out' if their arguments of principle are never reconsidered, or if they are in effect permanently discounted by constitutional entrenchment of the opposing view, as well as when they are ignored altogether. As Waldron puts it, of constitutionalizing moral and political principles (although what is said applies equally to ordinary legislation that Governments will in practice not review):

> To think that a constitutional immunity is called for is to think oneself justified in disabling legislators in this respect (and thus, indirectly, in disabling the citizens whom they represent).... To embody a right in an entrenched constitutional document is to adopt a certain attitude towards one's fellow citizens. That attitude is best summed up as a combination of self-assurance and mistrust... mistrust, implicit in [the] view that any alternative conception that might be concocted... next year or the year after is so likely to be wrong-headed or ill-motivated that her own formulation is to be elevated immediately beyond the reach of ordinary legislative revision.[363]

This takes us back to a point made right at the start of this chapter.[364] To avoid adopting such an attitude of mistrust towards fellow citizens, the reform process in relation to violative crime should seek to make moral progress by showing what Sellers calls 'decent humility'.[365] This requires, on the one hand, that principled objectors to legislation give it time to prove its worth, and to gain (or to lose) moral legitimacy. This insight explains the justifiability of relatively lengthy 'cooling-off' periods before the policy of legislation is subject to formal review. However, the same humility should be expected of Parliament, which brought the legislation into effect. As Sellers puts it, 'the great value of public deliberation about ultimate truths is that it helps us to correct our own moral mistakes'.[366] So, Governments passing key legislation on, say, murder, abortion, or euthanasia, should as a matter of course build into that legislation provision for policy review within (say) twenty years. In so doing they would be doing something of importance in the public sphere to fulfil what Finnis describes as the 'indispensible conditions for worthwhile discussion', namely respect for 'truth (and knowledge of it), and friendship (goodwill towards other human persons)'.[367]

In this respect, the policy of successive Governments does not stand up particularly well to scrutiny, in spite of the fact that there have been periodic debates on some controversial issues such as the death penalty and voluntary euthanasia. On the one hand, Governments have been reluctant to re-open many key questions of principle in relation to killing and the ending of life, even in the face of a great deal of medical and technological development and change affecting the terms in which the debates are now conducted. So, for example, when setting up the review of

---

[363] Waldron (1993), at 27. [364] Text at n 6 above, onwards.
[365] Sellers (1991), at 276. [366] *Ibid*, at 273. [367] Finnis (2007), at 11.

murder in 2005, the Government deliberately kept broader considerations arising from euthanasia, suicide, and abortion off the agenda for reform, without consulting in advance on whether that was, for example, what the public would have preferred.[368] To be sure, this follows the Government's own code of guidelines on consultation, which allows official bodies to decide the agenda informally through a discussion with 'stakeholders':

> It will often be necessary to engage in an informal dialogue with stakeholders prior to a formal consultation to obtain initial evidence and to gain an understanding of the issues that will need to be raised in the formal consultation. These informal dialogues are also outside the scope of this code.[369]

This guidance may be right for many potential consultation issues. However, in relation to the moral principles at stake in a review of the law of homicide, the use of the guidance to exclude 'end of life' issues from the review may raise the suspicion that Government is treating the current legal position as, in effect, constitutionally all-but untouchable when, of course, it is not.

On the other hand, that lack of what Sellers called 'decent humility' has been accompanied by an unhealthy determination constantly to tinker with some kinds of homicide-related legislation, in order to achieve a greater measure of control over conduct, without much—or any—consideration of the principles that may be at stake.[370] We deserve better. Some people may not like the idea that hard-won policy victories on key issues such as abortion or euthanasia should, at a future point, be reconsidered, because they would prefer (wouldn't we all?) to be what I referred to above as 'perpetual winners' in the legislative process.[371] Such people should be willing to grant that republican impartiality requires such reconsideration, because the alternative is to accept that there can (should?) be an under-class of what I referred to as 'doomed losers' in political and moral debate, even on matters of high principle about which reasonable people disagree. Showing proper respect to fellow citizens demands that we do not tolerate such a situation.

3. Liberal-progressives and democratic criminal law-making

At first blush, this chapter may seem like a sustained critique of liberal-progressive influence on the law of homicide, but it is not. As I said earlier, there is much to be said for many liberal-progressive principles, and for their influence within the criminal law in general,[372] and on the law of homicide in particular. My focus

---

[368] See Law Commission (2005), at 1 (Terms of Reference). That is not to say that the Law Commission would have been the right body to consider such matters. The issue is whether, at the same time as the Commission's review, the Government would itself undertake review of the broader issues.

[369] <http://webarchive.nationalarchives.gov.uk/+/http://berr.gov.uk/policies/better-regulation/consultation-guidance>.

[370] See the discussion of road traffic legislation in Ch 2.

[371] See the passage cited from Waldron (1993) at n 363 above.

[372] See, eg, Jeremy Horder (2004), chs 4 and 5; and text at n 139 above.

has been on the way in which Governments, law reformers, and scholars have sought to secure and retain that influence within, and beyond, the law of homicide. As we have seen, one or more such groups have at different times dressed up liberal-progressive principles as technical or craft matters best left to the experts, excluded these principles from testing at the bar of professionally researched public opinion, or protected these principles—once embodied in legislation—from systematic subjection to periodic review. None of these strategies is right, or fair to those who oppose such principles. Liberal-progressives in universities, the professions, and Government should have the confidence, as well as the decent humility, to seek to secure ideals through, rather than insulated from, the influence of public opinion and public debate.[373] As Waldron puts it:

> Things might be different if principles of right were self-evident or if there were a philosophical elite who could be trusted to work out once and for all what rights we have and how they are to be balanced against other considerations. But the consensus of philosophers is that these matters are not settled, that they are complex and controversial. . . . [So, the] question, 'Who gets to participate?', always has priority over the question, 'How do they decide, when they disagree?'.[374]

Waldron, and others in this 'republican' tradition of constitutional thinking naturally see the 'who gets to participate?' question as concerned primarily with elected representatives. By contrast, in this context, elected representatives can sometimes be part of the problem, as well as part of the solution, in so far as they seek (in the name of the public) to impose their preferred reforms on the public, without any kind of investigation of what the public wants. Giving proper effect to the republican ideal, for the purposes of homicide law reform, entails seeking a role for members of the public (having been selected such that as a group they adequately reflect the public[375]) as representatives of the public. A thorough-going and good faith commitment to this ideal could mean such groups eventually attaining the kind of status, in relation to law reform, that juries now have when determining the outcome of individual criminal cases.[376] Their contribution could jointly come to be understood and appreciated as having distinctive and intrinsic

---

[373] The same remark could be made, of course, to those with right-wing views about the structure of the substantive criminal law; but since such people are non-existent in academia, and few and far between elsewhere, I have not concerned myself with them. Right-wingers on matters of sentencing and criminal procedure abound, of course, in Parliament, even if they remain as rare as hens' teeth amongst experts in England and Wales.

[374] Waldron (1993), at 50.

[375] By way of contrast with juries, who also *represent* the public, but on a basis for selection, given the logistical and cost constraints involved, that even when relatively randomized cannot be *representative* of the public in each and every case. It is doubtful, in any event, if only 12 people can be sufficiently representative of the public.

[376] I hope (without much confidence) that this reference to the 'status' of juries will not mislead readers into thinking that I am suggesting that there is a direct analogy between the role of juries and the role of the public in evaluating law reform proposals. The selection of each is clearly for very different purposes, and the method of selection (amongst other things) reflects that fact. I am concerned only with establishing that the very different roles of both juries and representative members of the public are linked by the fact that their roles provide intrinsic, and not merely instrumental, value to the practice of law and law reform.

value in the governance of the polity. Famously, for Blackstone, the jury was 'looked upon as the glory of the English law'.[377] This was, amongst other things, because on the one hand, if left to officials the administration of justice might fall victim to, 'an involuntary bias towards those of their [the officials'] rank and dignity',[378] and because 'it is not to be expected from human nature, that the few should always be attentive to the interests and good of many'.[379] On the other hand, if the administration of justice was left to lay people outside the governance of legal rules, 'at random in the hands of the multitude, their decisions would be wild and capricious . . . '.[380] Homicide law reform (and the reform of other violative crimes), informed and guided by properly researched and representative public opinion, is meant to be a way of plotting a course between broadly the same undesirable extremes. I do not believe it is altogether fanciful to suggest that, if a determined and consistent effort were engaged in to make the law reform process pursue that course, the process could itself in time become one of the 'glories' of English criminal law.

---

[377] Blackstone (1765–69), book 3, ch 23.
[378] *Ibid.*   [379] *Ibid.*   [380] *Ibid.*

2

The Rise of Regulation and the Fate
of the Common Law

I. Introduction

I shall try to show how the development of and demand for discrete, specialized, and context-sensitive offences of homicide reflects the modern emergence of a distinctive cast of thought about the nature and function of homicide law reform. This is the regulatory or bureaucratic–administrative cast of thought, according to which law is understood mainly as a malleable tool to be fashioned in a way that will promote the achievement of specific ends in a particular context, when the public interest demands this. We encountered it in Chapter 1, when we saw how Government uses consultation at least in part as a way to garner a range of expert and more or less specialist opinion on homicide, to increase the element of the '*zweckrationell*'[1] in homicide law reform. In the present context, this Weberian idea[2] is taken much further, becoming an important motivating force behind legislation. The predictability of, and hence control over, desired results (the reduction of unjustified killing) in a particular context takes precedence in the definition of offences over the element of the '*wertrationell*'[3] that is so central to traditional offences of homicide at common law. The bureaucratic–administrative cast of thought has in effect come to rival an older tradition of thought about the nature of law that I shall (somewhat misleadingly) call the 'traditional–codificatory' ideal. As we shall see in the next section, the traditional–codificatory ideal, focused on common law offences, began to come to prominence over 200 years ago, and since then has influenced almost all formal proposals to reform the law of murder and manslaughter up to the present day. Those who think in a traditional–codificatory style see law reform as involving the retention, with a greater or lesser degree of modernization, of traditional crimes involving *mala in se* (murder, manslaughter, burglary, arson, rape, and so on). They seek, though, to improve on the definition of such crimes by turning them into more general, and more readily comprehensible rules and principles, applicable to all persons irrespective of the context in which the harm is inflicted.

The bureaucratic–administrative style of thought is here to stay, and can undoubtedly add an important new problem-solving dimension to reform of the law of homicide. No one should mourn the loss of total hegemony in the field of

---

[1] 'Goal-rationality'.   [2] Weber (1947), at 337.   [3] 'Value-rationality'.

homicide by the crimes of murder and manslaughter, the crimes that exemplify the traditional–codificatory cast of thought in the domain of homicide. However, I shall argue that something worth retaining may indeed be lost—most particularly in point of legitimacy—by simply abandoning traditional–codificatory styles of thinking (and with them, common law crimes) when shaping homicide law reform. It may sometimes be better to use regulatory forms of law to *support* the application of murder and manslaughter to homicides committed in contexts where the application of the law has proved difficult or controversial. This may enhance the law's legitimacy more effectively than replacing those two crimes with newly minted homicide offences purportedly tailored to suit those contexts more precisely.

II. Homicide Offences: The Traditional–Codificatory View

There have always been competing accounts of what I am calling the traditional–codificatory perspective on law and law reform.[4] The perspective that I have in mind first comes to prominence in the late eighteenth and early nineteenth centuries, as part of a critique of what was perceived at that time to be the haphazard and piecemeal nature of reform effected by statute.[5] It is focused more on the form than on the substance of the law, in that its principal aim is to make the criminal law more systematic and hence accessible (hence the 'codificatory' element in its name). However, its substance usually takes the form of a more or less modernized version of common law offences (hence the 'traditional' element in its name). In so far as the traditional–codificatory model does draw for its substance on a version of the common law, its ideal is law comprised of accessibly formulated general rules, applicable to all persons largely irrespective of the context in which they act. Ironically, the ambitions of the traditional–codificatory view, in terms of the law's form rather than its substance, were an important part of the reforming agenda of Jeremy Bentham, in other respects the common law's most trenchant critic. This is because not only does the traditional–codificatory view by its nature require embodiment in statute, but because it is perfectly consistent with—indeed, may exemplify—rule utilitarianism of a kind favoured by Bentham. What are the origins of this traditional–codificatory perspective (about which more detail will be given in due course)?

Famously, Bentham caricatured Sir William Blackstone as concerned only with the law as it is, he—Bentham—being concerned with the law as it ought to be.[6] Nonetheless, they shared the view that parliamentary intervention in the law (the Murder Act of 1752 being an example[7]) had to that point been entirely unsatisfactory because of its concern largely for the ephemeral, as opposed to the enduring,

---

[4] See Postema (2003); Farmer (2000).
[5] See generally, Farmer (2000).
[6] Bentham (1789), ch XVII.
[7] See Law Commission (2005), at para 1.94.

and for the particular over and above the general. Encouraging legislators to avoid 'quackery in Government', Blackstone complained that:

To say the truth, almost all the perplexed questions, almost all the niceties, intricacies and delays (which have sometimes disgraced the English . . . courts of justice) owe their origin not to the common law itself, but to innovations that have been made in it by Acts of Parliament.[8]

With this observation, of course, he coupled the view that it would be 'too Herculean a task' for a popular assembly to replace any 'fundamental point' of common law,[9] a view with which Bentham famously and vehemently disagreed.[10] However, Bentham's views on Parliament's record in legislating within the criminal field were strikingly similar,[11] albeit expressed in more lurid terms:

The country squire who has his turnips stolen, goes to work and gets a bloody law against stealing turnips. It exceeds the utmost stretch of his comprehension to conceive that the next year the same catastrophe may happen to his potatoes. For two general rules . . . in modern British legislation are: never to move a finger until your passions are inflamed, nor ever to look further than your nose.[12]

Whether—and if so, why—twentieth and twenty-first century homicide legislation suffers from a modern-day version of such vices will be questions addressed in later sections. What did Blackstone, Bentham, and others who shared their views, see as the remedy for such 'particularism' in statutory law reform?[13] One theme in particular predominates. For Blackstone, the criminal law 'should be founded upon principles that are permanent, uniform and universal'.[14] For Bentham, the law must be comprised of 'written, visible, and intelligible and cognoscible rule[s] of action and guide[s] to human conduct'.[15] To similar effect, for other commentators, such as Anthony Hammond,[16] what was needed was the 'substitution of general rules for particular decrees',[17] or, as one commentator put it: 'We would melt down the old, alloyed, and shapeless coin, in order to recast, in a pure and symmetrical shape, the large quantity of precious metal which it contains.'[18]

---

[8] Blackstone (1765–69), vol 1, at 10, cited by Smith (1998), at 73.

[9] Blackstone (1765–69), vol 3, at 267, cited by Smith (1998), at 73.

[10] See Schofield and Harris (1998), at 20–1.

[11] See Smith (1998), at 73–4.

[12] Bentham MSS in the library of University College, London, cxl 92, cited in Postema (1986), at 264.

[13] On the vice of particularism in legislation, see Horder (1994).

[14] Cited by Smith (1998), at 20.

[15] Cited by Schofield and Harris (1998), at 18–21.

[16] Principal author of the 1824 Report of the Select Committee on Criminal Law: see the useful discussion in Smith (1998), at 80–3.

[17] Hammond (1829), Introduction, at xiv–xvi, cited by Smith (1998), at 82.

[18] Anon (1830), at 333, cited by Smith (1998), at 75. The commentator goes on to say, 'Mr Bentham would throw away the whole, silver as well as copper'; but that is an observation on differences of opinion about the content the new rules should have (the point about 'precious metal' supposedly contained in the common law), and not on the form the law should take to accommodate the content.

To be sure, there were great differences of opinion amongst these authors about the content the new model criminal law should have. Should it, for example, be shaped by the existing common law—the 'large quantity of precious metal'—or be determined instead by the new principle of utility?[19] For Sir James Stephen, for example, whose efforts to produce a criminal code comprised of general rules had such great influence on the development of the criminal law in the Commonwealth, 'two things only remain, positive rules, the will of ... a legislator, and the principle of general utility'.[20] However, what united this disparate group of commentators was the sense that, whatever the principles governing its content ought to be, law should be comprised of general, uniform, or universal rules. Moreover, these rules were to take a form such that they were 'intelligible and cognoscible' (in Bentham's words), or as William Eden put it, 'clearly obvious to common understandings and fully notified to the people'.[21] The rules were, in other words, to be addressed (or at least address-able) to citizens rather than just to lawyers. Sir James Stephen argued that reform must take a form such that 'the old law books and reports must be distilled into a portable and intelligible form, so that the nation at large may have some conception of its rights and obligations'.[22] To underline his point, in this respect, Stephen sought to make actions speak as loudly as words by giving a (well-received) lecture on codification to a meeting with the Trades Union Congress, which lasted several hours in 1877.[23] To similar effect, the Attorney-General said, in a speech on 3 April 1879:

Surely, it is a desirable thing that anybody who may want to know the law on a particular subject should be able to turn to a chapter of the Code, and there find the law he is in search of explained in a few intelligible and well-constructed sentences ... [having] a succinct and clear statement before him.[24]

How should the traditional–codificatory account of law-making be understood, in theoretical terms?

III. The Traditional–Codificatory Account Theorized

1. Reform proposals inspired by common law principles

In answering this question, let us take, by way of example, the 1878–79 Homicide Bill and its successor, the Law Commission's recommendations for reform of

---

[19] See n 18 above.

[20] Stephen (1892), at 210 and 219, cited by Smith (1988), at 50. As it turned out, for Stephen what Stephen took to be consonant with the principle of general utility were largely the requirements of the existing common law: see Horder (2002b), at 461–2.

[21] Eden (1771), at 312.

[22] Stephen (1856), at 252.

[23] For an account of the proceedings, see Hostettler (1995), at 165–70. Hostettler notes that Stephen observed, in relation to the TUC's dislike of common law principles, 'their dead silence when I said anything in its praise and their eager applause when I found fault with it. I felt very queerly towards them' (*ibid*). Stephen's Code even received the commendation of the normally satirical *Punch* Magazine, which on 20 July 1878 said, 'Punch takes off his cap and bells to Sir James Stephen— Protomendor, and not also, strange to say, as yet, Proto-martyr, of our criminal law' (*ibid*, at 179).

[24] *Hansard*, HC 3 April 1879, Vol 245 (3rd Series) col 316, cited by Bingham (1998), at 696.

the law of murder. They are both attempts to give effect to a broadly common law model of murder within the law of homicide. The 1878–79 Bill's traditional–codificatory element, as I have explained that notion *qua* the ideal of law-making, can be found in its attempt to define the primary offence of murder (excluding felony murder) through a general rule expressed in ordinary language:

Culpable homicide is murder...

  (a) if the offender means to cause the death...

  (b) if the offender means to cause to the person killed any bodily injury which is known to the offender to be likely to cause death, and if the offender, whether he does or does not mean to cause death, is reckless whether death ensues or not...

  (c) killing with intent to inflict grievous bodily harm in order to facilitate [a certain range of offences].

The Law Commission's recommendation that there should be created offences of first and second degree murder is a recommendation from the same intellectual stable. The Commission's recommendation for the offences of first and second degree murder (setting aside the effect of defences), for example, is that they should be comprised of:

  (a) Killing intentionally [first degree murder].

  (b) Killing where there was an intention to do serious injury, coupled with an awareness of a serious risk of causing death [first degree murder].

  (c) Killing where the offender intended to do serious injury [second degree murder].

  (d) Killing where the offender intended to cause some injury or a fear or risk of injury, and was aware of a serious risk of causing death [second degree murder].[25]

These recommendations, like the rules of common law homicide on which they are founded,[26] are a classic embodiment of what has been called the '*gesellschaft*' ideal of law, law that involves: 'pervasive and essentially exhaustive rules of conduct for all relations between individuals, which are to be applied to any circumstances at all'.[27] As we will see in the next section, it is this—*gesellschaft*—aspect of common law homicide that has come to be seen as inimical to a primarily regulatory, context-dependent and means-end dominated scheme for the reduction of lethal harm, especially lethal harm caused on the roads.

However, in its dependence on primarily value-laden as opposed to predominantly descriptive labels ('murder' and 'manslaughter', as opposed to, say, 'causing death by dangerous driving'), common law homicide—and the proposals to reform it—also hark back to a pre-modern '*gemeinschaft*' ideal of law, in which:

---

[25] Law Commission (2006), at para 1.67. For a comparison between the 1879 Bill and the Law Commission's recommendations, see Ch 3 below.

[26] Such as Coke's famous definition of murder, still in small part good law today: see the discussion in Law Commission (2005), at para 1.52.

[27] Kamenka and Tay (1975), at 319.

the emphasis is on law and regulation as expressing ... internalised norms and traditions of an organic society.... Here there tends to be no sharp distinction, if there is any formal distinction at all, between ... legal issues and moral issues.[28]

This feature of the common law ideal of homicide remains attractive,[29] even in the regulatory context that (as we shall see in the next section) has come to exercise such an important influence on the law of homicide in relatively recent years. The enduring nature of public identification with an internalized norm such as 'manslaughter', has led reformers to embrace some intermingling of the *gemeinschaft* forms of law and administrative-regulatory forms of law, to give the latter greater moral credibility. The creation of an offence of 'corporate manslaughter' perhaps best encapsulates this phenomenon.[30] The new crime involves the adaptation of a general common law crime, with its value-laden and retribution-orientated *gemeinschaft* label (manslaughter), to fit a specific regulatory context: that of accident caused by gross breach of a duty of care resulting at least in part from, 'the way in which any of [an] organisation's activities are managed or organised by its senior managers'.[31]

2. The impact of regulatory thinking on the common law model

There are dangers in seeking to splice together forms of law from such different traditions of legal thought. The creation of the crime of corporate manslaughter can be seen as a classic illustration of what Lacey, Wells, and Quick have identified as an important tension within modern criminal law between kinds of law:

That between the older ideas of crime as public wrongdoing and the modern reality of criminal law as a predominantly administrative system managing enormous numbers of ... 'regulatory offences': between the older, quasi-moral and retributive view of criminal law and the instrumental, regulatory aspect of criminal law which has become increasingly dominant under modern and late modern conditions.[32]

The rise of the regulatory state involves challenges to the traditional reliance on the impartial application of very general rules of law that cut across any concern for contextualization, challenges generated by new demands for specialized governance of professions and industries, in the public interest:

[T]he growing concern with and interest in the law of certain areas—broadcasting, fishery, trade practices, the environment—is necessarily one that requires bureaucratic-administrative

---

[28] *Ibid.*

[29] In its review of homicide, for example, the Law Commission found almost unanimous support for the retention of the terms 'murder' and 'manslaughter', even if there was less agreement on the wrongs that each should represent: see Law Commission (2006), at para 2.2.

[30] See the Corporate Manslaughter and Corporate Homicide Act 2007, discussed in Ch 4 below. On the draft proposals, see further, Sullivan (2001).

[31] Section 1(3). The regulatory dimension to the offence is brought out in s 8(2), where the 'gross' character of any breach of duty is to be determined by the jury in part by consideration of whether—and to what extent—the organization was in breach of existing health and safety legislation.

[32] Lacey, Wells, and Quick (2003), at 7–8.

forms and attitudes: it seeks to regulate an activity and not to adjudicate in collisions between individuals; its fundamental concern is with consequences rather than with fault or *mens rea*, with public need or public interest, or the interest of the activity itself, rather than private rights and individual duties.[33]

In the case of homicide, the process of adjudicating in cases of 'collisions between individuals' may come itself to be shaped by regulatory, public interest-based demands. In some instances—the road traffic context being the prime example— these demands have led to an effective displacement from the relevant legal space of rules of homicide (and of manslaughter in particular) that embody common law principles. To replace such rules, offences specially tailored to the regulatory context[34] have from time to time been created and subsequently reformed, to reflect—amongst other things—the changing demands of that regulatory context.

However, tension of the kind referred to by Lacey, Wells, and Quick is not to be found only between the forms of law. It may also be found in the way that each form of law generates different expectations about labelling and punishment, expectations that may prove hard for the state to 'manage' (the management of expectations being yet another emerging task for the modern state). A conviction for 'manslaughter' implies serious wrongdoing and at first blush the need, unless there are exceptional circumstances, for harsh punishment. By way of contrast, conviction for a regulatory offence need carry no such implications on its face.[35] So, the severe limitation on punishment for corporate manslaughter (no sentence of imprisonment can be imposed[36]) creates the appearance of legal paradox: a serious crime without serious penal consequences.[37]

Conversely, consider the effective confinement of criminalization of death on the roads to the regulatory offences of causing death by various forms of dangerous or careless driving.[38] This way of dealing with homicide, arising in the course of regulated activity, arguably carries an implication that offenders will be punished in a way substantially more reflective of the need to secure their future compliance with regulations, than of any need to reflect simple public condemnation and demands for vengeance. The implication is reinforced by the presence of such offences in Road Traffic Acts otherwise much taken up with road *safety* issues, rather than in a homicide statute.[39] Yet, the maximum sentence for causing death by dangerous driving has now been increased to fourteen years' imprisonment. This is a maximum sentence once considered appropriate by the Law Commission as a maximum for the substantive offence of manslaughter itself, a crime whose

[33] Kamenka and Tay (1975), at 138–9.

[34] Such as causing death by dangerous driving, or causing death by careless driving.

[35] In fact, I shall suggest later that if the labelling is regarded as part of the punishment, then the labelling may be regarded as an integral element in what it means to satisfy legitimate expectations that corporate killing is taken seriously, quite apart from any other element of punishment imposed.

[36] Corporate Manslaughter and Corporate Homicide Act 2007, s 1(6).

[37] But see section VIII. below.

[38] To be considered in further detail in ensuing sections.

[39] On the appropriateness of the legal 'location' of homicide-related law, see Ch 3 below. On the 'road safety' dimension to dangerous and careless driving, see Cunningham (2007).

rationale is focused principally on the demand for public condemnation in individual cases rather than on the possibility of securing future compliance in the context in which the offence took place.[40] The offence of causing death by dangerous driving (together with its punishment) has in effect outgrown its origin merely as a heavy-duty tool for reinforcing a deterrent regulatory message about road safety. The offence has become more like a traditional common law crime, in which the public interest in securing retribution typically predominates over other (more forward-looking) concerns. It has proved difficult, then, for Governments to have their cake and eat it too. It has not been easy to satisfy the perceived need, for deterrence reasons, to increase road safety through increasing numbers of prosecutions and convictions for causing death on the roads (taking the administrative-regulatory approach, rather than leaving homicides to be dealt with as potential manslaughters), whilst also satisfying the demand for sentences of a retributive kind that would certainly have fitted the crime, had it remained manslaughter.[41]

Nonetheless, support should be given to the way in which, for example, the corporate manslaughter offence seeks to combine forms of law reflecting different casts of legal thought. Seen in a positive light, such a strategy can be regarded as a way of helping traditional ways of thinking and categorizing to find continued meaning and relevance in a modern regulatory context: here, in the shape of a 'bureaucratic–administrative' form of law[42] with a *gemeinschaft* label, 'manslaughter'.[43] The argument may turn out to be, then, that reformers should have adopted such an approach, an approach more supportive of the common law's mixture of *gesellschaft* and *gemeinschaft* forms of law, in the road traffic and perhaps also in other contexts. This is a theme to which I will return later.

IV. Homicide Offences: Competing Models

In the work of some thinkers, the preservation or pursuit of the *gesellschaft* element in the common law has been turned into an ideology of freedom under the rule of law. In FA Hayek's writing on the rule of law, for example, he suggests that:

When we obey laws, in the sense of general abstract rules laid down irrespective of their application to us we are not subject to another man's will and are therefore free. It is because the lawgiver does not know the particular cases to which his rules apply . . . that it can be said that laws and not men rule. . . . As a true law should not name any particulars, so it should especially not single out any specific person or group of persons.[44]

The idea that there might be a unique association between this view of law (a version of the common law ideal of law-making described in section I. above) and freedom under the rule of law was shown to be wrong some years ago.[45] Kinds of law that are very far from the *gesellschaft* form of law may still be perfectly capable

---

[40] See generally, Law Commission (1996).

[41] Similar problems have been identified in relation to the new offence of causing death by careless driving: see Cunningham (2007), at 297–302.

[42] Explained in section IV.   [43] See further, Clarkson (1998).

[44] Hayek (1944), at 54.   [45] See Raz (1979), ch 11.

of satisfying the demands of the rule of law. Nonetheless, Hayek's exposition of the *gesellschaft* form of law captures something of importance, when applied to the criminal law. It links modern departures from that form of law to a wish, through law, to subject people—'specific... group[s] of persons'—more closely to another's (the legislator's) will. The latter approach is what, building on the analysis in the preceding section, we can call the bureaucratic–administrative or regulatory model of law. This model has (misleadingly) been associated by some with the rise of legal positivist thinking. So, for example, Richard Tur has suggested that, '[I]deal-typically, positivism may be characterised by such notions as "fact", "will", "power", "instrumentalism", "discretion", "*mala prohibita*", etc.'.[46] To similar effect, Lon Fuller spoke of legal positivism in terms of a 'managerial' or 'top down' one-way projection of power and authority.[47] Whatever the merits of the association of these notions with legal positivism, they are most certainly associated with the regulatory model of law.

Very broadly, some of the contrasting aims and elements of the bureaucratic–administrative or regulatory model, as compared with the common law or the traditional–codificatory models, might be summarized as follows (it is far from an exhaustive list):

Common law/traditional–codificatory model

1. General applicability (not context specific).
2. Application to all citizens equally.
3. Fault element required.
4. Classical view of responsibility and causation.
5. Comprised of *mala in se.*
6. Legitimacy not tied to consequentialist evaluation.
7. Labels descriptively evaluative.[48]

Regulatory or bureaucratic—administrative model

1. Context-specific application.
2. Targeted at particular groups.
3. Fault elements dispensable or watered down.
4. Responsibility and causation elements malleable.
5. Blurring of *mala in se/mala prohibita* distinction.
6. The outcomes that law produces are crucial to legitimacy.
7. Labels descriptively factual.[49]

---

[46] Tur (1986), at 23. It seems rather doubtful that legal positivism can be associated with any particular style of legislation, let alone a particular style of government or administration.

[47] Fuller (1969), at 139.

[48] In other words, they seek not merely to describe an activity, but simultaneously to mark its wrongfulness. Examples are not only murder and manslaughter, but also arson, burglary, and rape.

[49] So, in contrast to examples given in n 48, examples under this heading would be causing death during unlicensed, disqualified, or uninsured driving (Road Safety Act 2006), or causing the death of a child or vulnerable adult (Domestic Violence, Crime and Victims Act 2004).

The aims and elements of the regulatory model are linked to the rise of a concern—outlined in the preceding section—for the management of sectors of society or specific fields of activity in the 'public interest', understood in terms of the achievement of certain public goods. Nonetheless, in spite of the positive listing of distinctive features of each model, it must be kept firmly in mind that these are ideal-types or casts of thought and not rigid categories that are designed to have thorough-going normative significance. Not all homicide-related offences fall clearly into one category or other, and not all offences clearly within one category will exemplify all the seven characteristics within that category: they may embody some of the characteristics listed in the other category. I am certainly not claiming, for example, either that the offences of murder and manslaughter have been developed without regard to the consequences of adopting certain kinds of definition (element 6); clearly, they have. It is not part of my plan to seek to place every homicide-related offence clearly within the province of one model or the other (a largely sterile and inevitably ahistorical exercise), but to chart the gradual emergence of the regulatory model as a force within a domain that was previously that of the common law or of the traditional–codificatory model.

The need for caution in allocating offences firmly to one model or another is illustrated by modern developments in relation to the offences of murder and manslaughter, offences one might think of as classic examples of homicide offences developed largely under the influence of the common law or traditional–codificatory models. Each of these crimes has been overlaid with a substantially regulatory covering, in the form of element 6 (making outcomes crucial to legitimacy). In the case of murder, that has come through the introduction of guidance—controlled by the Secretary of State for Justice—on the extent of punishment that should follow conviction for murder in particular kinds of circumstances.[50] This is an attempt to introduce a degree of direct (regulatory) Government influence on when the punitive outcomes of murder cases are to be regarded as legitimate. Similarly, the classes of person who stand to be convicted of corporate manslaughter have been placed under the control of the Secretary of State for Justice, who may change them by amending the relevant schedule.[51] This provision obviously brings element 2 (is there equality of application, or are some groups (dis)favoured?) into play; but element 6 is at issue, in that there is manifestly a wish to ensure that the new law's legitimacy is not undermined by application in what are regarded by Government as inappropriate contexts. So, even in the heartland of the common law, as Hayek impliedly suggested, the rise of regulatory forms of legal intervention may lead to attempts to subject some groups rather than others more closely to the legislator's will, thus blurring the line between 'purely' common law offences and regulatory offences.

---

[50] Criminal Justice Act 2003, s 269 (sch 21).
[51] Corporate Manslaughter and Corporate Homicide Act 2007, ss 21 and 22.

V. The Regulatory Model Exemplified

What might be examples of offences classically regarded as regulatory or bureaucratic–administrative in nature? The most obvious examples are the specific offences concerned with death on the roads, of which more will be said below. As is well-known, these offences began with the creation of the offence of causing death by 'reckless or dangerous' driving under the Road Traffic Act 1956, with a maximum sentence (at that time) of five years' imprisonment. By its very nature, this offence fulfils elements 1 and 2 of the regulatory model of law, being context-specific and targeted at particular groups (driving and drivers, respectively). Further, in the way that its wording has come to be reformed—it is now causing death by 'dangerous' driving rather than by grossly negligent driving[52]—it fulfils element 3 by watering down the fault requirement (as, *a fortiori*, is the case with the new offence of causing death during unlicensed, disqualified, or uninsured driving[53]).[54] This change to the offence also means that it has come to fulfil element 5, in that causing death by dangerous driving now rests on a blurred line between *mala in se* and *mala prohibita*, a development reinforced by the reliance on more descriptive than evaluative labels ('causing death by dangerous driving', as opposed to 'manslaughter'). Element 5 has been further reinforced by the indication from the Crown Prosecution Service that a manslaughter charge should not be brought in a case where death has been caused by dangerous driving, even if the elements of that offence may well have been fulfilled, unless it is a 'case of the utmost gravity'.[55]

More than a hint of element 4 can be found in the offence of 'aggravated vehicle-taking' contrary to the Theft Act 1968, section 12A. Broadly speaking, for this offence to be committed, it is only necessary for D, knowing that a vehicle has been taken without authority, to 'allow...himself to be carried in it', and for it then to be proved that (fatal) injury was caused by the driving of the vehicle. D will be guilty unless he or she can show inter alia that he or she was not in or in the immediate vicinity of the vehicle when the driving, or the accident, occurred. When, in such circumstances, death is caused, a sentence of up to fourteen years' imprisonment may be imposed. It might be thought hard to imagine, in any criminal offence, a more tenuous connection in terms of responsibility and causation between what D 'did' and any death that occurred.

However, an approach as broad or even broader has been adopted by some state legislatures in the United States to provide a means of securing additional deterrents to, as well as retribution against, those involved in supplying illegal drugs that have

---

[52] As a result of the changes effected by the Road Traffic Act 1988, s 1.

[53] See the Road Safety Act 2006, s 21.

[54] It is worth emphasizing that the very broad notion of 'danger' that governs the offence under s 1 of the Road Traffic Act 1988—see text at n 86 below—has not been narrowed (still less has any enhanced fault requirement been introduced) to reflect the fact that the maximum penalty has over time almost tripled to 14 years' imprisonment.

[55] <www.cps.gov.uk/publications/prosecution/pbd_policy.html>.

killed a user. An example is the creation of the offence of 'third degree murder' in Pennsylvania, defined as follows:

Section 2506. Drug delivery resulting in death.

(a) General rule.—A person commits murder of the third degree who administers, dispenses, delivers, gives, prescribes, sells or distributes any controlled substance or counterfeit controlled substance . . . and another person dies as a result of using the substance.[56]

This offence, punishable by a minimum of five years' imprisonment, may be committed even when the actions of a third party or the victim him or herself—with no less knowledge of the risks than the accused—have occurred between the act of the accused person who sold, delivered, gave, or distributed (and so on) the drug, and the victim's 'resulting' death. Notoriously, the Court of Criminal Appeal at one time took some faltering steps towards a similar position, through manipulation of common law doctrines,[57] although these steps were decisively halted by the House of Lords' decision in *Kennedy*.[58] The very fact that such developments have been mired in confusion and controversy is a sure sign that the attenuated forms of responsibility and causation that may connect a drug supplier to an ultimate user's death, whilst capable of being addressed through malleable regulatory forms of law, cannot easily be adapted to fit the principles constitutive of a common law or traditional–codificatory framework.[59]

However, it is the emergence of element 6 that is perhaps the most interesting in this context. It has long been a strongly held opinion amongst most lawyers that common law offences, such as murder and manslaughter, should not have their meanings unduly twisted or distorted by judicial interpretation, solely in order to capture particular forms of wrongdoing that might otherwise fall outside their scope. In other words, element 6 of the common law or the traditional–codificatory models is an important criminal law principle (even if frequently honoured in the breach[60]). By way of contrast, frequent change in the nature, scope, and quantity of offences, in the name of the public interest (element 6 under the regulatory model), can be an acceptable norm in the regulatory sphere. In recent years, the offences connected with death on the roads have multiplied (there are now at least four such

---

[56] Pennsylvania Consolidated Statutes, Crimes and Offences (Title 18), c25, s 2506.

[57] For analyses of the case law, and opposing views about the direction the law should take, see Ormerod and Fortson (2005); Jones (2006).

[58] *Kennedy (No 2)* [2007] UKHL 38.

[59] See Ormerod and Fortson (2005). It is worth noting, in passing, how the existence of regulatory crimes such as the one under discussion ought to be regarded as casting a significant shadow over the modern demand for a more 'contextual' approach to criminalization. We can now see how the left-liberal cast to many such demands stems solely from their partisan nature: they typically focus on the contextual circumstances that show up the offender in a favourable light. But if a truly contextual approach is to be taken in a non-partisan way, then law reformers would be free additionally to focus on—perhaps obliged additionally to focus on—circumstances that aggravate the offence, such as secondary or 'knock-on' harms or setbacks to the relatives of victims, to those living in the locality, and so on.

[60] A thesis developed with all the indignation he could muster by Williams (1983). He said of judicial activism in the criminal law, 'the expansion of the law is unavowed . . . the judges keeping up the pretence that they are mere mouthpieces of the law . . . [whereas] . . . to the discerning eye [a judicial decision] is often no more than . . . rationalisation accompanied by misdirection and legerdemain' (*ibid*, at 16).

offences[61]) as new policy concerns have emerged, such as concern about a rise in the number of unlicensed or uninsured drivers. Further, as I have already mentioned, there has been tacking to and fro between narrower and broader versions of some offences, in response to real or perceived difficulties in prosecuting different versions. So, for example, having begun with causing death by reckless or dangerous driving, in the Road Traffic Act 1956, we moved through its narrower version— causing death by reckless driving[62]—to the current offence of causing death by dangerous driving in the Road Traffic 1988.[63]

Let me put on one side the questions whether these changes of policy tack have been effective, and whether they have been motivated more by a wish to placate vocal pressure groups and newspaper editors than by a genuine concern for public policy.[64] What is significant in this context is how an overriding public interest concern (howsoever construed) in enhanced road safety has led to continued experimentation in different forms of offence. We have moved towards what Hayek might have referred to as the greater subjection of the regulated group to the 'will' of the legislator, in a way that might be regarded by many as unacceptable or dysfunctional had it occurred with the development of a common law offence.[65]

VI. Murder and Manslaughter: The Growing Crisis of Confidence

1. Breaches in the wall: three early examples

Let me now set the discussion in a broader context. The last 100 years have seen a wide-ranging erosion of the legal hegemony previously enjoyed by the common law crimes of murder and manslaughter in the domain of homicide.[66] Even so, Parliament has not (other than in the road traffic context) gone so far as to make 'causing death' an aggravating factor of a whole range of non-fatal offences, in the

---

[61] See Cunningham (2007), at 288.

[62] The Criminal Law Act 1977, s 50 abolished the 'or dangerous' element of what had been the offence of causing death by reckless or dangerous driving.

[63] Similarly, having begun with the offence of taking and driving a vehicle away without authority, contrary to the Road Traffic Act 1960, we moved to the somewhat broader offence of simply 'taking' a vehicle without authority, created by the Criminal Justice Act 1982 (amending the Theft Act 1968, s 12), which was then supplemented by the offence of aggravated vehicle-taking, in the Aggravated Vehicle Taking Act 1992, the offence that involves a further 'aggravating element' when death is caused: see text following n 55 above.

[64] For discussion on this point, see Cunningham (2007), at 301–2.

[65] However, such developments have begun to affect both murder and manslaughter. The development of the common law is not, of course, immune from 'tacking to and fro' with regard to fault or other elements of offences, or from policy-related changes. The difference lies in the fact that, under the regulatory model, experimentation and (occasionally) 'tacking to and fro' may be intentionally adopted as a medium- to long-term *strategy*, whereas this is difficult or impossible in a precedent-based system of case-by-case common law development.

[66] See further, Lacey, Wells, and Quick (2003), ch 6. I put on one side here consideration of the old offence, supervening on murder in certain circumstances, of so-called 'petty treason'.

way that some legislatures have done.[67] Nonetheless, Parliament has intervened to create specific homicide offences of infanticide,[68] 'child destruction',[69] 'assisting suicide',[70] causing death by dangerous driving,[71] and causing or allowing the death of a child or vulnerable adult.[72] In the first three instances (infanticide; child destruction; assisting suicide), the crime of manslaughter could quite easily have been used to achieve one of the effects desired: criminalization other than through the crime of murder. Instead, an entirely context-specific homicide offence was preferred, henceforth cutting off the homicides in question from association with the culturally and historically rich offence label, 'manslaughter'.[73] The contrast, then, is with the approach taken in 1957 to death caused as a result of a partly completed suicide pact.[74] In this instance, there was a wish to avoid the murder label, even when the survivor or survivors of the pact had intentionally caused the death of another member of the pact.[75] However, the solution was to treat such killings as manslaughter, consistent with the traditional approach also taken to provocation (and to diminished responsibility),[76] rather than to create a new offence of 'suicide-pact killing', or the like. The often arbitrary nature of the choice[77] in effecting legal change during the twentieth century, between creating a new specific offence or applying manslaughter, underscores the sense in which it is increasingly no longer seen as morally and legally important to maintain manslaughter's hegemony outside those homicides appropriately labelled as the greater offence of murder.

2. Vulnerable victims: on the road and in the home

In the second set of instances (causing death by dangerous driving; causing or allowing the death of a child or vulnerable adult) the practice of charging manslaughter was perceived to be part of the problem, rather than a potential solution.[78] Let me take first the case of causing death by dangerous driving. It is commonly supposed that it was (at least historically) simple jury reluctance to convict of 'manslaughter' in such circumstances, because of a distaste for the label, that led to

---

[67] See Spencer and Pedain (2005), ch 10. The road traffic context is, of course, the exception in England and Wales: see, eg, Road Safety Act 2006, s 20.

[68] Infanticide Act 1922.

[69] Infant Life (Preservation) Act 1929.   [70] Suicide Act 1961.

[71] Road Traffic Act 1956. See the discussion of this offence in the next section.

[72] Domestic Violence, Crimes and Victims Act 2004.

[73] I should not be taken to be saying that manslaughter would have been an equally appropriate label in each instance. On the face of it, that label seems more appropriate in the case of infanticide than child destruction, given the traditional view that neither murder nor manslaughter apply before a victim has been born alive; but there is clearly room for legitimate disagreement on this point.

[74] Homicide Act 1957, s 4.

[75] For further analysis of the operation of s 4, see Law Commission (2005), pt 8, and Ch 8 below.

[76] Although the pleas of provocation and diminished responsibility are clearly somewhat different in nature to a plea of failed suicide pact, as the latter involves no overt 'subjective' condition in the form of emotional over-reaction or mental disorder: see Law Commission (2005), pt 8.

[77] I do not say that the choice has always been arbitrary. Assisting suicide, for example, seems perfectly appropriately dealt with as a discrete homicide offence.

[78] In that, on the typical set facts at issue in such cases, it was thought to be too difficult to obtain convictions for manslaughter.

ex hypothesi unmerited acquittals.[79] However, if that is so, other solutions more supportive of the continued use of the common law offence of manslaughter could have been adopted to address this problem more directly. An example would have been to require (as is the case more generally with trial by jury in France) that the jury in 'motor manslaughter' cases contain a proportion of lawyers, who could be expected—or even required—to exercise influence on lay members in favour of the strict application of the law to the facts.[80] Furthermore, there is no conclusive evidence that the creation of 'lower impact' labels for offences to make conviction easier actually leads to higher proportions of convictions in the relevant cases. An example, in this context, involves changes to fault requirements. For example, of those charged with causing death by reckless driving, 89 per cent of those prosecuted were convicted in spite of the need to show a high degree of moral fault on the part of the driver;[81] whereas, of those prosecuted for the offence that replaced it, causing death by dangerous driving (involving a wholly objective test), the conviction rate has been 79 per cent.[82] One might seek to argue that the high conviction rate for causing death by reckless driving must reflect the fact that only the worst cases were ever prosecuted; but in fact, prior to the Road Traffic Act 1991, prosecutions for that offence ran at no less than 86 per cent of offences reported, a fractionally higher proportion than has been maintained since 1991.[83]

That brings us directly to the perceived problem that the gross negligence test for liability for manslaughter did not, in any event, cover sufficient ground in this context, because not all 'dangerous' conduct on the roads that may cause death will amount to gross negligence. As Lord Atkin remarked in *Andrews v DPP*:[84]

[The Road Traffic Acts] ... have no direct reference to causing death by negligence ... s. 11 imposes a penalty for driving recklessly or at a speed or in a manner which is dangerous to the public. There can be no doubt that this section covers driving with such a high degree of negligence as that if death were caused the offender would have committed manslaughter. But the converse is not true, and it is perfectly possible that a man may drive at a speed or in a manner dangerous to the public and cause death, and yet not be guilty of manslaughter.[85]

The existence of this 'justice gap' should be acknowledged. However, it is hard to see how the gap can be regarded as having been filled in a way that adequately respects the interests of drivers, when 'dangerous'—for the purposes of the offence of causing death by dangerous driving—includes not only danger of death, but

---

[79] See Ormerod (2005), at 1016.

[80] I accept, of course, that a judgment whether negligence is 'gross' is a matter for each juror, and not something on which advice about the need to apply the law to the facts will necessarily assist; but the point is that once one has accepted that negligence as to causing death was indeed gross, then there should be no shirking the duty to bring in a verdict of manslaughter.

[81] It would be pointless to enter here into the old debate whether so-called '*Caldwell*' recklessness (see *Caldwell* [1981] AC 341) really did involve an assessment of moral fault. In factual terms, if not in strict legal terms, it probably did involve such an assessment in most cases.

[82] Pearce *et al* (2002), ch 4.

[83] *Ibid.*

[84] [1937] AC 576.

[85] *Ibid*, at 583.

danger of any injury or even of nothing more than serious property damage.[86] It is hardly a statement of any originality to point out that such an extensive definition of danger renders the link with causing death opaque, and hence makes questionable the moral basis for the offence as defined.[87] What would have been the difficulty about creating an offence of 'causing death, injury, or serious property damage by dangerous driving', where the meaning of 'dangerous' in relation to each harm means the danger of bringing about that very harm?[88]

So, how should the relationship between causing death by dangerous driving and gross negligence manslaughter have been addressed, given the gap that Lord Atkin rightly saw as existing between them? For what it is worth, the public interest in strong measures being taken against those whose driving poses a danger of death seems to me to justify in law *treating* a death so caused as gross negligence manslaughter.[89] That would be a way of marrying a wish to preserve a common law structure to homicide offences, with the desire—as part of a regulatory scheme—to do justice to the public interest in safety on the roads. It would fit with research into public opinion that, as we saw in Chapter 1, supports the view that killing through some kinds of driving, especially driving whilst drunk, deserves the label, 'manslaughter'.[90] Yet, successive governments have shown little interest in supporting the application of manslaughter to instances where death has been caused on the road. Classic recent examples are the creation of the specific offences of (a) causing death whilst driving both carelessly and under the influence of drink or drugs,[91] and (b) causing death whilst driving unlicensed, disqualified or uninsured.[92] In both of these instances, it seems highly likely that D could—and should—be found guilty of unlawful and dangerous act manslaughter.[93] Each involves the commission of an unlawful act—respectively, driving under the influence of drink or drugs, and unlicensed, disqualified, or uninsured driving—that may pose a danger of causing some harm, but is not unlawful solely in virtue of

---

[86] Road Traffic Act 1988, s 2A(3). It is, no doubt, the influence of element 3 (fault elements may be watered down) in the regulatory model that provides at least part of the explanation.

[87] See more generally, Ashworth (1993), and the discussion of the correspondence principle in Ch 5 below.

[88] For the view that a correspondence between the nature or degree of fault required and the outcome produced, is defensible where *objective* fault elements are at issue, see Horder (1995). I leave open the question whether 'dangerous' should be (perhaps in part) defined by reference to engagement in specific acts such as 'tailgating', racing another driver, and so on: see on this kind of suggestion, Spencer (1988); Cunningham (2007), at 307–10.

[89] Perhaps subject to a provision that the defendant may raise evidence of an exceptional circumstance, and then show why that should block the inference from dangerousness to gross negligence.

[90] See Mitchell (2000).

[91] Road Traffic Act 1988, s 3A.

[92] Road Safety Act 2006, s 21, inserting s 3ZB into the Road Traffic Act 1988: see further, Cunningham (2007), at 288.

[93] In a slightly different context, see the discussion of this species of manslaughter in Wells (2001), at 117–20. In the case of causing death by careless driving whilst under the influence of drink or drugs, what is the argument that a jury could not or would not find such a person—on a holistic view—to have driven 'dangerously', and hence to be guilty of causing death by dangerous driving in any event? See the scathing comments of the Royal Commission on Transport 1929 about the Ministry's proposal at that time to distinguish between dangerous and careless driving, cited by Pearce *et al* (2002), ch 5.

involving negligent or careless conduct. As is well-known, it is only the latter kinds of unlawful act that may not form the basis of an unlawful and dangerous act manslaughter charge.[94]

Turning to the offence of causing or allowing the death of a child or vulnerable adult, this is an offence of simple negligence, by way of contrast with 'gross' negligence manslaughter.[95] I shall focus on the version of the offence that involves 'allowing' a child or vulnerable adult to be killed by another's unlawful act. The offence is committed if D (a member of the same household as V and having frequent contact with V) ought to have been aware that there was a significant risk of serious harm being unlawfully caused to V, and V's death was so caused by another member of the household in frequent contact with V.[96] D commits the offence if, in such circumstances, D fails to take such steps as could reasonably have been expected to protect V from the risk, and the unlawful act killing V takes place in circumstances of the kind D ought to have foreseen. It is, to say the least, a complex offence. Further, it remains a controversial question whether it should ever be possible to find someone guilty of a homicide offence when they have been guilty of no more than simple negligence.[97] Was the new offence, one that imposes liability on the basis of simple negligence, really necessary?

The Law Commission argued that the offence of manslaughter was inappropriate in this context, because there was doubt whether it could be manslaughter when X—through his or her own carelessness—failed to prevent Y from unlawfully killing V through some deliberate act.[98] It is, though, hard to see how there could be much doubt on that score where X and Y jointly and severally share responsibility for V's welfare, and it is not just a case of Y being V's parent but X only having a separate duty towards V in virtue of being, say, V's doctor.[99] Further, we are still left with the question of why the fault element should be simple negligence rather than the more restrictive gross negligence (in some form). To that question it is not easy to find a clear answer in either the Commission's Report or in the Consultative Report that preceded it.[100] Part of the problem may lie with the traditional unwillingness of criminal lawyers to recognize any legitimate kind of fault other than subjective fault.[101] Having, thus, no high-profile advocates, 'gross' negligence has received no scholarly—and little judicial—analysis and defence,[102]

---

[94] See *Andrews v DPP* [1937] AC 576. Again, it has been, no doubt, a relative lack of concern under the regulatory model for evaluative labelling considerations (element 7) that has led to the failure to place prosecutorial emphasis on this route to conviction.

[95] See Domestic Violence, Crime and Victims Act 2004, s 5.

[96] *Ibid*.

[97] This is perfectly possible in France, for example, but the introduction to England and Wales of an offence of causing death by careless driving has been heavily criticized: see Cunningham (2007).

[98] Law Commission (2003b), at paras 5.55–5.62.

[99] The Australian courts have found a husband liable for manslaughter when he culpably failed to prevent his wife killing their children: *Russell* [1933] VLR 59. In its evidence to the Law Commission, the Crown Prosecution Service argued that the law could be adapted in a way that would enable proof of manslaughter in the difficult cases.

[100] See Law Commission (2003c), at paras 6.20–6.27; Law Commission (2003b), at para 7.18.

[101] For criticism, see, eg, Wells (1982).

[102] See Horder (1997a).

and has hence been treated by the legislature and the Law Commission as involving no difference worth attending to from simple negligence, other than in cases of manslaughter by gross negligence itself.[103]

With these two instances, we see legal change favouring the creation of specific offences, ahead of the provision of support for the application of manslaughter to the supposedly problematic cases. That development has come about, even though there were either ways in which the application of manslaughter could have been better supported, or there is scant evidence that improvements in conviction rates would result from creating a new (lesser) specific offence to displace the application of the more serious offence of common law origin. Once again, thus, we find evidence of a growing loss of faith in the importance of maintaining manslaughter's hegemony in cases of homicide unintentionally caused.

VII. Pressure Group Politics and Specialized Offences

To some extent, these and other related developments reflect two influences whose growth has been an important factor in twentieth century legal politics. These are the increasing significance of the regulatory arm of the state,[104] but also the increasing prominence in legal politics of highly specialized expert or 'single issue' pressure groups.[105] We can detect their influence in more than one legislative change or law reform proposal of recent years that has or would have involved an erosion of the authority or scope of the common law homicide offences.[106] For example, in proposing the creation of an offence of causing or allowing the non-accidental death of a child, effectively displacing manslaughter in the relevant circumstances, the Law Commission said in its 2003 report:

Our inspiration for undertaking this project was the work of the National Society for the Protection of Children ('NSPCC') 'Which of You Did It?' Working Group.... We have benefited greatly from their efforts and the generosity with which they have shared their time and their thoughts.[107]

The central concern of the NSPCC was not in fact the question whether any new offence should be created, as opposed to legal support being given to the application of manslaughter to new circumstances. Its concern was the ineffectiveness of the law in attributing responsibility when the death of a child must have been at the hands of one or other of its parents, but there was no proof or insufficient

---

[103] An example from a different context involves sexual offences. Having consistently held out for subjective tests of fault, and been unwilling to defend 'gross' negligence tests in relation to the consent or the age of the victim, 'subjectivist' judges and scholars now find the reformed law of the Sexual Offences Act 2003 centred on tests of simple negligence.

[104] See section III.2. above, and Lacey, Wells, and Quick (2003), at 6–8.

[105] This issue was also discussed in Ch 1 above.

[106] An important example, not discussed in further detail here, is the influence of the Centre for Corporate Accountability (<www.corporateaccountability.org>) in getting the offence of corporate manslaughter on to the statute book.

[107] Law Commission (2003c), at para 1.8.

proof that it was one parent in particular or both acting in concert. Nonetheless, the specialized focus provided by 'single issue' politics in the field of homicide has a tendency to produce proposals eroding the authority of the more generally applicable common law offences.[108]

An example, where an expert perspective has exerted such influence, can be found in the draft Bill that was to legalize assisted dying for the terminally ill.[109] In supporting the Bill at the second reading stage, Lord Joffe (the sponsor of the Bill) said, even before he gave the statistics relating to public opinion:

Let us *start* with the experts. There is a strong division of opinion among them. For example, the Royal College of Physicians was in favour of neutrality when it gave evidence to the Committee but later, after a consultation process, decided to oppose the Bill. The British Medical Association was against the Bill when it gave evidence, but subsequently changed to a position of neutrality. The Royal College of Nurses was against the Bill, but a survey in the Nursing Times found 60 per cent of nurses in favour of the law being changed.[110]

The balance of expert opinion was clearly regarded by Lord Joffe as a key element in the justification for the proposals: hence his attempts to present the balance as at least neutral, or as marginally favouring the proposals. The importance of this is the way that this focus on an experts' perspective is linked to a narrow or specialized approach to the offences that are to hem in or restrict acting on a permission to provide assistance to die to terminally ill people. Under clause 4 of the Bill, such a permission would not be valid without a declaration given in advance that the patient wished to be assisted to die. Accordingly, clause 11 of the Bill included the following proposed offence:

(1) A person commits an offence if he wilfully falsifies or forges a declaration made under section 4 with the intent or effect of causing the patient's death. A person guilty of an offence under this subsection shall be liable, on conviction on indictment, to imprisonment for life or for any shorter term.

But, if someone 'wilfully' falsifies or forges a section 4 declaration, 'with the... effect of causing the patient's death', then, under the existing law that must surely be at least manslaughter, and might well be murder. For such falsification will almost necessarily be done with the awareness that V may, or with the knowledge that V will, be killed in consequence. What compelling purpose, then, is served by the creation of this offence?[111] If a declaration was forged in order to facilitate by

[108] An example is a recent attempt to introduce an offence creating liability for causing another's suicide. On 18 October 2006, Iain Duncan Smith MP introduced into Parliament a Bill to create a specific offence of causing another to commit suicide, based on a recommendation by Refuge (also supported by Southall Black Sisters). *Hansard*, HC Debs 18 October 2006, 877–9. Laura McGowan and I have argued that a context-specific offence of this kind is unnecessary because the conduct in question is adequately covered by gross negligence manslaughter: Horder and McGowan (2006).
[109] Assisted Dying for the Terminally Ill Bill: <www.publications.parliament.uk/pa/ld200304/ldbills/017/04017.1-4.html>.
[110] HL Debs 12 May 2006, col 1185 (my emphasis).
[111] In a case where D falsifies or forges the s 4 declaration 'with the intent' of causing the patient's death, this would presumably be preparatory conduct falling short of an attempt to kill, and so there is logical space for this part of the s 11 offence.

concealing the nature of what was intended to be, and was, an unlawful killing, then there seems to be scant justification for permitting the killer to escape the mandatory life penalty for murder.

There seems little doubt that the adoption of a context-bound approach to criminalization of homicide, undermining the authority of murder and manslaughter, is more likely to be taken when pride of place in the reform process is afforded to interest or expert groups. This is not, of course, to question the value or importance of such groups. It is simply to observe that such groups now frequently seek not only in practice to enhance the welfare and status of those they represent, but also to secure a discrete legal basis for such enhancement. As the Charity Commissioners observed, speaking of groups representing disadvantaged people:

> Many organisations now feel that it is not sufficient simply to alleviate distress arising from particular social conditions.... They feel compelled also to draw attention as forcibly as possible to the needs which they think are not being met... *and to press for effective official provision to be made to meet those needs.*[112]

Activists must all be (would-be) law reformers, it seems, in that an attempt to increase the perceived importance in society at large of particular interests would nowadays scarcely be complete without a distinctively *legal* as well as political programme of reform. How should criminal lawyers respond to such developments?

VIII. Homicide: Reconciling Common Law and Regulatory Values

Appearances notwithstanding, my argument for homicide reform is not meant to be against the intrusion into homicide law of a regulatory approach, and hence in favour only of a traditional–codificatory approach to reform. The conclusion I seek to draw from the foregoing analysis and critique is a slightly different one. It is that a wholesale shift from a common law to a regulatory approach in the law of homicide may have few clearly proven advantages, and many real disadvantages, most especially in relation to fault or to punishment, and hence in relation to legitimacy. As we have seen, in these respects a regulatory approach may sometimes be too harsh on accused persons (causing death on the roads; causing the death of a child or vulnerable person), but sometimes also too generous to them (Assisted Dying for the Terminally Ill Bill). The direction of my argument is towards a system of criminal law in which common law and regulatory approaches are regarded as mutually reinforcing, rather than as rival claimants to exclusive occupancy of the relevant legal space.[113] How can such a system be developed?

The offence of corporate manslaughter provides one model, through its use of a *gemeinschaft* concept—manslaughter—to give effect to a regulatory objective:

---

[112] Cited in Sheridan (1973), at 47 (my emphasis).

[113] For a broader perspective on the relationship between common law and regulatory approaches, see Brudner (1993).

ensuring that a company can in appropriate circumstances be found liable for homicide brought about at least in part by glaring deficiencies in the senior managers' management or organization of the company's activities.[114] The common law and regulatory approaches are mutually reinforcing in this sense. The powers available to the court upon conviction are classically regulatory in form. The punishment can only be a fine, a punishment well suited, of course, to the special kinds of defendants at which the offence is aimed (profit-making organizations and public bodies with necessarily deep pockets).[115] Further, the courts are entitled to order specified steps to be taken by a convicted defendant to remedy a breach, a clearly regulatory provision beyond the scope of 'remedy' through punishment at common law.

However, most importantly, these regulation-orientated powers available upon conviction—probably far less punitive than many groups advocating corporate liability would have liked—are themselves in part reinforced and supported by the way in which the offence takes a common law approach to labelling and fault. Liability is for 'manslaughter', and the fault element—'a gross breach of a relevant duty of care'[116]—mirrors the common law requirement in manslaughter for gross negligence. In taking this approach, the new offence recognizes that the labelling element of conviction for the common law homicide offences (murder; manslaughter) can *itself* be regarded as a part of the punishment, as long as its currency has not been debased by substantial diminution of fault requirements. The contrast, then, is with some of the offences concerned with causing death on the road, and with offences that borrow elements of common law terminology (such as the offence of 'third degree' murder[117]) whilst replacing the common law content with elements less sensitive to the common law's concern with fault, responsibility, and causation. Here, regulatory law has replaced rather than supported common law offences, with the result that ever-increasing levels of punishment have had to compensate for the absence of a truly condemnatory label for offences (with a fault corresponding to that label) to do some of the punitive work.

An alternative model may be more appropriate where the proposal is otherwise to create specific homicide offences applicable to 'specialists' who kill (typically, through negligence) in the course of their duties when these duties by their nature create risk. Two classic examples of such specialists would be armed police officers, and doctors, who kill through negligence (respectively) in shooting at those considered to be dangerous suspects and in attempting to treat patients.[118] Given that these professionals' execution of their duties necessarily involves subjecting the suspects (and bystanders) or patients respectively to a risk of being killed, the thought may arise that to deal with them through the law of manslaughter is inappropriate for one of two reasons. First (the 'pro-specialist' view), some may consider that the risk of conviction for manslaughter when a bad mistake has been

---

[114] Corporate Manslaughter and Corporate Homicide Act 2007, s 1.
[115] See elements 1 and 6 of the regulatory model of law, in text following n 49 above.
[116] Corporate Manslaughter and Corporate Homicide Act 2007, s 1.
[117] See text at n 56 above.
[118] See Ch 8 below for further discussion of the position of armed officers.

made is inappropriate, given that the chance of such a mistake is a professional—and perhaps daily—hazard even for generally competent professionals.[119] Secondly (the 'anti-specialist' view), the difficulty of securing a manslaughter conviction—given the stigma attached to conviction—may mean that too many badly incompetent or even uncaring officers or doctors who kill might escape criminal prosecution for homicide altogether. These views may coalesce in a proposal to create an offence of, say, 'unlawful killing in the (purported) execution of duty', or the like, that will play something like the same regulatory role as is played by the offence of causing death by dangerous driving in relation to death on the roads.

There is little doubt that the regulatory context in which such killings take place (the conduct of armed police officers and surgeons is certainly regulated by professional codes of conduct) makes specialized and separate treatment by the law of homicide—following the regulatory model—a legitimate possibility.[120] However, the specialists in question may themselves prefer to be judged by the same broad standards—and to stand to be convicted of the same offences—as ordinary people. Further, there is a not inconsequential risk that the way in which they conduct their duties may change, to the detriment of the public, if they are not so judged. Most importantly, though, in this context it is possible to keep faith with the application of common law offences to the lethal conduct of such specialists, *and* account for the regulatory context, other than through the creation of new homicide offences.

There is more than one way to seek to do this. It would be possible, for example, to ensure that in appropriate cases the jury is given pre-prepared evidence drawn up by the relevant professional bodies (and approved by the relevant Government department) on the frequency with which their members must pose risks of a similar kind, and the conditions of work under which they are expected to do so.[121] More substantially, it is perhaps not impossible to imagine prosecutions in such cases having to be approved in advance—in something like the style of the old grand jury—by a specialized body including (perhaps) members of the relevant professions and their regulators, members of complaints authorities, victims' family groups, and so forth.[122] Whether the current system for prosecuting doctors or armed officers is so defective that a radical scheme of this kind (and *a fortiori* the creation of new offences) is really necessary may be open to doubt, although it is perhaps worth further consideration.

The significant point, in the present context, is that the mere identification of a 'killing field' with a regulatory backdrop to it need by no means lead straight to the adoption of an approach to the application of homicide offences shaped by the regulatory model. As the development of the corporate manslaughter offence illustrates, there is plenty of scope for imaginative solutions that seek to support rather than erode the continued use of the common law offences.

---

[119] For further discussion, see Quick (2006).

[120] See Quick (2008).

[121] Naturally, it would have to be possible for the prosecution to seek to show how that evidence has no weight or bearing when considering D's conduct in the individual case in question.

[122] Obviously, I cannot here go into how exactly such a body should be constituted, or how it should go about its work.

PART II

HOMICIDE OFFENCES: DISPUTING THE BOUNDARIES

3

On Being, Morally and Legally
Speaking, a 'Murderer'

I. The Law Commission's Three-tier Structure
for Homicide

Building on its Consultation Paper, in 2006 the Law Commission published a final report recommending a new structure for the law of homicide in England and Wales.[1] Replacing the current two-tier structure comprised of murder and man-slaughter was to be a three-tier structure. The top tier in this structure was to be 'first degree murder', the middle tier 'second degree murder', and the lowest tier manslaughter. The existing, familiar terminology—murder; manslaughter—was thus to be retained, but murder was sub-divided as (but not in the same way as) in most American state penal codes. As we will see, the adoption of such a structure involves a rejection of the more liberal-progressive structures found in French and German law (structures that informed Macaulay's Code) where intentional killing is in key respects the central concept.[2] The structure is comprised of the following elements:

First degree murder: (a) intentional killing; (b) killing with an intention to do serious injury in the awareness that there is a serious risk of causing death.

Second degree murder: (a) killing with the intention to do serious injury; (b) killing with the intention to cause injury or a fear or risk of injury, in the awareness that there is a serious risk of causing death; (c) the result of a successful partial defence plea to first degree murder.

Manslaughter: (a) causing death by gross negligence; (b) causing death through a criminal act intended to cause injury, or in the awareness of a serious risk that injury may be caused.

Why put a three-tier structure in a place of the two-tier structure that has been in place for 500 years or more? For one simple reason. The two-tier structure is no longer able to meet the increasing demands being made of it.

---

[1] Law Commission (2005); Law Commission (2006).
[2] See Ch 1 above. See further Spencer (2007) and Du Bois-Pedain (2007). That is not to say that the Law Commission's recommendations are 'illiberal': far from it.

First, pressure is being placed on the two-tier structure by developments in the partial defences. 400 years ago, there was only one partial defence to murder: provocation (although at that time it was not clearly distinguished from excessive defence). As a result of the changes made by the Homicide Act 1957 ('the 1957 Act') and the Coroners and Justice Act 2009 ('the 2009 Act'), there are now three, or arguably four, partial defences—provocation, excessive defence (under the aegis of loss of self-control), diminished responsibility, and half-completed suicide pacts.[3] At present, in England and Wales, an offender who pleads any of these defences successfully has his or her crime reduced to manslaughter, even though he or she may admit having intended to kill. This is controversial or problematic because, as a substantive offence, manslaughter is a crime that may involve relatively low culpability. It can be committed with a fault element well short of an intention to kill. So, it is not obvious that the partial defences should have the effect of reducing murder to manslaughter, thus lumping together in the same offence category those who killed intentionally in excusing circumstances and those who may not even have intended to do someone an injury. In general terms, it is, of course, not wrong to use the same offence category for a successful lack-of-intent plea as for a successful excusatory plea.[4] The question is whether better labelling of offenders who may have intended to kill but have an excusatory partial defence can be achieved. An obvious solution is to place them in a new offence category with those who, whilst they lack the fault element for the highest category of homicide offence, are significantly more blameworthy than those committing manslaughter as a substantive offence.

Secondly, the existing structure must now seek to accommodate a whole variety of different fault elements without being able to rely, as in the past, on the inherent flexibility or vagueness of 'malice aforethought' as an umbrella term capable of covering them all. The 1957 Act restricted the scope of malice aforethought,[5] although it quite clearly anticipated that this term would continue to express the fault element for murder. However, since 1957, the judiciary have been increasingly uncomfortable using the term, in spite of the clear implication in the 1957 Act that it should remain the relevant term of art.[6] The House of Lords has now said that malice

---

[3] The state of Victoria, to give one example, also has a narrow half-completed suicide-pact defence to murder: Crimes Act 1958, s 6(b). More generally, practice regarding these defences varies considerably world-wide: see now Reed and Bohlander (2011). Some jurisdictions have no defence of provocation, as in French law: see Spencer (2007). Some have no defence of diminished responsibility, as in some American jurisdictions: see Finkelstein (2007). In Germany, there is a very wide 'consent' defence going well beyond the English defence of half-completed suicide pact: see Du Bois-Pedain (2007), and the discussion in Ch 1 above.

[4] See Tadros (2005b), at 136: '[a] criminal offence might quite properly reflect overlapping values, or vices, whereby two instances of behaviour that fall within that offence do not share all of the salient and distinctive elements that make any particular token of the offence wrongful.'

[5] By abolishing so-called 'constructive malice' in the law of murder.

[6] See, in particular, the criticisms of Lord Bridge in *Moloney* [1985] AC 905, at 920. In fact, immediately after the passing of the 1957 Act, courts were already suggesting that malice aforethought was merely a term of art, standing for nothing beyond 'intention': see *Vickers* [1957] 2 QB 664.

aforethought is not to be regarded as a suitable term for the fault element in murder. 'Intention' has become the judiciary's favoured term, but this change of use has led to new set of difficulties. Intention does not have the narrowest possible meaning in English law.[7] Nonetheless, malice aforethought was clearly capable of covering highly culpable states of mind, such as a willingness or preparedness to kill in the course of conduct, which intention, as such, is not. Cases that would have been treated as murder cases fifty years ago, when the term malice aforethought was still in use, must now be treated as cases of manslaughter because there was no actual 'intention' to kill or to inflict serious injury.[8] The policy question whether that development is desirable has never been directly addressed in the case law. That is, perhaps, understandable. An acute policy dilemma is raised by any attempt, through case law development, to change the definition of murder within the two-tier structure. As much by accident as by design, in abandoning the use of 'malice aforethought' the courts have narrowed the definition of murder from what it was when Parliament reformed the law in 1957, whilst making 'intention' itself something of a term of art rather than a term only to be interpreted by the jury itself as a matter of ordinary language.[9] That has left the law with a crime of manslaughter that has an unacceptably broad scope. Manslaughter is now unable to reflect the legitimate demand that the offence label reasonably accurately reflect the nature of the wrong done. However, were the courts consequently to widen the law of murder at manslaughter's expense, that would entail the broadening of the class of offenders on whom the mandatory life sentence must be passed, a matter that ought above all else to be regarded as a matter for Parliament.

As we saw in Chapter 1, there have been previous attempts to persuade Parliament to strike the right balance between murder and manslaughter. The last attempt to do so through provision of a full definition of murder was in the Homicide Bill of 1878–79. The relevant provision ran as follows:

Culpable homicide is murder . . .

(a) if the offender means to cause the death . . .

(b) if the offender means to cause to the person killed any bodily injury which is known to the offender to be likely to cause death, and if the offender, whether he does or does not mean to cause death, is reckless whether death ensues or not . . .

(c) Culpable homicide is also murder . . . if [the offender] means to inflict grievous bodily injury for the purpose of facilitating the commission of any of the offences hereinafter mentioned.

---

[7] *Woollin* [1999] AC 92 (HL).

[8] The classic case is setting fire to a building known to be occupied by sleeping inhabitants, where the claim is that the intention was only to frighten the occupants, but someone was killed in the conflagration. In 1975 this was treated as murder if the defendant knew it was likely that someone would die: *Hyam* [1975] AC 55. With the complete demise of malice aforethought as a term of art broader than intention, by the 1980s such cases had to treated as ones of manslaughter: see *Nedrick* [1986] 3 All ER 1, and the discussion of other such cases in Wasik (2000).

[9] See, eg, Simester (1997).

'Maybe next time you'll
think twice before
murdering someone'

When the Law Commission's Consultation Paper on murder was published in 2005, the Daily Telegraph (Matt included) took the view that the proposals would weaken the law; but when the final Report was published in 2006, a leading editorial in the paper called on the government to reform the law in accordance with the recommendations. The Daily Telegraph, 21 December 2005 Image produced with the permission of the Telegraph Media Group Limited © Telegraph Media Group Limited 2005.

The provision formed the basis for the existing Canadian law of homicide, and it is not far removed from the Law Commission's recommendations for the fault element in first and second degree murder combined. The provision does succumb at the end to the temptation to retain a (watered down) version of the felony-murder rule. Although that rule has a wide currency in the English-speaking world,[10] it has been heavily criticized and was rightly consigned to legal history by Parliament through section 1 of the 1957 Act. Like the overwhelming majority of its consultees, the Commission resisted the temptation to re-introduce it (although 'criminal act' manslaughter remains). Putting this point on one side,

[10] See, eg, Finkelstein (2007).

what is the function of defining murder in the way the 1878–79 Bill does? Over 100 years later, William Wilson expresses the function thus:

> The key task, for the purposes of fair labelling, is to cut up the murder-manslaughter cake in a way which renders the two wrongs meaningfully distinct and makes it clear exactly how citizens must behave to avoid the relevant prohibition.[11]

To regard this as *the* key task is, however, to take the existing 'two-layer cake' structure for granted. The Commission no longer believes that is the right thing to do. A 'three-layer cake' structure makes it possible to distinguish between wrongs, and hence to respect principles of fair labelling, in a more sophisticated way. To achieve this, each of the three tiers within the recommended structure has two morally equivalent wrongs, each (with first degree murder at the top) being in principle lower down in the scale of severity than the wrongs in the tier above.[12]

Furthermore, a three-tier structure would enable a greater measure of justice to be brought to sentencing in homicide cases. The mandatory life penalty cannot be taken as seriously as it ought to be when such a diverse range of offenders as at present falls within it. Suppose D is provoked by V to lose his self-control and strikes V on the knee with a baseball bat, breaking V's kneecap. V goes to hospital, but his knee becomes infected and he dies. If D's reaction to V's conduct does not surmount the tests set down in the 2009 Act for a successful plea of loss of self-control, D can be convicted of murder if his intention was to inflict an injury with the bat that the jury judges to be serious. It is murder even if in the heat of the moment D had no idea that his action would lead to V's death. In such a case, therefore, D will receive the mandatory life penalty. However, the judge is likely to impose a tariff or initial period in custody of perhaps only eight to ten years (conceivably less), given D's provoked loss of self-control and the absence of an intention to kill.[13] If he is a man in his 30s, D therefore stands to spend eight to ten years in custody, but perhaps another thirty to forty years out on licence. Such cases, where the tariff period must inevitably be relatively short because there was both a lesser degree of culpability and some element of partial defence, form a significant proportion of the total.[14] They raise questions about the width of murder in the context of the obligation to pass a life sentence upon conviction. As Martin Wasik has argued:

> the principled development of sentencing guidelines requires the avoidance of overly broad offences. Such offences fail to make explicit the moral distinctions which should be reflected in the law, and they lump together very different forms of conduct under a single, misleading, offence label. Sentencing coherence in homicide, it seems, depends on offences being arranged hierarchically, and with gradations within those offences being clearly based upon the different degrees of offender culpability for causing death.[15]

---

[11] Wilson (2000), at 38.

[12] It might be said, alternatively, that each tier has what might be thought of as a principal wrong, and a subsidiary wrong that can be regarded as morally equivalent to it. Not much hangs, however, on the characterization.

[13] Both of these are expressed to be mitigation factors in murder cases under the Criminal Justice Act 2003, s 269 and sch 21.

[14] See the analysis of such cases in Law Commission (2005), app E.

[15] Wasik (2000), at 192.

To restore some moral authority to the mandatory sentence (if it must remain), it should be confined to the offence of homicide with the highest degree(s) of fault. Further, to ensure not only fair labelling but also justice in sentencing for homicide offences ranked below the top-tier offence, manslaughter should cease to remain an all-encompassing jumble. That means the introduction of a three-tier structure;[16] but how should the offences within it be defined? I will concentrate on the less familiar and more controversial of the offences in the three-tier structure, first and second degree murder.[17]

II. The Fault Element for First Degree Murder

Under the Commission's proposals, first degree murder will be committed when someone kills intentionally, or kills with an intention to do serious injury, in the awareness that there is a serious risk of causing death. This involved a change from the provisional proposals in the Consultation Paper, where the proposal was that first degree murder should be confined to intentional killing. There was considerable support amongst the Commission's consultees for confining first degree murder (and, hence, the mandatory life sentence) to intentional killing. That said, the Commission decided that to confine it so closely would have meant that some killings morally just as heinous as intentional killings would have escaped categorization as first degree murder. An example might be the person who tortures his victim through the infliction of a series of horrific injuries over a prolonged period, but the victim dies of a resulting heart attack before the torturer has forced the information from him. In such a case, the desire to continue the application of the torture is inconsistent with an intention to kill through the act of torture. However, there are compelling grounds for regarding the torturer as guilty of murder, if he or she has intentionally inflicted serious injury, especially if he or she is aware of a serious risk that the victim will die in the course of the torture, whether or not the information demanded has yet been revealed. Under the expanded definition of first degree murder recommended by the Law Commission, the torturer in such a case will be guilty of first degree murder. In more commonplace cases, the expanded definition also gives greater reassurance that a charge of first degree murder is appropriate. If, say, D shoots or stabs V in the head or heart, then, in the absence of any special explanation about his or her intentions, D can readily be found to have had the fault element for first degree murder.

The recommended definition of first degree murder does little more than update the proposal made for reform of the law of murder in England and Wales in

---

[16] The three-tier structure relates to general offences of homicide but, for the sake of completeness, it ought to be added that there is a notional fourth tier. This is comprised of specific homicide offences regarded as in principle less serious than manslaughter, such as causing death by dangerous driving, infanticide, or causing the non-accidental death of a child or vulnerable adult. See further, the discussion in Ch 2 above.

[17] For discussion of manslaughter, see Ch 5 below. For discussion of partial defences, see Ch 8 below.

the Draft Criminal Code of 1989.[18] What is different are the recommendations for the new middle-tier offence of second degree murder. Second degree murder is made to do a great deal of work under the Commission's recommendations. It functions both as a free-standing offence in two different situations, and as the crime to which first degree murder is reduced when a plea of loss of self-control, diminished responsibility, or half-completed suicide pact is successful on a first degree murder charge. I shall be concerned here with its function as a free-standing offence.

III. Second Degree Murder: Cases of Intending Serious Injury

The first situation in which second degree murder is committed, as a free-standing offence, is when someone kills having intended to do serious injury, even if they were *un*aware of a serious risk of causing death (compare first degree murder, above). Under the current law, killing in these circumstances is murder. Broadly speaking, that reflects the position in jurisdictions in, or influenced by, the English-speaking world, although in mainland European jurisdictions killing in such circumstances would commonly be a lesser offence.[19] The current position in English law can lead to injustice, because it means that the mandatory sentence of life imprisonment must be passed on someone who may have had no idea that his or her actions might cause death. Such a person should not fall within the highest category of homicide, as is recognized by those jurisdictions that treat it as second degree murder or as some other offence. Under the draft code of 1989, someone who killed having intended to do injury regarded as serious by the jury would have been guilty of manslaughter. The Commission does not now regard this as a satisfactory solution. Manslaughter is widely considered to be an over-broad crime even as it stands. It would have become still wider with the inclusion of killing where there was an intention to do serious injury. This would have been a serious matter, because it is likely that a large proportion of killings currently categorized as murder take place when there is an intention to do serious injury but no intention to kill.

Moreover, there are sound moral reasons for thinking that killing with intent to do serious injury should be treated as a crime of murder, even if not as first degree murder. The nature of the harm intentionally done will in many cases mean that the defendant has made death a foreseeable consequence of his or her action. To launch an attack of that severity against another person demonstrates a disregard for the vital interests of others deserving of the label 'murderous' even if it would not be right to regard the crime as one of first degree murder. As a matter of grading, liability for second degree murder is justified by the fact that when death occurs, albeit unfore-

---

[18] Clause 54: 'A person is guilty of murder if he causes the death of another—(a) intending to cause death; or (b) intending to cause serious personal harm and being aware that he may cause death.'

[19] See respectively, Finkelstein (2007) and Leader-Elliot (2007), as compared with Spencer (2007) and Du Bois-Pedain (2007).

seen, D is not being held responsible for harm done out of all proportion to the harm intended.[20] Consequently, there is no need to add, as the 1878–79 Bill does, the further restriction that the intentional infliction of serious injury must have been for the purpose of facilitating the commission of a range of specified offences. The history of such 'felony murder' provisions has not been a happy one, although, as indicated above, many jurisdictions have retained them and they have a small band of spirited and ingenious contemporary defenders.[21] Such provisions lead to the drawing of arbitrary distinctions between offenders.[22] They entail secondary litigation, often leading to further complexity and arbitrariness, over the meaning of terms such as 'for the purpose of facilitating'.[23] We are better off without them.

IV. Second Degree Murder: Tackling Reckless Killing

Under the Commission's recommendations, the second situation in which second degree murder would be committed as a substantive offence arises when D intends to cause some injury, or a fear or risk of injury, in the awareness that he or she is posing a serious risk of causing death. This is similar to the proposal in the 1878–79 Bill (above), although I will be explaining how the extension of it in the Law Commission's recommendation to include cases where D intended to cause a *fear or risk* of injury is significant. However, unlike the 1878–79 Bill, the Commission's recommendation eschews use of the term 'recklessness'. Here is an important change from the Consultation Paper. In that paper, the Commission provisionally proposed that someone should be guilty of second degree murder if they killed another person through 'reckless indifference'.[24] The aim of that proposal was to ensure that two kinds of reckless killer fell within the scope of second degree murder, and that a third kind fell outside its scope (manslaughter being the appropriate crime in latter case).

The first kind of reckless killer meant to fall within second degree murder is (in general terms) the kind regarded under the old law as acting out of malice aforethought, and hence guilty of murder, but currently falling outside the scope of murder because there is no actual intent to kill or to inflict serious injury:

Recklessness Case 1: D injects V with an illegal drug, realizing that the drug may amount to an overdose or contain potentially lethal impurities. The drug is an overdose or does contain such impurities, and V dies in consequence.[25]

Recklessness Case 2: D sets fire to V's house where V is asleep, intending to cause V to run in terror from the house, but knowing that V may be killed if he or she does not escape. V fails to escape and is killed.[26]

In both cases, D's potentially harmful act is aimed at V in the knowledge that the act poses a risk of death. Under the Commission's provisional proposals, in both

---

[20] On this point of principle see Wilson (2000), at 36; Horder (1997a), and Ch 5 below.
[21] See Wilson (2000).   [22] See Finkelstein (2005).
[23] Turner (1964), at 487–8.   [24] Law Commission (2005), pt 3.
[25] See *Parfini* (2003) 2 Cr App R (S) 362.   [26] See text at n 8 above.

cases, D could be regarded as acting with 'reckless indifference'. The question was to be whether D's attitude towards injecting V was 'if this causes V's death, so be it', or 'so what?'[27]

The second kind of killer meant to be caught by the provisional proposal was one who, without aiming any potentially harmful act at V, nonetheless acted with such a high degree of recklessness that his or her attitude could be regarded as one of indifference:

Recklessness Case 3: D overloads a lorry with people hoping to obtain entry to Britain illegally. Although (as D knows) there is no way of ensuring that fresh air enters the locked compartments where the people are hidden, D completes a long journey into Britain without stopping to check on the people's condition, in order more quickly to obtain his payment. A number of people in the compartments are suffocated to death.[28]

In this example, likewise, it seems plausible to suppose that D's attitude is 'if death is caused, so be it'. That would make him recklessly indifferent, and hence guilty of second degree murder even though no act of his was aimed at causing injury or the fear or risk of injury.

The insistence that a lethal act manifest reckless *indifference*, if it is to amount to second degree murder, was meant to ensure that not all killing by advertent risk-taking became second degree murder:

Recklessness Case 4: D is an electrician. D has installed wiring that he or she knows does not meet official safety standards, because he or she is highly sceptical about the value of the 'officious meddling' involved in setting standards. The poor quality of the wiring leads to V being electrocuted and killed.[29]

In this case, it seems unlikely that D could fairly be said to be manifesting a callous attitude towards potential victims, although his or her conduct is reprehensible and in a basic sense 'reckless'. D's distrust of officialdom may explain his or her actions better than a disregard for the safety of electricity users. D could be found guilty of manslaughter by gross negligence, but should not (at least on these facts) be guilty of second degree murder.

Some commentators on the Commission's provisional proposals were sharply critical of 'reckless indifference' as a test of liability, principally on the grounds that it was too vague[30] or left too much unstructured discretion to the jury.[31] There would certainly be no improvement on the present law if a whole series of cases had to be taken to the appeal courts to determine meaning of 'reckless indifference'. Consequently, in its final recommendations, the Commission dropped the reckless indifference term and substituted a test with clearer (albeit more complex) language. This was the test of whether D, 'intended to cause injury, or a fear or a risk of injury, and was aware of a serious risk of causing death'. The question is whether that test fulfils the same function as the test of reckless indifference. How does it

---

[27] Law Commission (2005), pt 3.
[28] The facts are not dissimilar to those in *Wacker* (2002) EWCA Crim 1944.
[29] See more generally, *Merrick* (1996) 1 Cr App R 130.
[30] See, eg, Rogers (2006), at 240–3; Wilson (2006), at 477–8.
[31] Wilson (2006), at 478–9.

apply to the recklessness cases 1–4 above? In case 1, D can be found guilty of second degree murder under the Law Commission's recommendations because D intended to cause injury (in the shape of the injection) and was aware of a serious risk of causing death. This would probably also have been the result under the 1878–79 Bill (above). Under that Bill, the jury was also required to be sure that the defendant acted recklessly as to causing death, but it is unclear what that really added to the other requirement that D knew that his or her unlawful action was likely to cause death.

Unlike the 1878–79 Bill, the Law Commission's recommendations for second degree murder extend to cases in which D intends to cause a *fear or risk* of injury, in the awareness that a serious risk of death is being posed. There is good reason for extending the mental element in this way, and it is illustrated by case 2. Here, D would not have been guilty of murder in the 1878–79 Code because he or she did not intend to cause bodily injury as such. Nonetheless, D intended that V should fear injury, and hence D falls within the scope of second degree murder because D was also aware of a serious risk that V might be killed. The Commission further extends the scope of second degree murder beyond the limits set by the 1878–79 Bill to cover cases where D intends to create a risk of injury, aware that there is a serious risk of causing death. What kinds of cases does this extension cover?

Recklessness Case 5: D intends to play 'Russian roulette' with V. D puts a single bullet into a revolver, spins the barrel and points the gun at V's head while V is not looking. Without checking to see whether the gun will actually fire, D pulls the trigger. The gun goes off, killing V.[32]

Here, D intends to subject V to a risk of injury and is aware that in so doing there is a serious risk of causing V's death. If the Commission's recommendations had stopped short at intending to cause a *fear* of injury, then whether D was guilty of second degree murder in this kind of example would have turned on whether or not V was sufficiently aware of what D was about to do to fear injury. The boundary between homicide offences ought not to turn on such an issue.

That leaves the contrast between cases 3 and 4. One reason that the Commission initially proposed the reckless indifference test, as opposed to an updated version of the 1878–79 Bill, was to ensure that examples like case 3 fell within the scope of second degree murder and were not confined to manslaughter. On re-consideration, it seems quite likely that many such cases will in fact fall within the now recommended definition of second degree murder. What must be borne in mind is that foresight of a consequence that is virtually certain to occur can be a basis for inferring 'intention' in law.[33] In case 3, when D continues on his long drive despite knowing the conditions that those hiding in the back must endure, it can readily be found either (a) that he foresees it as virtually certain that they will eventually fear injury, or (b) that he foresees it as virtually certain that there will be a risk of injury. That being so, the jury is free to infer that D intended to subject the victims to the fear of or to a risk of injury. If the jury does so infer, then if it is also found that

---

[32] See *Faure* [1999] VSCA 166, discussed by Leader-Elliott (2007).
[33] See *Woollin* [1999] AC 92 (HL).

D was aware of a serious risk of causing death, he or she can be found guilty of second degree murder under the recommended test almost as easily as if the reckless indifference test were being applied.

By way of contrast, it is less likely that D in case 4 foresees a risk of injury as certain to be posed. Even if he or she did, it is highly unlikely that a jury would infer from this that D intended to subject potential electricity users to a risk of injury. That being so, there are good grounds for thinking that in case 4 D will be found guilty only of manslaughter, not of second degree murder, even if he or she was aware of a risk that someone might be killed by electrocution. Allowing for variations in the facts of particular cases (clearly, it is not inconceivable that a 'corner-cutting' electrician could, and should, in some circumstances be found guilty of second degree murder), this seems to be the right result.

There are no easy or perfect solutions to be found in this hinterland between murder and lesser homicide offences. What takes some of the heat out of the debate is the three-tier structure. The Commission recommended a discretionary life maximum penalty for second degree murder, just as there is for manslaughter. So, whilst the labelling issue will continue to divide commentators, the sentencing consequences are not so stark as under a two-tier structure.[34] What might add further subtlety is the adoption of a special regime for sentencing in second degree murder cases where a fixed term of years in custody is the appropriate sentence. This could involve a change to the current, controversial system in which the judge states the maximum term of custody that may be served, but the offender can be released at a much earlier point. Instead, the judge could state the minimum that must be served, and a formula (say, one quarter of that minimum) would determine the maximum. Second degree murder cases are likely to attract long determinate prison sentences, even when a life sentence is inappropriate. The longer the sentence the more anomalous it seems when someone stands to be released at an early point relative to the maximum. Under the current system, if a judge wishes to ensure that an offender spends, say, fifteen years in prison under a determinate prison sentence, he or she must pass a sentence of thirty years' imprisonment. Small wonder that so many life sentences are passed in such cases, inappropriate though they may be. It would make more sense in such a case for the judge to be able to say that the offender must spend at least fifteen years in prison and allow a formula to determine what the maximum period will be.

V. Taylor's Criticisms of the Final Recommendations

Following publication of the Law Commission's final recommendations, Richard Taylor has offered some trenchant criticism of some aspects of the second degree murder category.[35] He recognized that there might be some merit in the creation of

---

[34] Although one can expect that sentences for second degree murder will be higher than they are for manslaughter: see Law Commission (2006), app A.

[35] Taylor (2007). I will not deal here with his criticisms of the place of partial defences to murder in the Law Commission scheme. Partial defences are dealt with in Ch 8 below.

a category of second degree murder offences, to accommodate cases falling just short of an intention to kill:[36] (i) intending to do serious injury in the awareness that there is a serious risk of causing death, and (ii) showing in one's actions a reckless indifference to causing death. He did not necessarily disagree with the Law Commission's recommended replacement for (ii), namely causing death through an intention to cause injury, or a fear of or risk of injury, in the awareness that there was a serious risk of causing death.[37] However, he argued that once (i) was moved by the final report into the first degree murder category, there was an insufficiently compelling case for leaving within second degree murder cases of death caused when intentionally doing serious injury, in the *absence* of any awareness of a serious risk of causing death.[38] He gives two reasons for this. First, in his view, even when a death has been caused by an intention to do serious injury, if D was not aware of a risk of causing death, then the death, if not simply accidental, 'is at worst negligent which sounds like manslaughter rather than murder of any degree'.[39] Secondly, on the positive side, if the replacement for (ii) became the only substantive offence within second degree murder, there would then be a greater degree of coherence in point of culpability between first and second degree murder. This would be because both categories would be united by having in common a focus on what he calls an 'advertently lethal attack'.[40] That is to say, in his view, in both first and second degree murder, a desirable common element would be the awareness of a serious risk of causing death (subsumed by, in first degree murder, the most serious kind of fault: the intention to cause death).

How convincing are these criticisms? Richard Taylor's view is very plausible, and widely shared by theorists and reformers going back as far as Macaulay, as we have seen.[41] I will return below to the case against including within second degree murder instances where there was 'only' an intention to do serious injury, in the absence of any awareness of a serious risk of causing death. Two initial points that arise, in relation to Taylor's critique of the inclusion, are these.[42]

First, it is misleading to describe death resulting from an intention to do serious harm as 'at worst negligent'. It is misleading, precisely because such a death stems from an attack on the victim (which we can call case 1), and not merely from the unwitting exposure of the victim to a risk of death (which we can call case 2).[43] That makes the two ways in which death comes to be caused in part incommensurable, from a culpability perspective. In case 1 (an attack on V), the intention to do some injury to V is in part the justification for convicting D of a homicide offence if death is thereby caused. Irrespective both of the likelihood that the death in question would occur and of whether D foresaw the risk in question, D's infliction of injury is an intentional violation of V's physical integrity, and not (like case 2) an instance in which D merely unjustifiably puts V's physical integrity at risk.

[36] Under the initial proposals on which the Law Commission consulted, intended killings were the only kind within first degree murder: Law Commission (2005).
[37] Law Commission (2006).   [38] Taylor (2007), at 355.
[39] *Ibid.*   [40] *Ibid*, at 356.   [41] See Ch 1 above.
[42] Considered in more detail in Ch 5 below.
[43] Wilson (2006), at 472–3. See Ch 5 below for fuller discussion.

Consequently, D may be liable for causing the ultimate extinction of the life force that animates and hence forms part of the value of that integrity.[44] This is because physical integrity (and the life force that animates it) must be regarded, as a distinct intrinsic value, as an undifferentiated whole. Damage to one aspect of it that leads to damage to another aspect of it (including the extinction of the life force that animates it) is not just linked by brute causation, unlike, say, the link between action damaging to physical integrity and the disturbance of the air by that action. Instead, the two are connected by the way that, together, they undermine a value, the intrinsic value of (V's) physical integrity.[45]

Building on this notion, it is, then, as a matter of grading, the seriousness of the injury *intentionally* inflicted—the degree of the intentional violation of V's physical integrity—that, when death is thereby caused, justifies the 'murder' label. That is so, even if, in such circumstances, the risk of death was (for some reason) no greater than if some lesser injury had been intentionally inflicted.[46] Contrast the case where V's death is caused solely by risk-taking (case 2). There is still, of course, damage to V's physical integrity and the extinction of the life force that animates it. However, it would be too harsh to ignore either a claim that the risk of death was too remote for there to have been negligence as to causing the death itself (as opposed to negligence as to some non-fatal injury or property damage), or a claim that D foresaw only the risk that non-lethal harm might be done and not that death might be caused.[47] It would be too harsh, because the (unjustified) posing of risks of harm should not be judged in the same way as intentionally causing such harm. An attack on physical integrity treats the value of physical integrity with a special kind of disrespect not necessarily present in conduct that only (unjustifiably) puts that value at risk in any given case.[48] One can reach the view that cases 1 and 2 are morally identical, in that death is purely accidental or at best negligent, only by ignoring these morally significant differences between the ways in which the deaths are caused.

Secondly, questions arise concerning whether Taylor's proposed scheme, whatever other merits it may have, is given the coherence he claims for it in virtue of being centred on the idea of an 'advertently lethal attack'.[49] To begin with a smaller point, it is not quite right to say that first and second degree murder can be given the requisite degree of coherence, in point of culpability, by confining the substantive offence of second degree murder to cases where there was, in addition to an intention to cause injury or a risk or fear of such injury, an awareness of a serious

---

[44] By contrast, in these circumstances, D would not necessarily be liable for, say, accidentally causing damage to V's property in the course of the intentional attack on V's physical integrity, unless D foresaw that outcome as a possibility: *Pembliton* (1874) LR 2 CCC 119. On this last point, see further, Ch 7 below.

[45] For more detailed discussion, see Ch 5 below.

[46] As Michael Moore points out, in so far as deaths are very remote from the intentional infliction of injury, the principles of causation may relieve D of liability for the death: see Moore (1997).

[47] These harsh rules of common law were effectively removed respectively by the decision in *Adomako* [1995] 1 AC 171 (HL), and *Moloney* [1985] AC 905 (HL). See further, Horder (1995).

[48] See, on the distinction between attacks and endangerments, Duff (1996), at 363–8; Duff (2007), at 148–58.

[49] Taylor (2007), at 356.

risk of causing death. To do that would, of course, create an affinity between the substantive offence of second degree murder and the variety of first degree murder in which D may be convicted if he or she intended serious injury when also aware that there was a serious risk of causing death. However, there would not, *pace* Taylor, be an affinity in this respect between the substantive offence of second degree murder and the worst kind of first degree murder, intentional killing. For, it has long been understood that, barring exceptional circumstances, intended consequences are never too remote.[50] If D shoots at V intending to kill V when V is standing on a hillside far away, D will be guilty of murder (other things being equal) if the shot does kill V, even though D may have believed there was only a remote chance of killing V from such a distance away. In such a case, surely there could be no reason to acquit D of murder simply because D believed that there was *not* a serious risk of causing death by shooting? Perhaps that reinforces the case for restricting first degree murder to cases of intentional killing, as the Law Commission initially proposed;[51] but such a recommendation is likely to divide opinion just as much, and possibly more, than the current law (Taylor does not himself seem to support it).[52]

Further, the notion of an 'advertent lethal attack' needs to be subjected to critical scrutiny, because it trades on ambiguity. An attack could clearly be 'lethal' either because it was lethal in intent, or because it had lethal consequences. Let us suppose that an 'intentionally lethal attack' is in principle murder because it was an attack undertaken with lethal intent. By contrast, let us suppose that an 'attack with lethal consequences' is in principle manslaughter because it did not embody such an intent, even though it caused death. Where does that leave (i) instances in which D kills by intentionally causing serious injury (second degree murder, under the Law Commission's scheme); (ii) instances in which D intentionally causes serious injury aware of a serious risk of causing death (first degree murder under the Law Commission's scheme); and (iii) instances in which D kills through intentionally causing injury, or a fear or risk of injury, aware—in so doing—of a serious risk of causing death?[53] Such cases do not involve intentionally lethal attacks, so they do not fall into that category. They might be regarded as instances of attacks with lethal consequences,[54] but that does not quite do them justice either. It seems more accurate to describe such cases as falling into a different category: what could be called 'potentially lethal attacks'. However, if that is right, then we need to recognize—as the Indian Penal Code recognized[55]—that the moral salience of the potential lethality in an attack may come out in different ways. Potential lethality may have moral salience because D is aware of that potential (aware of a serious risk

[50] See, on this issue, Gardner (1994).

[51] Law Commission (2005); Ashworth (2007).

[52] The issue was discussed in Ch 1 above, in relation to Ashworth's critique of the Law Commission proposals: Ashworth (2007).

[53] Such cases will be second degree murder, in the Law Commission's scheme, unless there was an intention to cause serious injury, in which case they will be first degree murder.

[54] Only instance (iii) is treated as manslaughter under the current law.

[55] Indian Penal Code, s 300; see Ch 1 above.

of causing death) in what he or she does, even though there may not, to the untutored eye, appear to be any such potential.[56] This is the form of potentially lethal attack on which Taylor focuses in seeking to give his scheme coherence; but there are other species of unlawful killing where the moral salience of potential lethality comes out in a different way: instances (i) and (ii) above. If D repeatedly stamps on V's head in order to coerce V into giving D vital information, D is not (*ex hypothesi*) launching an intentionally lethal attack (V must be kept alive to provide the information). D's attack is only potentially lethal, whether (should V die as a result of the attack) it falls into instance (i) and hence amounts to second degree murder, or into instance (ii) and hence amounts to first degree murder. In such cases, the attack is by its nature potentially lethal, whether or not D is aware of that fact; that is why to kill through intentionally inflicting an injury of that nature is murder under the Indian Penal Code even in the absence of such awareness.[57] When this analysis is put alongside the earlier criticism of the place of intentionally lethal attacks within 'advertently lethal attacks' in Taylor's scheme, it seems that this notion cannot provide the coherence to the law of murder that Taylor believes it has the capacity to do.

Taylor poses another challenge to the inclusion within second degree murder of cases in which there was an intention to cause serious injury, in absence of an awareness of a serious risk of causing death. Under the Law Commission's recommendations, (a) first degree murder includes the cases where serious injury is intended and there is an awareness of a risk of causing death, and (b) second degree murder includes cases of an intention to cause some injury, or a fear or risk of injury, in the awareness of a serious risk of causing death. That being so, if a jury also has the option of convicting of second degree murder where there was an intention to cause serious injury, there will be too great a risk of juries being unable to reach a verdict because they are split between the options. He says:

> Suppose that six jurors think D intended serious injury with no awareness of a serious risk of death but the other six jurors think there was only an intent to cause injury but these second six consider that there was awareness of a risk of death.... [T]here can be no conviction since although both sets of jurors are convinced of facts which independently amount legally to second degree murder, they do not all (or a majority of them) agree that any single one of the relevant facts (intention to cause *serious* injury or awareness of serious risk of death) is proven. This problem is likely to occur not simply in relation to alternative verdicts but also where the prosecution case from the outset is second degree murder on one or other of these alternatives.[58]

As Taylor points out,[59] the Law Commission was itself taken up with the problem of split juries, but focused on avoiding any problems that might arise, in that

---

[56] Perhaps, to give a somewhat fanciful example, D is V's doctor, and knows that V has a weakened skull on one side of his or her head, so when D loses his or her temper with V, D deliberately inflicts a blow with a fist on that side of the head. See Ch 5 below for further discussion.

[57] See Ch 1 above. After quite extensive discussion, the Law Commission rejected the creation of such a category: Law Commission (2005), at paras 3.93–3.114.

[58] Taylor (2007), at 357–8.   [59] *Ibid*, at 356.

regard, in relation to pleading different partial defences. It did not consider whether, and to what extent, the problem of split juries might arise from the way in which the substantive offences of first and second degree murder were defined. In Taylor's view the problem would be much reduced, were cases in which D intended serious injury but was unaware of a serious risk of causing death treated as manslaughter, rather than as second degree murder. Then, assuming D did not intend to kill, in relation to a murder verdict the jury would be faced with a more straightforward choice between deciding that D intended serious injury (aware of a serious risk of causing death), which would be first degree murder, and deciding that D intended to cause some injury, or a fear or risk of such injury (aware of a serious risk of causing death), which would be second degree murder. The case in which D could be also be guilty of second degree murder if he or she intended serious injury in the absence of the relevant awareness would no longer complicate this choice.

It would be right to acknowledge the force of this objection to the inclusion of 'plain vanilla' cases of intention to do serious harm (i.e. where there is no awareness of a serious risk of causing death) within the scope of second degree murder, even though it is difficult for anyone to predict how much of a problem the Law Commission's recommended scheme would prove to be in practice. However, its force is diminished if the substantive offence of second degree murder is confined to cases where there was an intention to do serious injury. Although it would be a conservative position to adopt, allowing to remain within manslaughter cases in which D caused V's death through an intention to cause injury (or a fear or risk of injury), knowing that a serious risk of death was involved, might have to be the price paid to avoid the problem Taylor raises. Arguably just as significant is Taylor's acceptance (with which I wholeheartedly agree) that cases of death caused through an intention to do serious harm are instances of homicide, worthy of labelling as (at least) manslaughter, and not merely accidental deaths for which D is not criminally responsible. I gave some reasons for that view above, and I return to it in Chapter 5.

VI. Questioning the Aspiration for a Codified 'Law of Homicide'

The Law Commission's Consultation Paper was entitled *A New Homicide Act for England and Wales?*[60] That gives an indication of the limits of the agenda given to the Law Commission for homicide law reform. The Homicide Act alluded to, the 1957 Act, was primarily concerned with aspects of the fault for murder (section 1) and with partial defences (sections 2–4).[61] That same agenda accounts for a substantial part of the Law Commission's work in its 2006 report, although there is a broader focus, in the sense that complicity in murder, the defence of duress and the offences of infanticide and manslaughter are also considered. What the report

---

[60] Law Commission (2005).   [61] For more detailed analysis, see Ch 8 below.

does not do is provide a 'codified' law of homicide in the sense in which that notion is commonly understood, namely a comprehensive statement of the entire law of homicide. Clearly, wholesale codification of the law of homicide would not, as such, be a bad thing. However, it is an open question whether codified law necessarily equals better or even simpler law.[62] Codification will not put an end to controversy over the structure and content of the law. It is hard to imagine that the pens of the criminal law's critics will be laid down once and for all if a criminal code for England and Wales is finally enacted; far from it. Criticism and pressures for change will begin almost from the moment of enactment. In any event, how plausible was it, or is it, to suppose that codification of any given part of the criminal law requires no more than, as a former Attorney-General once suggested, 'a few intelligible and well-constructed sentences'?[63]

The former Attorney-General's claim seems politically naïve because it overlooks the priority commonly given by the legislature to the particular over the general. This political priority was acknowledged by Bentham who, in addition to his relentless attacks on judge-made law, also directed his critical fire (as we have seen[64]) at what he called the 'two rules... in modern British legislation', namely: 'never to move a finger till your passions are inflamed, nor ever to look further than your nose'. Examples of these two 'rules' in operation in the modern era abound in the law of homicide. Examples include the creation of the offence/defence of infanticide in 1922 (but no defence of diminished responsibility until 1957); the creation of the 'killing in pursuance of a suicide pact' partial defence in 1957 (before the review of the law governing suicide itself, leading to the Suicide Act 1961); and the tacking to and fro between 'recklessness' (Road Traffic Act 1988) and 'dangerousness' (Road Traffic Act 1991) as the wrongful element in what was, at the start, the offence of 'causing death by reckless *or* dangerous driving' (Road Traffic Act 1956), along with the ad hoc creation of allied offences such as causing death by careless driving when under the influence of drink or drugs.[65] A credible law reform policy for England and Wales has to try to make a virtue of this overriding concern with the particular. The Law Commission's report attempts to do just that, for the law of homicide.

The late Sir John Smith memorably declared:

I am in favour of codification of the criminal law because I see no other way of reducing a chaotic system to order, of eliminating irrational distinctions and of making the law reasonably comprehensible and certain.[66]

I think this over-states the case for codification. Whatever one may say in specific criticism of, for example, the Accessories and Abettors Act 1861, the 1957 Act, section 3 of the Criminal Law Act 1967, section 8 of the Criminal Justice Act 1967,

---

[62] See, eg, Holland's criticisms of the Canadian Criminal Code: Holland (2007).
[63] HC Debs 3 April 1879, vol 245 (third Series), col 136.
[64] See Ch 2 above.
[65] Road Traffic Act 1988, s 3(A). See, on the road traffic legislation more generally, Ch 2 above.
[66] Smith (1986), at 290.

the Theft Acts 1968 and 1978, the Criminal Damage Act 1971, the Criminal Law Act 1977, the Criminal Attempts Act 1981, the Computer Misuse Act 1990, the Sexual Offences Act 2003, the Fraud Act 2006, and even the Offences Against the Person Act 1861,[67] they together constitute considerably more than just legalized chaos. They are a vast improvement, for example, on the preceding criminal law that had been developed at common law, derided by Bentham as 'this impostrous law, the fruits, the perpetual fruits [of which] are . . . in the breast and in the hands of the judge, power everywhere arbitrary, with a semblance of a set of rules to serve as a screen to it'.[68]

Sir John's real complaint in the passage just cited is that these offences have not been gathered together in a single code and 'rationalized', so that the guidance of a single thread of principle moulds them into a univocal system. There are, for example, what he would have regarded as 'irrational distinctions' between the objective standards of liability employed in the Sexual Offences Act 2003 and the more subjective standards that run through the Criminal Damage Act 1971, distinctions he believed ought to be erased in favour of the latter. With all due deference to Sir John, his appeal for the elimination of such so-called 'irrational distinctions' seems less than compelling. It has for some time ceased to be clear that subjective standards of liability are appropriate in, say, rape cases, in the way that they may be in, say, conspiracy or criminal damage cases. The beguiling thought that it might actually be *irrational* (not just unfair, from one—contested—point of view) to distinguish between crimes by applying objective standards to some and subjective standards to others, rests on the outdated picture of the world of criminal law reform as an apolitical, technocratic realm dominated by (liberal-progressive) experts, a misleading picture that was criticized in Chapter 1. That said, perhaps I am being too harsh by taking this line of criticism of the aims of would-be codifiers of the criminal law in general. So let me turn to the specific question of how high a priority we should give the embodiment of the entirety of the law of homicide in a single Homicide Act.

VII. Plural Values and the Virtues of Piecemeal Reform

It is commonly assumed that there are advantages to wholesale codification of the law of homicide, as compared with more piecemeal reform aimed at making particular parts of the law of homicide more just, accessible, and humane, as the 1957 Act in some measure did (for all its flaws). I have doubts about whether the Law Commission should give wholesale codification a high priority, even though its statutory duty is to move towards codification of the law. Quite simply, it is unclear how much intellectual or moral coherence there would be to an Act that sought to address all homicide-related law. As I shall now suggest, such an Act might fail to recognize the pluralistic basis on which legislation on particular

---

[67] On which, see Gardner (1994).   [68] See Schofield and Harris (1998), at 20–1.

homicide-related issues comes to be nested in a variety of different social and political contexts.

At present, England and Wales has many different statutes dealing, directly or indirectly, with the preservation of life or with the ending of life. Examples include: the Treason Act 1351, the Offences against the Person Act 1861, the Infant Life Preservation Act 1936, Article 2 of the European Convention on Human Rights 1950, the 1957 Act, the Abortion Act 1967, the Suicide Act 1961, the Internationally Protected Persons Act 1978, the Road Traffic Act 1988, the Law Reform (Year and a Day Rule) Act 1996, the UN Personnel Act 1997, the Terrorism Act 2000, and the 2009 Act. To these, of course, must be added judicial decisions concerning the meaning of life (for the purposes of the law of homicide[69]) and on when it is acceptable to end life, such as *Airedale NHS Trust v Bland*[70] (patients in a persistent vegetative state), and *Re A (Conjoined Twins).*[71] The case for an all-embracing 'Homicide' Act rests on the assumption that it would be beneficial legislatively to integrate under the rubric of 'homicide' all of the instances—addressed by such laws—in which death has been unlawfully caused. In other jurisdictions, some steps have been taken towards this end. So, for example, the Californian Penal Code includes the following provisions:

187.(a) Murder is the unlawful killing of a human being, or a foetus, with malice aforethought.

(b) This section shall not apply to any person who commits an act that results in the death of a foetus if . . . the act complied with the Therapeutic Abortion Act . . .

191.5 Manslaughter is . . .

(c) vehicular . . . driving a vehicle in the commission of an unlawful act . . . with gross negligence.

However, there are some important moral, social, and political complexities that this kind of unifying legislation threatens to erase, sometimes at the level of fundamental values.

To begin with a simple example, how convincing is the case for extracting the offence in England and Wales of 'causing death by dangerous driving' from its road traffic context,[72] and placing it in a new Homicide Act? The offence seems at least as at home alongside its road traffic-related siblings, such as the offence of 'dangerous driving', which is the lesser included offence under the Road Traffic Act 1988. That is probably where the lay person in search of guidance on his or her legal obligations—Hart's 'puzzled man'[73]—would expect to find it. More importantly, offences concerned with dangerous driving can be thought of as belonging naturally to the regulatory realm of health and safety. A similar point has been made, in criticism of the offence of corporate manslaughter, in supporting the case for an alternative offence of causing death through breach of health and safety laws.[74] The

---

[69] *Poulton* (1832) 5 C & P 329; *Enoch* (1850) 5 C & P 539; *Malcherek* (1981) 2 All ER 422.
[70] [1993] AC 789 (HL).   [71] [2001] Fam 147 (CA).
[72] Road Traffic Act 1988, s 1. See Ch 2 above.   [73] Hart (1961), at 193.
[74] See Glazebrook (2002).

fact that death has been caused need not, in and of itself, inevitably lead us to regard as inappropriate the placing of the relevant prohibition in its regulatory context.[75] Causing death by dangerous driving is one unacceptable face of what is, in general, engagement in an activity—driving—that is regarded as acceptable

To provide an extreme contrast, in its worst form as an intended killing, murder is not the unwanted by-product of permitting people to engage in risky activity.[76] Successfully to kill someone and hence commit murder is by definition to engage in a kind of conduct that is unacceptable; and in so far as there are serious doubts about that—as in the case of 'mercy' killing—then the question arises whether such killings should continue to be regarded as murder.[77] Other forms of murder and manslaughter straddle the border between the two kinds of crime, regulatory and non-regulatory. In some instances (say, a gang attack that ends in another's death) the conduct in question that led to the death will—as in cases of intended killing— be unacceptable, period. In other cases—say, deaths caused through medical malpractice or through dangerous (but consensual) sports—murder and man-slaughter are being relied on to do much the same job as causing death by reckless driving: condemning those who step beyond the boundaries of otherwise tolerated but risky conduct. In such cases, perhaps there is a case for a 'culpable homicide' offence based on negligence (below manslaughter) to catch such 'regulatory' cases and protect the offender from the harsher 'murder' or 'manslaughter' label; but consideration of that is beyond the scope of this chapter.[78]

Similar issues arise at a more fundamental level. What is commonly considered to be the law of 'homicide' is that part of the law concerned with the prima facie wrong of ending of another's life when that life is already 'in being'.[79] The defences commonly regarded as available wholly to justify or excuse the intentional com-mission of that prima facie wrong are, correspondingly, focused on the preservation of a life that would otherwise wrongly be ended (self-defence; necessity).[80] Tradi-tionally, this has been more or less the full extent of the criminal law codifier's menu, and it is not hard to see why. A true and full account of justifications for killing would have to address much more controversial instances where the justifi-cation is not (or may not be) the preservation of life, as such: examples are abortion, killing in war, taking one's own life, deciding not to resuscitate a dying and untreatable patient, and withdrawing life support from a patient in a persistent

---

[75] In saying that, I am not, of course, in any sense suggesting that deaths caused on the roads or in the workplace are in some sense less serious than deaths caused in other contexts and treated as murder or manslaughter. Even if the offence of causing death by dangerous driving were regarded as so serious as to warrant the death penalty, that would not in any way diminish the case for keeping that offence in a Road Traffic Act.

[76] Subject to what will be said below about death caused in the course of engagements with dangerous people involving armed police officers.

[77] The Law Commission recommended that the area of mercy killing is the subject of a special review: see Law Commission (2006).

[78] See Quick (2008); Glazebrook (2002). See further, Ch 4 below.

[79] In other words, when someone has been 'born alive': see n 69 above.

[80] In circumstances where the individual has no choice but to act him or herself if life is to be saved.

vegetative state. Take, by way of example, suicide and abortion. Without entering into the rights and wrongs of these instances where life is ended unnaturally, they may all stand to be justified or excused, if at all, by values unconnected to the preservation of life. The lawfulness of suicide and abortion stems from the belief that (in some or all circumstances) to permit these practices shows a proper concern for civil liberty and for the right to self-determination. One might question, then, the recent innovative use of anti-social behaviour orders to prevent people seeking to take their own lives, even when a social cost is imposed when such people must be rescued and treated.[81] A society that can afford to rescue reckless people trying to have fun by crossing the Atlantic on a rubber inflatable hardly needs to trespass on the right to self-determination in the interests of cost-saving.

Contrariwise, the decision not to resuscitate a dying and untreatable patient or to withdraw life support from a patient in a persistent vegetative state may (in many instances) be better justified by considerations of what is in the patient's best interests, rather than by an appeal to the right to self-determination.[82] Something similar might be said about many instances of 'mercy' killing. Nonetheless, these examples share with suicide and abortion the absence of any justification founded in the preservation of life itself. As suggested above, each of these sets of homicide-related concerns (suicide; abortion; withdrawing patient life-support; 'mercy' killing) is best located in its own political or moral—and hence legislative—context, a context partly distinct from that in which the would-be codifier of the law of homicide shapes his or her frame of reference. What lesson, then, should one draw from these examples?

They suggest that the criminal lawyer's ambition to codify the entire law of homicide, if not actually incoherent, rests on the false premise that either the 'preservation of life' or the 'ending of life' itself provides a sufficiently substantial focal point for legislation on all end-of-life issues. In questioning this ambition I should obviously not be taken to be saying that, for example, the question whether life can be ended ceases to be an issue within the domain the law of homicide simply because the killer is a doctor or mother and the victim a patient or foetus. However, the fact that the killing of patients or foetuses can be murder or manslaughter is a conclusion to an argument about the legal status of those killings. That argument should be in part shaped or determined by moral and political principles outside the life-preservatory domain of homicide. That point, at least, is recognized under Californian penal law relating to abortion, in the legal connection that it establishes between homicide law and abortion law.[83]

---

[81] In January 2006, Amy Dallamura found herself banned under such an order from visiting any beach in Aberystwyth, where she had repeatedly tried to drown herself; and Kim Sutton from Bath was likewise banned from jumping into rivers, canals, or onto railway lines.

[82] Obviously, I am putting aside here the issues raised when someone has made a 'living will' with instructions on how they are (not) to be treated when terminally ill.

[83] See text following n 71 above.

Shamefully, England and Wales still lacks proper medical ethics legislation that would relieve the courts of the primary duty to resolve intractable life-or-death medical dilemmas using doctrines ill-fitted for the purpose, like necessity, drawn from the domain of life-preservation.[84] The issue has, by and large, simply been ducked by the legislature. In an ideal world, we would not have an all-embracing codified law of homicide so much as separate pieces of legislation divided, according to respect for the plural and conflicting nature of values, very roughly as follows:

1. *Life preservatory domain* (homicide law):

Issues: e.g. definition of murder and manslaughter; justifications and complete excuses for murder and manslaughter concerned with life-preservation, such as self-defence and necessity.

2. *Quality of life domain* (medical ethics law):

Issues: e.g. 'mercy' killing; assisted suicide; cessation of life-support for patients.

3. *Domain of self-determination* (law of civil liberties):

Issues: e.g. abortion; suicide.

4. *Regulatory domain* (law of health and safety):

Issues: e.g. causing death by dangerous driving; corporate manslaughter (i.e. causing death through breach of health and safety at work rules).

5. *Domain of national and international security*:

Issues: e.g. genocide; use of weapons of mass destruction; jurisdiction to try non-nationals for homicide committed overseas.

As indicated above, although each domain is context-sensitive, there can be overlapping and controversy over the territory claimed by each of them. Take the examples where patients die needlessly on the operating table, and where armed police shoot someone wrongly thought to be armed and dangerous. Some might argue that unjustified killing in these kinds of cases should be regarded, however serious, first and foremost as a regulatory offence, even if life-preservation was the purported justification for the action that led to the death.[85] They should be regarded as regulatory offences, so the argument runs, because doctors and armed police officers face life-threatening choices as part of their professional, rule-following duties and not—as is the case for ordinary citizens—as unexpected, once-in-a-life-time emergencies for which the doctrines of necessity and self-defence (on which professionals currently have to rely) were designed.[86] Some would also regard

<hr/>

[84] See *Re A (Conjoined Twins)* [2001] Fam 147 (CA).

[85] In that regard, it is perhaps not insignificant that when in 2005 an armed policeman shot an innocent man on the London underground system because he mistook him for a terrorist, the only charges brought concerned breach of health and safety laws in connection with the way the operation as a whole was run: <www.bbc.co.uk/1/hi/uk/5186050.stm> (17 July 2006).

[86] See further, Rogers (1998).

'mercy' killing as having no claim to special status under any 'quality of life' rubric because it is a straightforward violation of the right not to be killed, protected within the life-preservatory domain. I hope I have done enough to suggest that it is right to regard reform of the law of homicide within the life-preservatory domain as a modest but coherent and achievable aim, unlike grandiose schemes for the codification of all the law relevant to the commission of homicide.

4

Corporate Manslaughter and Public Authorities

I. A Public Culture of Neglect: Employers, Employees, and Consumers

Scholars have long called for the introduction of a specific offence of 'corporate' manslaughter,[1] and their wish was (to a greater or lesser extent) granted when Parliament passed the Corporate Manslaughter and Corporate Homicide Act 2007 ('the 2007 Act').[2] Under section 1 of the 2007 Act, an organization will be liable for corporate manslaughter ('corporate homicide' in Scotland) if 'the way in which its activities are managed or organised':

(a) causes a person's death, and

(b) amounts to a gross breach of a relevant duty of care owed by the organization to the deceased.

In that respect, the way in which an organization's activities are managed or organized by its 'senior management' must be a 'substantial element' in the breach of the duty of care (section 1(3)).[3] 'Senior management' is defined by section 1(4)(c), in relation to an organization, in terms of persons who play, 'significant roles in—(i) the making of decisions about how the whole or a substantial part of its activities are to be managed or organised, or (ii) the actual managing or organising of the whole or a substantial part of those activities'.

In the lead up to, and subsequently in response to, the passing of the 2007 Act, many criminal law scholars focused and continue to focus almost exclusively on the application of the 2007 Act to companies, rather than to public bodies.[4] In one way, that is perfectly understandable. Although the fatal injury rate at the workplace in Britain is one of the lowest in Europe,[5] in 2010–11 there were still 171

---

[1] See, eg, Slapper and Tombs (1999); Wells (1993); Wells (1989).

[2] Naturally, there have been many academic criticisms of the 2007 Act, but I am not directly concerned with these here: see, eg, Gobert (2008).

[3] This is perhaps unlikely to prove to be a very significant restriction on the scope of liability, as the courts do not interpret the term 'substantial' to mean 'main' or 'major'. They understand it to mean simply 'not insignificant' or 'not wholly trivial': see *Cato* [1976] 1 All ER 260, at 265–6. For the Law Commission recommendations on which this section is based, see Law Commission (1996).

[4] There have been some important exceptions. See, eg, Allen (2007).

[5] <www.hse.gov.uk/statistics/fatals.htm>.

deaths amongst Britain's workers and most occurred in the pursuit of private corporate activity. So, in 2010–11, the distribution of fatalities in main industrial sectors was as follows:

Agriculture: 34
Construction: 50
Manufacturing: 27
Waste and Recycling: 9
Services sector: 47.[6]

By contrast, in the health and social care sector, for example, there have been only four work-related fatal accidents since 2000–01.[7]

However, a focus on workers in industry who have died in accidents gives a misleading picture of where real dangers lie in the public services—in particular, in the health service—and hence gives a distorted picture of the kinds of avoidable deaths the 2007 Act has the potential to deter. To begin with, as it was put in debate on the Bill that preceded the 2007 Act in the House of Lords:

[T]here is no reason why the death of an individual in one situation should be considered less of a death, or less deserving of justice, merely because that situation was presided over by Government officials as opposed to privately employed foremen. Indeed, it is all the more of a tragedy and contravention of the natural principle of justice where the state itself acts with such gross negligence that the very lives of its own citizens are forfeit.[8]

The use of the term 'citizen', rather than 'employee' at the end of this passage is highly significant. For, taking the management and organization of the health service as a focus, it is patients—not workers—who are unjustifiably and inexcusably being systematically exposed to unacceptable risks of death, or even being assaulted, and who in consequence are dying in considerable numbers.[9] A Marxist obsession with the moral and political significance of the relationship between workers and their employers[10]—a preoccupation characteristic even of liberal scholarship on the 2007 Act—has meant that this ugly side of public service activity has never been subjected to much scrutiny by criminal law scholars who support the new manslaughter offence.[11] Even scholars who have moved beyond the narrow confines of the Marxist perspective tend to expand their focus in ways that exclude examination of public authorities as criminals: by concentrating on, for

---

[6] *Ibid.* It is perhaps worth noting that more than half of fatal injuries were of three kinds: being struck by vehicles, being struck by falling objects, or falling from height. By contrast, slipping or tripping, and handling accidents predominate in non-fatal injury, including major injury.

[7] <www.hse.gov.uk/statistics/industry/healthservices/health.pdf>.

[8] 688 HL Official Report (5th Series) col GC 189 (Lord Ramsbotham).

[9] See the discussion in section III. below.

[10] See Marx (1975), at 385–6 on the significance of the employer-employee relationship. Marx was never noted for showing much moral concern about consumers, as opposed to the employers and their employees who provide services for consumers.

[11] Apart from Allen (2007), before the 2007 Act, and Griffin and Moran (2010) after it, comment on the applicability of the 2007 Act to the NHS has largely been confined to specialist clinical journals: see, eg, White (2008).

example, criminal activity by Governments themselves or by Mafia-like organizations and criminal gangs.[12] Yet, the dangerous perpetuation of negligence, idleness, indifference, inefficiency, and arbitrary cost-cutting does not only affect the safety of workers. Consumers of public services also suffer from the effects of an all-too human set of institutional failings, a collective culture of neglect, that can readily be found at work in Government departments, hospitals, schools, and prisons not motivated by profit.[13] What is more, the perpetuation, along with the concealment, of institutional failings that lead to consumers' deaths by gross negligence may well be one of the few things which, for whatever reason, management and its workforce in the public sector jointly tolerate or at which they connive.[14]

The Government was prepared to acknowledge this point, and hence to extend the offence in the 2007 Act—albeit in too limited a way[15]—to cover at least some deaths caused by gross negligence (speaking loosely) in the provision of public services. Yet, this reflects little more than the fact that public authorities have very broadly similar sorts of obligations to third parties—i.e. those who are neither employers nor employees—under the Health and Safety at Work Act 1974 ('the 1974 Act').[16] The intensively examined 1974 Act has for many years imposed a duty on employers to make their places of work safe for third parties (including patients), as well as for employees.[17] Yet, the silence of most criminal law scholars on the issue of public authority liability for corporate manslaughter, both before and after the passing of the 2007 Act (with the odd exception[18]), has been truly deafening. Yet, for those criminal lawyers willing to make the intellectual leap out of the Marxist moral-political rut in which corporate manslaughter scholarship has largely been stuck,[19] the rewards are considerable. There is, for example, a real possibility of exploring ways in which the deterrent effect of the threat to public authorities of criminal liability under the 2007 Act can, in spite of its severe limitations (discussed in due course), do at least something to make idle, indiffer-

[12] See, eg, the thoughtful work in this area of Harding (2007).
[13] For a broader examination of the explanations for crime within organizations, see Gobert (2007).
[14] See the discussion of the report on Stafford Hospital, in text at n 34 below. Naturally, such an anti-consumer attitude, that draws both employers and employees into a kind of conspiracy, may be found as much in the private as in the public sector; but—consistent with the theme being developed here—the links between corporate manslaughter and consumer protection are yet fully to be explored.
[15] See, eg, section V. below.
[16] I say, 'very broadly' similar, in that the obligations under the 1974 Act are wider. In establishing an offence bearing on s 3(1) of the 1974 Act, for example, there is no need to prove gross negligence on the employer's part, and no need to show that third parties exposed to risk were within the scope of a pre-existing duty of care owed by the employer.
[17] Section 3(1) of the 1974 Act imposes a duty on an employer to conduct their undertakings in such a way as to ensure, so far as is reasonably practicable, that persons not in his employment who may be affected thereby are not thereby exposed to risks to their health and safety.
[18] See, on the potential liability of the police under the 2007 Act, Griffin and Moran (2010). For an early study that sought to anticipate the effects of the 2007 Act on NHS Trusts, see Allen (2007).
[19] Which is not to imply that scholarship conducted from this perspective is not of outstanding quality: see, eg, Wells (2001); Gobert and Punch (2003).

ent, or cost-obsessed NHS Trusts engage in much more serious efforts to prevent the large number of unnecessary deaths being caused in their hospitals. Before returning to this issue, though, we should examine the way in which the liability of public authorities arises under the 2007 Act, and the considerations bearing on it when compared with the potential liability of private firms.

II. The Reach of the Duty of Care: Public and Private Organizations

The offence of 'corporate' manslaughter applies not only to private companies—the traditional focus of scholars who have argued for the imposition of liability on organizations—but also to a large range of public bodies (including the police) for the most part set out in Schedule 1 of the 2007 Act.[20] It is worth noting that under Schedule 1, the new offence will apply to the Ministry of Defence, to the Department of Health, and to HM Prison Service.[21] The 2007 Act applies in some measure to all the public bodies the performance of whose functions are most likely to involve causing deaths, whether these occur (for example) in custody or in hospital. Having said that, as we will see, the 2007 Act restricts in important ways the range of activities engaged in by public bodies in respect of which a duty of care and hence liability can be imposed. The Act includes these exemptions for public bodies even though the Government itself indicated that the Health and Safety Executive has censured a Crown Body only four times in the last six years in relation to the causing of a death.[22]

The 2007 Act certainly spreads the liability net wider than some jurisdictions have thought appropriate. For example, in the Australian Capital Territory ('ACT'), the crime of 'industrial manslaughter' can only be committed by an employer against a worker in the course of their employment.[23] It would not apply to a case in which, for example, a member of the public was killed by a workplace explosion or by a company's defective products or dangerous services.[24] By way of contrast, in virtue of section 2, the 2007 Act is of wider application. Section 2(1) sets out the scope of the duty of care not to cause deaths imposed on organizations to which the 2007 Act applies:

---

[20] The fact that public bodies are set out in the Schedule means that they may be added to or subtracted from relatively easily by the Secretary of State for Justice, who thus retains bureaucratic control over who can be an offender.

[21] For some of the background, see the statement of the Secretary of State for Justice, at 463 HC Official Report (6th series), col 331.

[22] Home Office (2006).

[23] Crimes Act 1900 (ACT), s 49A, inserted by the Crimes (Industrial Manslaughter) Amendment Act 2003.

[24] See the discussion in Tasmanian Law Reform Institute (2007), at para 6.3.5.

(1) A 'relevant duty of care', in relation to an organisation, means . . .
    (a) a duty owed to its employees or to other persons working for the organisation . . .
    (b) a duty owed as occupier of premises;
    (c) a duty owed in connection with —
        (i) the supply by the organisation of goods or services (whether for consideration or not),
        (ii) the carrying on by the organisation of any construction or maintenance operations,
        (iii) the carrying on by the organisation of any other activity on a commercial basis, or
        (iv) the use or keeping by the organisation of any plant, vehicle or other thing;
    (d) a duty owed to a person who, by reason of being a person within subsection (2) [a detained person], is someone for whose safety the organisation is responsible.

It is clear from the wording that the scope of the duty is very considerably wider than that imposed under the legislation in the ACT, mentioned above. Third parties, such as those occupying neighbouring properties and consumers of public services, including health care services, may fall within the scope of the duty not to cause death (respectively, under section 2(1)(b) and under section 2(1)(c)(i)) just as easily as employees (under section 2(1)(a)). In that regard, whether there was a duty on a particular organization not to cause the death of a particular individual will be a question of law for the judge and not a jury question.[25] As well as making it possible to maintain consistency between the civil and the criminal law on this point, this precautionary measure will prevent a jury working backwards from the mere fact that death has been caused by the (in)action of an organization to the conclusion that there must have been a duty not to cause it. On the other hand, the question whether there was a 'gross' breach is one for the jury. The jury must decide, 'if the conduct alleged to amount to a breach of that duty falls far below what can reasonably be expected of the organization in the circumstances' (section 2(4)(b)). In that respect, a good deal of scholarly attention has been focused on how extensive the notion of 'in the circumstances' is meant to be. The Law Commission, in suggesting the phraseology, said that it would encompass:

such matters as the likelihood and possible extent of the harm arising from the way in which the company conducted its operations [as compared with] the social utility of its activities and the cost and practicability of taking steps to eliminate or reduce the risk of death. . . .[26]

---

[25] 2007 Act, s 2(5). The offence of corporate manslaughter is triable on indictment only. Under s 2(5), the judge is entitled to make any findings of fact necessary to come to a decision on the duty question.
  [26] Law Commission (1996), at para 8.6.

The courts have been resistant to the idea that unprofitability is a 'cost' factor that can legitimately entitle a private company to cut corners on health and safety.[27] Contrariwise, Government departments are likely to benefit (a) from the fact that what they can spend overall is ultimately determined by central Government, and (b) from the fact that they will almost always be able to play the 'social utility' card in a broader range of circumstances than private firms.[28] Nonetheless, the 2007 Act's starting point is that whether an organization is providing a public service free or for a charge, or is a private company devoted to profit-maximization, that organization may find itself liable for homicide if it has caused death because it wrongly allowed its premises, plant, or vehicles (or the like), or the working conditions that it sustained, or the way that it provided its services, to become highly dangerous for employees or others who came into contact with or used them.[29]

III. The Potential Impact of the 2007 Act on Negligent NHS Trusts

The moral significance of the silence of criminal law scholars on the applicability of the 2007 Act to services provided under the auspices of NHS Trusts can only be properly understood when one considers some figures. The Care Quality Commission recorded some 1.25 million 'incidents' occurring in NHS hospitals in 2010–11, meaning patient safety incidents and 'near misses'.[30] To put that overall figure in perspective, around 32 per cent of staff in major surveys conducted by the Care Quality Commission between 2009 and 2011 said that they had witnessed at least one error or 'near miss' that could have led to injury (or worse).[31] So far as deaths in hospitals are concerned, overshadowing the figure of roughly 170 deaths annually occurring nationwide in a private employment context,[32] are two figures discussed here. First, there is the figure of 1,800 deaths (along with approximately 1,600 severe injuries) attributable to the unnecessary administration of anti-psychotic drugs to some 120,000 dementia patients in a single year: 2009.[33] Secondly, there is the figure of nearly 500 deaths—500 above and beyond the figure that could ordinarily be

---

[27] See *F Howe & Son (Engineers) Ltd* [1999] 2 All ER 249, and the good discussion of this issue in Gobert and Punch (2003), at 105–7.

[28] See the discussion in section V. below.

[29] The 2007 Act, s 2(6) specifically disapplies certain common law restrictions on liability: 'For the purposes of this Act there is to be disregarded—(a) any rule of common law that has the effect of preventing a duty of care from being owed by one person to another by reason of the fact that they are jointly engaged in unlawful conduct; (b) any such rule that has the effect of preventing a duty of care from being owed to a person by reason of his acceptance of a risk of harm.'

[30] <www.cqc.org.uk/public/reports-surveys-and-reviews/reports/state-care-report-2010/11/quality-and-safety>.

[31] <www.cqc.org.uk/media/nhs-staff-have-their-say-results-national-survey-are-published>.

[32] See text at n 6 above.

[33] Department of Health (2009), at para 5; discussed in the text at n 50 below. Only about 20,000 patients out of 180,000 treated with anti-psychotic medication in any given year were found by the report to derive, on balance, a benefit from the treatment.

expected in the period in question—that occurred in one hospital alone (Stafford Hospital) from 2005/06 to 2007/08.[34] I will consider the latter first.

Of some of the causes of the approximately 500 deaths, the Chair of the Inquiry into the deaths, Robert Francis QC, concluded (inter alia):

The omissions [by hospital staff] left patients struggling to care for themselves; this led to injury and a loss of dignity, often in the final days of their lives. The impact of this on them and their families is almost unimaginable. Taken individually, many of the accounts I received indicated a standard of care which was totally unacceptable. Together, they demonstrate a systematic failure of the provision of good care. . . . It is difficult to believe that lapses on the scale that was evidenced could have occurred if there had been an adequately implemented system of nursing and ward management.[35]

Staff at the hospital were found (a) to have left patients in soiled sheets (even those infected with *Clostridium Difficile*) at a hospital suffering from infection control problems; (b) to have failed to record incidents when patients had fallen; (c) to have made patients share razors and washbowls; (d) to have left meals out of reach and to have provided no or inadequate supplies of water (no adequate charts of nutrition and hydration were kept); (e) to have made a number of misdiagnoses, in circumstances where the patients' families were not listened to, investigations were not followed up, and information about them not shared; (f) to have discharged patients at inappropriate times; and (g) to have failed to report 'incidents', some of which were subsequently the subject of coroners' inquests. Of such failings, the Chairman indicated that they were the result of 'systemic failings', and were hence 'more than can be explained by the personal failings of a few members of staff'.[36] He drew attention, in that regard, amongst other things, to the influence of target-driven priorities,[37] a lack of openness, acceptance of poor standards of conduct (including toleration of bullying by staff), and a culture of 'denial' on the part of the Trust.[38] The Chairman concluded:

[The Trust's] culture is characterised by introspection, lack of insight or sufficient self-criticism, rejection of external criticism, reliance on external praise and, above all, fear. I found evidence of the negative impact of fear, particularly of losing a job, from top to bottom of this organisation.[39]

In that regard, in 2011, the Care Quality Commission found that just over one in ten of the 100 acute NHS hospitals it inspected were not meeting one of two essential standards in relation to the treatment with dignity and respect of older people, and nine other hospitals were meeting neither of these standards.[40]

---

[34] *Mid Staffordshire NHS Foundation Trust Inquiry* (2010), vol 1, at 360 (figure 5).

[35] *Ibid*, at paras 21–2.

[36] *Ibid*, at 12 (para 30).

[37] The Trust was faced with finding cuts of £10 million by the end of 2006–07.

[38] *Ibid*, at 16 (para 43). A fuller list of concerns about systemic failure can be found at *Mid Staffordshire NHS Foundation Trust Inquiry* (2010), vol 1, at 24 (para 80).

[39] *Mid Staffordshire NHS Foundation Trust Inquiry* (2010), vol 1, at 184 (para 135).

[40] <www.cqc.org.uk/public/reports-surveys-and-reviews/reports/state-care-report-2010/11/quality-and-safety>. It should be noted that not every failure to meet these standards is itself potentially

The Chairman's conclusion can usefully be compared with a statement of intent by the Department of Health in a memorandum of understanding concerning prosecution of criminal offences drawn up between the National Health Service, the Association of Chief Police Officers, and the Health and Safety Executive, in 2006.[41] In that document, the Department of Health said that it was:

Pursuing its commitment to patient safety among other things by encouraging a shift in the NHS from a prevailing culture of blame to one that is fair and just. All experience in other high risk industries shows that a culture in which blame predominates in the handling of errors and adverse incidents creates a climate of fear leading to concealment of safety problems. The can lead potentially to more, rather than fewer incidents.[42]

Clearly, Stafford Hospital had taken on board the need to move away from a 'culture of blame', since it failed to engage in any self-criticism and rejected external criticism. Manifestly, though, this move was not accompanied by any serious attempt on the Hospital's part to replace a culture of secrecy and blame with a culture of openness and dedication to achieving the highest standards achievable in the circumstances. In that respect, the Department of Health's statement is curiously vague on such a crucial point. It is unclear what it means to replace a culture of 'blame' with a culture that is 'fair and just', since blame allocation is one—albeit only one—potentially important feature of achieving justice and fairness. If the Department of Health was itself unclear what its priorities were in 2006, in the way that NHS Trusts should shape their management policies, how could an NHS Trust be confident that it was providing an authoritative lead in that respect?

Stafford Hospital is, of course, not the only one to have caused deaths through systemic failures. Criminal lawyers are familiar with the case of *Misra*,[43] in which two junior orthopaedic surgeons at Southampton University Hospitals NHS Trust were both convicted of gross negligence manslaughter; but they are often less familiar with the fact that there was also a successful prosecution of the NHS Trust under the 1974 Act and a fine of £100,000, based on the Trust's failure adequately to supervise the surgeons in question. In *Great Western Hospitals NHS Trust*,[44] a nurse mistakenly gave a healthy woman patient (herself a hospital employee), who had just given birth, a powerful anaesthetic instead of a saline solution. The patient died an hour later from a heart attack. Although both substances had similar packaging, an inquest into V's death had found that the storage system for drugs at the hospital was 'chaotic'. A joint police and Health and Safety Executive ('HSE') investigation showed that there was no management

---

lethal. Rudeness, although wholly unacceptable, is an example. However, staff rudeness may make a patient or his or her relatives more reluctant to complain about incidents or treatment that do threaten a patient's safety.

[41] <www.hse.gov.uk/foi/internalops/fod/oc/100-199/165-10.htm>.
[42] *Ibid*, Foreword.
[43] [2004] EWCA Crim 2375.
[44] Unreported; see <www.hse.gov.uk/press/2010/coi-sw-783sww10.htm>.

system for the storage of drugs, at board, pharmacy, and ward level.[45] Following the subsequent trial, the judge attributed the error not only to the fault of the nurse who administered the anaesthetic, but also to what he called, 'systematic fault'.[46] In this case, though, the NHS Trust was prosecuted under section 3(1) of the 1974 Act, as the incident occurred in 2004 before the passing of the 2007 Act.[47] In a different context, in March 2011, the Care Quality Commission noted failures on the part of an NHS Trust to do enough to prevent suicides by patients in its care with mental health problems disposing them to commit suicide.[48] At least one NHS Trust has been found to have been badly at fault in relation to one such death, as a result of failures of communication and risk-assessment, and of a failure to remove or render safe known ligature points in patients' rooms (despite a Care Quality Commission report five months previously warning of the dangers these ligature points posed).[49]

Few lessons can necessarily be learned from isolated cases, unless they are symptomatic of widespread malpractice. However, more than one study has shown strong evidence of potentially lethal malpractice on an impressive scale, some of which borders on the murderous. As I have indicated, in 2009, a Department of Health report estimated that roughly 1,800 people annually suffering from dementia die prematurely, and many more suffer serious side-effects, from the administration without clear clinical justification of the so-called 'chemical cosh', a strong anti-psychotic drug wrongly used merely to sedate agitated or distressed (i.e. 'difficult') patients.[50] The report went on to recommend the reduction in the use of such drugs as a first resort by no less than two-thirds. Criminal lawyers will not need reminding that such conduct, when unjustified, amounts to the infliction of grievous bodily harm. In cases where death has been caused thereby, such conduct may amount to manslaughter or even murder; but to focus on the fault of those acting on the front line may in many instances be to miss the point. A key element of support for the offence under the 2007 Act comes from the fact that it enables a switch of focus within the law of homicide from malpractice of individual employees, to the 'facilitative' culture of neglect to which the employees' managers contributed through their own shortcomings. Why the importance of such a switch of focus in the public sector, as well as in

---

[45] *Ibid.*

[46] <www.guardian.co.uk/society/2010/may/17/mother-killed-myra-cabrera-bupivacaine>.

[47] The Trust was fined £75,000, and required to pay £30,000 costs. Under the current Protocol governing prosecution, the police have primacy in relation to any potential corporate manslaughter prosecution, if manslaughter is suspected, but the HSE will investigate possible breaches of the 1974 Act in parallel with any such investigation: <www.hse.gov.uk/foi/internalops/fod/oc/100-199/165-10.htm#The-protocol>.

[48] <www.cqc.org.uk/media/regulator-tells-lincolnshire-partnership-nhs-foundation-trust-improvements -are-necessary>. As of 1 September 2011, the 2007 Act applies to deaths in custody and deaths of detained mental patients.

[49] <www.bindmans.com/index.php?id=961>.

[50] Department of Health (2009), at para 4. See further text at n 32 above, and *Daily Telegraph*, 1 November 2011.

the private sector, should have excited so little interest or support from criminal law scholars is anyone's guess. I have suggested it is likely to be a product of the lingering influence, even on liberal scholars, of narrow Marxist presuppositions about the relations that have predominant moral significance in the workplace, namely relations between employer and employee.[51]

More commonly, poor management leads to either or both of the widespread toleration of inherently risky conduct and high error rates in the provision of care. Taking the former first (inherently risky conduct), a 2008 study showed a non-compliance rate with hand-hygiene standards amongst staff in four acute NHS hospitals in Ireland of 30 per cent overall, a figure that rose to 41 per cent for doctors and medical students. Non-compliance rates ran at 43 per cent in the period just before clinical procedures began, rising to 49 per cent after the completion of such procedures.[52] In more recent times, the Care Quality Commission has found that about 30 per cent of hospital staff surveyed in England and Wales said that hot water, soap, and paper towels or alcohol rubs were not always available when they were needed.[53] Turning to the latter (error rates), a 2008 study of the use of anaesthetics in Australian hospitals found that system-based or organizational factors were influential in 90 per cent of anaesthetic accidents, key factors being:

teamwork and communication problems;
problems with the design, construction, maintenance, and standardization of equipment;
problems with drugs: labelling, purchase, stock control, delivery to and from storage etc;
problems with the assessment and scheduling of patients;
problems with the planning and co-ordination of anaesthetists and their co-workers.[54]

In Holland, a 2001 study suggested that in 25 per cent of the anaesthesia-related deaths, inadequate preparation of the patient was to blame, whilst inadequate patient monitoring as a contributing factor was attributable to organizational failures in some 40 per cent of cases.[55] Most deaths resulting from anaesthesia-related accidents in England and Wales are considered to be avoidable.[56]

It is probably unrealistic to expect many of the kinds of cases just discussed to result in a prosecution under the 2007 Act when death has been caused, whether this is attributable to diffusion of responsibility by staff,[57] to difficulties in proving a causal link between malpractice and the death of, say, an already elderly and sick patient, or to other factors. As a matter of law, rather than of practice, so far as prosecution is concerned, two issues must now be addressed: proof of fault under

[51] See text at n 10 above.
[52] Creedon *et al* (2008).
[53] <www.cqc.org.uk/media/nhs-staff-have-their-say-results-national-survey-are-published>.
[54] For further detail, see Reason (2005).
[55] Arbous *et al* (2001).
[56] K Gannon, 'Mortality Associated with Anaesthesia' 46 (1991) Anaesthesia 962. For a Scottish case from 2010, see <www.scotcourts.gov.uk/opinions/2010FAI15.html>.
[57] On which, see Gooderham (2011).

the 2007 Act and the exemptions from liability for public authorities provided by the 2007 Act itself.

IV. Proving Fault under the 2007 Act

The 2007 Act takes a significant (albeit limited[58]) step beyond the limitations of corporate liability at common law. At common law, a company could only be found liable for an offence (such as manslaughter) with a fault element if that fault element was possessed by someone, such as a director or chief executive, who could be identified with the company itself (the 'identification doctrine'). In *Lennard's Carrying Co Ltd v Asiatic Petroleum Co Ltd*,[59] Lord Haldane said:

Mr Lennard was the directing mind of the company... his action was the action of the company itself... [his] fault is not merely that of a servant or agent for whom the company is liable upon the footing *respondeat superior* but somebody for whom the company is liable because his action is the very action of the company itself.[60]

In searching for criminal fault, the 'simplistic'[61] identification doctrine treats companies as if they were individuals, confining liability to instances in which someone who can be said to be 'the company itself' had the fault necessary for the commission of the offence. That has always been a major limitation on liability, for the simple reason that it fails to take account of the degree to which in medium- to large-sized organizations crucial strategic decisions are frequently delegated to lower levels of management than those granted plenary authority over the organization's affairs (in the case of private companies, in their articles of association). It is true that the vast majority of British firms are very small, and are hence unlikely to have many, if any, layers of management. Nonetheless, it is unacceptable that an organization should be able to escape liability for serious crime, even when the fault element for the crime was possessed by someone with authority to take strategic decisions, simply because that person was not a director or chief executive.

As Simester and Sullivan rightly pointed out,[62] the narrowness of this approach is illustrated in a private sector context by the case of *Redfern and Dunlop Ltd (Aircraft Tyres Divisions)*.[63] In this case, the knowledge of no less a person than the European sales manager was considered insufficient to fix a company with liability when charged with knowingly exporting combat equipment to Iran. Similarly, in *P&O Ferries (Dover) Ltd*,[64] the company escaped liability for manslaughter following the Zeebrugge ferry disaster in which 192 people were drowned, in part because the ship's master was not someone who could be identified with the company itself. In consequence, the only successful prosecutions for manslaughter against companies have involved very small companies where the directors are necessarily them-

---

[58] On the limitations, see, eg, Gobert (2008).
[59] [1915] AC 705, [1914–15] All ER Rep 280.
[60] [1915] AC 705 at 713, [1914–15] All ER Rep 280, at 283.
[61] Simester and Sullivan *et al* (2010), at 274.   [62] *Ibid*, at 275–6.
[63] (1992) 13 Cr App R (S) 709.   [64] (1991) 93 Cr App R 72.

selves involved in day-to-day management and decision-making.[65] A similar point can obviously be made about the operation of many kinds of public authorities. In *Great Western Hospitals NHS Trust*,[66] the immediate cause of the mother's death was a mistake (in itself, perhaps, negligent rather than grossly negligent) by a nurse who mistook a package containing a powerful anaesthetic, that the nurse wrongly attached to the mother's intravenous drip, for an almost identically wrapped package containing saline solution that should have been attached to the drip. An HSE enquiry found systematic fault at ward level in that it was the practice to keep the two packages in the same cupboard.[67] However, such negligence on the part of ward managers could not necessarily be attributed to the hospital itself, let alone the NHS Trust. So, even though the Trust was itself found to have been negligent, in that it had no policy on drug storage, in itself that might not amount to 'gross' negligence. It is only when the negligence of all these parties is aggregated that the case for finding gross negligence is strong; but such aggregation was never possible at common law.

In some jurisdictions, the net of liability is also cast more widely by statute than by the common law but in a different way. For example, under section 12.3(1) of the Australian Model Criminal Code, the fault element of an offence can be attributed to a corporation if it expressly, tacitly, or impliedly authorized or permitted the offence to take place. Section 12.3(2) sets out four means by which such authorization or permission may be proved:

(a) proving that the body corporate's board of directors intentionally, knowingly or recklessly carried out the relevant conduct, or expressly, tacitly or impliedly authorised or permitted the commission of the offence; or

(b) proving that a high managerial agent of the body corporate intentionally, knowingly or recklessly engaged in the relevant conduct, or expressly, tacitly or impliedly authorised or permitted the commission of the offence; or

(c) proving that a corporate culture existed within the body corporate that directed, encouraged, tolerated or led to non-compliance with the relevant provision; or

(d) proving that the body corporate failed to create and maintain a corporate culture that required compliance with the relevant provision.

The Tasmanian Law Reform Institute recommended adoption of these provisions as a basis for corporate criminal liability in general, with the exception of (d) as a basis for liability. It regarded (d) as going too far in that, while undoubtedly a species of corporate fault, it is a negligence-based form of liability and hence an unsound basis on which to attribute to the company an offence involving intention, knowledge, or recklessness.[68] Would provisions (a) to (c) have been a better model

---

[65] See, eg, *Kite and OLL Ltd* (unreported) 8 December 1994.

[66] Unreported; see <www.hse.gov.uk/press/2010/coi-sw-783sww10.htm>. For details, see text at n 44 above.

[67] See text following n 44 above.

[68] See Colvin (1995), at 2–3 and 37, '[it is] questionable . . . whether it is an appropriate ground on which to hold a corporation responsible for the intentional, knowing, or reckless commission of an offence'.

for corporate manslaughter and corporate liability in the United Kingdom more generally?

It seems obvious that if fault can be attributed to a 'senior manager' (2007 Act), or to a 'high managerial agent' (Australian Model Criminal Code), then a case against a corporation involving proof of fault against a European sales manager, or hospital ward manager, is likely to be soundly based. Furthermore, in its concentration on 'the way in which [the organisation's] activities are managed or organised', section 1 of the 2007 Act goes beyond simply fixing an organization with liability by taking account of the individual culpability of a wider range of individuals within the organization—under section 1(3), senior managers—than was possible at common law. As is the case with the 'corporate culture' test under the Australian Model Criminal Code, the 2007 Act makes it possible to convict an organization on the basis of collective failings that (in the case of the 2007 Act) must include, but are not restricted to, failings on the part of senior managers. How much wider in this particular respect, if at all, is the 'corporate culture' test of liability? A test case for any differences between the 2007 Act and the Model Criminal Code might be *P&O Ferries (Dover) Ltd*.

In this case, the company's ferry overturned having left Zeebrugge harbour with its bow doors open, leading to a large number of deaths. P&O Ltd and seven individuals (two of whom were sufficiently senior to be identified with the company itself) were prosecuted for manslaughter. The trial judge (Turner J) directed that the defendants be acquitted. As a matter of common law, the judge was not prepared to aggregate the fault of the defendants, such that a 'global' judgment could be made that there had been, collectively, a reckless disregard for safety.[69] In the circumstances, that was fatal to the prosecution's case. Moreover, evidence that the assistant bosun responsible for shutting the bow doors had fallen asleep, that the chief officer whose responsibility it was to ensure that the bow doors were shut had failed to do so, and that there was no means by which the captain could confirm from the bridge that the bow doors were shut, did not assist the prosecution's case against the company. For this evidence did not show that the company itself, as opposed to these individuals, had behaved with reckless disregard for safety.

Would that all still be true under the 2007 Act? Arguably, it would not. At best, the individuals just mentioned would be regarded as no more than junior—rather than senior—managers, since they do not really have, to use the words of the 2007 Act, 'significant roles in—(i) the making of decisions about how the whole or a substantial part of [the company's] activities are to be managed or organised, or (ii) the actual managing or organising of the whole or a substantial part of those activities' (section 1(4)). However, it must be kept in mind that whilst any case of corporate manslaughter must rest, as a necessary condition of success, on proof of a breach of a duty of care on the part of senior managers, under section 1(3) the prosecution's case need only be that such a management failure was a 'substantial'

---

[69] At that time, the fault element for manslaughter was considered to be recklessness; it is now gross negligence: see *Adomako* [1995] 1 AC 171.

element in the breach.[70] The prosecution would also be able to rely on the conduct of others involved in management or organization at lower levels (like the ship's chief officer and captain) to construct its case that the way in which the organization was organized or managed as *a whole* caused death through a gross breach of a duty of care.

So, had P&O been prosecuted under the 2007 Act, it is likely that the case would have succeeded. The Sheen Enquiry into the Zeebrugge ferry disaster had concluded that, 'from top to bottom the body corporate was infected with the disease of sloppiness',[71] and added that:

[A] full investigation into the circumstances of the disaster leads inexorably to the conclusion that the underlying or cardinal faults lay higher up in the company. All concerned in management, from the members of the Board of Directors down to the junior super-intendents, were guilty of fault in that all must be regarded as sharing responsibility for the failure of management.[72]

That being so, it would have been easier to convict the company under the 2007 Act. The Act permits evidence of fault to be aggregated to the extent that under section 1 the jury is entitled to consider in a holistic manner 'the way in which [the company's] activities are managed or organised', so long as the role of senior management was a substantial contributing factor to a gross breach of a duty of care. For the same reasons, in the case discussed earlier, it would have been in principle possible to convict Great Western Hospitals NHS Trust of corporate manslaughter, had the 2007 Act been in force at that time.[73] The fault of the nurse, the ward managers, and of the NHS Trust could have been aggregated in deciding whether or not there had been a gross breach of the duty of care to the mother.

The difference under the Australian Model Criminal Code would be the relevance of head (c) above,[74] because this has no precise equivalent under the 2007 Act. In other words, there would be a possibility of proving guilt through a finding that 'a corporate culture existed within the body corporate that directed, encouraged, tolerated or led to non-compliance with the relevant provision'. What, if anything, does this add? According to the Model Criminal Code Officers' Committee, one function of the 'corporate culture' basis for attributing fault to a company is to catch the unwritten rules by which a company operates. It is meant to permit the prosecution:

to lead evidence that the company's unwritten rules tacitly authorised non-compliance or failed to create a culture of compliance. It would catch situations where, despite formal documents appearing to require compliance, the reality was that non-compliance was expected. For example, employees who know that if they do not break the law to meet production schedules (e.g. by removing safety guards on equipment) they will be dismissed. The company would be guilty of intentionally breaching safety legislation.[75]

---

[70] See n 3 above.

[71] Herald of Free Enterprise Report of the Court (1987), at para 14.1, cited by Wells (2001), at 109.

[72] *Ibid*, at para 14.1.

[73] See text at nn 44 and 66 above.

[74] See text following n 67 above.

[75] Model Criminal Code Officers' Committee (1992), at 111–13; See further Bucy (1991), at 1128–46.

So understood, the 'corporate culture' basis for convicting organizations does not add significantly to the 2007 Act, because breaches of a duty of care by senior managers themselves—here, through the expectation that employees would ignore safety procedures—play a role in causing the offence to be committed. However, under section 12.3(6), the Model Criminal Code defines a corporate culture as 'an attitude, policy, rule, course of conduct or practice existing within the body corporate generally *or in the part of the body corporate in which the relevant activities take place*' (my emphasis). This seems to be suggesting that the prosecution would have been able to rely on proof of a 'culture of sloppiness' on *the Herald of Free Enterprise* alone, as a basis for their case against P&O, if the ship and its crew could be regarded as the 'part of the body corporate in which the relevant activities [took] place'. The prosecution would then have needed to look no further than evidence of the culture of neglect amongst those on board responsible for the ship's safety—such as the bosun, the chief officer, and the captain—whatever might have been going on in terms of (perhaps harder to prove) management practices higher up in the corporate chain of command.[76] Similarly, had it been possible to prosecute on such a basis the Mid-Staffordshire NHS Foundation Trust in the Stafford Hospital case,[77] the prosecution might have had to look no further than the culture of neglect that had developed in some (but not all wards) at the hospital, without concerning itself with what was going wrong at higher levels of management. That is not necessarily much of an improvement.

It is not necessarily a criticism of the 2007 Act that it failed to extend the bases for establishing corporate liability to include proof of a 'corporate culture' of neglect or indifference, whether in the organization as a whole *or* in some part of it. To begin with, although such a thing undoubtedly exists, there is an inherent vagueness in the notion of 'corporate culture'—something that can apparently be found in any one or more of 'an attitude, policy, rule, course of conduct or practice'—that makes it of doubtful value in the context of criminal liability. Further, in so far as 'corporate culture' can be proved in law if it existed only in the part of the body corporate where the relevant activities took place, even if it was condemned by or completely unknown to the board of directors and senior managers, then (in the absence of a due diligence defence for the company) the doctrine in effect makes the company vicariously liable for the acts of those further down the chain of command who sustained the culture and hence committed the offence.[78] Whilst vicarious liability for fault-based offences is possible in some jurisdictions,[79] and has gained a foothold in England and Wales,[80] it is unlikely to be the approach taken across

[76] See further, the Australian Model Criminal Code, s 12.3(4).
[77] See text at n 34 above.
[78] Under s 12.4 of the Australian Model Criminal Code, if an employee reasonably believed that a high managerial agent would have authorized or permitted the commission of the offence, that is a factor relevant to whether there was a 'corporate culture' in which the commission of such offences was tolerated; but this factor is not decisive.
[79] See the discussion of United States law in Wells (2001), at 132–6.
[80] See the discussion in Simester and Sullivan *et al* (2010), at 263–72.

the board in the United Kingdom.[81] Making it easier to prosecute organizations for the wrongdoing of their employees may come at a moral cost, namely the absence of a need for the prosecution to focus, at least in part, on the wrongdoing of those with overall responsibility. As Wells puts it (although not necessarily as a criticism of vicarious liability, as such):

[The 2007 Act] has elements of 'organisational' liability in allowing the jury, when it decides whether there has been a gross breach of duty of care, to consider whether elements of corporate culture—attitudes, policies, systems or accepted practices—contributed to the failure to comply with health and safety legislation.[82]

In an important way, had the prosecution in a hypothetical corporate manslaughter prosecution been able to focus solely on the activities of some wards in the Mid-Staffordshire NHS Foundation Trust case, whilst that would have made prosecution of the Trust easier legally speaking, it would, ironically, at the same time have let those with ultimate responsibility for its running off the moral hook. It may be true, as Wells argues, that whatever model of criminal responsibility is adopted, 'it is the corporation that is being held liable';[83] but 'liable' and 'liability' are slippery concepts. It is arguable that if these concepts are to have some intrinsic value, and not merely instrumental value, those found liable for offences involving proof of fault—including organizations—must, even if only through a minor contribution (or through a failure to prove due diligence), be found to have been at fault themselves.

Having said that, the notion of corporate or organizational culture can play an important evidential role. It may provide support both for the view that an organization tolerated the commission of criminal offences by its employees, and for the view that senior managers individually consented to or connived at such criminal activity. Moreover, section 8(3) of the 2007 Act makes what looks very like organizational culture a factor that may be taken into account in deciding whether there was a 'gross' breach of a duty of care. To that end, section 8 requires the jury to consider whether and to what extent the organization failed to comply with health and safety legislation, and adds:

The jury may also—

(a) consider the extent to which the evidence shows that there were attitudes, policies, systems or accepted practices within the organisation that were likely to have encouraged any such failure . . . or to have produced tolerance of it. . . .

The law thus makes proof of a culture of neglect a possible building block in establishing a case that the required fault element has been made out, rather than turning proof of it into a necessary part of such a case, or even making proof of it

---

[81] There is, of course, less of an objection to vicarious liability if senior managers of the organizations have a 'due diligence' defence. For further reflections on this, and discussion of a more sophisticated version of the 'corporate culture' theory, in terms of whether an organization's, 'system, its operating policies, displayed a reckless attitude to safety', see Wells (2001), at 158.

[82] Wells (2010), at 386.

[83] *Ibid.*

ipso facto sufficient to establish such a case. With such an ambiguous notion as organizational 'culture', that may be the best approach.

V. Privileging the Public Sector: the Exemptions from Liability

1. Introduction

Under the 2007 Act, there is an extensive set of circumstances in which public organizations, but not private ones, are exempted from a duty of care under the 2007 Act. Particularly common is an exemption bearing on any function public bodies have relating to the all-important section 2(1)(c) above, namely the supply of goods and services, construction and maintenance, commercial activities, and the use or keeping of vehicles or plant etc. A cynic might say that the 2007 Act in fact does little more than the ACT legislation, mentioned above. The 2007 Act certainly goes somewhat beyond the ACT's extension of liability to cover the deaths of employees (section 2(1)(a)), in that under the 2007 Act liability can also be extended to deaths arising from occupation of premises (section 2(1)(b)). However, the 2007 Act does not go much further, so far as most of the public sector is concerned (and in some instances, not even as far as that[84]). Unsurprisingly, the Government has said that it expects no more than a single prosecution against a public body annually.[85] The cynical view need only to some degree be tempered by acknowledging that (at the House of Lords' insistence) there are now relatively extensive duties that will be owed to prisoners and detained patients under section 2(1)(d) and section 2(2), duties which cannot be reduced to duties owed by the relevant public organization in its role as an occupier of premises where such people reside.

2. Are the exclusions too wide? Decisions based on 'public policy'

The cynic can point to the fact that, although the extension of criminal liability to the public sector is the 2007 Act's starting-point, the exclusions of liability from which the public sector benefits are very broad. In that regard, it is appropriate to begin with an examination of section 3(1). This section excludes from the scope of the 2007 Act's duty of care not to cause death, 'any duty of care owed by a public authority in respect of a decision as to matters of public policy (including in particular the allocation of public resources or the weighing of competing public interests)'. The exclusion was justified by the Government on the basis that decisions involving matters of public policy are subject to other kinds of account-ability, such as public inquiries or reports; but the Government itself has the power

---

[84] See s 3, which gives a blanket exemption in respect of deaths stemming from decisions by a public authority based on public policy considerations, and s 4 giving a blanket exemption for deaths arising from hazardous military activities of an operational or training nature.
[85] Home Office (2006).

to resist calls for a public inquiry or a report, reducing the significance of that route as a means of ensuring that there are independent forms of accountability.

The exclusion brings into play the well-known distinction between 'operational' and 'public policy' matters.[86] This is a distinction employed by the courts to assist in drawing the boundaries of the duty of care for the purposes of adjudicating civil claims against public authorities in the tort of negligence. In *X v Bedfordshire CC*,[87] Lord Browne-Wilkinson said that 'a common law duty of care in relation to the taking of decisions involving policy matters cannot exist',[88] and added:

[the factors public authorities take into account when making decisions] will often include policy matters, for example social policy, the allocation of finite financial resources between the different calls made upon them or . . . the balance between pursuing desirable social aims as against the risk to the public inherent in so doing. It is established that the courts cannot enter upon the assessment of such 'policy' matters.[89]

In that regard, Lord Browne-Wilkinson drew a distinction between, on the one hand, (a) the manner in which a public authority exercises a statutory discretion and, on the other hand, (b) the way in which its duty has been implemented in practice. He thought that, for example, the exercise of a discretion to close a school would be an illustration of the former (policy factor), whereas the actual running of the school in accordance with statutory duty would be an illustration of the latter (operational factor). So, decisions taken falling within (b) would attract a duty of care at common law, whereas decisions taken falling within (a) would not.[90]

What might be examples of how the distinction will work in the present context? Arguably, deaths attributable to a Health Trust's decision to economize by reducing certain kinds of expensive medical services could not lead to a prosecution for corporate manslaughter, no matter how poor the management thinking behind the decision. By way of contrast, a crass decision in furtherance of such a policy to change a series of individual patients' medication to something cheaper but entirely unsuitable that then caused those patients' deaths, might fall outside the scope of the exemption in section 3(1). The same will be true of toleration of the kind of callous, homicidally indifferent conduct of the kind discussed elsewhere in this chapter. In like manner, a decision not to use limited resources to build more prison accommodation, with the result that prisoners must share cells because there is no other way of accommodating rising numbers, could not, in and of itself, give rise to liability for (say) a consequent suicide, even if that decision reflected glaring failures of strategic planning. On the other hand, management bungling that led to a decision to make two particular prisoners share a cell, with the entirely foreseeable

---

[86] See *Anns v Merton LBC* [1978] AC 728 (HL). The distinction caused difficulty in the examination of the conduct of the NHS Trust in the Mid-Staffordshire case: see Mid Staffordshire NHS Foundation Trust Inquiry (2010), vol 1.

[87] [1995] 2 AC 633 (HL).

[88] *Ibid*, at 738.

[89] *Ibid*, at 737.

[90] The 2007 Act specifically excludes from the scope of the duty of care the kind of decisions at issue in *Anns v Merton LBC* [1978] AC 728, namely inspections carried out as a matter of public duty: see s 3(3).

result that one killed the other would—it is submitted—be a course of conduct falling outside the scope of the exemption in section 3(1) and would hence be covered by section 2(1)(d).[91]

It is, perhaps, ironic that the 2007 Act relies on the 'public policy' nature of a decision as a basis for excluding the duty of care, because the courts have moved away from such a simplistic 'all-or-nothing' test in determining whether a common law duty of care exists, for the purposes of the law of negligence.[92] For example, in *Barrett v Enfield LBC*,[93] Lord Slynn of Hadley held that:

Policy and operational acts are closely linked and the decision to do an operational act may easily involve and flow from a policy decision. Conversely, the policy is affected by the result of the operational act.[94]

To similar effect, in *Phelps v Hillingdon LBC*,[95] Lord Clyde held that:

A distinction may be suggested between on the one hand matters of policy or discretion and on the other hand matters of an operational or administrative character. *But this kind of classification does not appear to provide any absolute test for determining whether the case is one which allows or excludes a duty of care.* The classification may provide some guide towards identifying some kinds of case where a duty of care may be thought to be inappropriate.[96]

The key question may, then, turn out to be whether the courts will hold that section 3(1) excludes a duty of care, for the purposes of the 2007 Act, when there was *any* policy dimension to the decision(s) allegedly taken through—in effect—gross negligence, and contravening section 1(1). For it may be open to the courts, as a matter of interpretation, to hold that section 3(1) only shields a public organization from the scope of the duty of care under the 2007 Act if the decision was *predominantly* one based on public policy considerations. This would accord with Lord Wilberforce's view in *Anns v Merton LBC*[97] that 'the more "operational" a power or duty may be, the easier it is to superimpose on it a common law duty of care'.[98]

Should the courts take the wider or the narrower view of the scope of the exemption? An argument in favour of the wider view of its scope may come from paying closer attention to the 'public' nature of the public policy basis for a decision that will take it outside the scope of the duty of care, for the purposes of the 2007 Act. When the courts have described the distinction between policy and operational matters, it has sometimes been in terms of whether or not the authority had a discretion or choice between courses of action (policy) or was simply implementing a policy previously decided on (operational).[99] However, there is more than one way to understand 'discretion', for the purposes of drawing the policy–operational

---

[91] See further, the discussion of the Zahid Mubarek case in the text at n 113 below.
[92] There is a good discussion in Booth and Squires (2006), at paras 2.29–2.54.
[93] [2001] 2 AC 550 (HL).   [94] *Ibid*, at 557.
[95] [2001] 2 AC 619 (HL).   [96] *Ibid*, at 673–4 (emphasis added).
[97] [1978] AC 728.   [98] *Ibid*, at 754.
[99] See *X v Bedfordshire CC* [1995] 2 AC 633, at 735 (per Lord Browne-Wilkinson).

distinction. As Aronson and Whitmore put it, the notion of discretion in this context:

> may indicate that the official has a power to choose between two or more alternatives.... Alternatively, it may be used to indicate that an expert's or professional's sense of judgment is called for.... Or it may be used to indicate the power given to an official to formulate policy, to balance competing public interests by criteria which a court is not equipped to evaluate in terms of 'reasonableness'.[100]

Aronson and Whitmore suggest that only the third kind of discretion is a kind that the courts should regard as outside the scope of any common law duty of care, and there is support for that interpretation in the case law.[101] On that view, perhaps, whenever a decision is based—even in part—on the exercise of discretion in this third sense, it is outside the scope of the duty of care for the purposes of the 2007 Act.

On the other hand, in favour of the narrower view of the scope of the exemption, it must be kept in mind that section 17 of the 2007 Act requires the consent of the Director of Public Prosecutions ('the DPP') to any prosecution for corporate manslaughter. This is a means of sifting out and halting claims of liability that are not in the public interest, something that has no equivalent in private law. As the Tasmanian Law Reform Institute pointed out,[102] the DPP may, in particular circumstances, refuse consent to a prosecution if some other more satisfactory means of holding the public body to account is being pursued, such as a public inquiry. It goes almost without saying that the scope of a criminal statute should normally be construed more strictly than a rule or principle imposing mere civil liability. However, the courts should be vigilant to ensure that the advantages, in terms of protection from liability, given to public authorities are not construed too widely. In particular, the courts should not find that such authorities will only be held liable in circumstances where a private organization would have been liable, if it had agreed with the public authority to carry out at operational level what turned out to be the death-dealing activity in question. Suppose, for example, that a death attributable to a gross breach of a duty of care can be put down to management failings in a joint venture between a public authority and a private organization, and they are both prosecuted. In such a case, whilst section 3(1) may well apply to the public authority, the courts should not go out of their way to find that the exclusion shields the authority from liability simply because its part in the joint venture involved some policy-making element. To do that would effectively mean that only the private organization was exposed to prosecution, something that may well leave not just the company itself, but also the victims' families and the general public, with a well-founded sense that justice has not been done.

---

[100] Aronson and Whitmore (1982), at 69.

[101] *Anns v Merton LBC* [1978] AC 728, at 754 (Lord Wilberforce), 'public authorities have to strike a balance between the claims of efficiency and thrift ... whether they get the balance right can only be decided through the ballot box, not in the courts'.

[102] Tasmanian Law Reform Institute (2007), at para 5.1.11.

Section 3(2) sets out a more limited exclusion in respect of anything done 'in the exercise of an exclusively public function', meaning a function that falls within the ambit of the Crown prerogative, or is by its nature only exercisable with the authority conferred by the exercise of the prerogative or by, or under, a statutory provision.[103] This exclusion relates only to the public functions involved in section 2(1)(c), such as the supply of goods or services, construction work, or the use of vehicles and the like. It does not exempt the relevant organization from liability arising from a breach of duty to an employee, or from a breach of a duty as an occupier of premises, or (perhaps most importantly) from a breach of duty owed to a detained person such as a prisoner or detained patient. The exemption was not supported by consultees in the Government's consultation exercise,[104] and it is worth noting that the Tasmanian Law Reform Institute rejected this basis for exempting public authorities. The Institute said:

> The Institute does not recommend a UK style exception for activities done in the exercise of a public function. Crown criminal liability is already possible in Tasmania in relation to some criminal offences. . . . While Crown prosecutions would no doubt be exceptional, as they are rarely in the public interest, a valuable message is sent by providing that all people, including the Crown and Government bodies must obey criminal laws.[105]

This is a point to which I will return in the next subsection. A similar exemption, limited to section 2(1)(c), is applied by section 5(3) to policing or law-enforcement activities other than operational or hazardous training activities (they have a broader exemption, examined below), and by section 7(1) to a variety of child-protection and probation functions.[106] So, the exemption from liability arising from activities covered by section 2(1)(c) is generous in terms of who it covers.

In fairness to the Government, and in response to the cynic's view, it would be right to say that even this cursory look at exemptions for public organizations reveals that there has at least been no attempt, other than in very limited circumstances, to give a blanket exemption to public organizations simply because they are by nature involved in controversial, sensitive, or dangerous work, such as managing prisoners, protecting children, or treating or detaining patients. Nonetheless, the question is whether the exemptions granted to some of these public bodies do indeed go too far.

3. Are the exclusions too wide? Prisons, the police, and the military

It will not be possible here to examine the proper scope of all the exemptions held out to public bodies, in particular the exemption applying to the provision of services under section 2(1)(c). However, a comparison can be made between the

---

[103] There is a further exclusion in s 3(3) respecting duties arising in respect of inspections carried out in the exercise of statutory functions, which disapplies the duty of care unless it falls within s 2(1)(a) or(b).

[104] Home Office (2005), at 9.

[105] Tasmanian Law Reform Institute (2007), at para 5.1.11.

[106] In the civil law context, see by way of contrast, *Vicar of Writtle v Essex CC* (1979) 77 LGR 656.

position in which prisons (and other custodial institutions) and secure hospitals find themselves, and the position in which police and armed forces organizations find themselves, so far as the scope of exemptions is concerned. It is arguable that the more generous exemption held out to army and police organizations is unwarranted. If one puts on one side for a moment the possibility of a prosecution of the employer for a simple health and safety offence, the wide scope of the exemption effectively leaves individual service personnel to 'carry the can' when a death has been unlawfully caused because something went badly wrong. Further, the exemption gives too little weight to the vital role of the DPP in preventing prosecutions under the 2007 Act when they are not in the public interest.[107]

Section 2(2) specifically provides that someone for whose safety an organization is responsible may be owed a duty when:

(a) he is detained at a custodial institution or in a custody area at a court or police station; ...

(c) he is being transported in a vehicle, or being held in any premises, in pursuance of prison escort arrangements ... ;

(d) he is living in secure accommodation in which he has been placed;

(e) he is a detained patient.

The inclusion of this subsection came at the insistence of the House of Lords, and was not in the original Government Bill.[108] Given that there were no less that 1,000 suicides in custody in the thirteen years leading up to 2007, it is hardly surprising that the subsection gave rise to controversy. By way of contrast, deaths caused during active service, or during training in a hazardous military or police operational context, are expressly excluded from the scope of the duty of care under section 2.[109] Under section 6, similarly exempted are (with limited exceptions) the actions of the emergency services in responding to emergencies.[110] No specific exemptions have been held out to prisons and secure hospitals.

The justification for this difference in treatment would seem to be this: it might be said that there is an overriding public interest in preventing what was described by the Government as the growth of a 'culture of defensiveness' in the conduct of military and police operations and training, because such a culture would be

[107] Under s 17, the DPP's consent is required for all prosecutions under the 2007 Act.
[108] 694 HL Official Report (5th series), cols 135–8.
[109] 2007 Act, ss 4 and 5 respectively.
[110] Other than a response that involves a medical treatment decision (excepting a decision concerning the order in which patients are treated): s 6(3) and 6(4). It is not made explicit that decisions taken by a prison governor during a prison riot would be covered by s 6, although it is almost certain that they are covered, because only duties at issue in s 2(1)(a) and s 2(1)(b) are 'duties of care' for the purposes of s 6 of the 2007 Act, even in an emergency. In other words, s 2(1)(d), concerned with prisoners and detained patients, is within the scope of the 'emergencies' exception. On a generous reading, prison governors' decisions in emergencies would be covered by s 6(2)(d)(ii): '... any other organisation providing a service of responding to emergency circumstances ... otherwise than on a commercial basis ...'. More probably, such a situation would be held to be covered by the 'law enforcement' exemption in s 5, on which see see later in this Chapter.

inimical to achieving the very aims of such activities.[111] So, if the introduction of an offence of corporate manslaughter in these contexts might encourage the growth of such a culture, then the offence should not be applied to such activities. By way of contrast, although the Government sought to apply the same reasoning when fighting its losing argument against the application of the offence to deaths in custody,[112] the growth of a 'culture of defensiveness' may, ironically, be precisely what is needed to promote good practice amongst staff and minimize the risk of deaths in custody or in hospital.

Here is a well-known illustrative example of this last point. In November 2000, Robert Stuart was convicted of the murder of Zahid Mubarek. Stuart was a prolific offender: disturbed, dangerous, and a known racist with a history of disruptive and bizarre behaviour whilst in detention. On arrival at Feltham Young Offenders' Institution, Stuart was placed in a cell with Mubarek, and brutally killed him. An inquiry conducted by Mr Justice Keith came to this conclusion in 2006 about the way Stuart and Mubarek were dealt with:

[B]ecause of a pernicious and dangerous cocktail of poor communications and shoddy work practices prison staff never got to grips with [Stuart]. . . . [There was] a bewildering catalogue of shortcomings, both individual and systemic, at Feltham at the time. . . . I name those members of staff who were in some way to blame for what happened to Zahid. But all this has to be seen in the context of the establishment as a whole. Feltham was identified in the mid-1990s as a prison which was failing on many fronts. . . . [A]t present there is a disconnection between aspiration and reality, because insufficient attention is paid to 'outcomes rather than processes'.[113]

The report added that the governor with line responsibility had very little operational experience, and did not get help from the manager of the department, 'who had become complacent as his retirement beckoned'.[114] This was not an isolated instance of poor staff practice and inadequate leadership in custodial institutions. Speaking of Wormwood Scrubs, Lord Ramsbotham, a former Chief Inspector of Prisons, said in the debate on the Corporate Manslaughter Bill that, 'although there was no case of manslaughter, there was extraordinarily bad behaviour by staff, brutality of prisoners and, over a number of years, management failure on a scale that I simply could not believe'.[115] Unsurprisingly, he concluded that:

this [amended] Bill, which is based on the duty of care and which should be shown to everyone in charge of these authorities, is an appropriate weapon. I seriously believe that the Bill would energise the management system in a way that nothing else that I have come across in the past ten years seems to have been able to.[116]

---

[111] This argument is critically examined below.
[112] See the response of Lord Bassam to the proposal to apply corporate manslaughter to the prison service, 688 HL Official Report (5th Series), col GC 198.
[113] Cited by Lord Hunt, 688 HL Official Report (5th Series), col GC 187–8.
[114] Cited by Lord Ramsbotham, 688 HL Official Report (5th Series), col GC 191.
[115] 688 HL Official Report (5th Series), col GC 192.
[116] *Ibid*, col GC 193.

It is also highly arguable that the almost complete reliance that a detained prisoner or patient must place in the relevant organization to ensure his or her health and safe-keeping during what may be a lengthy period of detention, overrides counter-vailing considerations and warrants placing the relevant organization under an ongoing duty of care. As Lord Hunt said in successfully arguing for the extension of liability to cover deaths in custody:

The power lawfully to deprive an individual of his or her liberty must be one of the most serious responsibilities there can be. The duty of care owed to an individual in detention, where he cannot act freely in his own interests, is onerous and profound, yet the way in which the Bill is currently ordered suggests that that responsibility is not so regarded by the Government.[117]

This second argument in favour of the imposition of liability on prison organiza-tions does not, of course, have the same application to police and army organiza-tions, because their personnel have freely chosen their employment and are to a much greater extent responsible for their own welfare. However, that leaves the question whether the 2007 Act is right to leave police and army organizations immune from prosecution for corporate manslaughter, so far as deaths arising from hazardous training or operations are concerned, because of a supposedly overriding need to prevent a 'culture of defensiveness' developing in training and operational contexts.[118]

The exemption for policing and law enforcement (the military activity exemp-tion in section 4 is in the relevant respects similar) in section 5 is as follows:

(1) Any duty of care owed by a public authority in respect of—
   (a) operations within subsection (2),
   (b) activities carried on in preparation for, or directly in support of, such opera-tions, or
   (c) training of a hazardous nature, or training carried out in a hazardous way, which it is considered needs to be carried out, or carried out in that way, in order to improve or maintain the effectiveness of officers or employees of the public authority with respect to such operations, is not a relevant 'duty of care'.

(2) Operations are within this subsection if—
   (a) they are operations for dealing with terrorism, civil unrest or serious disorder,
   (b) they involve the carrying on of policing or law-enforcement activities, and
   (c) officers or employees of the public authority in question come under attack, or face the threat of attack or violent resistance, in the course of the operations.

---

[117] *Ibid*, col GC 187.
[118] I will in fact leave on one side here the s 6 exemption for organizations involved in the provision of emergency services in the course of which someone is unlawfully killed. The law is reluctant even to impose civil liability in such circumstances, let alone criminal liability: see *Church of Jesus Christ of Latter Day Saints (Great Britain) v West Yorkshire Fire and Civil Defence Authority* [1997] QB 104, [1997] 2 All ER 865 (CA), approved on this point by Lord Hoffmann *in Gorringe v Calderdale* MBC [2004] UKHL 15, at [32].

The weakness of the argument for this immunity is that, first (and most unfairly), the existence of the exemption for police and army organizations may mean that *individual* police officers or army personnel are now more likely than individual prison officers or nurses to find themselves prosecuted when deaths have been caused through serious negligence. This will be for the simple reason that sections 4 and 5 prevent the relevant police or army organization itself being prosecuted for corporate manslaughter, so recourse against individuals is more likely.[119] By contrast, in a similar situation there is no such legal protection for the prison or hospital. As the European Court of Human Rights pointed out in the introduction to its judgment in *McCann v UK*:[120]

> The most important point which emerges from any study of the law on this subject is that the responsibility is an individual one. Any police officer who uses a firearm may be answerable to the courts or to a coroner's inquest and, if his actions were unlawful (or improper), then he as an individual may be charged with murder, manslaughter or unlawful wounding.... The fact that a police officer used his firearms under the orders of a superior does not, of itself, exempt him from criminal liability....[121]

Secondly, it may seem right to prevent a 'culture of defensiveness' developing in the way that individual police or army personnel carry out their duties in hazardous situations.[122] Nonetheless, it is questionable whether the same considerations apply with the same degree of force (in so far as a 'culture of defensiveness' is just a negative term for the positive virtues of a 'health and safety culture', or of a 'human rights culture') to the organizations tasked with planning the context in which those duties will be carried out. I would not myself presume to pass judgment on the conduct of the authorities that led up to the killing of the IRA terrorists that was the subject of the litigation in *McCann*. However, the European Court was not persuaded that the killing of the three terrorists constituted a use of force which was no more than absolutely necessary in defence of persons from unlawful violence within the meaning of Article 2(2) (a) of the European Convention on Human Rights. A (bare) majority of the court found that:

> there was a serious miscalculation by those responsible for controlling the operation. As a result the scene was set in which the fatal shooting... was a foreseeable possibility if not a likelihood.... [There was] a lack of appropriate care in the control and organisation of the arrest operation.[123]

---

[119] Although it would be right to qualify this claim by re-emphasizing that a prosecution of an employer under the 1974 Act may be undertaken, in part, to avoid making individuals 'carry the can' for what were really organizational and management failings.

[120] *McCann v UK* (1996) 21 EHRR 97.

[121] *Ibid*, at para 137.

[122] In the civil law context, some doubt has been cast on whether unwarranted 'cultures of defensiveness' really do develop as a response to the fear of litigation: see Halliday *et al* (2011).

[123] *McCann v UK* (1996) 21 EHRR 97, at paras 205 and 212.

The authorities had been planning the operation on Gibraltar for some months. In that regard, among the serious miscalculations and failures to which the court pointed were the decision by the authorities not to prevent the suspects from travelling into Gibraltar and their failure to make sufficient allowances for the possibility that the intelligence assessments relied on might, in some key respects, have been erroneous. Crucially, the court cast doubt in that respect on whether the authorities adhered to their obligation to respect the right to life of the suspects. The court doubted 'whether they [the soldiers] had been trained or instructed to assess whether the use of firearms to wound their targets may have been warranted by the specific circumstances that confronted them at the moment of arrest'.[124] It is, of course, an open question whether the failures of the authorities to respect their obligations under Article 2(2)(a), as found by the court, would necessarily amount to the kind of 'gross' breach of duty of care due in part to management or organizational failings on the part of senior management (had there been no exemption in this respect) that is required for conviction under the 2007 Act. The latter does not necessarily follow from the former. The question is, should an exemption from liability be granted to the authorities in this kind of situation, even though it leaves as the only possible targets for prosecution respecting deaths caused individual soldiers who receive *(ex hypothesi)* erroneous advice that they will in all probability have to shoot to kill?

There is a case for saying that the exemption is undesirable and unnecessary. It means, for example, that military authorities will still be exempted from prosecution under the 2007 Act, even if they ignore or tolerate the development of a 'shoot-to-kill culture' amongst soldiers called in to non-military operations, simply because such a development is seen as good for morale in that it is more 'macho' than the culture developed by their counterparts training armed police officers.[125] It would have been better, in this context, to have taken the approach of the Tasmanian Law Reform Institute to the 'exclusively public function' exemption, cited above.[126] In other words, it would have been better to have relied on the proper exercise of prosecutorial discretion and in particular on the judgement of the DPP (in deciding whether to give consent to a prosecution) as to whether the prosecution is in the public interest. As the Institute said, '[t]he exercise of prosecutorial discretion should result in only appropriate cases being prosecuted. A factor relevant to this would no doubt be the extent to which the potential defendant had already been held accountable in another arena.'[127] It is unlikely to be easy to secure convictions or even to find adequate grounds to commence a prosecution, in these kinds of circumstances, and hence the police and military authorities would have scant grounds to fear that ill-founded prosecutions would ever be undertaken or succeed.

---

[124] *Ibid*, at para 137.
[125] On this point, see *ibid*, at para 211.
[126] Tasmanian Law Reform Institute (2007), at para 5.1.11.
[127] *Ibid*.

5

Violating Physical Integrity: Manslaughter by Intentional Attack

I. The 'Pure' Form of Manslaughter

In *Mawgridge*,[1] Holt CJ gave the following example as an instance of manslaughter:

Suppose upon provoking language given by B to A, A gives B a box on the ear, or little blow with a stick, which happens to be so unlucky that it kills B who might have some impostume in his head or other ailment which proves the cause of B's death, this blow though not justifiable by law, but is a wrong, yet it may be manslaughter, because it does not appear that he [A] designed such a mischief.[2]

This example is one I shall treat as a 'pure' form of manslaughter by intentional attack. Subject to an assumption that the attack involved a wounding or some actual bodily harm, I shall defend the continued existence of this form of unlawful homicide. Its status has been questioned by those who defend the view that someone should not be found criminally liable for harmful consequences he or she brings about, unless he or she intended those consequences to come about or realized that they might come about.[3] Additionally, whatever the justification for its existence may be, the appropriateness of the label 'manslaughter' for such a form of homicide has been regarded by some as too severe.[4] I will argue that neither of these arguments, plausible though they may be, is very convincing. If anything, when thinking in terms of a three-rung homicide 'ladder' (say, first degree murder; second degree murder; manslaughter) the pure form of manslaughter has the best claim of all the forms of unintentional homicide to a place on the third rung with the label 'manslaughter'.[5] I will start with an account of the moral significance of the pure form of manslaughter.

II. The Two Essential Features of the Pure Form of Manslaughter

The 'pure' form of manslaughter is rightly considered to be criminal homicide in virtue of two features that it possesses. First, it involves an intended attack on the

---

[1] (1707) Kel 119.   [2] *Ibid*, at 131.
[3] See, eg, Ashworth (1993); Ashworth (2008).   [4] Mitchell (2009).
[5] See Ch 3 above for a discussion of the homicide ladder.

victim. This was a feature of this species of manslaughter central to the wrong in issue, until the species evolved through development of the common law during the nineteenth century. It evolved into a far less satisfactory—indeed, almost indefensible—mongrel variety commonly known as 'unlawful and dangerous act' manslaughter.[6] Although it requires that D have engaged in criminal conduct, this mongrel variety is largely reliant, for its justification, on the danger of harm posed by D's criminal conduct: whether D intended any harm to come about is not in itself necessarily legally significant. As we shall see, this has led to a number of anomalies, not least in how this form of manslaughter relates to a separate form of manslaughter directly dependent on the nature and degree of unacceptable danger posed: manslaughter by gross negligence.

Antony Duff has explained the special moral significance of intentional attacks, as compared with endangerments.[7] In the sense adopted here, intentional attacks have the causing of prima facie unlawful harm as their end or as their means to an end.[8] An attacker is guided by the wrong reasons, rather than simply (whether or not knowingly) failing to abide by the right reasons.[9] Attacks necessarily engage D's (ill-) will, whereas that is not necessarily true of potentially harmful endangerments.[10] As Duff puts it:

A certain hostility towards its object is intrinsic to an attack—a practical hostility towards the interests or people it attacks, in that it is aimed against those people or their interests.... This hostility is not an attitude lying behind and motivating the action that constitutes the attack.... It is a practical attitude intrinsic to, and constituted by, the action as an attack: to attack another person *is* to display hostility towards them.[11]

The second feature of this species of manslaughter (perhaps not so clearly implicit in the example given by Holt CJ) is the need for the intended attack to be on V's physical integrity. It must amount to more than a simple trespass to the person such a minor push, slap, or prod. The attack must go beyond such incursions on V's rights and amount to a violation of V him or herself:[12] something so serious that (in the absence of special circumstances) V is not permitted by law to consent to it.[13] The major injustice in the present law of manslaughter by 'unlawful and dangerous act' is that it permits criminal liability for homicide brought about

---

[6] Horder (1997a), at 107 and 111–12.

[7] Duff (1996), at 363–8; Duff (2007), at 148–58.

[8] Including the infliction of pain so severe it is tantamount to a loss of physical integrity, and is not merely transient and trifling. Physical integrity naturally includes the integrity of mental functioning: see *Chan-Fook* [1994] 2 All ER 552.

[9] Duff (2007), at 151.

[10] In saying this, I am, of course, putting on one side instances in which there is interference with my responsibility for an intentional attack: where my mind is under the control of another, or something of that kind.

[11] Duff (2007), at 149–50.

[12] See Ch 1 above, for this distinction between incursions on rights and violations of the person. See further section III. below.

[13] In broad terms, it must be an attack intended to cause at least bodily harm (as, *ex hypothesi*, in Holt CJ's example at n 2 above): *Meachen* [2006] EWCA Crim 2414: but see, *contra*, *Boyea* [1992] Crim LR 574.

through conduct posing a risk of non-lethal harm. It permits this, if the conduct in question also amounts to whatever the law happens to regard at that particular time as 'criminal' (in a sense excluding negligence-based crime).[14] A simple criminal trespass to the person such a push or slap, or putting someone in fear of attack, could lead to a manslaughter verdict if there was a danger of some physical harm involved and V consequently (say) fell over, hit his or her head, and died. D may even be convicted of manslaughter if he or she commits criminal damage, in circumstances where the damage posed a danger of some harm to the person and someone is thereby killed. In such a case the killing will be manslaughter, even though D's crime was a property crime and not an offence against the person, notwithstanding the fact that the inherent danger in D's conduct would never in itself provide an adequate basis for a prosecution for gross negligence manslaughter.

Mitchell has said that a conviction for homicide in such cases—so long as the label 'manslaughter' is removed—may be defensible on the grounds that:

> [T]he argument in favour of recognizing criminal liability for what might loosely be called 'unlucky deaths' is based on a combination of the criminal context (the unlawful act) and its dangerousness. . . .[15]

There can be little doubt that D's normative position can sometimes change in virtue of committing a criminal act.[16] However, even Mitchell himself seems unclear how much difference the commission of a criminal act should in itself make if the main reason for V's death is the dangerousness of D's conduct.[17] Suppose that it is not disputed that D killed V, when V fell over hit her head and died. However, the prosecution and the defence dispute whether D killed V in this way by actually punching her: on the facts, it might have been that D aimed a punch at her that missed when V ducked to avoid the blow, but that in having to move so suddenly V thereby fell over hit her head and died. In such a case, the judge will have to tell the jury that if D actually punched V thereby causing her death, then so long as D delivered the punch intentionally or recklessly, D will be guilty of manslaughter. In particular, there will be no need for the judge to refer to the 'dangerousness' of D's act. As the danger need only be an almost inevitable danger of some harm,[18] it is irrelevant in this case because D by his intentional assault has in fact already caused some harm. By contrast, if D aimed a punch at

---

[14] For discussion, see Simester and Sullivan *et al* (2010), at 402–9.

[15] Mitchell (2009), at 510.

[16] This is crucial, for example in the law governing complicity in crime: see *Chan Wing-siu v R* [1985] AC 168 (HL). More commonly, it is the possession of fault elements that can change D's normative position, and not simply bear on the degree of D's blameworthiness. This can occur in relation to liability for remote consequences. For example, suppose that an aircraft I am responsible for maintaining crashes because of an extremely rare structural defect. I cannot rely on the extreme rarity of that defect to escape criminal liability for damage or death caused, if I personally knew or suspected that plane suffered from the defect. My knowledge or suspicion estops me from relying on what would otherwise be a powerful argument against holding me liable; my normative position has in that respect changed.

[17] The danger posed need only be a danger of some harm, not of death or even of serious injury: *Church* [1966] 1 QB 59 (CA), at 70.

[18] *Ibid.*

V and missed, the judge will have to tell the jury that the question is whether D's attempt to punch V was not only unlawful but also dangerous, in the sense of posing an almost inevitable risk of at least some harm. Whilst such a case is not very likely to arise, it illustrates a problem with the rationale for the mongrel variety of manslaughter. Nonetheless, Mitchell concludes that a crime of unlawful and dangerous act homicide, 'should suffice to satisfy the interests of the deceased's next of kin'.[19] As he must surely recognize, that is not really an adequate justification for a homicide offence, whether or not labeled 'manslaughter'. I will consider the issue of dangerous or risky conduct in section VII.

As I will seek to show in the next section, understanding manslaughter in terms of killing by intentionally attacking V's physical integrity is not to understand it simply as the placing of a more-or-less arbitrary restriction on the over-broad scope of the common law crime (the mongrel variety of manslaughter). Further, understanding it in this way is not to make an implicit claim that attacks on physical integrity are more dangerous to life than attacks on property. That may be a false claim, for example, in cases of arson. Manslaughter committed through an intentional attack on V's physical integrity does not rely *at all* for its rationale on an assessment of the danger to life or limb posed by such conduct. It is enough that D caused death, in the meaning given by law to the notion of 'caused', by such an attack.

III. The Importance of the Intrinsic Value of Physical Integrity

Relying on Duff's arguments,[20] let us assume that there is something of distinctive moral significance about an intentional attack, as compared with an act (albeit, perhaps, a criminal act) that is merely endangering in nature. What is also morally distinctive about intentional attacks on someone's 'physical integrity'? What is special about attacks that go beyond mere incursions on V's rights and amount to (attempted) violations of V him or herself, attacks of a kind that V may not, absent special circumstances, consent to suffer?[21] An answer to these questions must be adequate to explain why, if such an attack leads to V's death, it should be manslaughter irrespective of whether death was foreseen or even likely to occur. In search of an answer, we need to start with an understanding of what is intrinsically valuable—and not merely instrumentally valuable—about V's physical integrity and the life force that adds constitutively to its value by animating it.

---

[19] Mitchell (2009), at 510.
[20] Duff (2007), at 148–58.
[21] See text at nn 12 to 13 above. This is meant to be a broadly cross-jurisdictional point. An attack on someone's physical integrity should not be permissibly consented to, barring special exceptions for surgery and the like, in any civilized legal system. That is not to say that English law has created the right kinds of special exceptions, and hence I should not be taken to be endorsing decisions such as *Brown* [1994] 1 AC 212 (HL).

There is intrinsic value in the body's indivisibility as an animate whole; hence, I have a reason not to permit any violation of it.[22] The simple fact, for example, that I have completely lost the use of an arm or a leg is in itself, without more, no reason to have the limb amputated. Further, the value of physical integrity or wholeness is a value that is not to be found solely in the way in which it may usefully serve, instrumentally, to promote some other value. Its intrinsic value lies in the constitutive part that it plays in something of ultimate value, a flourishing human life. There is, of course, much that is of intrinsic value in human lives, and physical integrity is only one such value. However, the distinctiveness of physical integrity as an intrinsic value is of central importance here. To acknowledge the intrinsic value of physical integrity is to accept that there is a perspective from which it may be wrong to employ some forms of consequentialist metric to value the existence and functioning of the body and its parts (or, at least a matter for moral regret if one must employ such a metric). For example, I might be able to function perfectly well with only one kidney; but that ought not to entail that it should mean 'nothing' to me or to others that I have one kidney removed, whatever the purpose of removing it. Morally speaking, I and others should regret the loss as involving damage to my physical integrity and diminution of its value, even if that regret is more than made up for by the good effects that come about (perhaps, a life-saving operation for a close relative). I may truthfully say that I can 'do without' one kidney much more effectively than my relative can do without any properly functioning kidneys, and that is why retaining both kidneys no longer has any meaning for me. However, the power of that kind of analysis stems from an assumption that the key moral assessment is a forward-looking one of how my life will run without one kidney, as compared with how it will run without both. That assumption simply makes the instrumental relevance of the future impact of different kinds of consequences the key consideration, without allowing that, in some important contexts, these consequences may be irrelevant to moral evaluation.[23] Losing a kidney should still have (negative) moral meaning for me, even if I know I am justified in sacrificing it.

So, to recognize the intrinsic value of physical integrity as such is not to deny that it is capable of being outweighed by other values, or to deny that it may be subject to a cancelling permission to act against it, in many sets of circumstances. The importance of (properly conducted and supervised) blood donation to the health services provides a very good example where the value of maintaining physical integrity may be put on one side by the donor, in the interests of promoting in the community at large the very value of which physical integrity is a constitutive part:

---

[22] One could go further, and say that even a dead body should not, without special reasons, be dismembered, disemboweled, and so on, and hence claim that the value physical integrity subsists even when the body is not an animate whole. However, such a line of thought is probably explained best in relation to values associated with respect for the dead. There can surely be little doubt that one's life force is a constituent element in the intrinsic value of physical integrity, something that makes it a phenomenon to be valued within the moral domain.

[23] See generally, Williams (1982). I hope no-one will fall into the trap of supposing that, in itself, this is an argument hostile to consequentialism in all its forms. Highlighting the intrinsic value of physical integrity, as a part of promoting a healthy lifestyle and human flourishing more generally, can form part of a consequentialist philosophy; but it is none the worse for that.

the ultimate value of maintaining life itself.[24] In such circumstances, the forward-looking consideration that I can continue to flourish perfectly well whilst making regular blood donations is part of what shapes the cancelling permission that allows me to agree that my blood can be taken.[25] But the legitimacy of having a cancelling permission at all, respecting actions that violate physical integrity, is in this instance tied to the link between the permission and the (state-regulated and controlled) promotion of the ultimate value in question.[26] That explains why I will not be permitted to dishonour the value of another's physical integrity in any way by violating it for any reason I judge sufficient, even with the other person's permission.[27] I can no more allow someone to extract some of my blood to assist them in their fantasies about becoming a vampire than I can allow my foot to be amputated so that I am rendered unfit to work,[28] allow a section of my skin to be removed so that someone can add it to their collection of animal hides, or allow myself to be decapitated so my head can be put on display in a museum.[29] Properly to respect the value of physical integrity is to respect it in all its aspects, by—save in legally designated circumstances—avoiding the least violation of another (taking a small sample of blood) as much as the greatest (killing), or by acknowledging the moral importance of regret even when a violation is permitted and justified.[30]

Naturally, it is possible to value the body (or its parts) in other ways, such that the value of physical integrity plays no part in the evaluation. For example, some parts of the body are obviously more essential to life than others, some parts are more aesthetically pleasing than others, some parts regenerate whereas others do not, and some parts are doubtless better to eat than others. It is, though, as we will see, mainly the value of physical integrity rather than one of these other values that best explains some key features of the law governing the offences against the person.

---

[24] For a thoughtful modern discussion, see Nuffield Council on Bioethics (2011). I say that the value 'may' be put on one side for this purpose, because in a liberal state there must always be room, for example, for an individual conscientiously to resist moral pressure to donate blood.

[25] On cancelling permissions, see Gardner (2010).

[26] See Nuffield Council on Bioethics (2011), at para 5.42.

[27] Herein lies an important contrast with physical objects and their ownership. Things can have a physical integrity just as much as human beings. To cut out the mouth of the Mona Lisa would be not simply to damage the painting but to destroy its integrity as a painting. Even so, if the painting were mine absolutely, I could in principle do such an act myself or lawfully permit you to do it (even if to commit or to allow such an act to be committed would rightly be condemned as a piece of 'cultural vandalism').

[28] See Coke, 1 Co Inst 127a and b.

[29] Of course, if in one of these examples I were to do the injury to myself (rather than allowing it to be done to me), I would incur no liability. That is because different intrinsic values limiting the scope of the law now hold sway, the values of self-expression and/or of self-determination. In the eye of the law, recognizing my freedom to choose my own path is one thing, but where I need or permit the intervention or assistance of others in order to exercise that freedom, other intrinsic values come into play that may limit the extent to which my normative freedom entails the normative freedom of those others to lend me assistance.

[30] In speaking of the 'least' violation, it needs to be kept in mind that merely transient or trifling violations should, as a matter of law, fall outside the scope of 'physical integrity', because it is obvious that I can and should be allowed (say) to consent to having my hair cut, my toe nails clipped, and so on. Such instances are normally covered by the 'ordinary social contact' exception, in any event.

IV. The Value of Physical Integrity and Fault Requirements in Homicide

In setting the terms on which basic (or, if you insist, prima facie) liability for injuries caused by intentional attacks is established in criminal law—the rules of liability, in Robinson's terminology[31]—English law is shaped by the intrinsic value of physical integrity and its constituent elements, as such. To understand how, we need to appreciate that the law is also shaped by what someone 'did' when they violated the physical integrity of another. If I intentionally punch you, but the ring I am wearing gouges out your left eye, I have blinded you in one eye. If the punch leads you to fall over, hit your head, and die, I have killed you. Blinding you in one eye and killing you are both things that I did, as well as punching you. The fact that only the latter was intended by me does not change the fact that all three things (punching; blinding; killing) were done by me.[32] That I did something, or that it occurred under my control,[33] is usually a condition of finding an individual liable for that something's occurrence, as much in civil law as it is in criminal law.[34]

It may be, for the purposes of the criminal law at any rate, that finding fault on my part respecting what I did (or at least the absence of any defence for doing it) is also a key aspect of basic liability. Legal liability, whether or not criminal, permits the state to visit adverse consequences on the person who did the deed in question simply because they did it; and it would be unduly harsh to visit such consequences on someone who cannot fairly be adjudged a wrongdoer respecting what was done. Having said that, it does not follow that rules of basic liability require that the element of wrongdoing relate in a very particular way to the very thing that I did. If I intentionally kill you, that is a wrong of a different order from the one I commit when I cause your death by punching you (leading you to fall over hit your head and die). What I did in killing you through my unlawful punch is nonetheless an unjustified harm, inflicted through wrongdoing, and the fact that your death was unintended or unforeseen does not change that. It is thus perfectly intelligible that the law fixes on the fact that an unjustified harm came about through wrongdoing, when establishing basic criminal liability.[35] Equally, it is only right that, having established the rules of basic liability, the law is willing in some cases to super-impose on these rules further rules concerning the grading of offences. These grading rules will reflect the seriousness of what was done by, for example, taking degrees of fault into account when labelling different manifestations of wrongdoing. So, for example, whilst killing through an intention to injure is

---

[31] Robinson (1993).

[32] See Gardner (1998c).

[33] On this alternative, see Shute, Gardner, and Horder (1993), Introduction.

[34] I put on one side here issues such as the vicarious liability of land-owners *qua* land-owners or of companies.

[35] It is perfectly intelligible, despite the heroic efforts of Alexander and Ferzan to convince us that it is wholly unfair, if not downright irrational: Alexander and Ferzan (2009). See further Ashworth (2008); Mitchell (2009).

manslaughter, killing through an intention to do serious injury is murder.[36] In both cases, the basic wrong may be the same (by way of contrast with cases involving intentional killing), but the greater degree of blame to be attached in the latter case is *ex hypothesi* enough to warrant conviction for murder.

The intrinsic value of physical integrity can play a role in explaining basic liability in offences against the person, by providing one way in which fault elements in relation to such liability can be understood. In the example in which I punch you, you fall over hit your head and die, in intentionally punching you I intentionally violate your physical integrity, whatever the nature or degree of harm I intended to inflict through the punch. What is more, the unjustified harm that comes to you (your death) through my intentional wrongdoing involves a destruction by me of the life force that is partly constitutive of the same intrinsic value. What I intentionally do to you—punch you—is thus not linked to your death only through brute causation ('taking the consequences'), but is linked to it in point of value, the intrinsic value of your physical integrity as an animate whole. Contrast this example (or that of Holt CJ with which this chapter began) with one in which I punch you, you fall to the ground and break a glass object in your pocket. In such a case, the law has for long held that I will not be liable for the breaking of the object unless I foresaw that it might be broken.[37] The explanation given for this in law is that my undoubtedly malicious intent towards you cannot be 'transferred' to your property, as a convenient substitute for proven malice towards your property.[38] Supporting this explanation is an understanding that the violation of the value of a person's physical integrity is not a violation of the values underpinning the need to respect proprietary interests. That is what generates the thought that the two kinds of offences belong in different 'families'.[39] Whilst I am linked causally, through my wrongdoing, to the damage done (indeed, I am the one who did it), I am not thereby linked to it by reference to the same value. So, the two kinds of offences should not be treated as commensurable, for the purposes of establishing fault in criminal law, and the law impliedly recognizes this by requiring malice proven towards your property if I am to be convicted of damaging it.[40]

Many theorists—although rarely, if ever, judges, legislators, and the public[41]—complain that liability for manslaughter in 'one-punch' cases when the punch has killed is unfair, because the offence is manslaughter whether or not the death (so long as it was caused by D) was foreseen.[42] What is the answer to this complaint?

---

[36] For further discussion, see Ch 3 above, section V., and Horder (1997a). Ashworth (2008) has offered some criticisms of my argument in Horder (1997a) that have led me to re-interpret what I said in the light of the distinction between rules of basic liability, and rules of grading.

[37] See the discussion in Ch 7 below.

[38] *Pembliton* (1874) L 2 CCR 119.

[39] For critical discussion of the notion of 'families' of offences, see Ashworth (2008), at 244. In a sense, my exploration of the role of respect for the value of physical integrity is an attempt to give more substance to the idea of a 'family' of offences against the person relevant to the pure form of manslaughter.

[40] See the discussion in the text at n 27 above.

[41] See Ch 1 above.

[42] Ashworth (2008); Mitchell (2009); Alexander and Ferzan (2009).

For the purposes of establishing rules of basic liability, it is not unfair to take the view that if D intentionally attacks V's physical integrity, and a violation of V's physical integrity (or the destruction of one of its constituent values, such as life force) takes place, then D may be found liable for that violation in whatever form it occurs. Respect for the value of physical integrity as such licenses such an approach. As a matter of basic liability, part of what it is to show respect for that value is to draw no distinctions between violations of physical integrity or its constituent values brought about by a piece of conduct.[43] Consequently, when D kills V through an intentionally harmful punch, kick, or stab (or through an attempt to perpetrate such an attack), D's intention to violate V's physical integrity changes his or her normative position with respect to whatever damage D does to V's physical integrity or to one of its constituent elements. In respecting the value of physical integrity and its constituent values in the rules of basic liability, we do not allow liability to be affected by D saying, 'But if you look at what I intended to do (say, cause actual bodily harm), it was not what actually happened to V (say, death) which was much worse.' D's basic liability is unaffected by this claim, because it appeals to a set of considerations that are not in play for the purposes of establishing such liability: forward-looking considerations such as the likelihood that an injury may prove fatal in any given instance. An intention to do an injury of the latter kind may affect the grading of an offence, but not basic liability for the wrong done. The salience, for the purposes of establishing basic liability, of the moral perspective provided by respect for the intrinsic value of physical integrity and its constituent elements is a matter of judgement and choice. However, the salience of any alternative moral perspective will in that regard also be a matter of judgement and choice, and is not compelled by inexorable logic, by 'Absolute Truth', by what would (supposedly) be 'rational', 'obviously fair', or whatever.[44]

What this analysis does leave open is the possibility that, in any pure case of manslaughter, it could be a denial of basic liability to show that one positively believed (and had good grounds to believe) that an intended violation of physical integrity would not take the form that it did. Instances in which such a claim could plausibly be made will not be common. In most cases, D will not advert to the possible ways in which V's physical integrity might be violated, when intentionally violating V's physical integrity; but there is still a reason to account for exceptional cases in which the claim can be made. An example might be one where, for use as paint, D takes some of V's blood under V's instruction as V is a doctor; but the wound becomes infected and V dies in consequence. In such a case, D can plausibly claim that, in these particular circumstances, at the time when the blood was taken he or she positively believed (for good reason) that V would not suffer harm other than the wound necessarily inflicted in taking the blood from V. Little or nothing is done to disrespect the value of physical integrity by providing for such an excuse, even when what is stake are the rules of basic liability. Such an ascriptive claim is capable of negating the effect of D's change of normative position, in intentionally

---

[43] See text at n 22 above.
[44] For the use of such terms in defence of liberal-progressive thinking, see Ch 1 above.

attacking V's physical integrity, with regard to the particular violation of physical integrity that D unintentionally brings about. It negates that effect, in much the same way as, for example, in civil law, an ascriptive claim that one was a bona fide purchaser for value *without notice* ('equity's darling') can negate what would otherwise be the effect of one's change of normative position vis-à-vis a right-holder when one acquires a title encumbered by the right in question. In the latter case, in establishing the ascriptive claim one may acquire title free from the right; in the manslaughter case, in establishing the ascriptive claim one may now deny liability for the unintended violation of V's physical integrity.

V. The Current Law and the Pure Case of Manslaughter Compared

It should be reasonably obvious which decided cases fall, and which do not fall, under the pure form of manslaughter, and which can be manslaughter only in virtue of the mongrel variety, 'unlawful and dangerous act' manslaughter. Even so, it is a useful exercise to provide some illustrations of how the former is narrower than the latter.[45]

(a) In *Mallet*,[46] D quarrelled with his neighbour, V, and punched him in the face. V fell awkwardly, hit his head on a paving stone and died. This is manslaughter according to both the pure and the 'unlawful and dangerous act' varieties of manslaughter.

(b) In *Ariobeke*,[47] D frightened V by following him to a railway station and looking for him on a train. V tried to escape by crossing a live railway track and was electrocuted. This is manslaughter according to the unlawful and dangerous act doctrine, but may not exemplify the pure form of manslaughter. It will only fall under the latter if D's conduct amounts to an attempt to attack V physically. It is not enough, for the purposes of the pure form of manslaughter that D intended simply to frighten V, even though this is technically an assault in law. To frighten someone, even intentionally, is not to attack their physical integrity.

(c) In *Watson*,[48] D burgled a property, frightening its occupant V who was old and frail. The shock of the burglary killed V. This is clearly unlawful and dangerous act manslaughter, but it does not exemplify the pure form of manslaughter: there is no intentional attack on V's physical integrity. In some circumstances, on these facts, manslaughter by gross negligence might be made out, although it may not be easy to establish a duty of care owed by the burglar to the householder not to cause physical harm arising out of the burglary itself. To that end, it might be necessary to show that D carried on with the burglary despite knowing that a frail householder was aware of his or her activities.

---

[45] These cases are helpfully discussed in Mitchell (2008).
[46] [1972] Crim LR 260.   [47] [1988] Crim LR 314.   [48] [1989] 2 All ER 865.

(d) In *Mitchell*,[49] D pushed an elderly person after an argument. The victim stumbled against V, leading V to fall, hit her head and die. This is a case of 'unlawful and dangerous act' manslaughter, if the push was such as to subject the person who stumbled in consequence to an almost inevitable risk of at least some physical harm. However, it is not an instance of the pure form of manslaughter, unless the push was itself so violent as to involve in itself a violation of V's physical integrity: there must be something going beyond a mere trespass to the person.

In his investigation of public opinion on worked examples of homicide,[50] Barry Mitchell gives members of the public a variation on *Mitchell* to test the limits of support for 'unlawful and dangerous act' manslaughter. In his example, D 'gently pushes' V during the course of an argument, V unexpectedly trips, hits her head against a wall and, having (as in Holt CJ's example) a thin skill, she dies from her injuries. Unsurprisingly, Mitchell found that the majority view was that the death was only accidental. I suggest that this is because D's conduct in making unlawful contact with V takes the form of no more than a trespass to the person. It does not involve an invasion of V's physical integrity. It is not an attack of a kind so significant that consent could not (in the absence of special circumstances) be given to it, thus relating that invasion to the same intrinsic value as unlawful killing itself. Mitchell adds that, in the public's view, 'only when the gap between what D intended or foresaw and V's death is narrowed down did they [the public] favour convicting D of criminal homicide'.[51] That might be taken as possible support for the pure form of manslaughter, but it must be kept in mind that this form of manslaughter does not depend for its legitimacy on the presence of any likelihood of death occurring from the intentional attack on V's physical integrity.[52] For that reason, the facts of *Mallet* (example (a) above) would provide a better basis for exploring the public's views on the legitimacy of constructive manslaughter than *Mitchell* or the 'gentle push' example.[53]

VI. The Place of Manslaughter in Homicide Law and Manslaughter in its Place

We should note the inherent suitability of manslaughter by intentional attack for a place in any ladder of homicide offences. It falls neatly behind death caused by an attack intended to kill or to inflict serious harm (both murder, or one first and the other second degree murder, depending on the law's structure), in that it involves death caused through an intention to attack V's physical integrity. In that respect, it

---

[49] (1983) 76 Cr App R 293.   [50] Mitchell (2000).
[51] Mitchell (2008), at 543.   [52] See text at n 18 above.
[53] What complicates the task of exploring the public's views on this point is that some intentional attacks on V will amount to a grossly negligent breach of a duty of care not to cause V's death, an alternative route to manslaughter that—whether or not the public are aware of its legal existence—may exercise an influence on their thinking. For further discussion, see Horder and McGowan (2006).

does not pose the problems for juries split between possible verdicts that are posed by risk-based forms of homicide.[54] Turning to the latter, as a variety of manslaughter, killing through gross negligence fits rather less easily into the homicide ladder. Not only is the fault element incommensurable with the fault elements for murder, but unlike the other forms of homicide it hinges entirely on a question of degree: the grossness of negligence (an aspect of its incommensurability). If there was any general homicide offence for which a different label was appropriate it is (by analogy with causing death by dangerous driving) manslaughter by gross negligence, and not manslaughter by intentional attack. Manslaughter by recklessness, of course, appears to suffer from the same problems of incommensurability and lack of 'fit'. Its wickedness, though, may make it in a broad way equivalent in point of culpability to manslaughter by intentional attack, or even to murder. Further, in some cases it may be a very fine line indeed that separates it from causing death through an intentional attack.[55] This leaves open the possibility that someone might simply dislike as lurid and unduly condemnatory the term, 'manslaughter'. If widely shared, that sentiment might amount to an argument against introducing it into a jurisdiction for the first time; but as an argument against a term long established in law, and understood and applied with little difficulty or protest by countless juries over centuries, it does not pass muster.

VII. Violations, Invasions of Interests, Recklessness, and Risking Death

1. Manslaughter by risk-taking

Alongside manslaughter by 'unlawful and dangerous act' in English law, there has for many years been the separate crime of manslaughter by gross negligence.[56] Broadly speaking, gross negligence manslaughter involves a breach of a duty of care by D not to subject someone to a risk of death, in circumstances involving gross negligence on the part of the person in breaching the duty of care and thereby causing death.[57] The focus is on the ascription of grave fault in relation to death caused by the impermissible taking of a risk that death might result.[58] The relationship between 'unlawful and dangerous act' manslaughter and gross negligence manslaughter is troubling. We have already encountered the problems with the relationship posed by the dangerousness element in 'unlawful and dangerous act' manslaughter.[59] A further anomaly arises from the way in which the element of

---

[54] Taylor (2001).

[55] See the discussion in Ch 3 above.

[56] I will not be concerned here with the possibility that there is a further species of involuntary manslaughter, reckless manslaughter: see Simester and Sullivan *et al* (2010), at 415–17.

[57] See *Adomako* [1995] AC 171 (HL).

[58] To that end, the courts have indicated that, in appropriate circumstances, they will regard reckless (advertent) risk-taking as a form of grossly negligent risk-taking: *A-G's Reference (No 2 of 1999)* [2000] 3 All ER 182.

[59] See text following n 18 above.

unlawful act is interpreted. In contrast to the pure form of manslaughter, for the purposes of 'unlawful and dangerous act' manslaughter, the criminal act engaged in by D suffices as a relevant form of unlawful act when it is committed recklessly as well as when it is committed intentionally.[60] Yet, in legal contexts, recklessness itself depends for its meaning on a normative judgement that there has been impermissible risk-taking. Like a judgement that someone has been grossly negligent, a finding of recklessness in the law of manslaughter is an ascription of (serious) fault in relation to the impermissible placing of another person in grave danger. As Duff puts it:

> One who recklessly endangers others does not thereby display active hostility towards them; but in her willingness to take the risk of harming them, and in her failure to take adequate precautions against doing so, she shows that she does not care as she should for their interests.[61]

It will often be unclear how the element of unjustified risk-taking in reckless conduct adds much to the dangerousness element, in the crime of 'unlawful and dangerous act' manslaughter. To give a classic example, imagine that D throws a brick from the roof of a high building, knowing that there may be people walking on the street below. The brick strikes V, and V dies when he or she hits his or her head on the ground when falling. Although D may not have intended to hurt anyone, D was reckless as to the causing of some harm. So, when the brick strikes the person below, D is guilty of (at least) assault occasioning actual bodily harm. The commission of this criminal act ought in theory to be the preliminary step in an analysis wherein the next step is deciding whether D's act was not only criminal but dangerous. But the next step is superfluous, on the facts of the example (as we have seen[62]). In law, the element of danger is an inevitable danger of some harm, but that is harm that D has already caused through the criminal act itself.

The element of impermissible risk-taking through recklessness only gains independent purchase when the risk-taking in question does not involve an inevitable risk of personal harm. Suppose that, to see how high I can throw it, I hurl a stone into the air, aware that it may come down on a glass roof. The stone does come down on the glass roof, breaking it, but additionally a splinter of glass flies into V's eye, killing him. In this example, I am reckless as to the causing of the damage done (the unlawful act element in the shape of criminal damage). Let us also say that, in the circumstances, there is an inevitable risk of at least some physical harm to another person (the dangerousness element) because a party was going on in the room under the glass roof. In this kind of contrived example, one can identify independent work to do for both the criminal act element committed through recklessness, and for the dangerousness element; but that is not saying very much. Where D's conduct in killing V is to be condemned because V's death came about through impermissible risk-taking, the proper course is to charge D with the variety of manslaughter focused on such risk-taking: manslaughter by gross negligence.

---

[60] See, eg, *Newbury* [1977] AC 500.
[61] Duff (2007), at 151.   [62] See text at n 18 above.

This analysis underscores, of course, the importance of focusing on intentional conduct in cases of pure manslaughter. To direct harm at V intentionally is to attack V, a qualitatively different kind of way in which to pose a risk to V. Indeed, engaging in an intentional attack is a way of posing a risk of harm that does not depend on the degree of risk that the harm may occur to justify convicting D for attempting to cause or for causing the harm.[63] The controversial element in the pure case of manslaughter is surely not this, but the fact that D is to be held liable for some of the unintended as well as some of the intended consequences of his or her intentional attack. I have sought to explain how the justification for this is to be found in the law's respect for the intrinsic value of individuals' physical integrity and its constituent elements.[64] It disrespects that value to regard it as a sound basis for denying liability when D says (in effect): 'I only intended to punch V; whether V lived or died in consequence, was seriously injured, or suffered a medically recognized psychiatric illness as a result, simply did not feature in my practical reasoning.'[65]

2. Manslaughter as a horrific crime

At the outset, in Chapter 1, I described murder and manslaughter as violative crimes. They involve violations of V him or herself, and not merely (and quite possibly, not at all) incursions on V's interests. In so doing, I cast doubt on whether the fact that murder and manslaughter are violative crimes means that they are also always 'horrific' crimes. Fleshing out that claim will shed some further light on the pure form of manslaughter.

In developing his original thesis that murder and manslaughter are horrific crimes, because they involve violations of V him or herself, even Stanton-Ife expresses some doubts about how comprehensive the analysis might turn out to be. With commendable candour, he asks rhetorically, 'is euthanasia at the competent request of a suffering adult best understood as horrific but justified, on the one hand, or not horrific in the first place?'[66] I think the answer to this question is that euthanasia consented to by a competent and fully informed adult, whether or not regarded as murder, is not a horrific crime in the first place. It involves a violation of V him or herself, but if it was committed at V's request, then it was arguably not committed in a way that constituted an invasion of V's interests. The act unlawfully caused V's death (a violation) but it did not invade

---

[63] See text following n 43 above. Even the most ardent subjectivist must surely accept the proposition in the text. If D aims a shot intended to kill at V from such a long distance away that D believes he or she has virtually no chance of killing V, but does successfully kill V, the low risk of killing V surely cannot figure in deciding whether or not to hold D liable for murder. For doubts about whether intention is especially significant in changing someone's normative position, see Ashworth (2008), at 241–2. I agree that intention is not the only fault element possession of which can change D's normative position: see, eg, the recklessness example given at n 16 above.

[64] See text following n 36 above.

[65] However, for a qualification see the 'reasonable belief' defence outlined above: text following n 44.

[66] Stanton-Ife (2010), at 139 fn 5.

V's interest in staying alive, because V had voluntarily surrendered that interest. In a case where a violation of V is not accompanied by an invasion of V's relevant interests, the violation will not be 'horrific'. Of course, in such cases—as in cases where V purports to sell him or herself into slavery—the law may as a matter of principle say that the relevant interest that V has (respectively in staying alive, and in retaining his or her freedom of choice in relation to labour) is 'not V's to give away'. If that were true, then a horrific crime would indeed have been committed. I suggest, though, that to say that V's interests are not his or hers to give away is a misleading way of putting the matter. A better analogy is with the making of a gift that, for whatever reason, the donee is not normatively free to accept. In such a case, we cast no doubt on the donor's normative freedom to make the gift. It is just that the purported gift will never take effect because the donee is not normatively free to accept it. Similarly, in the example of euthanasia, we should maintain the view that V is normatively free to relinquish his or her interest in remaining alive.[67] It is just that in these circumstances, for a variety of well-known reasons, the law will not accept that V's surrender of his or her interest in remaining alive changes the killer's (D's) normative position. In killing V at V's request, in the eye of the law, D is the same murderer he or she would have been had V given no consent to the killing at all, even if the crime D commits is not a 'horrific' one.

Mala in se may or may not include within their scope invasions of interests as such, in addition to or alongside violations of persons themselves, of property itself, or of some other intrinsic value. Having sex with human remains involves the *malum in se* of a violation of a dead person and hence of an intrinsic value concerned with respect for the dead.[68] It is a strong candidate for being considered a horrific crime; but such a sex act does not involve the invasion of someone's interest (there is no rights violation). How does manslaughter fit in to this picture, as a *malum in se*? Consider my earlier example in which the doctor consents to have blood taken, the wound becomes infected, and the doctor dies.[69] Can it be argued that this is not an instance of 'horrific' crime? The doctor's consent to the initial taking of blood, although a consent that in the circumstances is not valid in law, might be thought to mean that D who takes the blood is not invading the doctor's interests in so doing, and that, consequently, although the consequences may be horrific the crime, arguably, is not. Such a line of analysis overlooks the difference between the things that D did that have moral salience in this example.[70] Whilst, in virtue of V's informed consent, D's assault on V may not be horrific, the unlawful killing that D perpetrates in consequence is indeed horrific; and it is D's liability for that (un-consented to) killing which is our concern.

---

[67] It is important to shake oneself free of the easy (and nowadays, very common) assumption that this is a peculiarly modern, 'individualistic' account of normative freedom. From time immemorial, people have regarded themselves, and have been regarded by others, as normatively free knowingly and willingly to sacrifice their own lives as, say, an offering to the gods, or something of that nature. Such normative freedom thrives in many social and political environments hostile to or uncomprehending of liberal individualism.

[68] Sexual Offences Act 2003, s 70.

[69] Text following n 44 above.　　　　[70] See the start of section IV. above.

3. Manslaughter and trespass to the person

On one view, no distinction can or should be drawn between assaults taking the form of mere touching (including more 'robust' forms of touching such as a mild slap, poke, or push), and assaults that damage V's physical integrity in itself, such as wounds or assaults occasioning actual bodily harm. So, the argument runs, if there is a case for regarding the latter as a basis for a manslaughter conviction, it extends to cover the former as well. This thesis could be supported by reliance on Blackstone's famous claim that:

The law cannot draw the line between different degrees of violence, and therefore prohibits the first and lowest stage of it; every man's person being sacred, and no other having a right to meddle with it, in any the slightest manner.[71]

Notice that this passage in fact makes two different claims. The second claim is the principled one that the body is sacred, and thus no-one has the right to interfere with it in any way. The fact that an assault in law may be committed by the merest touching (falling outside any of the exceptions to the rule) is evidence of this. By contrast, the first claim is more of a policy claim. It is saying that the difficulty of distinguishing satisfactorily between different degrees of physical interference with another person (touch, poke, prod, slap, blow, etc) means that the distinction is not worth making. One may surmise that, in Blackstone's view, to try to make the distinction would be to send an unclear message to people about what they can and cannot do, and that is undesirable in the field of personal violence.

Perhaps Blackstone is right on both points. However, his points relate to the case for criminalizing as such non-fatal assaults of varying degree of severity. That leaves open an important possibility. If we go behind the policy point that the law cannot be seen to draw distinctions between 'degrees of violence', we can see that it may still be possible and appropriate, for certain purposes (such as determining the scope for a 'victim' to consent to the conduct in question), to make a distinction between kinds of physical interference with another person.[72] It has been my argument that, in determining the scope of manslaughter, an invasion of physical integrity is qualitatively different from an interference with the right not to suffer a trespass to the person. It can be argued that the latter offends more against a different intrinsic value. A mere trespass to the person seems close to offences involving insults, scaring people, or making frightening or (unwanted) sexually explicit telephone calls, remarks, or gestures in public. Trespass to the person is close to these wrongs because its prohibition appears capable of justification in terms of the intrinsic value of respect for the non-domination of personal space. By 'non-domination', I mean the freedom from unwanted contact (especially contact with no intrinsic value) that consumes or demands, or is liable to consume or

---

[71] Blackstone (1765–69), vol 4, at 120.

[72] See text at n 13 above. In saying this, I do not overlook the possibility that repeated shoving, slapping, poking, etc could go beyond a simple trespass to the person and amount to an attack on V's physical integrity.

demand, an unfair share of D's attention.[73] By 'personal space', I mean the flip-side of non-domination. This is the (heavily culturally influenced) set of understandings about the ways in which one may go about one's business, take one's plans forward, relax, and so on, without the interference of others, including within interference many instances of well-meaning assistance.[74] Both the non-domination of personal space and the preservation of physical integrity are intrinsic values that can be important contributors to an autonomous life. Nonetheless, they are not the same value. In our efforts to simplify the criminal law, we are wont to simplify and standardize the values that inform it. So much the worse for the theoretical basis on which the law stands.

[73] It may be objected that the pain they cause would seem to be a good reason to prohibit even minor pokes, slaps, and prods, and perhaps it is; but notice that the experience of pain does not feature in the justification for prohibiting invasions of physical integrity any more than it features in the prohibition of trespasses to the person. In the present context, what is significant about pain is that, like a fright or like someone persistently blocking V's way, it consumes an unfair share of V's attention.

[74] See generally, Von Hirsch and Simester (2006). Even if you wake me unsolicited from sleep on a train to offer me a fantastic bargain, this may be the wrong thing to have done, however much the bargain may suit me.

6

Joint Criminal Ventures and Murder

I. Murder during a Joint Criminal Venture: The Failures at Common Law

The Law Commission's final report on murder, manslaughter, and infanticide in 2006 had specifically addressed the problem of complicity in murder. Even so, the Government eventually decided against reform of the law of complicity, in so far as it applied to homicide.[1] However, the original Government Consultation Paper on homicide law reform had contained proposals for reform of the law in this crucial area.[2] These included proposals for reform of the principles governing when D can be held liable for a murder committed by P, when D and P were engaged in a joint criminal venture. This issue will be the main focus here. We need to consider why these proposals were abandoned, and to reflect more generally on the liability of D for murder committed in the course of a joint criminal venture.

As is well-known, the courts have struggled to find clear or just principles to govern D's liability, in cases where P kills V in the course of a joint criminal venture with D.[3] That is not, though, because 'joint criminal ventures' are by their nature hard to understand or generally difficult to make the subject of rules and principles; they are not. For example, there is little or no difficulty about the justice of finding D guilty of murder alongside P, when the joint criminal venture between them was itself aimed at murder. In such a case, the 'joint venture' basis of the liability of D and P is analogous to, but not the same as, the basis of liability in cases in which, with murder in mind, D assists or encourages P from the sidelines to commit the murder P intends to commit, without being part of P's murderous plan as such.[4] More difficult to resolve have been cases where D and P have been

---

[1] See respectively, Law Commission (2006); Ministry of Justice (2009), at para 106.

[2] See Ministry of Justice (2008), and House of Commons' Justice Committee (2010–12).

[3] See the discussion in Law Commission (2007), app B. For a general theoretical discussion of someone's complicity in another's act, see Kutz (2007). More specifically, on theorizing English law, see Sullivan (2008).

[4] It is important to understand why the two cases are not identical, even if they are analogous in terms of the moral basis they provide for regarding D as complicit in P's crime. Consider a joint venture case taking the form of a large international conspiracy whose members are recruited over time, and not all of whose expertise or labour is eventually used when P commits the agreed offence. In such a case, a member whose experience or labour is eventually not used (D) has not assisted or encouraged P, who may never know that D was involved at all. Nonetheless, D may be complicit in P's crime in virtue of D's agreement to be a part of the joint venture: see further, text at n 89 below.

engaged in a joint venture aimed at the commission of some crime other than murder, and in the course of the commission of that crime P has committed murder. When (if ever) should D be regarded as guilty of murder, along with P, in such a case, as well as being guilty of the crime that was the subject of the joint venture? The starting-point is the courts' view that D may be found guilty of the murder by P, if D entered into or participated in the joint criminal venture (whatever the crime that was the subject of the joint venture) realizing that P might commit murder in the course of that venture.[5] This answer does draw something of special legal significance out of the participation of D in a joint criminal venture with P. As Hughes LJ put it in *R v ABCD*:

The liability of D2 . . . rests . . . on his having continued in the joint venture of crime A when he realizes (even if he does not desire) that crime B may be committed in the course of it. Where crime B is murder, that means he can properly be held guilty if he foresees that D1 will cause death by acting with murderous intent. . . . He has associated himself with a foreseen murder.[6]

Having entered into or participated in the joint venture (crime A) out of which crime B arose, in the realization that crime B might arise in that way, D will not be heard to dis-associate him or herself completely from the commission of crime B. This illustrates the application of a familiar and simple principle of responsibility arising out of joint activity (an issue considered further in section VII.3. below). The principle was reflected in the draft Bill attached to the Government's original consultation proposals. Clause 3 said:

(1) Where—
  (a) two or more persons participate in a joint criminal venture, and
  (b) one of them ('P') commits the offence of murder in the context of the venture, another participant ('D') is guilty of murder if . . .
(2) . . . D foresaw that in the context of the venture a person might be killed by a participant acting with intent to kill. . . .[7]

However, the fault element for murder in English law goes beyond an intention to kill (the 'more culpable' fault element), and is broad enough to include cases in which someone kills having intended to do no more than serious harm (the 'less culpable' fault element).[8] It is this that should be regarded as the source of the difficulties for the law of complicity, and not the basic principles of complicity themselves. Consider a case of joint criminal venture on D and P's part (for

---

[5] *Powell & Daniels; English* [1999] 1 AC 1 (HL).

[6] *R v ABCD* [2010] EWCA Crim 1622, at 27. It has been suggested that the joint venture basis for D2's liability in respect of crime B, in Hughes LJ's example, is a kind of tacit 'encouragement': see Lord Phillips in *R v Gnango* [2011] UKSC 59, at 38. That is an artificial explanation that loses plausibility when the joint venture is large and not all participants in it know each other, or each other's roles, even though they share a common criminal purpose (perhaps orchestrated by a single criminal 'mastermind') and realize what may arise out of the perpetration of the agreed crime: see n 4 above.

[7] Ministry of Justice (2008), Annex C.

[8] The legal sufficiency of both these fault elements was confirmed in *Cunningham* [1982] AC 566 (HL).

example, burglary) in the course of which D realizes that P may inflict serious harm on someone—say, the householder—but P's attack on the householder goes beyond that, and is intended to and does kill him or her. D realized that P might act with the (less culpable) fault element for murder, but not the (more culpable) fault element with which P in fact went on to act. Should D still be found guilty of the murder by P?[9]

The familiar difficulty about giving an unequivocally affirmative answer to this question is the problem of the 'moral remoteness' of what P intentionally did, from what D anticipated that P might do.[10] It must be kept in mind that it is P's act in respect of which D is to be convicted of murder, not his or her (D's) own act. That being so, is the simple fact that D realized that P might act with the less culpable fault element for murder during the joint venture, but not with the more culpable fault element with which P in fact acted, sufficient to justify convicting D of murder?[11] The common law has sought to address the problem of the 'moral remoteness' of the murder by P from what D anticipated. At common law, a special test has been introduced that is meant to prevent D from being found guilty of the murder by P in cases such as that just discussed. This is the test of whether what P did was 'fundamentally different' from what D anticipated.[12]

Consider an example in which, in the course of a burglary, D anticipated that P might inflict serious disabling harm on V with a club, but P pulled out a gun and intentionally shot V through the head. In such a case, there are grounds for saying that there was a 'fundamental difference' between what P did and what D anticipated that P might do, and hence that D should not be found guilty of the murder by P. By way of contrast, suppose that, in the course of a burglary, D anticipated either (a) that P might seek to incapacitate V by shooting V in a non-vital part of the body, but P in fact intentionally shot V through the head, or (b) that P might intentionally inflict a serious disabling injury with a club that could (as D realized) itself kill V, but P in fact intentionally shot V through the head. On such facts, what D anticipated that P might do (intentionally cause serious harm) is not what P did (intentionally killing). Nonetheless, there is perhaps far less of a case than in the previous example for saying that what P did was 'fundamentally different' from what D anticipated, and a jury should be able to convict D of murder in cases such as (a) and (b).[13] In the first alternative (a), the lack of moral remoteness comes from the fact that D anticipates the same mode of attack as P in fact launches, just not its lethal intent. In the second alternative (b), the lack of moral remoteness comes from the fact that D anticipated that the victim

[9] Most particularly, on the assumption that D did not, in addition, anticipate that the victim might die as a result of P's (anticipated) infliction of serious harm.
[10] For a further factor bearing on the moral remoteness question, see n 9 above.
[11] Keeping in mind the point made in n 9 above.
[12] *Powell & Daniels; English* [1999] 1 AC 1 (HL).
[13] For general discussion, see Law Commission (2007), app B. What result an application of the common law yields in case (b) is rather less clear than the result that will be reached in (a), namely that D is guilty of murder.

might die as a result of the attack D anticipated, even if D did not anticipate either the mode of or the lethal intent behind P's attack.

I will not go over the problems that have arisen with the 'fundamental difference' rule, as a way of seeking to resolve the problems of moral remoteness, in a way that is both ethically acceptable and readily comprehensible to a jury.[14] Suffice to say that, amongst others, the following problems have arisen with the application of and consequences of applying of the rule:

1. It is unclear whether the rule is capable of application when D anticipated that P might intentionally kill (or that V might die).[15]

2. There has been doubt concerning whether it is P's 'act' (say, stabbing) that must be fundamentally different from what D anticipated, or the 'intention' with which P does an act, or both.[16]

3. It is unclear whether D can succeed in a plea of 'fundamental difference' if the act alleged to be fundamentally different is committed with a weapon D realized that P had with him or her.[17]

4. There has been uncertainty over whether the application of the 'fundamental difference' rule is a matter wholly for the jury. It could be that some facts— such as D's realization that P was in possession of the weapon eventually used—will mean that D cannot take advantage of the rule as a matter of law.[18]

5. A successful plea of 'fundamental difference' may mean that D may escape not only conviction for murder, but also conviction for manslaughter. It is not entirely clear if this remains true even if, say (and subject to a resolution of point 4 above), D was aware that P had the weapon eventually used to kill V.[19]

In my view, most of these problems were left unresolved, and were arguably exacerbated, by the decision of the House of Lords in *Rahman*.[20] It is, thus,

---

[14] See Law Commission (2007), app B.

[15] *Rahman* [2008] UKHL 45, at paras 65 and 68, where Lord Brown appears to be suggesting that the wholly unanticipated nature of P's 'act' (considered apart from the intention with which it was done) may make that act 'fundamentally different' from what D anticipated, even if D anticipated that P might do an act (of some kind) intended to kill.

[16] See *Van Hoogstraten* (unreported), 2 December 2003; *Rahman* [2008] UKHL 45. Rahman appears to shift the law decisively in favour of the 'act' rather than the 'intention' approach.

[17] *Rahman* [2008] UKHL 45. At para 66, Lord Brown appears to indicate that such awareness would be inconsistent with taking the benefit of the 'fundamental difference' rule.

[18] For equivocation on this issue, see *Powell & Daniels; English* [1999] 1 AC 1 (HL). See further *Rahman* [2008] UKHL 45, at para 66, where Lord Brown says that a jury 'must convict' if D realized that P was in possession of the weapon used to kill V (see further Lord Rodger's remarks at para 47). By way of contrast, at para 26, Lord Bingham says that the term 'fundamental difference' is 'not a term of art', and that its meaning needs no explanation to a jury.

[19] *Powell & Daniels; English* [1999] 1 AC 1 (HL); *Rahman* [2008] UKHL 45.

[20] *Rahman* [2008] UKHL 45. As my concern in this chapter is with general principles, we will not go into the facts of the case here. For an examination of the facts, and of the decision of the Court of Appeal, see Law Commission (2006).

something of an irony that Sir Richard Buxton has recent suggested that, at least in cases where the joint venture contemplates serious violence:

[T]he law is now settled by . . . the speech of Lord Brown of Eaton-under-Heywood in *Rahman* (at [68]). Given that guidance . . . it will only tempt providence or cause confusion to seek to improve the law by legislation.[21]

On the contrary, I believe that little if anything was settled by the decision of the House of Lords, and that the problems I have listed above, amongst others, will persist until they have been resolved by legislation. Even so, I will not concern myself here with point 5, with whether the law should be reformed such that D can be found guilty of manslaughter, even if acquitted of murder in virtue of an application of (some reformed version of) the fundamental difference rule.[22] I will concentrate on proposed reform of the rule itself.

II. Murder in a Joint Criminal Venture: The Abandoned Path to Reform

The Government accepted the Law Commission's criticisms of the 'fundamental difference' rule.[23] The Government's initial proposals would have replaced it with the following provisions (alongside a provision making it clear that D will be guilty of murder if D realized that P might intentionally kill[24]):[25]

(1) Where—

    (a) two or more persons participate in a joint criminal venture, and

    (b) one of them ('P') commits the offence of murder in the context of the venture, another participant ('D') is guilty of the offence of murder if subsection . . . (3) applies . . .

(2) [omitted]

(3) This subsection applies if—

    (a) D foresaw that, in the context of the venture, serious injury might be caused to a person by a participant acting with intent to cause such injury, and

    (b) P's criminal act was within the scope of the venture.

(4) P's criminal act was within the scope of the venture if it did not go far beyond that which was planned or agreed to, or which was foreseen, by D.

---

[21] Buxton (2009), at 243.

[22] For discussion of this point see Ministry of Justice (2008), at paras 108–110; Law Commission (2007), at paras 4.42–4.46.

[23] Ministry of Justice (2008), at paras 76 and 94–107.

[24] Clause 3(2), reversing the effect of Lord Brown's opinion in *Rahman* [2008] UKHL 45: see n 16 above.

[25] Clause 3 of the draft Bill, n 3 above, annex C.

The crucial provisions here are clause 3(3)(b) and 3(4). In a case where D realizes that P may intentionally cause serious injury (but not kill), D may be convicted of murder if P's act was still 'within the scope of the venture'. P's act will be within the scope of D and P's joint criminal venture if it did not go 'far beyond' what was planned, agreed to, or foreseen by D. The language of 'far beyond' what was agreed etc, although obviously not more certain in scope, is arguably more apposite for jury trial than the language of 'fundamental difference' to what was agreed etc. The notion of 'far beyond' invites consideration of a simple quantitative question of degree. By way of contrast, the notion of 'fundamental' difference invites consideration of a seemingly qualitative question of kind. Clearly, although what P does may indeed be qualitatively different to that which D anticipated (for example, use of a taser, as compared with use of a shod foot), it is probably more helpful to a jury to present such differences more straightforwardly as essentially quantitative ones. The question should be, quite simply, how relatively distant or remote is what P did from what D anticipated P might do? I will return to consideration of this test shortly.

Nevertheless, the Government has decided not to take forward clause 3. The Government has said:

[W]e have now received [the Law Commission's] full report on complicity, and we accept the weight of opinion expressed in response to the [Government] consultation that any legislation in this area should address the Law Commission's proposals for a *comprehensive* reform of the law on secondary liability.[26]

That turns the spotlight on the Law Commission's recommendations. What did the Commission recommend should be the approach to joint venture cases in which murder was committed?

III. Codifying Complicity Law: How 'Benthamite' Should One Be?

Unlike the Government's abandoned reform proposals, the Commission's *Participating in Crime* report[27] does not contain specific clauses dealing with homicide cases. All cases of crime committed in the course of a joint venture are to be addressed through application of clause 2 of the draft Bill attached to the report:

(1) This section applies where two or more persons participate in a joint criminal venture.

(2) If one of them (P) commits an offence, another participant (D) is also guilty of the offence if P's criminal act falls within the scope of the venture.

The Commission took the view that, in applying these clauses, the courts should hold that D will be guilty of P's offence—because it is within the scope of the joint

---

[26] Ministry of Justice (2009), at para 106 (Government's emphasis). It seems unlikely that anything further is to be done to bring about such comprehensive reform.

[27] Law Commission (2007).

venture, broadly construed—if D realized that, in the course of the joint venture, P, in engaging in the conduct element, might commit the crime in question.[28] In broad terms, this would mean that, to be convicted of murder by virtue of this clause, D must foresee that P may intentionally kill V, or foresee that V might die as a result of the intentional infliction of serious harm on V by P.[29] It was decided not to complicate the Bill by including provisions specifically addressing homicide (which was in any event being simultaneously separately considered by the Commission[30]), to ensure that the courts reached this result. In the Commission's view, the courts could and should be trusted to reach it through judicial law-making, building on clause 2. In that regard, there is some jurisprudential history worth considering in this context.

Any codifying project may be pulled in different directions by a conflict between the demands of clarity and simplicity in drafting, on the one hand, and on the other hand, the demands of comprehensiveness and attention to detail. The Law Commission found itself caught in the conflict when moving towards general codification in the 1980s. The 1985 draft Code had included provisions on interpretation (including illustrative examples) meant to limit the scope for judicial law-making, thus placing the emphasis on the comprehensiveness of the statutory detail.[31] However, the revised code of 1989 removed these provisions. The Commission was now anxious to stress that 'the interpretive role of the judiciary will continue to be important',[32] because it found it could not otherwise maintain the required degree of simplicity in drafting. In few areas on which the Commission has worked (although intoxication is a notorious example[33]) has this conflict proved to be more difficult to manage than in the attempt to reform the law governing assisting and encouraging crime.[34] In large measure, this is because the doctrines governing liability for assisting and encouraging crime are examples of the 'auxiliary' part of the criminal law, the part meant to buttress the fair and effective operation of individual criminal wrongs.[35] Accordingly, like the rules governing intoxication, these doctrines consist of rules that must be capable of application to almost all crimes within the jurisdiction (and to some outside it). They must be capable of doing this, whatever the complexities and deficiencies in the definition and scope

---

[28] *Ibid*, at paras 3.166–3.169. The Commission thus rejected the view later adopted by Lord Brown in *Rahman* ([2008] UKHL 45, at para 63) that an act is within the scope of a joint venture only if it is within the 'common purpose' shared by D and P. That may be the ordinary meaning of 'joint venture', but there is no reason why the law should have to follow ordinary meanings, if justice is more clearly and simply done through departing from such meanings.

[29] See the discussion in the text following n 12 above.

[30] Law Commission (2006).

[31] Clauses 3 and 4 of the draft code.

[32] Law Commission (1989), at para 2.6, although as de Búrca and Gardner point out, there is some equivocation in the report over the right approach to take to the role of the judiciary: de Búrca and Gardner (1990), at 560.

[33] See now, Law Commission (2009).

[34] A version of the Commission's recommendations for inchoate offences of assisting and encouraging crime (recommendations that prioritized comprehensiveness) has become law following the passing of the Serious Crimes Act 2007, pt 2.

[35] See Gardner (1998c).

of such crimes, and whether or not the punishment regime following conviction can take account of differing modes of participation.

In its *Participating in Crime* report, having decided on the principles that it wished to see in statutory form,[36] a difficult choice had to be made by the Commission between two alternative Bills it had drafted to embody them, each of which took a different approach:

One approach ... [was] to express the policy in a relatively open-textured form, focusing on general principles. Under this approach, it would be for the courts, guided by our report feeding into Judicial Studies Board specimen directions to juries, to fill in the details in particular cases. The other approach ... [was] a Bill which itself provid[es] the details. Nowhere is the contrast between the two approaches more pronounced that in the respective clauses dealing with D's liability for participating in a joint venture.[37]

From a longer-term perspective, of course, the difficulty of reconciling the two approaches emerged at the same time as reformers began to take seriously the notion that the common law should be reformed and replaced on a systematic basis by statute. On the one hand, for example, Bentham was famously of the view that:

so long as there remains any, the smallest scrap, of unwritten law unextirpated, it suffices to taint with its own corruption—its own inbred and incurable corruption—whatsoever portion of *statute* law has ever been, or ever can be, applied to it.[38]

On the other hand, Bentham was a strong supporter of the view that the conduct-guiding rules of a legal system legal system should be, 'written, visible and *intelligible, and cognosible*';[39] yet, these two views may come into conflict. This may happen if it is too difficult to replace an entire complex body of common law with straightforward and readily comprehensible statutory rules. For the Commission, this poses a particular difficulty. This is because a key *raison d'être* for the Commission is, to use the language of the White Paper preceding the Law Commissions Act 1965, to reduce the law to a form that is, '*accessible, intelligible,* and in accordance with modern needs'.[40]

The Commission ultimately opted for the first (simple) approach outlined above[41] and hence the Bill favouring—in so far as is possible—statements of general principle (relying on judicial law-making to fill out the details). This Bill, and its more comprehensive rival, had both been considered by the Commission's criminal law advisory group,[42] the overwhelming majority of whom supported the first approach. Consequently, as we have seen, so far as joint criminal ventures

---

[36] It is outside the scope of this chapter to discuss the merits of these principles. It would hard to improve on the critical analysis of what they should be to be found in the following sources: Wilson (2008); Simester (2006); Sullivan (2008); Smith (1997); Smith and Hogan (2008), at 211–19.

[37] Law Commission (2007), at para A.15.

[38] Cited in Schofield and Harris (1998), at 20–1.

[39] Schofield and Harris (1998), at 18 (my emphasis).

[40] Lord Chancellor's Department (1965), at 2 (my emphasis).

[41] See the passage cited at n 37 above.

[42] Consisting of, amongst other specialists in crime, a Lord Justice of Appeal, a High Court Judge, a Crown Court Judge, three QCs, and three professors of criminal law.

are concerned,[43] the report's Bill says little more that what has been set out in clause 2 above.[44] The question whether or not D is to be found guilty of P's offence because it fell 'within the scope of the [joint] venture' is ultimately one for the jury. However, the jury is to be assisted to answer the question by rules and principles designed to give more detailed legal meaning to the notion of 'the scope of the venture'. These rules and principles will come from the report itself, and from guidance based on it issued to judges by the Judicial Studies Board.

In that regard, it is important to note that although under the Commission's recommendations the common law is to be abolished,[45] the cases at common law will remain as an important legal context against which the rules and principles set out in the report can be understood and interpreted. That is what is implied when the Commission indicates that reliance may be placed by judges, in developing the law on the basis of clause 2 above,[46] on the report itself (feeding into the guidance issued by the Judicial Studies Board).[47] So, I respectfully disagree with Sir Richard Buxton when he suggests that the Commission's approach is contrary to principle because 'it is Parliament, not the Judicial Studies Board, that should make the law'.[48] The Commission has never suggested otherwise. Under the Commission's recommendations, it will indeed be Parliament that makes the law—through enacting clause 2—on the basis of which judges will then develop and apply it, drawing on pre-existing case law, as they have for many years done with, for example, the law of attempts under the Criminal Attempts Act 1981. As with overruled cases or dissenting judgments, abolished common law retains its status as a form of contextual, background 'legal material' (persuasive authority), even if it has no binding force.[49] In my view, one of the major steps forward to result from the enactment of the Commission's recommendations would be to turn case law that is theoretically binding, but in fact ambiguous and contradictory, into a source of (no more than) guidance for the establishment of better law in the future.

IV. Clause 2, Uncertainty, and Article 7 of the European Convention

Would the enactment of clause 2 above[50] (considered alongside the supporting legal context just explained), without specific provision for murder cases, do enough to produce satisfactory reform? Sullivan has argued that it would not be sufficient.[51] He is critical of the Commission's decision to adopt the first approach to the drafting of clause 2 dealing with joint ventures (as well as opposing

---

[43] The Commission had adopted the approach aiming at comprehensiveness in its report on inchoate offences of assisting and encouraging crime, an approach that found favour with Government in pt 2 of the Serious Crime Act 2007.

[44] See text following n 27 above.

[45] Law Commission (2007), (Jurisdiction, Procedure and Consequential Provisions) Bill, cl 8.

[46] Text following n 27 above.   [47] Law Commission (2007), at para A.15.

[48] Buxton (2009), at 240.   [49] See the brief discussion in Horder (2006), at 81 fn 55.

[50] Text following n 27 above.   [51] Sullivan (2008). See further Buxton (2009).

the Commission's stance on the substantive rules and principles that should govern this area of the law).[52] Although his criticism of the Commission's adoption of the first drafting approach is very tightly tied to his criticism of the policy recommendations the clauses embody, he has two specific criticisms of the Commission's drafting approach.

The first criticism is that he believes that clause 2, in particular, will be an 'incomplete' rather than a 'self-contained' statement of the law governing liability for wrongs committed in the course of a joint venture, requiring clause 2 to be 'replaced' by the disinterring of the old cases.[53] I do not agree that clause 2 is an incomplete statement of the law governing joint ventures (although it is not 'self-contained' either, if that is meant to mean that it can be applied in some sense acontextually). An incomplete statement of the law governing joint ventures would be one that, for example, deliberately sought to address joint ventures where only the agreed offence is committed, whilst leaving the principles governing other instances of joint venture to the common law.[54] Clause 2 is not incomplete in that way, and is intended to cover the whole ground.

I believe that the phrase, 'within the scope of the [joint] venture' has a high degree of linguistic determinacy, whilst nonetheless being in important respects context-dependent.[55] The context on which its meaning and scope depends is, of course, the need to employ some of the conceptual apparatus of the common law whose binding character clause 2 is intended to replace. Sullivan objects to this on the grounds that the old common law is full of 'uncertainty and complexity'.[56] However, as I indicated at the end of the last section,[57] much of that uncertainty and complexity was generated by the fact that, in theory, cases deciding different— or even contradictory—things were *all* meant to bind the judges who had to interpret and apply or explain them. Such cases would lose their binding force, were the Commission's Bill to become law. Courts would then have the freedom

---

[52] Sullivan (2008), at 20–1.   [53] *Ibid*, at 21.

[54] Sullivan distinguishes three situations in which joint venture liability may arise. In addition to 'agreed offence' joint ventures, he lists joint ventures where an offence collateral to the joint venture is committed, and joint ventures where there is no agreement to commit a criminal offence. It should be noted here that I do not believe that the latter kind of joint venture is a *separate kind* of joint venture from a joint venture involving agreement to commit an offence (this may not be Sullivan's argument either: see Sullivan (2008), at 22). Agreements are merely one way in which joint ventures may arise. Another way is when D2 joins D1 in the commission of an offence against V, and they end up committing the offence together (a 'collaborative' venture). One should not be led into error by the thought that joint venture can be no less (or, indeed, no more) than conspiracy turned-into-action. Further, whether joint ventures in which it is the offence collateral to the agreed offence that is in issue are a *distinct* form of joint venture may also be doubted. The issue in such cases is whether the collateral offence was within the scope of a joint venture that (by definition) included an agreed or collaborative venture.

[55] For this distinction, see Endicott (1996), at 685–6. Endicott gives the example of the word 'tomorrow', which is highly determinate linguistically, but obviously radically context-dependent when it comes to identifying the day to which it refers. The point made in the text is somewhat obscured by the Commission's unfortunate use of 'open-textured' to describe the phrase 'within the scope of the venture'. Sullivan rightly picks up on this misleading way of putting the matter: Sullivan (2008), at 21 fn 9.

[56] Sullivan (2008), at 21.   [57] Text following n 49 above.

to affirm—as I fully expect that they would—that the rules and principles drawn from the cases supporting the Commission's understanding of the scope of clause 2 form the correct background against which to interpret and apply clause 2.

Sullivan suggests that a judge might legitimately interpret clause 2 in such a way as to confine it to joint ventures involving the commission of the agreed offence alone,[58] because that is arguably the 'natural meaning' of joint criminal venture as well as being a reading that favours the accused.[59] This does not seem very plausible to me, for the excellent reason given by Simester and Sullivan, namely that (as argued above) the context in which words are used is all-important in statutory interpretation:

Modern statutory interpretation, both civil and criminal, should first take the form of ascertaining the *ordinary meaning in context*. The reference to context is particularly important. It is a feature of language that meaning is not merely lexical, but also depends on the surrounding words and the purpose of the writer.[60]

Quite so. The context in which clause 2 has been drafted makes it abundantly clear that collateral offences may legitimately be regarded as in some circumstances part of a 'joint criminal venture'.

Sullivan's second criticism of the Commission's approach to drafting concerns Article 7 of the European Convention on Human Rights, guaranteeing that there can be no crime without a (prior) law creating it: the principle of legality. It is a development of the first criticism, in that he claims clause 2[61] may fail to provide the kind of certainty required to satisfy Article 7, even though, as Emmerson and Ashworth have observed, 'the standard of certainty required under the Convention, and under comparable constitutional principles, is not a particularly exacting one'.[62] Sullivan says:

[The Commission] intends that a subject who is party to a joint criminal venture may be guilty of a criminal offence despite a lack of intent to commit the offence, a lack of an agreement to commit the offence, a lack of any involvement in the commission of the offence and a lack of any assistance or encouragement to those involved in its commission. A citizen is entitled to know, in the clearest terms, when such a singular form of criminal liability . . . may be incurred. The language of clause 2 does not of itself alert the reader to this possibility. If clause 2 were to be enacted in its present form, doubt will arise about its compliance with Article 7 of the ECHR.[63]

There is a substantial element of hyperbole about this passage, because the common law already imposes liability in all or almost all of the circumstances mentioned, and (as Sullivan is aware) clause 2 is intended largely to replicate key elements of the present law. So, if thus interpreted, clause 2 will not impose liability in a way or

---

[58] Excluding joint ventures where an offence that was not the agreed offence is committed.
[59] Sullivan (2008), at 25. See my comments on this view at n 28 above.
[60] Simester and Sullivan *et al* (2010), at 47 (authors' emphasis).
[61] Text following n 27 above.
[62] Emmerson and Ashworth (2001), at paras 10–23.
[63] Sullivan (2008), at 21.

in circumstances that are in any real sense 'singular' in form, however much Sullivan may dislike that result as a matter of principle.

The European Court has indicated that the criminal law will not fall foul of the Convention if 'the individual can know from the wording of the relevant provision and, if need be, with the assistance of the courts interpretation of it, what acts and omissions will make him liable'.[64] I believe that clause 2[65] more than adequately meets this test. Further, Simester and Sullivan cite an important passage from *SW v UK*[66] that (I suggest) removes the element of doubt over whether clause 2 complies with Article 7:

[I]n the United Kingdom, as in the other Convention States, the progressive development of the criminal law through judicial lawmaking is a well-entrenched and necessary part of legal tradition. Article 7 of the Convention cannot be read as outlawing the gradual clarification of the rules of criminal liability through judicial interpretation from case to case, provided that the resulting development is consistent with the essence of the offence and could reasonably have been foreseen.[67]

So far as the first of these two important qualifications at the end of this passage is concerned, it has already been held that the basic doctrines of complicity in English law are consistent with the 'essence of the offence', in the sense of providing sufficient detail such that the accused knows the case against him or her when accused of committing a crime through secondary participation.[68] So far as the second qualification is concerned, as I have already said, the intention underlying clause 2 is substantially to replicate the key elements of the current law, as explained in the Commission's report. Accordingly, to use Lord Bingham's words,[69] '[a] legal adviser asked to give his opinion in advance' on the scope of clause 2 would be able to do so.

I hope that I can be forgiven for having taken the opportunity to defend the adoption of the first approach to drafting described above,[70] the approach prioritizing clarity and simplicity. What, though, of the discarded second approach to drafting, prioritizing comprehensiveness and attention to detail? I will not repeat the arguments for rejecting it. I hope that it will be kept in mind that even very experienced judges and barristers at the higher reaches of the profession who were consulted rejected the discarded Bill, taken as a whole, as beyond redemption in its complexity. Even so, as indicated at the start, the Commission drafted one particular clause, later discarded, that would have added detail to clause 2[71] by directly addressing the question of when D should be found guilty of murder, when V was killed by P in the course of a joint criminal venture undertaken by D and P. I will now consider this clause in detail.

---

[64] *Kokkinakis v Greece* (1993) 17 EHRR 397, at 423.
[65] Text following n 27 above.   [66] (1995) 21 EHRR 363.
[67] *Ibid*, at 398.
[68] *Mercer* [2001] EWCA Crim 638.
[69] *Rimmington; Goldstein* [2005] UKHL 63, at para 36.
[70] See text at n 37 above.   [71] Text following n 27 above.

V. Murder and Joint Ventures: The Provisions of the 'Discarded' Bill

Parliamentary Counsel began work on the Commission's discarded Bill before the Commission embarked on its project on the law of homicide.[72] Accordingly, the instructions to Counsel were drafted on the premise that a reformed law of complicity would operate within the context of an unreformed law of homicide. The relevant clause, clause 15, thus remains of particular significance, given that the Government has (for the time being) decided not to take forward the Commission's recommendations for a division of the crime of murder into first and second degree murder.[73] Clause 15 provided:

> (1) If P commits an offence of murder, D is not guilty as a result of clauses 2 and 3 of that offence if—
>   (a) P's criminal act is not what D anticipated,
>   (b) there was no real possibility that the victim would have died had P done what D anticipated,
>   (c) D did not believe that there was any possibility that someone would die (if a person were to do what D anticipated), and
>   (d) the fact that death (rather than a less serious injury) occurred is not attributable to any accidental behaviour of P's or to any feature of P's criminal act of which P was unaware.

Clause 15 would have replaced the common law rule that D's liability for the murder by P cannot result from an act that was 'fundamentally different' from the act D anticipated.[74] In that regard, clause 15 imposes stringent conditions for escaping liability for another's murder, all of which would have to have been satisfied in any individual case. What clause 15(1)(a) requires in practice is that P's criminal act involved unlawful killing, and that D did not anticipate that P would do such an act.[75] However, even if D did not anticipate that P would kill V, both clause 15(1)(b) and 15(1)(c) must also be satisfied. What this means is that (15(1)(b)) the act D anticipated on P's part must have been essentially non-lethal in character, such as punching, and (15(1)(c)) D must have believed it to be essentially non-lethal in character. Finally, clause 15(1)(d) deals with cases in which, although D can satisfy clauses 15(1)(a) to 15(1)(c), the reason they are

---

[72] Law Commission (2006).

[73] Under the Commission's recommendations, second degree murder would have included cases in which P killed intending to do serious injury (even though P did not intend to kill). Accordingly, in at least some such cases when they occurred in a joint venture context, if D foresaw that P might act with the intention to do serious injury D could be convicted of second degree murder. Under the Commission's recommendations, the sentence for second degree murder was to be a matter for the judge. So, in such cases, there would no longer have been a need to take the difficult decision whether to convict D of plain 'murder', with the result that he or she received a mandatory life sentence.

[74] *Rahman* [2008] UKHL 45.

[75] See the discussion in the text following n 12 above.

satisfied is that V's death was attributable merely to an unforeseen or accidental feature of P's action. An example would be where D anticipates that P will stab V in a non-lethal attack, but neither of them realizes that there is a lethal fungus on P's knife and it is the fungus that proves fatal to V.

Taken together, these conditions were intended to put severe constraints on the ability of D to claim that a murder by P was not within the scope of the joint venture. However, they were meant at least to embrace the possibility that, albeit rarely, it could be right to acquit D of murder even when he or she realized that P might commit murder (in the form of killing through action intended to do serious harm) in the course of a joint venture. A key issue is thus whether, such is the importance of getting both a right and a stable solution in such cases, it is worth complicating what is currently the simplicity of the Law Commission's recommended 'joint venture' clauses by adding clause 15 to them.

VI. The Problem of Distinguishing the General from the Particular

I will resist the temptation to offer an opinion on whether the discarded Bill might, especially in the homicide context, have proved to be a better solution than that offered at common law in *Rahman*,[76] or by the Government in the abandoned provisions of its recent Consultation Paper.[77] The Law Commission's criminal law advisory group rejected the Bill as over-complex, and at that point it came to the end of its useful life.[78] However, in the context of this article, it is perhaps more important to conclude with some brief observations about the function of codification.

Spencer has recently complained about the complexity of modern legislation, which he ascribes amongst other things to a desire to 'micro-manage the criminal justice system by means of over-detailed and prescriptive legislation'.[79] He suggests that an end could be put to this by confining primary legislation to 'rules at a high level of generality', whilst 'matters of detail usually can and should be left to the judges to sort out, by case-law . . . '.[80] This would seem to be, of course, exactly the approach taken by the Law Commission—and so roundly criticized by Sullivan[81]—to the scope of criminal liability in the course of a joint venture, through clause 2.[82] Even so, one of the difficulties with Spencer's otherwise sensible-sounding suggestion is the difficulty in practice of knowing when rules 'at a high level of generality' (for Parliament) end, and 'matters of detail' (for judicial law-making) begin. For example, is the question whether a special

[76] [2008] UKHL 45.   [77] Ministry of Justice (2008).
[78] See text at n 42 above. It must be kept in mind that the Commission has already conducted a formal consultation exercise on this area of the law: see Law Commission (1993). There would have been scant justification for a further Consultation Paper going over the same ground with consultees.
[79] Spencer (2008a), at 594.   [80] *Ibid*, at 600.
[81] Sullivan (2008).   [82] See text following n 27 above.

complicity rule should be adopted in murder cases, where D anticipated the infliction of serious harm but P intended to cause death, a rule 'at a high level of generality', appropriate for parliamentary definition? Or, is it one of the 'matters of detail' that can safely be left to the courts? I can think of no easy way of deciding, and there may be no right answer. Moreover, deciding that an issue is a 'matter of detail' does not in truth resolve the question of whether it is more important for Parliament, or for the courts, to address it. The discarded Bill treats murder in the course of a joint venture as a matter to be addressed by Parliament, whereas the Law Commission's draft Bill (and the Government's abandoned draft Bill) treat it as a matter to be addressed by the courts. Opinions may legitimately differ on which approach is right, and it is unrealistic to suppose that even the Law Commission will or should always favour one approach over the other.[83]

Bentham, at least, was clear that the attempt to distinguish the two realms (of generality, and of detail) would not only be pointless, but would guarantee the continued subjection of the nation, on crucial issues, to the inescapably haphazard, often unstable, non-consultative and democratically unaccountable species of law-making known as 'common law development'.[84] Notwithstanding the almost immeasurably higher quality of judges developing the criminal law now, as compared with Bentham's day, nowhere are the defects of continuing to permit common law development (other than where absolutely necessary) more evident than in the law currently governing the 'matters of detail' bearing on joint ventures in the course of which murder is committed.

VII. A Viable Alternative?

Sullivan is not simply a critic of the Law Commission's recommendations, but has his own powerfully presented alternative.[85]

1. Sullivan's account of complicity

To begin with, on his view, the conditions under which D may be liable for a murder committed by P depend on whether the form of participation engaged in by D is, 'tantamount in terms of culpability to directly and intentionally carrying out the killing itself'.[86] He believes that only in three sets of conditions (alternatives to each other) will that requirement be satisfied:

1. When D both intends V's death at P's hands, and does something necessary for P to murder V.

2. When D, intending V's death at P's hands, agrees with P that P should kill V.

---

[83] Perhaps the Government's now abandoned cl 3 dealing with issue is the 'Goldilocks' clause ('just right') for which we have all been searching (see text at n 7 above). That issue is likely to remain unaddressed in the immediate future.

[84] See text at n 38 above.   [85] See Sullivan (2007).   [86] *Ibid*, at 287.

3. When D encourages or assists P to murder V, intending to encourage or assist P in that regard (and the encouragement has some impact on P in respect of his murderous actions).[87]

It might forcefully be said that very much in favour of this scheme is the fact that it makes proof of intention—the intention that V be killed, or that P be encouraged or assisted to kill V—a normative condition of secondary liability. The effect of that is to restrict the scope of D's complicity in a clear and morally unambiguous way, a restriction of a kind that is in principle always welcome in law, perhaps most of all in criminal trials before juries. So, what is to be said against this scheme, as a law reform proposal? I will draw attention only to two points.

2. Sullivan's account: too many cases excluded?

First, I believe Sullivan's scheme carries an inherent risk of systematically producing what other legal systems[88] regard as unjustified acquittals. For example, in set of conditions 2, Sullivan stipulates that D must not only agree that V should be murdered by P, but should also intend that V be murdered by P. So, consider this example:

D agrees to take part in P's plan to rob V of valuable drugs, and to murder V if V does not reveal the drugs' location. However, D does not reveal to P that he (D) has no view one way or another on whether V should be killed. This is because D's secret intention is to run off with the drugs as soon as D and P have found them. When D and P meet V, and V hands some drugs over, D runs off with the drugs. P still goes on to kill V because V will not reveal whether D now has V's entire store of drugs.

On these facts, D cannot be implicated in the murder through the application of set of conditions 1 or 2, because D never intended V to be killed, even though D agrees with P that V shall be killed.[89] Further, it is unclear that D can be implicated through application of set of conditions 3, because it seems equally unlikely on these facts that D intended to encourage or to assist P to murder V. Especially given that it was P's plan to kill V to obtain the drugs in the first place, it cannot be assumed that D's agreement with the plan in and of itself involved an intention to assist or to encourage P to murder V. Yet, some might say—the Law Commission certainly did[90]—that by agreeing to a criminal enterprise in which V was to be murdered by P in certain circumstances, D has already done enough to implicate

---

[87] I have distilled the three instances from Sullivan's discussion of the issues: Sullivan (2007), at 287.

[88] See text at nn 95 to 97 below.

[89] I trust that it needs no substantive argument that, because an agreement has an objective existence, it can be reached through conformity with the relevant social practice, even if one or more people do not intend it to be carried out. An agreement that someone intends to renege on is still an agreement. Nonetheless, this point leaves logical and moral space for the view that if two or more people agree to do something illegal, but *none of them* actually intends to carry it out, none should be found liable in respect of that agreement in itself: see Smith and Hogan (2008), at 414.

[90] Law Commission (2007).

himself in the murder if it took place. No doubt there is plenty of room for argument, but it seems to me highly plausible to maintain that D's kind and degree of fault—a callous indifference to whether the agreement to kill V ends in V's murder by P—is such that it is, in Sullivan's words, 'tantamount in terms of culpability to directly and intentionally carrying out the killing itself'.[91]

What is more, under Sullivan's scheme, the prosecution will have what seems to me to be an unjustifiably hard time showing beyond reasonable doubt that D, in agreeing that P should murder C if need be, was not merely indifferent to whether P went ahead as agreed, but intended P to do so. Given that the prosecution must (*ex hypothesi*) show that there was an agreement between D and P that P would commit the crime, why should it have to go further and show beyond reasonable doubt precisely what D's state of mind was—as between intention or (mere) indifference—in relation to P's fulfilment of the proven agreement? That will commonly be a matter of pure speculation, when what must be shown is that the intention in question (that the agreement be fulfilled) related not to D's own conduct but to someone else's: P's. Indeed, in *Rahman*, Lord Brown went so far as to say that the need to prove intention in these circumstances would be 'absurd':

At what point is it suggested that the actual killer's intention is to be determined? He may have embarked on the venture intending at most to cause gbh but later, in the heat of the moment, for any one or more of a host of possible reasons, changed his mind and decided to kill or perhaps merely become reckless as to whether he killed or not. It is absurd that the criminal liability of secondary parties should depend upon such niceties as these.[92]

Sullivan maintains that, in the example given at the beginning of this paragraph, that:

it [would be] unjust to find him [D] liable for first degree murder... if one is committed to a parity of culpability between the principal offender to first degree murder and any accomplice to that offence.[93]

His opinion is, of course, perfectly defensible, but it is curious that he does mention that the contrary view—cited by the Law Commission in its report[94]—is maintained not only in English law, but in Australian and New Zealand law as well. In *Rapira*,[95] the New Zealand Court of Appeal held that D will be guilty of a crime committed by P if D foresees that P, in carrying out an unlawful plan, may commit a crime of the type in question (in that case, murder). The High Court of Australia has consistently taken a very similar line.[96] I believe that the fact that these humane and sophisticated systems of criminal law take broadly the same approach significantly undermines the moral case for saying that, in my example, D is treated unduly harshly at common law, or under the Law Commission's recommendations.

---

[91] Sullivan (2007), at 287.   [92] *Rahman* [2008] UKHL 45, at 70.
[93] Sullivan (2007), at 286.
[94] Law Commission (2007), at paras 3.148–3.150.   [95] [2003] 3 NZLR 794.
[96] *Darkan* [2006] HCA 34; *Clayton v The Queen* [2006] HCA 58. To similar effect, see *Te Moni* [1998] 1 NZLR 641.

I believe that the case in favour of Sullivan's account is given disproportionate weight by, amongst other factors, an assumption that the crime foreseen by D as a possible incident of the joint venture is (much) worse than the crime to which D meant to be a party: the subject of the joint criminal venture. Reform of the law of complicity should involve making no such assumption. Consider, for example, a case in which the collateral offence is criminal damage of some kind, and the agreed offence is murder, rather than the other way around:

In the carrying out of a joint venture with P to commit murder, D foresees that P may start a fire to burn down V's house thus destroying evidence of the murder. D does not want P to do this because of the risk that D will himself be hurt, but D nonetheless carries through the joint venture, and P does set the house on fire during the commission of the murder.

Sullivan is perfectly entitled to take the view that, in such a case, D should not be convicted of arson, even if D may be convicted of murder. However, I maintain that it is perfectly fair to convict D of arson in these circumstances, because D took part in a criminal enterprise with P, realizing that the very crime in fact committed by P (arson) might be committed in the course of that enterprise. My view does not—and the law's view should not—change if matters happen to be reversed and it is arson that is the subject of the joint venture, and murder the crime foreseen as a possible incident of that joint venture.

3. Sullivan's account: the reliance on 'constructive' liability

There is a more theoretical question whether Robert Sullivan finds himself having to rely, for the plausibility of his scheme to be maintained, on a 'constructive' basis for liability whose presence in the Law Commission's recommendations he so strongly criticizes.[97]

Sullivan draws on a superseded Law Commission Consultation Paper on homicide[98] to suggest that, in the Commission's view, 'foresight that P might commit a crime is to encourage or assist P to commit the crime',[99] a proposition he criticizes as a fallacy. That presentation of the Commission's work on complicity in murder does no justice to the Commission's actual viewpoint. The Commission has expressly repudiated the 'fallacy' as an element in its justification for D's liability in the circumstances under discussion.[100] The Commission's viewpoint can be explained as follows, using the well-known distinction between normative and

---

[97] An element in liability is 'constructive' if it involves, for example, an irrebuttable presumption of some kind of wrongdoing or of a fault element, if particular facts are proved, rather than requiring proof that actual wrongdoing took place or that actual fault was possessed. A milder—less objectionable—form of constructive liability may be found when proof of guilt of (lesser) crime A suffices—possibly, only if certain further conditions are also met—to establish proof of guilt of (greater) crime B, irrespective of whether crime A is itself a crime of comparable gravity to crime B. This is a rough and incomplete sketch, deserving of greater attention that cannot be given to it here.

[98] Law Commission (2005), superseded by Law Commission (2006).

[99] Sullivan (2007), at 286.

[100] See Law Commission (2007), at paras 3.54–3.57.

ascriptive rules.[101] Normatively, in this context, what connects D to crimes committed by P is the occurrence of those crimes as an execution of, or in connection with, the perpetration of the joint criminal venture to which D was a party.[102] Ascriptively, what makes it fair to blame D as well as P for the commission of those crimes, is the fact that D foresaw that they might be committed by P in the relevant normative context (even then, D may in some circumstances still escape liability[103]). In such circumstances D may not, morally or legally, dis-associate him or herself from P's crimes. Controversial though it may be, this view involves no reliance on the fallacy to which Sullivan alludes.[104] What the Commission's scheme does do is incorporate a 'constructive' element into its normative foundations. The normative building-block is the proposition that one reason to avoid participation in a joint criminal venture is that the execution of that joint venture may give rise to other—perhaps worse—forms of criminality. Other than in exceptional cases,[105] D will not be permitted to say that, when participating in a particular joint venture (say, burglary) there was in the particular circumstances no reason to avoid its commission because of a possibility that another crime (say, arson or murder) might be committed. The law simply presumes that there was such a reason, and it does so with good cause. In relation to collaborators in crime, research has shown that gang members commit five times more crime than non-gang members, and that they are far more likely (due to peer pressure, amongst other factors) to carry guns and knives.[106] That gives empirical backing to Lord Steyn's justification for the current law: 'experience has shown that joint criminal [ventures] only too readily escalate into the commission of greater offences'.[107] Indeed, other research has confirmed that collaborators in crime tend to 'psych each other up,' with the result that:

[A] study of active burglars...found that people in groups are more likely to be aroused, raising the possibility that group crimes lead to unplanned violence.[108]

In that regard, the 'constructive' element to this normative building-block comes through reliance on the existence of a joint 'criminal' venture with P as the normative foundation for D's liability, irrespective of the nature of the criminality

---

[101] See Raz (1990), at 11–12.

[102] The normative rule could perhaps be expressed, in rough-and-ready way, as, 'do not join in a criminal venture that may give rise to the commission by the participants of crimes connected to the venture'. For a defence of the Commission's broad approach in this regard, see Simester (2006).

[103] Law Commission (2007), at paras 3.153–3.162.

[104] The way in which Sullivan presents the fallacy is also puzzling, because the fallacy could (surely?) only begin to look plausible in cases where P *knew* that D realized what P might do in the course of the joint criminal venture, and gained succour from that knowledge; but there has never been any requirement of such knowledge in the rules of complicity, and the Commission has never recommended that there should be one.

[105] Where P is wholly on a frolic of his or her own: Law Commission (2007), at paras 3.153–3.162.

[106] Marshall, Webb, and Tilley (2005).

[107] *Powell & Daniels; English* [1999] 1 AC 1.

[108] Cromwell (1991), at 586. See further Simester (2006), at 599; Katyal (2003), at 116 and 117: 'where the responsibility for a single crime is spread over many persons...diffusion can...remove internal constraints to crime'.

involved. If D foresees that the joint criminal venture may end in murder arising out of the venture (and it does), whether the criminal nature of the joint venture was burglary, robbery, rape, or the infliction of serious harm, for example, will not influence D's liability for the murder.[109] Bearing in mind the conclusions of the empirical research just mentioned (in particular, the unplanned way in which collaborative criminal activity may escalate), it would inevitably involve arbitrariness to seek to distinguish in law between kinds of joint criminal venture, for the purposes of determining the normative basis of complicity in murder or in any other crime.

Whatever one's view about that, admittedly controversial, claim, Sullivan is not in a good position to criticize such a way of building normative foundations for liability, because he employs a form of constructive liability in his own account. In set of conditions 2, where D has agreed with P that V will be murdered, and P commits the murder, Sullivan justifies D's conviction for murder with the following claim:

> P's killing of V is something done on behalf of both of them. The fact of agreement of itself suffices to implicate the parties.[110]

This seems to me to be simply an irrebuttable presumption or constructive element in the normative basis for convicting D. It is, after all, perfectly possible for D and P to agree to kill V, but for P to perpetrate the killing in circumstances expressly disavowed by D, with the result that the killing would not, in context, seem to be done 'on behalf of both of them'. Here is an example:

> D expressly tells P not to use a gun to perpetrate a killing they have agreed to commit, because of the greatly increased penalties that will imposed should they be convicted of murder with a firearm.[111] However, excited by the prospect of using a gun when they encounter V, P uses a gun he has concealed from D to murder V.

In such circumstances, English law justifies convicting D of the murder committed by P, because V's death is what D agreed with P to bring about.[112] If one adds a gloss that, when P kills V, it must be done 'on behalf of both' D and P (and one really means that), one risks a jury acquitting in such cases. Suppose D agrees with P that P will kill D's wife, but not on the day of atonement. P knowingly kills V on that day. Is that killing done 'on behalf of both of them'? In English law, D would

---

[109] See Sullivan (2007), at 286. In Sullivan's view, the law's insistence on there being a joint *criminal* venture is, in this respect, arbitrary. Surely, he says, a lawful venture such as an agreed 'pub crawl' might equally be foreseen as likely to give rise to (say) violence used by one of the pub crawlers in the group? True, but not a reason to abandon the law's focus on joint *criminal* venture. Valuing civil liberties means valuing them even when—as in the case of pub crawls or demonstrations—some participants may be led into unplanned criminal activity. That issue is by-passed when the joint activity in question is (I assume, justifiably) criminal in nature already, because there is no civil liberty to commit theft, burglary, robbery, and so on.

[110] *Ibid*, at 278. He relies on an old dictum to the effect that, 'if several persons act together in pursuance of a common intent, every act done in furtherance of such intent by each of them is, in law, done by all': per Alderson B, in *Macklin* (1838) 2 Lew CC 225.

[111] Criminal Justice Act 2003, s 269, sch 21.

[112] See *Rahman* [2008] UKHL 45, at 33 (per Lord Rodger).

be liable for the murder, because a conditional intent is nonetheless an intent, and a conditional agreement nonetheless an agreement.[113] I doubt that Sullivan would disagree. However, only by reliance on a constructive form of liability, only by stripping the 'on the behalf of both' criterion of real ascriptive or normative significance, can such cases be regarded as ones where P necessarily acts 'on behalf of both' D and P in killing V.

VIII. Concluding Remarks

Research into public opinion on the scope of joint criminal venture has shown some surprise and dissatisfaction on the part of members of the public with the wide scope of the current law.[114] Consistent with the approach taken in Chapter 1 to the importance of public opinion on such matters, were such an attitude to be replicated in a more detailed and deeper investigation into the principles of joint enterprise as a whole, I would have to agree that a scheme such as Sullivan's may be better able to reflect public opinion and should be preferred for that reason. Even so, a deeper investigation would be needed, so that participants could be made aware how important the current law is in, for example, the international context. In *Tadic*,[115] D, a Bosnian Serb, was charged under the Statute of the International Criminal Tribunal for the former Yugoslavia with 34 crimes, amongst which was an allegation that he was complicit in the murder of five men in a village called Jaskici. He was an armed member of a group, some of members of which entered the village and killed the victims, as part of a joint criminal venture—ethnic cleansing—to drive the non-Serb population out of the area by inhumane acts. There was no proof that D had himself killed any of the five men. The Tribunal concluded that D could be found guilty of the murders, on the following basis:

> While murder may not have been explicitly acknowledged to be part of the common design, it was nevertheless foreseeable that the forcible removal of civilians at gunpoint might well result in the deaths of one or more of those civilians. Criminal responsibility may be imputed to all participants within the common enterprise where the risk of death occurring was both a predictable consequence of the execution of the common design and the accused was either reckless or indifferent to that risk.[116]

If these elements were found as a matter of fact, I have no hesitation in agreeing with the Tribunal, and with Court of Appeal which analysed the Tribunal's opinion,[117] that Tadic was both a war criminal and a murderer. Whilst not identical to the Law Commission's recommendations, the Tribunal's understanding of

---

[113] See *Saik* [2006] 1 AC 18, at para 5 (per Lord Nicholls).
[114] See Mitchell and Roberts (2011); Mitchell and Roberts (2012).
[115] 15 July 1999.
[116] Cited by Toulson LJ in *R (JS) v Secretary of State for the Home Department* [2009] EWCA Civ 364, at para 41.
[117] *R (JS) v Secretary of State for the Home Department* [2009] EWCA Civ 364.

complicity is far closer to those recommendations than it is to Sullivan's account of complicity. The Tribunal's understanding is also very close to the current law of complicity in England and Wales, Australia, New Zealand, and doubtless in many other countries too. If Sullivan's account of complicity precluded Tadic's conviction for murder, on the principles set out by the Tribunal above, then so much the worse, I fear, for his account.

7

Transferred Malice and the Remoteness of Outcomes from Intentions

I. The 'Impersonality' and the 'Prohibited Outcome' Doctrines

For several hundred years, the doctrine of 'transferred malice' was taken to apply when the actual, unintended victim was killed in the *same way* that the intended victim was meant to be killed. In such cases, the intention to kill (in that way) aimed at the intended victim is simply transferred to the actual victim(s). I will call this the 'impersonality' doctrine. The doctrine stands for the view that the identity of the victim is irrelevant, when a victim has been killed as D intended. An old example is *Agnes Gore's Case*.[1] D put poison in a drink that was meant for her husband, but the poison killed another man. The judges found her guilty of murder because 'the law conjoins the murderous intention of Agnes [D] in putting the poison into the electuary to kill her husband, with the event which thence ensued'. The ruling continued:

When one prepares poison with felonious intent to kill any reasonable creature, whatsoever reasonable creature is *thereby* killed, he who has the ill and felonious intent shall be punished for it, for he is as great an offender, as if his intent against the other person had taken effect.[2]

The law is explained in similar terms by Sir Matthew Hale later in the seventeenth century. He says:

If A by malice aforethought strikes at B and missing him strikes C *whereof* he dies, though he never bore any malice to C yet it is murder, and the law transfers the malice to the party slain.[3]

However, in later years, in explaining transferred malice, writers abandoned the assumed requirement that the actual victim had to die in the same way that the intended victim was meant to die. The change is foreshadowed in the Fourth Report of the Criminal Law Commissioners in 1839, where it is said that if D aimed to kill V1 and killed V2 instead:

---

[1] (1611) 9 Co Rep 81.   [2] *Ibid* (my emphasis).
[3] 1 *Pleas of the Crown*, at 465 (my emphasis). The same way of explaining the doctrine is to be found in the work of writers a century later. For Sir William Blackstone, for example: '[I]f one shoots at A and misses him, but kills B, this is murder; because of the previous felonious intent, which the law transfers from one to the other. The same is the case, where one lays poison for A; and B against whom the prisoner had no malicious intent, takes it, and it kills him; this is likewise murder' (Blackstone (1765–69), vol 4, ch 14). A similar view is expressed by Hawkins (1824), at 126, and by East (1803) at 230.

[h]e intended to kill and did kill; whether, therefore, the crime can be estimated by the intention or the result, its magnitude cannot be affected by the consideration that the mischief did not light where it was intended.[4]

By implication, at least, this analysis makes crucial to a murder conviction the mere proof of a causal link between the act D intended to be the killing act, and the killing, irrespective not only of who is killed, but also irrespective of exactly how. Of great importance, in developing this approach, was the influence of Sir James Stephen's work on the systematization of the law of homicide, for the purposes of his draft Code.[5] He explained transferred malice in this way:

Culpable homicide is murder... if the offender means to cause death... to one person, so that if that person be killed the offender would be guilty of murder, and *by accident or mistake* the offender kills another person, though he does not mean to hurt the person killed.[6]

This explanation has found expression in section 229 of the Canadian Criminal Code:

Culpable homicide is murder... where a person, meaning to cause death to a human being... by accident or mistake causes death to another human being, notwithstanding that he does not mean to cause death... to that human being....

The explicit reference to the possibility that the killing may take place 'by accident or mistake' makes it clear that *how* D causes the actual V's death is of no legal importance (if it ever really was). So long as D acts with the fault element of murder, and kills in consequence, they may be convicted of murder (other things being equal). As Stephen says of murder, 'There must be an act causing death; an intention accompanying the act, and death resulting as a fact.'[7] The justification for convicting of murder in such cases is the assumed moral insignificance of the way someone is killed, as well as of the identity of the person killed (the latter being the central issue, according to the impersonality doctrine), when death has been intentionally caused. In that regard, the transferred malice doctrine is really better understood as an application of what I will call the 'prohibited outcome' doctrine. So long as the prohibited outcome is caused (intentional killing), it matters not how.

II. Transferred Malice and the 'Remoteness' Principle

There has been an understandable difference of opinion amongst scholars over whether a murder conviction is ever appropriate when D killed someone they did not attempt to kill, even though D's attempt to kill did in fact end in a killing.[8] I will assume that, at least in some instances, it can be appropriate to convict D of

---

[4] Criminal Law Commissioners (1839), at 254.   [5] Draft Code, cl 274.
[6] Stephen (1883), vol 3, at 80 (my emphasis).   [7] *Ibid*, at 84.
[8] Contrast the views of, for example, Ashworth (1978), at 77, who is against the doctrine of transferred malice, with the views of Simester and Sullivan *et al* (2010), at 164–6, who are broadly in favour of it.

murder in these circumstances. However, I will argue that the range of instances in which this is appropriate is now rightly coming to be circumscribed by what I will be calling the 'remoteness' principle. The remoteness principle may serve to prevent conviction in the following kinds of example:

Example 1. D fires a gun at V1 intending to kill V1. D misses, but the noise of the gun being fired startles a bystander, V2, who consequently dies of a heart attack.

Example 2. D shoots V1, intending to kill V1. V1 is wounded and taken to hospital. Whilst waiting for treatment, V1 is seen by his father, V2. V2 is so aghast at the sight of V1 covered in blood that the shock kills him. V1 survives.

Example 3. D shoots at V1, intending to kill. The bullet misses, but enters a munitions factory behind V1. The bullet sets off an explosion that kills a large number of people.[9]

Broadly speaking, Andrew Ashworth is right to argue that the appropriate charges, on facts such as these, are attempted murder in relation to the intended victim, and (where appropriate) manslaughter in relation to actual victim(s).[10] A conviction for murder—a crime of specific intent—would often fail to label D's crime in a 'morally representative' way in any of these kinds of instances.[11] Sensible use of prosecutorial discretion is, though, probably the best way to ensure that this unrepresentative labelling is avoided, rather than creating a legal barrier to conviction for murder. In part, this is because one should not, in fact, completely bar murder convictions in such cases.

For Glanville Williams, a murder conviction in relation to the actual victim would be appropriate as long as 'the consequence was brought about by negligence in relation to the actual victim'.[12] I share Williams' instinct that a murder conviction should not be completely ruled out in such cases. Williams purports to give legal effect to this instinct through the inclusion of a specific further fault element of negligence in relation to the actual death, alongside the intention to kill. However, I believe that this—the presence or absence of negligence—does not adequately conceptualize the basis for determining whether a murder conviction is or is not appropriate in the three examples. What should matter in these examples is not only that the actual victims were unintended victims, but also that they died in an unanticipated way. This double element of deviation from D's plan is what, in principle, may make the deaths too *remote* from what D intended for murder to be a representative label. This idea of 'remoteness' provides a better way of understanding when a murder conviction would or would not be justified, in terms of representative labelling. In developing this point, it is necessary to analyse the decision of the House of Lords in *Attorney-General's Reference (No 3 of 1994)*.[13]

The case was concerned with the problems that arise when the 'person' to whom it is sought to transfer a murderous intent was, at the time of the relevant act, not someone who can be the victim of murder or manslaughter. A person cannot be the

---

[9] See further, the examples given by Stephen (1883), vol 3, at 15–16.
[10] Ashworth (1978).
[11] For an explanation of fair or representative labelling in criminal law, see Ashworth (1981).
[12] Williams (1961), at 132.   [13] [1998] 1 Cr App R 91.

victim of murder or manslaughter if they have not been 'born alive'. The first victim, M, was, to the offender's knowledge, 22–24 weeks pregnant with the offender's child. The offender, B, quarrelled with M, and stabbed her in the face, back, and abdomen with a long-bladed kitchen knife. M received hospital treatment, and was later discharged, still pregnant. Seventeen days later, M went into premature labour, and her baby, S, the second victim, was born alive. S lived for 121 days before dying of broncho-pulmonary dysplasia, caused by the effects of premature birth. S had a knife wound needing surgical repair, stemming from B's attack on M, but no connection could be made between S's death and the wound. The Crown's case against B was that the wounding of M, done with at least the intent to do grievous bodily harm, had set in motion a train of events that left S as a barely viable foetus, thus causing her premature death, once born alive. The Crown relied, in other words, on Sir James Stephen's simple test: was the death of a person born alive ultimately caused as a result of an act intended to kill or to do grievous harm (albeit that the person killed was not the intended victim, and was killed by accident or mistake)?

The judge ruled that B had no case to answer in respect of S, so far as murder and manslaughter were concerned. He said that at the time of B's act, S was not a live person, and that the cause of death was the wounding of the mother rather than of S. The judge ruled out the operation of the doctrine of transferred malice in relation to the murder charge, because an intention to cause serious injury to a person in being could not be transferred to someone, a foetus, who was not at that moment in being and thus not capable of being the victim of murder. So far as manslaughter was concerned, the judge ruled that the Crown's case must fail for similar reasons: the victim had to be a person born alive, at the time of B's unlawful and dangerous action. On appeal from a reference by the Attorney-General, the House of Lords agreed that B could not be found guilty of the murder of S. The House found, instead, that B could have been convicted of the manslaughter of S. So far as manslaughter is concerned, their Lordships' reasoning is straightforward and convincing. Their Lordships' reasoning where the murder charge was concerned is perhaps less convincing. The result *may* well have been correct—namely that B was not guilty of murder—but this should not have been regarded as inevitable, as a matter of law. The question should have been one for the jury: was what happened too remote from what B intended to happen (notwithstanding that the result was undoubtedly caused by B) to make a murder conviction a representative label? In that regard, the fact that B knew very well that M was pregnant could have been regarded as a crucial factor rendering S's death by no means too remote from what B intended to make a murder conviction appropriate.

So far as manslaughter was concerned, as an appropriate charge in this case, the issue of transferred malice did not arise. B intentionally committed an unlawful and dangerous act against his *intended* victim, M. No further fault is required for manslaughter, should death result from acting on such an intention. So, the fact that S died rather than M is quite irrelevant to B's liability, so long as B can objectively be shown to have caused S's death when S was a person in being. As Lord Mustill put it:

In a case such as the present, therefore, responsibility for manslaughter would automatically be established, once causation has been shown, simply by proving a violent attack even if (which cannot have been the case here) the attacker had no idea that the woman was pregnant.[14]

So far as murder was concerned, albeit with some reluctance, Lord Mustill was willing to uphold the doctrine of transferred malice. He said of the doctrine:

like many of its kind [it] is useful enough to yield rough justice, in particular cases, and it can sensibly be retained notwithstanding its lack of any sound intellectual basis. But it is another matter to build a new rule upon it.[15]

Giving the other main speech, Lord Hope concurred in this view. Lord Clyde, Lord Slynn, and Lord Goff agreed with the speeches of Lords Mustill and Hope. So, the House of Lords supported the view that the doctrine of transferred malice should continue to apply in the kinds of simple cases commonly used for centuries to illustrate its nature and scope, but that it should be extended no further. So, is the House of Lords excluding from the scope of the doctrine cases such as Examples 1–3 above? To answer this question, we need to conduct further analysis of the reasoning of Lords Mustill and Hope.

On the facts of the case in question, Lords Mustill and Hope explained their refusal to countenance a murder conviction in terms of their dislike for what they considered to be the need, to justify the conviction, for a 'double' transfer of malice. They thought that malice would have to be transferred first from the mother to the foetus, and then, secondly, from the foetus to the child.[16] Such a degree of artificiality to the mental element in murder they would not tolerate. The dislike of artificiality is to be commended, but it is hard to accept that this kind of artificiality, a 'double transfer' of malice, really occurs on the facts of this case. Quite simply, malice cannot be transferred from the mother to the foetus, because (as the House of Lords was at pains to point out) an unborn foetus cannot be the victim of murder. That being so, an intent against a mother that is in law murderous, can no more be changed into such an intent against her unborn baby, than English pounds can be changed into Spanish doubloons. The only possible transfer of malice is the transfer from the mother to the baby subsequently born alive; and that is a single transfer of malice, from one person who can be the victim of murder to another such person.

---

[14] *Ibid*, at 108. Similarly, the remoteness issue does not arise in a pure form when the charge is manslaughter by recklessness or gross negligence, where the issue is whether the death occurred through breach of a duty of care. It is only in an exceptional case, where it was such a breach that was itself intended to lead to death or serious harm, that a conviction for murder turns on this issue. It is one thing to say that a death was too remote from what was actually intended properly to be called an 'intentional killing', and hence murder. It is a rather different thing to say that a death was too far from the reach of a duty to take care not to cause death, to be something D should have guarded against. These are, in effect, the answers to two very different questions.

[15] [1998] 1 Cr App R 91, at 105. He is discussing *Latimer* (1886) 17 QBD 358.

[16] [1998] 1 Cr App R 91, at 106 (Lord Mustill), and at 113–14 (Lord Hope). For criticism, see Gough (1999).

However, Lord Mustill gives a more convincing argument against transferring intent in this case. Lord Mustill goes on to say:

The cases are treated as if the actual victim had been the intended victim from the start. To make any sense of this process there must, as it seems to me, be *some compatibility* between the original intention and the actual occurrence, and this is, indeed, what one finds in the cases. There is no such compatibility here. The defendant intended to commit and did commit an immediate crime of violence to the mother. He committed no relevant violence to the foetus . . . and intended no harm to the foetus or to the human person which it would become. . . . I would not overstrain the idea of transferred malice by trying to make it fit the present case.[17]

In this important passage, in seeking to ensure that there is 'some compatibility' between the original intention and the actual occurrence, Lord Mustill is rightly seeking to confine the scope of the doctrine other than by simply ruling out so-called double transfers of malice. In my terms, 'compatibility' can be maintained by asking the jury to consider whether the way in which the death of an unantici-pated victim resulted was too remote from the death that the defendant intended or anticipated, for a conviction for murder (a crime of specific intent) to constitute a representative label.[18]

Rather than being a factor that is always in issue in murder cases, the remoteness principle comes into play only when (a) the victim was not the intended victim, and (b) the victim was not killed in the way intended. These two conditions were met in *Attorney-General's Reference (No 3 of 1994)*. Although they are necessary conditions, they should not be treated as sufficient conditions for the purposes of the remote-ness principle. Crucial in that regard is the evidence that B deliberately stabbed M in the abdomen, knowing that she was pregnant. If D is aware that something may go awry, and *a fortiori* of how it may go awry, when he or she tries to put his or her intention into effect, that awareness is highly relevant to the question of how far, morally speaking, D can distance him or herself from the unintended outcome. Morally speaking, it makes the outcome less remote from what B intended, and more compatible with it.

III. Is There Simply a Break in the Causal Chain in Examples 1–3?

Here is one attractively simple way to split the difference between, on the one hand, traditional examples of the transferred malice in operation, and on the other hand,

---

[17] [1998] 1 Cr App R 91, at 106 (my emphasis).

[18] In some respects, the language of 'incompatibility' as between the actual outcome and D's intention is better than the language I am employing, that of 'remoteness', which is language also employed in causal doctrines from which my remoteness doctrine is meant to be distinct. However, the advantage of the language of 'remoteness' is that it carries with it an implication that the issue is one of fact-and-degree. By way of contrast, an outcome would seem to be either compatible (in some respects) or incompatible (in some respects) with an intention, rather than an issue of fact-and-degree, in that regard.

Examples 1–3 above. This is to say that death is caused by D in the traditional examples, but is not caused by D in Examples 1–3. In other words, one deals with the difference between the examples by treating it as a difference in point of legal causation, rather than a difference in the extent to which intention has gone awry. This is the approach taken by Simester and Sullivan *et al.* They say:

A proviso: transferred malice is unproblematic only if causal principles are properly observed. This explains the otherwise troubling case of *Heigho* 18 Idaho 566 (1910)....In that case, D assaulted W, and an onlooker died of fright. D was convicted of the manslaughter of W. It is submitted the conviction was wrong; D was not causally responsible for the onlooker's death.[19]

I beg to differ on this point. To begin with, the English case of *Towers*[20] seems to be inconsistent with the claim. In that case, D violently assaulted a girl who was holding a young baby. The girl screamed, frightening the baby. The baby then cried until its face turned black. From then on, the baby had convulsions until dying a month later. In Denman J's view, 'if the man's act brought on the convulsions or brought them to a more dangerous extent, so that death would not have resulted otherwise, then it would be manslaughter'.[21]

If D was not causally responsible for V's fright and consequent death, in *Heigho* and in *Towers,* then who or what was? It must be kept in mind that a cause can be a substantial and operating cause, in law, without being the only or even the main cause of an outcome.[22] So, the fact that V may in each case have had some unknown physical weakness that put his life at risk when exposed to sudden shock, or the like, cannot prevent the shocking event or action itself being regarded as in law a cause of death.[23] It will be a matter for the finder of fact, in each case. Both in *Heigho* and in *Towers,* there was an intentional assault that caused a death. By way of contrast, an outcome can be causally too remote to attribute it in law to the defendant, irrespective of what he or she intended or anticipated. Suppose D deliberately knocked V out in an area of town D knew to be notorious for its violence, and left V to his fate. As D fully realized might well happen, V is subsequently intentionally killed by a robber. V's death cannot in law be attributed to D because the law regards the free, deliberate, and informed act of a third party as breaking the chain of causation.[24] Reprehensible though it is, thus, D's action is in such cases merely the historical setting in which the real cause of death, the robber's act, operated. Simester and Sullivan *et al* have suggested that in *Heigho* the chain of causation was likewise broken, albeit in this instance because the outcome was not 'reasonably foreseeable'.[25] However, this test is surely a matter for the jury to

---

[19] Simester and Sullivan *et al* (2010), at 165 fn 224.   [20] (1874) 12 Cox CC 530.

[21] *Ibid*, at 533. A broadly similar approach is taken in the law of tort: *Bourhill v Young* [1943] AC 92 (HL).

[22] For the contrast between the mere historical setting in which a new cause operates, and a cause which is still a substantial and operating cause, see *Smith* [1959] 2 QB 35.

[23] This is a very old principle: see *Mawgridge* (1707) Kel 119, at 131 (Holt CJ).

[24] *Kennedy (No 2)* [2007] UKHL 38.

[25] Simester and Sullivan *et al* (2010), at 165 fn 224. See section VI. for further discussion of this point.

decide, and once the jury found the chain of causation established in *Heigho* and *Towers*, a manslaughter verdict was the right result.

So, the remoteness of a consequence from what someone intends or anticipates need not necessarily be treated as the same idea as that of causal remoteness. In *Attorney-General's Reference (No 3 of 1994)*, it is right to assume that B caused S's death. That being so, as the House of Lords indicated, if B is to be acquitted of murder it must be through the deployment of a principle limiting the scope of the doctrine of transferred malice. The principle of 'no double transfer' of malice is not up to the task. I suggest that the remoteness doctrine works much more effectively. It is now time to set the so-called doctrine of transferred malice, and the remoteness doctrine, in a proper theoretical context.

IV. The Prohibited Outcome and Remoteness Doctrines, Transferred and Translated Intent

The transferring of malice is really the application of a doctrine in particular circumstances, rather than a doctrine in itself. I am calling the doctrine of which it is an application the prohibited outcome doctrine. The prohibited outcome doctrine is 'permissive', in that it allows liability when a particular kind of interest has been culpably invaded or destroyed, even when the victim was not the intended victim, or the interest was not invaded or destroyed in the way intended. By way of contrast with the prohibited outcome doctrine, the remoteness doctrine is a restrictive doctrine. It constrains the reach of liability that would otherwise be justified by the prohibited outcome doctrine, by factoring in consideration of how the remoteness of outcome from intention (or foresight) affects the representative character of conviction for a particular offence. The remoteness doctrine is, in turn, related to but distinct from a separate rule that restricts the reach of the prohibited outcome doctrine in justifying criminal liability. This is the rule that a fault element for one offence cannot be 'translated' into the fault element for another offence.

So, in explaining the legal concept of transferred intent, we need to concern ourselves with four doctrines, principles or rules (terminology, in this respect, is not so very important):

(a) prohibited outcome doctrine (the transferring of malice being a warranted application);

(b) the labelling principle (conviction must constitute a representative label for D's wrong);

(c) the remoteness doctrine (transfers of intent must not compromise the labelling principle); and

(d) the 'no-translation' rule (different fault elements cannot be transferred between crimes).

The so-called doctrine of transferred malice operates as a residual example of a 'common law doctrine' within the criminal law. That is to say, it must be grasped through an appreciation of the examples in which it has been held to apply, or not to apply, rather than through the application of a general rule. The higher courts have not as yet made a decisive move to place the doctrine within the scope of such a rule or principle that, having been made legally authoritative, must thereafter be employed to decide particular cases. For example, in the Court of Appeal in *Attorney-General's Reference (No 3 of 1994)*,[26] Lord Taylor CJ said:

It is, therefore, necessary to consider the concept of transferred malice.... At its simplest the concept is that if a defendant intends to kill or to cause really serious bodily injury to A but instead kills B, he is as guilty of the murder of B as if the object of his intentions had been B rather than A.[27]

Two points should be made about this passage. First, in true common law style, the Lord Chief Justice here explains transferred malice by example. The Lord Chief Justice's explanation is not, then, an exposition of a *concept* of transferred malice, as such. His explanation is a demonstration of how an underlying legal proposition works when applied to a set of facts. The underlying proposition might be expressed thus: 'in law, fault elements relate to the relevant harm prohibited or interest violated'. Accordingly, the following are sufficient but not necessary conditions for a murder conviction: that D intended to kill V, that V was the person actually killed, and that V died in the way D intended. If, instead, D intended to kill V1 but his shot missed, and killed V2 instead, or V1 died when he fell under a speeding car, having been hit by the bullet, acceptance of the underlying proposition means that the intention to kill in each case satisfies the fault element. D can, then, be convicted of murder because he did an act intended to kill and did thereby kill (the prohibited outcome). D intentionally brought about the relevant harm, violating the protected interest, irrespective of whom was actually harmed or how, as things turned out. Accordingly, it is more accurate to speak of a 'prohibited outcome' doctrine, rather than of a 'transferred malice' doctrine.[28]

Secondly, the Lord Chief Justice's explanation seems to carry with it an implicit moral endorsement of the outcome. In his view, D is rightly convicted of murder in the example given. Such an endorsement is warranted only if the outcome respects the remoteness principle, namely that the more remote from the actual outcome the outcome intended by D is, the weaker the moral case for convicting. Murder is a crime of specific intent, and where an actual outcome (albeit caused by D) is too far removed from the outcome specifically intended, a conviction for murder will not be a representative label for the offence.

The remoteness principle affects the prohibited outcome doctrine, as it applies to murder cases, in two ways. One we have already discussed. Suppose that when D intended to kill, not only was the person killed not the person D intended to kill (unintended V), but the person killed also died in an unexpected way (unintended

---

[26] [1996] 1 Cr App R 351.   [27] *Ibid*, at 362–3.

[28] There is an added advantage to using the 'prohibited outcome' doctrine, rather than 'transferred malice', which is that the former doctrine is apt, in a way the latter is not, to explain the reach of liability in crimes where malice cannot be transferred, such as compassing the death of the Monarch.

mode). Then, the outcome, even if still caused by D, may be too remote from what D intended for a murder conviction to be a representative label. The second way in which the remoteness principle may impact on the applicability of the prohibited outcome doctrine is discussed, although not in these terms, by the Law Commission in its Consultation Paper on reform of the law of murder.[29] The prohibited outcome doctrine (the Law Commission uses the terminology of 'transferred intent') has the potential to cause injustice when D intended to do only serious harm, as the law currently understands that notion, to V1 but by his action killed V2. Where the harm intended would have been serious if done to V1 (hence fixing D with an intent to do 'serious' harm, for the purposes of culpability), but was not serious in itself when done to V2 even though it caused V2's death, an issue of remoteness of what D did from what D intended arises.

Before moving to discuss this last point, it may be helpful to distinguish the remoteness doctrine from another restrictive doctrine or rule that impacts on the scope of the prohibited outcome doctrine. This is what can be called the 'no-translation' rule. Every first-year law student knows that subjective fault elements cannot be transferred from crimes against the person to crimes against property, or vice versa. Suppose D throws a brick at V intending to harm V. The brick misses V, but damages V's car window. D's intention to harm V cannot be transferred to the damaging of the window. Whilst fault can be transferred, it cannot be 'translated'.[30] So, when throwing the brick at V, either D also realized they might damage V's property, or D did not advert to that possibility. The prosecution must prove that D had that fault element in relation to V's property, independent of any fault in relation to the harming of V's person that D may have had. One might legitimately ask why there can be no translation of fault from a crime against the person to a crime against property, when the two events are as closely connected as in this example. For, given the closeness of the connection, it cannot be the remoteness principle that explains the bar on liability. The answer is that the harm done is too *unlike* the harm intended or foreseen for the crime charged to be a truly representative label. As was argued in Chapter 5, there is an important moral distinction between crimes against property and crimes against the person. The prohibition on the translation of fault helps to sustain that distinction.

Does this mean that there cannot be a translation of fault, even when there is less moral significance to the difference between the crime intended or foreseen, and the (conduct element of the) crime committed? Smith and Hogan's *Criminal Law* tackles the issue cautiously, by saying only that 'as a general rule' one cannot mix together the fault element for one crime and the conduct element of another to render D guilty of the latter.[31] The caution is understandable, but may be

---

[29] Law Commission (2005).

[30] *Pembliton* (1874) L 2 CCR 119. I do not overlook the point that some items of property can in some circumstances rightly be regarded as part of 'the person', as in the case where D touches V through touching her clothes: *Thomas* (1985) 81 Cr App R 331. An issue of malice translation does not arise in such a case.

[31] Smith and Hogan (2005), at 114. Simester and Sullivan *et al* are bolder, saying (at 164) that 'it is not possible to convict someone on the basis of an *actus reus* for one offence accompanied by the *mens*

unjustified. Such doctrinal 'alchemy' is inconsistent with ensuring that offences are representative labels.

Example 4. D picks up a full rubbish bin he finds on a bridge, and seeing V walking under the bridge, tips the contents of the bin over the bridge and down on to V. V's arm is pierced by a discarded needle from the bin. The needle contains a dangerous drug, some of which enters V's bloodstream. D is charged with maliciously administering a noxious thing so as to endanger life, contrary to section 23 of the Offences Against the Person Act 1861.

Suppose that D admits having been aware that he might cause some harm to V when he tipped the contents off the bridge, but says he was wholly unaware that he might administer a noxious thing. It is trite law that, had D's sole intention been simply to cause damage to V's clothing, he could not be found guilty in these circumstances.[32] However, D admits having had the fault element for malicious wounding, contrary to section 20 of the Offences Against the Person Act 1861.

In the circumstances, some may argue that the fault element actually possessed is sufficiently similar to the fault element of maliciously administering a noxious thing, to mean that D is not *mis*-labelled, if convicted of the latter crime through a translation, as opposed to a transfer of the former fault element into the latter. Against this, others may say simply that this argument for translating kinds of intent presupposes a criminal code in which morally and legally similar offences are permitted to co-exist, and are not amalgamated. If such amalgamation took place, so the argument runs, there would inevitably be larger moral differences between the (fewer) crimes that remained, and translation of intent would always produce unrepresentative labelling. If, for example, there was no offence of maliciously administering a noxious thing, and one stood to be convicted only of recklessly causing harm, the 'translation' issue simply disappears. The right response to both of these arguments is this. The amalgamation of offences, and the translation of a fault element of one crime into that of another, both threaten to undermine the moral distinctiveness of separate offences, such as the section 23 offence and the section 20 offence. This distinctiveness may in some contexts be essential to the representative labelling of offenders.[33]

V. The Serious Harm Doctrine, the Prohibited Outcome Doctrine, and the Remoteness Principle

If D intends to cause serious harm to V, and thereby kills V, D is guilty of murder. This is the 'serious harm doctrine' in operation.[34] In that regard, 'serious harm' is in law to be given its ordinary and natural meaning by the jury.[35] In murder cases, the law relies on juries to reject the view that harm intentionally inflicted was 'serious'

---

rea for a different offence'. The example they give is one in which it is property damage that occurs, but intention was to cause harm to the person.

[32] *Cunningham* [1957] 2 QB 396. [33] See, eg, Gardner (1994); Horder (1994).
[34] *Vickers* [1957] 2 QB 664. [35] *Smith* [1961] AC 290, at 334 (Viscount Kilmuir LC).

when D has caused death thereby, if D would not be justly convicted of murder in consequence. The Law Commission rejected the view that this state of affairs is satisfactory, not least because D stands to receive the mandatory life sentence if convicted of murder. The Commission's recommendation was that D should be convicted of a new crime of 'second degree' murder in such instances, a crime with a discretionary life sentence attached to it.[36]

The problems with the law as it stands (one category of murder, but encompassing those who killed intending only serious harm), are the current width of the law's understanding of 'serious harm', and the capacity of that understanding to work injustice when the serious harm doctrine operates in tandem with the prohibited outcome doctrine. Injustice can be done because whereas the prohibited outcome doctrine is an 'agent-neutral' doctrine involving insensitivity to the vulnerability of the individual victim, the law's understanding of serious harm is 'agent-specific'. It can depend on the individual vulnerabilities of the victim. Harm that would be regarded as non-serious if inflicted on a more robust person, can be regarded as serious if inflicted on a less robust person. The two doctrines' contrasting agent-neutral and agent-specific approaches to victims can clash, opening the way to injustice, when harm intentionally aimed at a vulnerable person is by accident or mistake inflicted on a less vulnerable victim, who nonetheless dies. In such a case, the jury may be stuck with the view that if D intended to do harm that would be regarded as serious if inflicted on the vulnerable person, D's intention must continue to be regarded as an intention to do serious harm, when that intent is transferred. This will be so, even when D's act caused the death of someone more robust in an unlikely and unforeseen manner. In such a case, D stands to be convicted of murder, even though his intention would not have been regarded as an intention to do serious harm, if aimed at the more robust person directly.

Although it is not a murder case, the important case of *Bollom*[37] provides a starting-point for the discussion. In *Bollom,* D was charged under section 18 of the Offences Against the Person Act 1861 with causing grievous bodily harm with intent to do grievous bodily harm to his step-daughter, who was then 17-months old. The child had sustained numerous bruises on different parts of her body, some of which looked as if they were the result of being jabbed hard with a hollow cylindrical object, such as part of a pen. None of the injuries, though, needed any kind of treatment. D was initially convicted on the section 18 charge, and appealed, on the grounds that the judge had failed to direct the jury that the cumulative effect of the injuries could only be relevant to the question whether the harm done was 'grievous' if the injuries were part of a single attack or course of conduct. On that ground, D's appeal was successful. So far as the meaning of 'grievous' (serious) was concerned, the Court of Appeal took the view that this term should be given an agent-specific meaning. In other words, the question must be: what kind of harm would ordinarily and naturally be regarded as serious, given the age and state of health of the person on whom it was inflicted? Giving judgment for the court, Fulford J said:

[36] Law Commission (2005), pt 3.   [37] [2003] EWCA Crim 2846.

To use this case as an example, these injuries on a 6 foot adult in the fullness of health would be less serious than on, for instance, an elderly or unwell person, on someone who was physically or psychiatrically vulnerable or, as here, on a very young child. In deciding whether injuries are grievous, an assessment has to be made of, amongst other things, the effect of the harm on the particular individual.[38]

In general terms, it is hard to find fault with this agent-specific view of grievous (serious) harm. However, it generates two problems for the law of murder.

First, as the question whether the harm intended should be regarded as grievous (serious) is solely one for the jury, the fact that D was unaware of, or not thinking of, any special vulnerability the victim had will in theory be irrelevant to the question whether D intended grievous (serious) harm. There is, then, in law still the possibility that D could be convicted of murder where what D intended was what he or she regarded as the equivalent of a 'pinprick',[39] but the jury take a different view of the seriousness of the harm done. In practice, though, it may be that the two issues (whether D intended serious harm, and whether he or she was aware of V's vulnerability) are merged in the minds of jurors, ensuring that D is not found to have had the intent to do serious harm if he or she did not know of V's vulnerability. Secondly, though, even in cases where D *was* aware of the special vulnerability of the intended victim, a conviction for murder may seem unjust if the actual victim did not have such a vulnerability:

Example 5. D aims four hard jabs with a pen at a young child, while the child is being held by her mother. His intention is to cause painful wounds. One of the jabs with the pen misses the child, but accidentally goes into the mother's eye when she moves suddenly. The mother is killed by the injury.

At the moment when D aims the jabs at the child, the *Bollom* test may be satisfied, and D can and should be found to have had the intention to cause grievous (serious) harm. This is the agent-specific view of the serious harm doctrine at work. It is irrelevant that the person D killed in consequence did not have any special vulnerability where the harm intended was concerned, and hence that, had he aimed his action at her directly, his intention would *not* have been regarded as an intention to do serious harm. That follows from the agent-neutral character of the prohibited outcome doctrine.

Pusillanimous though it may seem, the Law Commission did not address these problems through tinkering with (still less by abolishing) the prohibited outcome doctrine, which retains significant legal and scholarly support. In its Consultation Paper, the Commission did canvas making the possibility of 'murder by pinprick' more remote by giving a restrictive definition to 'serious harm' (as under the Indian Penal code). Taking this option might mean defining serious harm along the following kind of lines:

---

[38] *Ibid*, at 52–3.
[39] For criticism of the possibility that there could be murder by pinprick, see *Cunningham* [1982] AC 566, at 577 (Lord Hailsham).

Harm is not to be regarded as serious unless it is harm of such a nature as to endanger life, or to cause, or to be likely to cause, permanent or long-term damage to a significant aspect of physical integrity or mental functioning.[40]

Taking this course might have done something to avoid potential injustice. Were the facts of Example 5 to occur, D would probably not be convicted of murder with harm defined in this way, as the harm intended is unlikely to be regarded as 'serious'. By way of contrast, consider a variation on Example 5, in which D meant harm to come to the child, the intended V, that the jury regard as genuinely serious on this definition (suppose D aimed a hard punch at the baby's head). It is perhaps then not unjust that D stands to be convicted of the murder of the actual V (the baby's mother). However, the Commission ultimately did not recommend a detailed or restrictive definition of harm.[41] So, injustice in such cases would have to be avoided through the fact that, on the Law Commission's recommendations, D stands to be convicted only of second degree murder, with a discretionary life sentence maximum. If that is not still enough, by way of amelioration, then the question must be whether the courts will apply the emerging remoteness doctrine to such cases, on the grounds that the way V's actual death came about was too remote from what D intended to make liability for murder a representative label.

VI. The Criticisms of Simister and Sullivan *et al*

The persistence of the impersonality and prohibited outcome doctrines is one manifestation of the law's hostility to the view that all elements of 'bad (outcome) luck' in bringing about a consequence must be eliminated, before one can begin proper moral assessment of the agent's action in bringing it about.[42] This is most obvious in the doctrines of causation. Consider an example in which D stabs V with intent to kill, and V only dies after negligent treatment at the hospital. There is little doubt that D may be guilty of murder, even if proper treatment might have saved V, unless the treatment was grossly (in itself, criminally) negligent. What will matter is whether the jury regard the stab wound as still an operating, albeit perhaps a now more minor, cause of death, or just the setting in which another cause, the negligent treatment, is operating.[43] If the jury do regard the stab wound as a still operating cause, D's 'bad luck' in actually causing V's death, as things turn out, will not affect his liability for murder.[44] Like the causal doctrines that operate to draw these distinctions, the remoteness doctrine is meant to ensure that, whilst bad luck need not be eliminated before moral responsibility can adequately be judged,

---

[40] Law Commission (2005), pt 3.

[41] Law Commission (2006), at paras 2.86–2.94.

[42] See further, Ch 5 above. See further, in this regard, the contrasting views of Ashworth (1993) and Duff (1993).

[43] *Smith* (1959) 2 QB 35.

[44] For a vivid example, see *Blaue* [1975] 3 All ER 446 (CA).

a wholly unexpected turn of events can provide a sound basis for denying criminal responsibility. The remoteness doctrine is, in other words, meant to operate in a way that parallels the doctrines of causation. The real burden is on theorists who would go further, by opposing *any* transfer of malice under the prohibited outcome doctrine. Such theorists must explain why luck should favourably affect D by allowing him or her to deny any criminal responsibility when things go awry in such cases, when they accept that bad outcome luck will not necessarily affect criminal responsibility in cases where it is the causal chain that takes an unexpected turn.[45]

In response to my theory, though, there has been criticism from those who, by contrast, support an application of doctrines of impersonality and prohibited outcome limited *only* by the principles of causation.[46] Of the theory of remoteness, developed here, Simester and Sullivan *et al* say, first:

> [S]uch a limiting principle should be rejected. First, it promotes uncertainty. When is the manner in which an outcome is caused sufficiently different and unexpected to count as incompatible? One might think that causation doctrines already have this in hand, but Horder's principle is meant to apply after causal responsibility for [V's] death is established. It is undesirable to compound the complexity of the enquiry into D's guilt, since the criteria of any additional limitation do not seem susceptible of clear enunciation.[47]

To begin with, we should note that the number of cases in any given year in which even the standard prohibited outcome and impersonality doctrines have to be applied is likely to be tiny. Obviously, the number of cases in which these doctrines would have to be supplemented with directions on the remoteness principle, because there was an unintended victim, *as well as* unexpected mode of fatal outcome, is going to be absolutely minute. Reasons to avoid uncertainty only become strong and compelling when uncertainty is likely to be encountered more often than once in a blue moon. We can, for example, live with causation doctrines based on the presence or absence of an inherently vague concept such as 'reasonable foreseeability', in part because we need to invoke such doctrines so rarely.[48] In any event, how uncertain really is the idea that—where my first criterion of remoteness is concerned—the killing of an unintended victim has taken place? As a test, it has about as much conceptual certainty as a test could have.[49] So far as my second criterion is concerned (the unexpectedness of the manner in which V died), to be sure, this does involve a notion less certain than the first criterion. But the doctrine that Simester and Sullivan *et al* suggest as necessary and sufficient in its stead—the test of 'reasonable foreseeability'—is just as uncertain;[50] but in context, it is none the worse for that.

---

[45] On this issue, see Moore (1997), ch 5.
[46] Simester and Sullivan *et al* (2010), at 165–6.   [47] *Ibid*, at 166.
[48] See, eg, *Roberts* (1971) 56 Cr App R 95.
[49] I am, of course, assuming that no reader would be foolish enough to confuse a test of conceptual certainty with a question of how hard something might be to prove as a matter of evidence.
[50] Simester and Sullivan *et al* (2010), at 165 fn 224.

It is true, of course, that the remoteness principle is to be applied after causation, with all its possible uncertainties in point of doctrine, has already been established. The remoteness principle is indeed by its nature an *ex post facto*, exculpatory doctrine relieving D of liability after the 'fact', but in itself that is no objection. The remoteness doctrine is apt to relieve D of liability in something like (but only something like) the way that, for example, the doctrines of loss of self-control and diminished responsibility may relieve D of liability for murder, only when D's causal responsibility for V's death has been established.[51] In other words, my test governs the propriety of labelling in respect of something (a death) admittedly caused. The principles of 'transferred malice' may be permitted to lead a double life, with some inculpatory doctrines serving to establish D's liability, alongside another doctrine—the remoteness principle—possibly exculpating D in some circumstances in the interests of fair labelling. This is one important respect in which the remoteness doctrine is similar to key doctrines of causation (despite the latter's relevance only to prima facie liability). Some such doctrines are designed to establish criminal liability, but some in addition are designed to restrict its scope. The fact that the principles of causation relate to the conduct element of a crime, and the principles of 'transferred malice' to the fault element, does not affect this basic similarity. The law could easily have insisted that D brings about (causes) an outcome when that outcome is merely 'foreseeable'. The law is not compelled by any special logic to require that the outcome be *reasonably* foreseeable before causation is established. That the law does require outcomes to be reasonably foreseeable, if they are to be attributable to D, reflects considerations of fairness in attribution, considerations running parallel to and in harmony with considerations of fairness in labelling.

Finally, Simester and Sullivan *et al* go on to consider a version of Example 3 above:[52]

D shoots at V1 intending to kill him. The bullet misses but enters a factory behind V1. There, it strikes an electrical transformer, causing the transformer to explode. The explosion kills a factory worker, V2.[53]

In this example, the remoteness principle would relieve D of liability for V2's death, because not only was the victim an unintended victim but the mode of killing was not the one intended. As Simester and Sullivan *et al* rightly point out, the application of the remoteness principle would mean that in this example, 'D would not be convicted of murder but, rather, of the attempted murder of V1 and of the manslaughter of V2'.[54] By contrast, Simester and Sullivan *et al* apply the impersonality and prohibited outcome doctrines to these facts, saying, 'D is straightforwardly guilty of murder, since by her act she intended to, and did, kill a human being'.[55] In criticizing the remoteness principle, they then go on to say:

---

[51] See, eg, *Blaue* [1975] 3 All ER 446.   [52] See text at n 9 above.
[53] Simester and Sullivan *et al* (2010), at 166.   [54] *Ibid.*   [55] *Ibid.*

Moreover, the moral case for a limitation seems unmeritorious. Suppose that the unexpected explosion had, in fact, killed V1. Convicting D of murder is then straightforward. Why should it make all the difference that it was V2 instead who died? Both are human beings. All the elements of the offence are present.... To convict D of unlawful act manslaughter, on the basis of an attempted murder causing death, is an unnecessary sophistication.[56]

In response to the final observation, I would say that the question here is not what is 'necessary', in order to develop an adequately morally sophisticated criminal law: that simply skews the debate in favour of an unrestricted application of the prohibited outcome and impersonality doctrines. The issue is whether a given sophistication makes the law fairer, in point of labelling, at little or no extra cost (given that so few cases are likely to arise in which the remoteness principle falls to be applied). The observation that both V1 and V2 are human beings, and that all the elements of the offence are present, adds nothing, because it is simply to reiterate the elements of the prohibited outcome and impersonality doctrines. The observation does not in itself do anything to reject the qualification of the prohibited outcome doctrine by the remoteness doctrine. On my account, a mistake or accident leading to the death of a different victim to the intended victim does not by itself generate a sufficient degree of unfairness to warrant finding D not guilty of murder. There must be the additional element that the killing came about in an unintended way.

[56] *Ibid.*

PART III

DEFENCES TO MURDER

8

Wrong Turnings on Defences to Murder

I. Civilized Law and Law Reform

1. Introduction

In this final chapter, I try to do three things. First, I will seek to move the debate about defences to murder beyond the issue of whether those defences should be characterized as permissions or excuses (without casting doubt on the importance of that distinction, for some purposes). I highlight a neglected perspective on the limits of such defences, in terms of whether those limits will make the law more 'civilized', as I will understand that notion. Secondly, I will consider the foundations on which much of the current law and a good deal of scholarly work are based: the relationship between the Report of the Royal Commission on Capital Punishment (1953) and the Homicide Act 1957 ('the 1957 Act'). As we will see, many of the Royal Commission's recommendations, like the provisions of the 1957 Act, had a civilizing inspiration and purpose. However, in taking forward the Royal Commission's recommendations, the Government of the day decided to adopt what we will see was a narrow, doctrinal approach to civilizing reform of the substantive criminal law recommended by the Royal Commission. This was an approach that gave a leading role to partial defences.[1] I argue that this proved to be a wrong turning. The Government could, and should, have opted for the Royal Commission's (only half-heartedly endorsed) more radical recommendations for civilizing sentencing duties and powers in murder cases. As we will see, these recommendations were not perfect, especially in their failure to make adequately distinct reform of the law as it governed D's suffering from abnormalities of mental functioning. These reforms would nonetheless have avoided some of the unintended consequences that, ironically, ultimately rendered the law of partial defences to some extent less rather than more civilized. Over time, these unintended consequences gave rise to the demands for change embodied in the Coroners and Justice Act 2009 ('the 2009 Act'); but the 2009 Act wrongly retained the partial defence structure left in place by the doctrinal path to reform ushered in

---

[1] I will not chop logic here on the question of whether it is better to refer to the defences introduced or modified by the 1957 Act as complete excuses to murder, or as 'partial excuses' (the more common term) to homicide. Both ways of referring to them can be perfectly acceptable, depending on the point at issue. For analysis of the appropriateness of the term, 'partial defences', see Husak (1998); Taylor (2007).

by the 1957 Act. Accordingly, I will, thirdly, conclude with a critique of partial defences. I will suggest that there should be little or no scope for partial defences in the law of homicide.

2. Civilizing defences: the case of permissions

In the middle years of the twentieth century, the scope of permissions[2] to use lethal violence was in some key respects being restricted. In the period under discussion (roughly, the 1930s through to the 1960s), the state restricted the scope for its own agents permissibly to kill in execution of justice. The death penalty was made inapplicable both to offenders under the age of 18 at the time of the offence's commission,[3] and to pregnant women.[4] The 1957 Act saw highly significant restrictions introduced to the scope of the crime of murder, and hence to the scope for the application of the death penalty, before the outright abolition of that penalty in 1965.[5] Further, the scope for an individual permissibly to use force in prevention of crime was reduced, and it became for the first time an offence of homicide to destroy a child in the womb.[6] We can think of these developments as part of a mid-twentieth century 'civilizing' process (an idea to be explained shortly[7]) in relation to the scope of permissions to kill. A more detailed example can be found in JWC Turner's discussion of the limits of permissible killing in prevention of crime.

As late as 1952, in relation to the use of force permissible in prevention of crime, Turner had conceded, in relation to homicide, that, 'Life may be taken with impunity, if it be necessary and reasonable for arresting a felon, or suppressing a felonious riot, or suppressing a crime of a forcible or atrocious nature'.[8] However,

---

[2] I will be using the term 'permissions' rather than 'justifications' for two reasons. First, I use this term because circumstances giving rise to a permission to invade another's interests, such as consent or an attack on oneself or another, do not necessarily carry with them any implication that it is right—'justified'—to do the action that is consented to, or that will negate or ward off the attack. It could be morally wrong to act, and yet be permissible. Secondly, I use the term 'permission' because it is conveniently vague in terms of whether it refers to a normative permission—a permission granted by law—or a 'default' permission that exists simply because there is no legal norm governing the conduct in question. Self-defence, for example, is a normative permission, a permission granted at common law. By contrast, the killing of a baby not yet 'born alive' (other than in order to procure an abortion) was permitted, but only by default, until the passing of the Infant Life (Preservation) Act 1929. I intend the term 'permission' to cover both kinds of example.

[3] Criminal Justice Act 1948, s 16, amending the Children and Young Persons Act 1933. The execution of those aged under 16 was prohibited by the Children Act 1908.

[4] Sentence of Death (Expectant Mothers) Act 1931.

[5] Murder (Abolition of the Death Penalty) Act 1965.

[6] Infant Life (Preservation) Act 1929, putting on one side cases in which the destruction occurred in the course of an attempt to procure an abortion. This is an example of the removal of a 'default' permission: see n 2 above. In the period under discussion, repeated attempts to introduce procedures under which euthanasia might become justified were firmly rebuffed. See the 1936 Voluntary Euthanasia (Legalisation) Bill, and the 1969 Voluntary Euthanasia Bill. I am grateful to Isra Black, King's College London for these references.

[7] See text at nn 27–29 below.

[8] Turner (1952), at 111.

he sought to qualify the scope of that permission. Citing the Report of the Royal Commission on Indictable Offences (1879),[9] he said:

We take one great principle of the common law to be that, though it ... permits the use of force to prevent crimes, to preserve the public peace, and to bring offenders to justice, yet all this is subject to the restriction that the force used is necessary; that is, that the mischief sought to be prevented could not be prevented by less violent means....[10]

Two points should be noted about this passage. First, Turner's comments are not directed at the status of killing to effect an arrest as a permission, as opposed to an excuse. Rather, they concerned the civilized limits of that permission.[11] Secondly, a broader point, there is nothing distinctively 'liberal' about this particular kind of civilization of the criminal law, so far as an individual's use of violence is concerned. It is part of a civilizing agenda that might be shared by many jurisdictions or ideologies, whether or not liberal, committed to reducing the incidence of violence or force used other than through the process of law.[12]

This point about criminal law and ideological context is important to an explanation of a seemingly contradictory trend developing at this time, so far as permissions and excuses are concerned. In the 1960s, suicide ceased to be a form of 'self-murder',[13] and the scope for abortion was very considerably widened.[14] These changes clearly broadened, in limited circumstances, permissions for killing other than in self-defence. However, unlike some of the restrictions on the scope for permissible killing just discussed, these examples represent a distinctively liberal turn in thinking about the civilization process in the criminal law. There can be decisive reasons not to criminalize harmful conduct or not to give it a highly condemnatory label, even conduct amounting to a killing that was not (say) self-defensive. There can be such reasons if criminalization or condemnatory labelling is pointless because no deterrent effect will be achieved, or because the taking of retribution or the imposition of the label will prove to be unduly harsh or disproportionate.[15] One might, for example, condemn abortion, whilst—however reluctantly—recognizing that it would be wrong to seek to deter or punish a

---

[9] Royal Commission (1878–79), at 11.

[10] Turner (1952), at 112; but see *Jerome v Phear* (1588) Cro Eliz 93 for an early example of legal insistence on restraint in this context.

[11] Not long thereafter, the law was changed by the Criminal Law Act 1967 to reflect this more civilized thinking about the need for restraint in law enforcement practice.

[12] In earlier times, for example, the restriction on suicide, as a form of lethal force, was justified through an anthropomorphization of civil society in Monarchist terms, an aspect of the so-called 'two bodies' theory; see Kantorowicz (1957). Suicide was regarded as impermissible, because it was, 'an offence ... against the King in that hereby he has lost a subject, and ... he being the head has lost one of his mystical members': *Hales v Petit* (1562–63) 1 Plowd 253. On the broader relationship between defences and liberalism, see Horder (2004), at 191–8.

[13] Suicide Act 1961, s 1. For a justification of the contrary view, see *Hales v Petit* (1562–63) 1 Plowd 253.

[14] Abortion to preserve the life of a mother had been made legal under the Infant Life (Preservation) Act 1929. The scope for abortion was more radically reformed by the Abortion Act 1967.

[15] I deliberately run together, in this passage, considerations of deterrence, of just deserts, and of cruelty in punishing. A flourishing system of criminal justice will see such considerations working in tandem just as often as in opposition to one another. See Gardner (1998a). See further the

perpetration of it through the law of murder, by making a foetus a potential victim of murder. It would be wrong because the labeling of abortion as murder is unduly harsh, a judgement reflected in the fact that for well over 150 years the performance of unlawful abortions has been regarded as a special offence with (only) a maximum life term.[16] When reforming the permissible limits of killing in the liberal state, preserving this common good—the humanity of the criminal law—must remain as much part of the civilizing picture as the promotion of values enhanced by self-restraint, and by the placing of strict limits on the authority of state officials to use lethal force.[17]

In that regard, it is easy to forget that the report of the Royal Commission on Capital Punishment, on which the 1957 Act's partially excusatory provisions were based, was itself concerned with placing restrictions on a permission for killing: killing through the application of the death penalty.[18] In this context, in developing its recommendations on the legitimate scope of that permission, we should note that the Royal Commission showed itself to be influenced by the need to promote the liberal common good just mentioned, the preservation of the humanity of the criminal law. In recommending (by a majority of 6–5) that no one under the age of 21 at the time of the offence should be executed, the Royal Commission said:

> We recognize that the primary purpose of inflicting the death penalty is to deter others. . . . Nevertheless, when the life to be terminated is a young life, the feeling is inevitable that the infliction of the death penalty may be a premature and over-hasty measure. There is today a widespread repugnance to the infliction of the death penalty. . . . This repugnance is especially acute when the offender to be put to death is young.[19]

The claim here is that, even if some deterrent effect is achieved by applying the death penalty to those under 21 years of age, the value of that is outweighed by the unacceptably harsh or disproportionate nature of the application of that penalty in the circumstances. A similar approach is implied in the Royal Commission's views on the possible execution of those found to be insane:

> If a medical inquiry is held and the doctors certify that the prisoner is insane, it is not only right and proper that the Home Secretary should respite the sentence of death . . . but it is his imperative duty to do so, both under the statute and because it is contrary to the common law to execute an insane criminal.[20]

3. Civilizing defences: abolishing an excuse for murder

Just as some permissions for killing other than in self-defence were being restricted or eliminated in the mid-twentieth century, so were some excuses for murder.

---

remarks of Lords Atkin and Hailsham debating the Infant Life (Preservation) Act 1929: <http://hansard.mill banksystems.com/lords/1928/nov/22/preservation-of-infant-life-bill-hl>.

[16] Offences Against the Person Act 1861, s 58, replacing earlier legislation.

[17] See text following n 33 below for more detailed discussion of common good or strategic concerns. I set out eight common goods of strategic concerns, bearing on permissions or excuses, in Horder (2004), at 16–17.

[18] Royal Commission on Capital Punishment (1953).

[19] *Ibid*, at paras 203 and 204.   [20] *Ibid*, at paras 368.

The demise of the 'chance medley' doctrine is a classic case in point. Shortly before Turner's sixteenth edition of Kenny's *Outlines of Criminal Law*[21] was completed, the case of *Semini*[22] was decided. That case saw the abolition of the old doctrine that killing—even intentionally—in the course of a 'chance medley' was manslaughter, not murder. In *Semini*, as D passed V in the street, D took umbrage at remarks made by someone in V's group of friends about a woman in D's company. D went back and struck one of V's friends (W) with his hand or fist. V encouraged (W) to fight D. W took off his coat in preparation for a fight, upon which D drew a knife and in the ensuing scuffle stabbed V fatally. D was convicted of murder and appealed to the Court of Appeal. He did so on the grounds that the jury should have been told that they could reduce the offence to manslaughter, on the grounds that the killing occurred in the course of a chance medley (a sudden and unpremeditated fight), even if any provocation from the deceased or from his friends was insufficient by itself to reduce murder to manslaughter. D's appeal was dismissed. Although the doctrine of chance medley is not very accurately described by the Court of Appeal,[23] it was declared obsolete, with Lord Goddard CJ having this to say about the rationale for its abolition:

At a time when society was less secure and less settled in its habits, when the carrying of swords was as common as the use of a walking stick at the present day, and when dueling was regarded as involving no moral stigma if fairly conducted, it is not surprising that the courts took a view more lenient towards provocation than is taken today when life and property are guarded by an efficient police force and social habits have changed.[24]

This is clearly an explanation for the removal of a defence in terms of the civilizing effect that it will have on the law (an effect with as much symbolic as real value, but no less important for that), notwithstanding the status of that defence as an excuse for murder, rather than as a permission to kill.[25] As a rationale for the removal of the defence, it owes much to Turner's explanation of the case for a more restricted permission to kill in prevention of crime.[26] In section 5 below, we will encounter another example of the civilizing process in relation to excuses, this time in relation to the doctrine of provocation.

4. Civilizing defences: beyond permissions and excuses

In that regard, so far as the civilizing of defences is concerned, I have argued that:

A civilized state claims ... the absolute right to cause significant harm in the name of retribution for wrongdoing. The civilized state claims this right because ... its trained officials are in the best position to give a public and impartial assessment, as civilized living

---

[21] Turner (1952).   [22] *Semini* [1949] 1 KB 405.

[23] The fact that Semini seemed to have no intention of fighting on equal terms (ie with the other party arming himself with a knife as well) would in fact have disqualified him from the defence when it was still a working feature of the law of homicide: see further, Horder (1992a).

[24] *Semini* [1949] 1 KB 405, at 409. The doctrine still has its defenders; see Leader-Elliot (2010).

[25] See further, the discussion of *Duffy* [1949] 1 All ER 932 in section 6(b) below.

[26] See text at n 9 above.

requires, of when, and how much, harm is retributively justified for the wrongdoing in question. Despite the fact that it is merely a partial excusatory defence, the doctrine of provocation... appears to derogate from the absoluteness of this right, and is to this extent the mark of a less civilised society.[27]

This argument has been criticized by Victor Tadros for failing to distinguish between the idea of provocation as an excuse for an impermissible act, and provocation as mixture of partial excuse (loss of self-control) and partial justification (justified retaliation) for action.[28] That criticism has some merit, but it does not engage with the main point of the passage. Whether holding out permissions *or* excuses, the state is under an obligation to ensure that those excuses fit with a civilized understanding of the role (both actual and symbolic) of the criminal law in society:

[The] very redefinition ('appropriation') of punishment as a manifestation of an official response to wrongdoing necessarily connects punishment to the state's broader vision for governance.... Let me define this broader vision in terms of a question that—for a consequentialist liberal—must be asked of all official responses to wrongdoing, including the structuring of substantive offences and defences. The question is: to what extent do those responses contribute to a more civilized and cultured, as well as more tolerant and humane, society, to that end helping to shape the ways in which, and the attitudes with which, individuals flourish in common?[29]

This test for the civilized quality of a defence applies irrespective of whether that defence is a permission or an excuse (and whether full or partial). The distinction between permission and excuse—made central to modern scholarly analysis of defences by Austin[30]—can be an important conceptual distinction that helps, inter alia, to enhance the quality and discernment of moral judgement of (in)action.[31] The distinction cannot, though, in itself tell us how far we can or should go in seeking to provide defences for aggression, and fatal aggression in particular. Of course, what is to count as a civilizing development in the law of defences is very much a contested matter. I have sought to give content to the idea through explanation of a range of 'strategic' concerns or common goods that set limits to, as well as providing scope for, the permissions and excuses for harmful conduct that a liberal state should seek to develop.[32] For example, overriding claims based on personal inconvenience, special pleading, and the like, are the following common goods (I set out six others):

(ii) Preventing the development [or maintenance] of defences perverting or distorting, amongst citizens and officials alike, a proper understanding of the importance (absolute and relative) of personal and proprietary interests, along with public or common goods...

---

[27] Horder (1992b), at 710.   [28] Tadros (2005a), at 304–5.
[29] Horder (2003), at 243.   [30] Austin (1956).
[31] On the importance of philosophy to this enterprise, see Shute, Gardner, and Horder (1993), introduction.
[32] Horder (2004), at 16–17.

(vi) The need to encourage citizens to seek redress through political or bureaucratic processes rather than resorting to 'self-help,' especially where the latter entails the use of force.[33]

It is not hard to see the influence of one or other of these strategic considerations or common goods at work in the restrictions developed both on the permission to use fatal violence in preventing crime, and on the abolition of the 'chance medley' excuse.[34] As we will now see, using as a case study 'infidelity' as form of provocation, civilizing influences have also shaped the much more important provocation excuse.

5. Infidelity: a case study in the quest to civilize an excuse for murder

At different times in different jurisdictions around the world, infidelity—and especially catching a spouse in the very act—has been regarded as a basis for reducing murder to a lesser offence, or for reducing the punishment.[35] Famously, at the beginning of the eighteenth century, Holt CJ regarded the killing of a wife in the act of adultery as a kind of excessive force used to prevent or stop a violation of 'property' (the spouse).[36] Holt CJ said in favour of regarding such lethal acts as manslaughter rather than murder, that 'adultery [is] the highest invasion of property', and that jealous anger at such a violation is 'the rage of the man'.[37] This is to give a predominantly normative explanation for regarding such a killing as only manslaughter.[38] In other words, the killing is impermissible because it involved a *somewhat* excessive use of force, in circumstances where some use of force—perhaps a considerable amount—would have been permissible. So far as it applies to catching an adulterous wife in the act, this kind of (monstrous!) explanation would probably have been accepted by most jurisdictions that had similar provisions up until the twentieth century and, in some instances, beyond.[39] Perhaps just as significantly, it is possible to give this predominantly normative explanation for the partial defence of provocation in its entirety, as it stood at the beginning of the eighteenth century. The other categories of admissible provocation endorsed by Holt CJ, all to some extent reflected circumstances in which, to the eighteenth- or

---

[33] *Ibid.*

[34] For a complete picture of common goods relevant to this discussion as a whole, we need to add to the list the liberal good (discussed earlier) of maintaining the humanity of the criminal law by avoiding pointless, unduly harsh, or disproportionate criminalization or labelling. The promotion of that good explains why some forms of killing (such as, in some circumstances, abortion or suicide) are not criminalized, and why some kinds of intentional killing are less harshly labelled (infanticide).

[35] There is an excellent analysis in Reed and Wake (2011).

[36] See *Mawgridge* (1707) Kel 119, referring to the earlier decision in *Manning* (1672) 1 Ventris 158.

[37] *Mawgridge* (1707) Kel 119, at 137.

[38] On the distinction between predominantly normative and predominantly ascriptive bases for explaining excuses, see Horder (2004), at 52–8. In short, normative analysis is concerned with what ought (not) to be done and what is (im)permissible, whereas ascriptive analysis is concerned, amongst other things, with blame(lessness) respecting something that, from a normative perspective, ought not to have been done.

[39] See the French Code Penal (1810), arts 324 and 326; Besse (1989); Reed and Wake (2011).

early nineteenth-century mind, some degree of force might have been permissible, normatively speaking: an insulting assault, coming to the aid of a friend or relative under attack, and seeing an Englishman unlawfully deprived of his liberty.[40] At least one strand of case law, developed in the late eighteenth and early nineteenth century, maintained this 'excessive defence' understanding of the provocation doctrine, concentrating on lethal force used in the heat of the moment in response to an attack of some kind.[41] Had that strand of case law been upheld by the House of Lords in the (in my terms) civilizing case of *Holmes v DPP* (discussed further below),[42] then the reforms of the doctrine effected by the 1957 Act might have taken a very different course.

In fact, Holt CJ had also explained the law's leniency in such cases in predominantly ascriptive rather than predominantly normative terms, saying that there could simply be 'no greater provocation'.[43] This theme was developed in some important nineteenth century cases and commentary, where the key issue was said to be whether the provocation might have been such as to lead a reasonable person to lose self-control, irrespective of whether D would have been justified in employing at least some force.[44] The increasing influence of thinking about provocation as a partial excuse, with a predominantly ascriptive rather than a predominantly normative basis, led some judges in later years to extend the scope for reducing murder to manslaughter in adultery cases. Mitigation of the offence came to include cases in which the 'property violation' constituted by adultery was over, and it was hence too late to use force to prevent its occurrence.[45] In particular, more-or-less sudden confessions of adultery were held to be, in ascriptive terms, potentially as worthy a basis for reducing murder to manslaughter on the grounds of provocation as catching a spouse in the very act.[46] Perversely (if predictably), though, the law retained some vestige of the predominantly normative 'invasion of property' basis for the law's leniency.[47] It refused to extend such leniency either to cases in which the man and the woman were merely engaged to be married or living together as husband and wife,[48] or to a case in which the man killed his brother on a mere suspicion (unfounded) that the latter had committed adultery,[49] or to cases in which the woman had declared that she was going to live with another man and commit adultery.[50]

---

[40] At that time, a lethal response to false imprisonment was also in some cases regarded, alongside the use or threat of violence, as sufficient grounds to reduce murder to manslaughter: *Buckner* (1641) Style 467; *Hopkin Huggett* (1666) Kel 59; *Goffe* (1672) 1 Vent 216.

[41] See Horder (1992a), at 93–4; *Sherwood* (1844) 1 C & K 556.

[42] [1946] AC 588.

[43] *Mawgridge* (1707) Kel 119. On the normative-ascriptive distinction, see n 38 above.

[44] *Welsh* (1869) 11 Cox 336; Royal Commission on Capital Punishment (1953), at para 137.

[45] The idea that force could be used to prevent an adulterous spouse from committing further adultery at some unspecified point in the future was regarded as perhaps going a little bit too far: see *Ellor* (1921) 15 Cr App R 41.

[46] *Rothwell* (1871) 12 Cox 145; *Jones* (1908) 72 JP 215.

[47] Presumably, simply to prevent over-extension of this basis for mitigation.

[48] *Palmer* (1913) 8 Cr App R 207 and *Greening* (1913) 9 Cr App R 105, respectively.

[49] *Birchall* (1913) 9 Cr App R 91.

[50] *Ellor* (1921) 15 Cr App R 41.

However, these broadening developments were reversed by arguably the most important case on provocation decided in the twentieth century, *Holmes v DPP*.[51] In that case, D killed his wife in a fit of temper following her confession of adultery. D was convicted of murder after the trial judge withdrew the issue of provocation from the jury. The House of Lords held that the judge had been right to withdraw the issue from the jury, on the grounds that no reasonable jury could have found that such a verbal provocation could on its own have led a reasonable person to do as Holmes did. The House of Lords overruled the case law developments (just described), that extended the adultery category to include confessions of adultery.[52] Giving the only speech, Viscount Simon said that these cases should not be followed because 'we have left behind us the age when the wife's subjection to her husband was regarded by law as the basis of the marital relation'.[53] The importance of this argument[54] is that it is a civilizing argument that transcends the hallowed distinction between permission and excuse. It derives much of its moral force from the view that, to use Viscount Simon's words, 'as society advances, it ought to call for a higher measure of self-control in all cases'.[55] For Viscount Simon, this argument holds true irrespective of whether the doctrine of provocation is best regarded as 'a limited concession to natural human weakness',[56] or as involving any element of normative permission. For Lord Simon what this meant, in civilizing terms, is that in the modern world there is symbolic moral and legal importance in refusing to allow confessions of adultery to form the basis for a provocation plea.[57]

The power of the judge to make such a symbolic statement, by refusing to put a 'confession of adultery' case to the jury, was removed by section 3 of the 1957 Act, not long after *Holmes* was decided.[58] Section 3 required the judge to put the provocation defence to the jury when there was *any* evidence of a provoked loss of self-control, irrespective of the nature or gravity of the provocation. The result was

---

[51] [1946] AC 588. I say this, of *Holmes v DPP*, because other important case law developments such as those in *Camplin* [1978] AC 705 were in a way anticipated by the Royal Commission on Capital Punishment (1953), at paras 141–45. The following analysis is taken from Horder (2005), at 132.

[52] See *Rothwell* (1871) 12 Cox 145; *Jones* (1908) 72 JP 215.

[53] [1946] AC 588, at 600. Lord Simon added (*ibid*) that only words 'of a most extreme and exceptional character' could amount to sufficient provocation to reduce murder to manslaughter. *Holmes* was rejected in Scotland, where confessions of adultery continued to be sufficient in principle to reduce murder to manslaughter: Royal Commission on Capital Punishment (1953), at paras 130–32.

[54] Which is obviously, in truth, an argument against the adultery category as a whole, not only against the category's extension to confessions of adultery.

[55] *Holmes* [1946] AC 588, at 600.

[56] Royal Commission on Capital Punishment (1953), at para 144.

[57] Just as, paradoxically, in the seventeenth century, there was symbolic moral importance in singling out certain cases of provocation—including the adultery category—for *favourable* treatment, even if it could theoretically have been subsumed within other categories.

[58] Section 3 of the 1957 Act sought to put the jury firmly in control of questions concerning the nature and degree of provocation that would warrant reducing murder to manslaughter. It read: 'Where on a charge of murder there is evidence on which the jury can find that the person charged was provoked (whether by things done or by things said or by both together) to lose self-control, the question whether the provocation was enough to make a reasonable man do as he did shall be left to be determined by the jury; and in determining that question the jury shall take into account everything both done and said according to the effect which in their opinion, it would have on a reasonable man.'

that judges and juries were free to regard adultery-related evidence as, in principle, evidence of grave provocation;[59] such an approach was no longer either compulsory (as it was, in 'caught-in-the-act' cases, before *Holmes*) or forbidden (as it was, in 'confession of adultery' cases, after *Holmes*). The moral damage to the authority of the criminal law as a repository of civilized values that ensued, in cases where a woman challenged a man's authority or self-esteem in some respect, is well illustrated by cases such as *Naylor*.[60] In this case, D picked up a prostitute (V) in his car, and then refused to pay, as agreed, for services rendered. V remonstrated with D, upon which he strangled her with such force that some of her neck bones were broken. The defence of provocation was put to the jury, as there was some evidence of a provoked loss of self-control, and the jury acquitted D of murder. In its recommendations on provocation,[61] the Law Commission sought to ensure that the moral integrity of the law was no longer undermined by the need to put the defence of provocation to the jury in such cases. The Commission sought to restore the civilizing developments initiated by the *Holmes* case, by recommending restoration of the judge's power to withdraw the issue of provocation from the jury, if no reasonable jury properly directed could conclude that the defence might apply.[62] It cannot be doubted that this recommendation (subsequently enacted[63]) is concerned not merely with cases where the evidence is factually weak, but also with cases—like *Naylor*—where it would, in a civilized society, be morally wrong even to risk the chance that a jury might show leniency to D. As the Law Commission said:

The current position does not serve the interests of justice because the need to put the defence to the jury in these circumstances increases the likelihood that an unmeritorious claim may succeed.[64]

Even so, as a civilizing influence on the law, reliance placed on the recommendation (embodied in section 54(6) of the 2009 Act) to restore the judge's power to withdraw the provocation issue comes at a moral cost. At the Law Commission's recommendation, the law now devolves to the trial judge in an individual case the role of guardian of civilized values, so far as the circumstances in which the defence may be withdrawn from consideration are concerned. Whilst that move admirably reduces the scope for litigation on questions of law, it also strips the law of the symbolic value it was given in *Holmes* when, in the name of upholding civilized values, the law itself singled out confessions of adultery for unfavourable legal treatment. To mark the law's disapproval of any lingering sense that marriage vows involved a wife's subjection to her husband, *Holmes* had stood for the view

---

[59] See, eg, *Mellentin* [1985] 7 Cr App R(S) 9.
[60] *Naylor* (1987) Crim App R 302.   [61] Law Commission (2004); Law Commission (2006).
[62] Law Commission (2006), at para 5.11.   [63] See now s 54(6) of the 2009 Act.
[64] Law Commission (2006), at para 5.15. This explanation involves reference to what I have elsewhere called 'strategic' considerations influencing the scope for excusing: Horder (2004), at 16–17. The Commission added, '[t]he current position may not even serve the interests of every D. Even if there is evidence of a loss of self-control, D may not want the jury to be side-tracked by a partial defence if his or her main claim is for a complete acquittal.'

that in *no case* was a confession of adultery to be regarded as provocation sufficient to go to the jury.

The Law Commission resisted any temptation there might have been to resurrect this kind of rule-focused symbolism, by placing emphasis on how nuanced ascriptive judgements (judgements of blame) must inevitably be in provocation cases, and hence on how such judgements are best left to judge and jury in individual cases:

It is a sad commonplace that when relationships break up there are often arguments and mutual recriminations. We think it would be seldom that words spoken in such a situation could legitimately make the other party feel severely wronged, to the extent that a person of ordinary tolerance and self-restraint in such as situation might have used lethal violence; but there may be cases where one party torments another with remarks of an exceptionally abusive kind . . . there are bound to be borderline cases.[65]

On this view, as the Commission candidly admits, it could be that, so far as adultery is concerned, 'one party's behaviour puts quite exceptional emotional pressure on the other',[66] and hence the defence could legitimately be put to the jury by the judge in such a case. However, at the stage of implementation, it proved too difficult for Government to withstand the powerful draw of normative thinking, and to resist the allure of the symbolic value with which such thinking can endow the law. From a normative perspective, the old law regarded catching a wife in the act of adultery as a situation involving a normative permission both to lose one's temper and use some force (to prevent the invasion of 'property'), whereas the new law turns such thinking on its head. The new law, building on *Holmes*, introduces a new kind of normative claim to endow the law with symbolic value, in the way that it addresses gender relations. In some circumstances, namely when confronted by infidelity, it is now both unjustified and inexcusable to react to provocation by losing self-control and killing. Under the new law, provoked loss of self-control may not be pleaded to reduce murder to manslaughter unless the provocation in question satisfies a threshold condition. This is that it amounts to a 'qualifying trigger' under the 2009 Act. By section 55(6) of the 2009 Act:

In determining whether a loss of self-control had a qualifying trigger . . .

   (c) the fact that a thing done or said constituted sexual infidelity is to be disregarded.

One should have some sympathy with the draftsman set the daunting task of turning this piece of symbolism into a workable law, but it has not proved difficult for commentators to find fault with it.[67] Putting aside contrived examples, it is not easy to see how something said, rather than something done, can 'constitute'

---

[65] Law Commission (2004), at para 3.147. For criticism, see Edwards (2011).

[66] Law Commission (2004), at para 3.147.

[67] See Miles (2009); Norrie (2010), at 288–9. The Court of Appeal has held that evidence of sexual infidelity must be disregarded only when it is the sole (or possibly also the main) piece of evidence relied on as provocation. It may still be admissible as evidence when presented merely as a part integral to a larger whole that constitutes the provocation complained of (and possibly also as the background necessary to understanding the true nature and gravity of the provocation): *Clinton, Parker and Evans* [2012] EWCA Crim 2. This implicitly affirms the mainly symbolic significance of s 55(6).

infidelity, as opposed to providing evidence of or anticipating it. It is not clear whether the quaint term 'infidelity', ironically far better suited to the world of marital relations derided by Viscount Simon in *Holmes* than the modern world, will be applied to unmarried partners, to married people between whom there is a separation order, and so on. The need for the courts to consider such questions simply resurrects lines of criminal jurisprudence long thought consigned to the history books.[68]

Section 55(6) of the 2009 Act also draws a seemingly arbitrary distinction between provocation founded on sexual jealousy and provocation founded in sexual envy. Jealousy is, broadly speaking, an emotion experienced at the (threatened) loss of possession of something regarded, whether or not correctly, as one's moral right or morally legitimate expectation.[69] Envy is, broadly speaking, an emotion experienced at the possession by someone else of something that one believes, whether or not justifiably, that one should oneself have instead.[70] Despite the closeness of the structural characteristics of each emotion, provocation based on sexual jealousy is now to be discounted as a qualifying trigger, whereas provocation based on sexual envy is not.[71] Someone (X) may be envious of a second person (Y), because Y has formed a romantic attachment to a third person (Z) whose affection X wants simply for him or herself. In itself, though, Y's attachment to Z does not involve any 'infidelity' to X. So, the envy that explains any loss of self-control by X can be a legitimate qualifying trigger. It is hard to understand the rationale of a law crafted in such a way that it relies on such a clear distinction being drawn between the two emotions, as potentially qualifying triggers. If D stalks a female celebrity he has never met, then flies into a rage and kills her when he (D) sees her passionately kiss someone, that provocation may in principle count a qualifying trigger, because no 'infidelity' is involved in the kiss. By contrast, if D flies into a rage when he sees his wife passionately kiss someone else, that will not count in principle as a qualifying trigger. Yet, if anything, the provocation (vestigial though it is) is surely stronger in the latter case than in the former.

Government deafness to such objections stems from the point being developed here. Section 55(6) of the 2009 Act is not designed either to embody the idea that ascriptive judgement about the gravity of provocation is inevitably nuanced and a matter of degree, or to simplify the tasks for judge and jury. It is designed to make a formal statement of symbolic value, in this instance by turning on its head the law's former implicit endorsement of male violence against unfaithful wives in the way that it shaped the categories of admissible provocation ('qualifying

---

[68] I refer not only to the line of authority already considered exploring the limits of the 'adultery' category, but also to the line of authority exploring the limits of marital rape, prior to the reforms effected by the Sexual Offences Act 2003.

[69] See Tov-Ruach (1980).

[70] Envy is, of course, often accompanied by a feeling—whether or not justified—that the other person only has the desired thing, or quality of excellence, by luck or undeservedly.

[71] Provocation founded on sexual jealousy is by implication largely discounted, as a qualifying trigger, because it is infidelity that induces it: the loss of a valued exclusivity in relation to another's devotion.

triggers').[72] The real problem with that, even if one accepts the legitimacy of what the law is seeking to do, is that the statement is only one of a number of such statements of symbolic value that could have been made, as part of the process of civilizing the law governing partial excuses. Consistent with the modern law's insistence on tolerant and restrained policing, why not have a clause disqualifying police officers from making use of the provoked loss of self-control (as opposed to the fear of serious violence) defence when the killing took place in the purported execution of their duty? Given the modern law's commitment to acting in the best interests of children, and bearing in mind that infants are the group of persons more likely than any other to be the victims of homicide, why not have a clause overruling *Doughty*[73] by disqualifying as provocation anything said or done by a child under the age of (say) 10?[74] If the use of primary legislation to make such statements seems awkward and litigation-prone, then, with relatively little loss of symbolic effect, they could instead have been incorporated into guidelines under secondary legislation.[75] However that may be, the suspicion must be that the commitment of legislators to thorough-going civilization of the provocation defence was only ever half-hearted, if the process was given any thought at all. That the 'infidelity' rule stands alone in this regard makes it appear to be little more than an example of gesture politics.

6. Loss of self-control: a threat to civilized values?

(a) Introduction

The requirement, in a provocation plea, that there have been a loss of self-control at the time of the killing provides a telling instance in which the law has struggled to reconcile competing values. On the one hand, there is naturally at least some sympathy for the person who has found themselves no match for the phenomenological strength of anger at a grave provocation, even though that person has killed in consequence. On the other hand, there is also a countervailing concern for an important common good.[76] A provoked killing, in the absence of any need to act defensively, would seem to be just the kind of case in which, by excusing murder, the law appears to say that it is prepared to look with some benignity on a kind of self-help remedy it is the very purpose of criminal law and punishment to replace: vengeful and lethal violence.[77] As we will see, the law sought at one point to reduce the moral and legal fall-out from this competition between values, by severely restricting the circumstances in which a killing following a loss of self-control was in

---

[72] With the important rider that the new law draws no distinction between unfaithful husbands and unfaithful wives.

[73] (1986) 83 Cr App R 319. In this case, D suffocated a baby, having allegedly lost self-control when he could no longer put up with the baby's crying: see Horder (1987).

[74] The age of criminal responsibility in England and Wales.

[75] For this suggestion, see Horder, <www.publications.parliament.uk/pa/cm200809/cmpublic/coroners/090203/am/90203s07.htm>.

[76] Common good (vi): see text at n 33 above, and Horder (2004), at 17.

[77] Gardner (1998a).

principle excusable: the loss of self-control had to be 'sudden and temporary'.[78] This restriction was meant to contain the moral and legal fall-out from the clash of values. The restriction meant that, in pursuit of the civilizing process, provocation could not be pleaded in any case where D, 'has had time to think, to reflect', and thus where D acts on the, 'conscious formulation of a desire for revenge'.[79] Hence, whilst maintaining a legally recognized measure of sympathy for the person who lost control and killed only in the face of grave provocation, the law could claim to have recognized only a narrow and exceptional departure from the pursuit of an important common good.[80]

Ironically, though, this intentionally restrictive element in the defence of provocation (the requirement for a loss of self-control to be sudden and temporary) became one of the most criticized, on the grounds of its narrowness, as we will see.[81] However, it is in fact more in line with recent civilizing developments in relation to other excuses. For example, in *Hasan*,[82] the House of Lords held that a plea of duress must not succeed unless the threat of death or serious injury is to be implemented 'immediately, or almost immediately on [D's] failure to comply with the threat'.[83] In that regard it will be irrelevant that, for example, D thought—even on reasonable grounds—that police protection would be ineffective to protect him or her and so did not seek it out although it was available. Harsh though it might at first sight seem, such a rule has a civilizing function. It affirms the need for citizens[84] to adhere to the ideal of an almost complete monopoly established by a flourishing and stable polity over the use of force, a monopoly that must be respected even at the risk of a degree of harsh treatment of individuals in some cases.[85] In his speech in *Hasan*, Lord Bingham placed reliance on Lord Morris' argument in *Lynch v DPP for Northern Ireland*[86]—an argument that implicitly relies on common goods (ii) and (vi) above[87]—that the defence of duress:

.... must never be allowed to be the easy answer of those who can devise no other explanation of their conduct *nor of those who readily could have avoided the dominance of threats* nor of those who allow themselves to be at the disposal and under the sway of some gangster-tyrant.[88]

---

[78] *Duffy* [1949] 1 All ER 932n.   [79] *Ibid*.

[80] Common good (vi): see text at n 33 above. As we have seen, this pursuit was symbolized by the contemporaneous abolition of doctrine of chance medley on the grounds that we no longer live in an age where lower temper flashpoints are tolerated, where many people carry swords and are prepared to use them, and when fairly conducted duels attract little moral stigma in practice. See *Semini* [1949] 1 KB 405, and the discussion at n 24 above.

[81] See further Mitchell (2011).

[82] *Hasan* [2005] UKHL 22.

[83] *Ibid*, at para 28 (per Lord Bingham). See, to similar effect, *MacGrowther's case* (1746) Fost 13.

[84] And for courts, in their development of the law.

[85] See passage cited from Horder (1992a), at n 27 above.

[86] [1975] AC 653.

[87] See text at n 33 above.

[88] *Lynch v DPP for Northern Ireland* [1975] AC 653, at 670 (my emphasis). The law now has a separate set of rules to deal with the ongoing influence of 'gangster-tyrants'. See, eg, *Sharp* [1987] QB 853. For similar kinds of reasons, in the USA, the rules regarding the pre-emptive use of self-defence

However, in the case of provocation, the restriction of the plea to instances of 'sudden and temporary' losses of self-control appeared merely to set its civilizing rationale in conflict with a different but equally important civilizing strategic concern: equal respect for both men and women in the design of defences. Suppose that, for a variety of reasons, women are far more prone to delay between the final act of provocation and losing self-control.[89] Then, the requirement for a 'sudden' loss of self-control, more or less immediately following the final act of provocation, puts women at a disadvantage in seeking to plead provocation, relative to men for whom such an immediate reaction comes more naturally.[90] I will suggest that, rather than seek to determine which strategic concern 'wins' in this particular clash, it is better to acknowledge that the stand-alone provocation plea (now under the umbrella of 'loss of self-control') is unworthy of continued recognition as an excuse for murder.

(b) The problem

Two closely related dilemmas confront would-be reformers of the doctrine of provocation, so far as the requirement of loss of self-control is concerned. The first one, the 'immediacy' dilemma, runs like this. On the one hand, an excusatory emphasis (to be found in a number of provocation defences in common law jurisdictions[91]) on the immediacy of violent retaliation stemming from a provoked loss of self-control seems to privilege those—perhaps typically, men—for whom such a reaction to a perceived insult may seem perfectly natural or acceptable.[92] In that regard, the legal concession dictates an excusatory focus on an unedifying side to human nature (a 'shoot from the hip' mentality, if you will), a side of human nature that commonly finds expression in the widespread use of domestic violence against women, of which provoked killings are but the tip of a large iceberg.[93] Moreover, the excusatory emphasis seems anachronistic and hence uncivilized. In spite of the excusatory character of the provocation defence, as currently defined, it seems out of place in a system of criminal justice fit for an age in which the most powerful justification for the monopoly claimed by the state over retributive

---

tend to be confined to situations where there is a need to act immediately or almost immediately to avert the threat: see the discussion in Horder (2002a) and Dressler (2002b).

[89] See, eg, the discussion in Baker (1998), at 198.

[90] See Horder (2005).

[91] See the codes set out in the comparative survey done by the Law Commission (2003), pt 5. A requirement for the defendant's reaction to be sudden or immediate can be found in the Northern Territory Code, s 34; in the Queensland Criminal Code, s 304; the Western Australia Criminal Code, s 281; the Indian Penal Code, s 300 (exception 1); and the Canadian Criminal Code, s 232. The requirement of loss of self-control is also retained in the proposals for reform of, for example, the New South Wales Law Reform Commission (1997). See further Dressler (2002a).

[92] It has been claimed that, in England and Wales, two women per week are killed by current or former (male) partners: see Edwards (1996), at 393–4; Edwards (2004), at 183. See further the studies done by the Law Commission (2004), app A, and app D, pt iii.

[93] There is, of course, a large literature on this. See, eg, Edwards (1996), ch 5. At the time Edwards was writing, one in every four violent crimes was a 'domestic' offence of some kind.

punishment is that the monopoly systematically eliminates and replaces (rather than tolerating or looking benignly on) the exaction of personal retribution for wrongdoing. On the other hand, legislative or judicial attempts to modify the defence to accommodate the morally significant claims of those (perhaps typically, women) whose reaction to provocation is not necessarily or usually a more-or-less immediate, violent explosion of temper, pose the risk of two unsavoury consequences. Such attempts may exacerbate the problem of anachronism, and, ironically, make it easier still for jealous and possessive men to claim an excuse for their angry violence against 'provocative' partners who cross them. Those attempts have involved permitting provocation to be pleaded even when there has been considerable delay between the last provocative event and D's alleged loss of self-control.[94] This development has certainly assisted some (battered) women whose lethal reaction did not immediately follow upon the final provocation. However, it has done so, in part, by downplaying the significance of evidence that D forearmed herself and was set upon revenge from the start.[95] This is evidence that ought to count tellingly against the possibility of excuse, if one takes the problem of anachronism seriously. It might, of course, sometimes be reasonable to forearm oneself where one has good cause to fear that one will otherwise be unavoidably overpowered by a particular aggressor.[96] Even so, such rational forward-planning seems inconsistent with the spontaneity of response at the heart of a plea of provocation. As Simester and Sullivan put it, the law required juries 'to consider an issue of provocation in circumstances where there seems to be ample evidence that the killing was a product of deliberation'.[97] As we may now see, this issue has not disappeared under the new law.

A simple answer to the problem of anachronism might seem to be the creation of a clearer distinction in law between evidence of mere delay, as such, and evidence of pre-planning or revenge-taking, the former being consistent with pleading

---

[94] In England, in that regard, the efforts have been made through judicial development of the common law: see, eg, *Ahluwalia* (1993) Cr App Rep 133; *Pearson* [1992] Crim LR 193; *Thornton* (1992) 1 All ER 306; but see further *Chhay v The Queen* (1994) 72 Australian Crim Rep 1. In some other common law jurisdictions, although there may be a requirement for a loss of self-control, there is no requirement that that loss of self-control be sudden: see, eg, Australian Capital Territory, Crimes Act 1900, s 13(3)(b); New South Wales, Crimes Act 1900, s 23(3)(b); New Zealand, Crimes Act 1961, s 169.

[95] See, in particular, *Ahluwalia* (1993) Cr App Rep 133. Forearming oneself is not, *ipso facto*, inconsistent with an adequate spontaneity of response for the purposes of a provocation plea. It all depends on whether the forearming was part-and-parcel of the (*ex hypothesi*) spontaneous angry response, or showed that the defendant was set upon revenge. For a long-forgotten expression of this point, see *Robinson's Case* Crompton's Justice, folio 26a–b, eg 9, and the better-known *Rowley's Case* (1612) 12 Co Rep 87. Likewise, a desire for revenge in the simple sense of retaliation is not inconsistent with spontaneously lost self-control; indeed, typically, it is the phenomenological strength of this desire that one finds oneself unable to control. However, to be 'set' upon revenge as a matter of practical reasoning, to have decided on it before one loses self-control, is inconsistent with a provocation plea: see *Ibrams and Gregory* (1982) 74 Cr App R 154. I am grateful to Professor Stephen Shute, of Sussex University, for his willingness to discuss this difficult point with me.

[96] See more generally, McColgan (1993).

[97] Simester and Sullivan (2003), at 347.

provocation and the latter not.[98] The 2009 Act seeks to make something of this distinction, by abolishing the supposed requirement for a loss of self-control to be 'sudden' (section 54(2)),[99] whilst at the same time placing outside the scope of the provocation plea killings motivated by a 'considered' desire for revenge (section 54 (4)). However, in this form, such a distinction is in practice likely to prove artificial. Juries sympathetic to D on the grounds of the provocation received (or for any other reason) will find that delay—even substantial delay—was not evidence that a considered desire for revenge had been formed, whereas juries unsympathetic to D (for whatever reason) will find that a delay clearly pointed to the formation of such a desire.[100] Ironically, thus, the distinction has the potential to throw an excusatory cloak around cases in which men have delayed using lethal violence against a partner or former partner, or her new lover (such killings being much more common than those in which a battered woman kills her abuser[101]). In such cases, Ds have been able to provide evidence that they lost self-control immediately before the killing itself, in spite of the delay between the killing and the last provocative act, or they have persuaded the jury that they (the Ds) might somehow have remained in a state of 'loss of self-control' throughout the period of delay. For example, in *Commonwealth v Andrade*,[102] D suspected his wife of infidelity, and observed her with another man. Seven hours after this observation 'confirming' D's suspicions, he killed his wife. In spite of this delay, the court found that 'the jury could have found that the defendant had lost, and not regained, control of himself at the time of the killing, and that this failure was not unreasonable in the circumstances'.[103] More generally, an important American study has found evidence of such a development in those US states which have adopted the Model Penal Code's concept of 'extreme mental or emotional disturbance', a concept that dispenses with any requirement for D's reaction to be immediate or sudden.[104] In those states, the number of cases that reach the jury when the 'provocation' is infidelity or simply a female (former) partner's decision to date another man, have dramatically increased, as compared with those states where the older view prevails, that the provocation must be such as might 'render... [someone] ... liable to act rashly or without due deliberation or reflection, and from passion rather than judgment'.[105] So, whilst some pressing gender problems with the defence of provocation may be addressed by relaxing the requirement of immediacy and

---

[98] See Horder (2005).

[99] Arguably, the requirement for a loss of self-control to be sudden had already disappeared at common law, following the decision in *Ahluwalia* (1993) Cr App R 133.

[100] See further, Gough (1999).

[101] Edwards (1996), at 393–400. See further the evidence gathered by the Victorian Law Reform Commission (2003), ch 2.

[102] 661 NE 2nd 1308 (Mass 1996), discussed in Dressler (2001), at 533 fn 218.

[103] *Commonwealth v Andrade*, 661 NE 2nd 1308 (Mass 1996), 1311. See further *Baillie* [1995] Crim LR 739.

[104] Nourse (1997).

[105] *Maher v People* (1862) 10 Mich 212, 220. See generally, Nourse (1997). At 1336, Nourse says: 'By broadening the time frame...the Model Penal Code makes the provocation claim available to defendants whose criminal acts appear not only intentional but premeditated. By contrast, such claims typically do not reach juries in traditional states.'

eliminating 'considered' revenge killings, others are left to become festering, open wounds.

This brings me directly to the second, closely related, dilemma facing would-be reformers. It concerns the very requirement that there should be a 'loss of self-control' (hence, by way of contrast, it can be called the 'loss of self-control' dilemma). A finding that D lost self-control at the time of the killing is crucial to mitigation by way of provocation across the (former) common law world. It has been abandoned perhaps only in the minority of US states in which the Model Penal Code's concept of 'extreme mental or emotional disturbance' has replaced it. Nevertheless, a good deal of mystery surrounds the concept.[106] The idea of losing self-control might be thought to be more metaphorically than psychologically descriptive. In the case law, it is elaborated on by Ds only through the use of further metaphors for their experience, such as the notion of 'exploding', 'cracking', 'snapping', and so forth (respecting which, of course, one will often have only their testimony as proof of the existence of the supposed loss of self-control).[107] Even so, there might be thought to be little excusatory weight to a claim that one was moved intentionally to kill another by a punitive retaliatory urge, even if it was provoked, were it not for the fact that it is claimed that the provocation in question led to an un-looked for loss of control of that urge, making D's reaction almost (albeit, obviously, not truly) 'instinctive' or only quasi-voluntary. Looked at in this way, there might be little to disagree with (whatever departure it may have involved from previous authorities[108]) in Devlin J's famous direction to the jury on the meaning of the subjective condition in provocation cases, approved by the Court of Appeal in *Duffy*:

> Provocation is some act, or series of acts...which...actually causes in the accused, a sudden and temporary loss of self-control, rendering the accused so subject to passion as to make him or her for the moment not the master of his mind.... Indeed circumstances which induce a desire for revenge are inconsistent with provocation, since the conscious formulation of a desire for revenge means that a person has had time to think, to reflect, and that would negative a sudden and temporary loss of self-control which is of the essence of provocation.[109]

Devlin J's clear and forthright interpretation of the 'essence of provocation' is tailor-made to answer the criticism that the concession the law thereby makes in homicide cases is anachronistic and hence uncivilized, because it is inconsistent with the law's abhorrence of 'self-help' punitive remedies for (perceived) injustice done. Not so, Devlin J might have said, because the condescension is based on the ethical proximity between sudden explosions of rage in which D lashes out with lethal intent, and other 'quasi-voluntary' conduct with an external cause, such as (say) D's sudden action in leaping through another person's glass window to avoid a runaway truck thought to be bearing down on her.[110] Quasi-voluntary actions, occupying

---

[106] See further, Horder (2004), at 76–98.   [107] See Horder (1992a), at 109.
[108] On which, see Horder (1992c).   [109] [1949] 1 All ER 932n.
[110] For this kind of analysis of the effect of provocation, see Hart and Honoré (1985), at 148–9 (obviously, I am not concerned with any possible defence of necessity or duress of circumstances in

the hinterland between the purely involuntary and the fully voluntary (albeit speedily decided on), pose no implicit threat to the law's monopoly on retributive punishment, so the argument goes, just in virtue of the fact that—unlike authentic expressions of justified retribution—they are not considered and reasoned responses to wrongdoing.

Even so, not only does Devlin J's explanation of the essence of provocation give rise to the immediacy dilemma, outlined above, but it raises the loss of self-control dilemma as well. An insistence that D have lost self-control, and been not for the moment the master of his or her mind, might be capable of giving genuinely excusatory colour to a retaliatory action. However, it is a yet further respect in which the operation of the doctrine of provocation indirectly discriminates in favour of those—largely, men—for whom a violent outburst of rage in the face of some kinds of provocation is understood to be perfectly natural (and, perhaps, regarded by some with sneaking admiration as 'manly'[111]).[112] Especially when we are concerned with men's angry violence against women, the tendency for violence to be expressed following a sudden loss of self-control seems likely to stem from a deeply ingrained assumption that there will be nothing much to fear by way of significant retaliatory (or other kind of) threat from women provokers, in general, or from an individual woman in particular, if and when the man's control is lost in the face of some perceived insult or wrongdoing on her part. What does this tell us about loss of self-control? Action that reflects a loss of self-control is commonly what Raz calls an 'expressive action'.[113] Such actions occur when, at least to some degree, the agent permits him or herself to lose control (they are thus not involuntary), although the loss of control is genuine enough once it occurs:

In all, purely expressive actions are almost like actions for reasons. They differ in that while they do not involve loss of control over their initiation they involve diminution of that control.... My suggestion is that we can think of people who perform normally expressive actions as people who let themselves express their emotions, feelings, or moods in action. They permit themselves to do so. ... In the case of purely expressive actions we ... allow the emotion to express itself, the will acting as a non-interfering gate-keeper.[114]

The taken-for-granted assumption that there will be no equal and opposite retaliatory, or otherwise threateningly negative, response from a (female) provoker is what nourishes some men's sense that they can 'permit themselves' to lose self-control when angered.

---

such an example). Plato put the point this way, '[t]he man whose anger bursts forth uncontrollably, whose action is instant, immediate, and without premeditation, resembles the involuntary killer', *Laws*, passage 9 (866d5–868a1) cited by Saunders (1991), at 155.

[111] One is reminded of Lord Holt CJ's view (cited earlier) that 'jealousy is the rage of the man, and adultery is the highest invasion of property': *Mawgridge* (1707) Kel 119, at 137.

[112] See Edwards (1996), at 379.

[113] Raz (1999), at 43.

[114] *Ibid*, at 43 and 44. In another context, a classic case of an expressive action, in Raz's sense, would be the reaction of members of a football crowd as a penalty in their favour is scored. Having waited with bated breath, the members of the crowd 'permit' themselves to lose control in a demonstrative way at the moment the goal is scored.

By way of contrast, especially when they are locked into relationships with violent men, women are far less likely to 'permit themselves' to lose self-control in the face of provocation. The reason is not far to seek. It is obvious that when D is taunted by V who is known or believed to be physically more powerful and aggressive than D, D's anger at the taunt is liable to be tempered by fear of the provoking victim's own reaction to any expressive display by D of annoyance at the taunt. So, D's reaction to the taunt will be one of mixed emotions—fear and anger—for which, in the most serious cases, it will be convenient to use the US Model Penal Code's term 'extreme emotional disturbance'.[115] The mixed character of D's emotional response to a taunt, in such circumstances, is liable to ensure that she does not lose self-control in an expressive way—whether or not immediately— of any retaliatory impulse she may be experiencing. However, depending on the gravity of the provocation (provocation of a kind that may have had a considerable cumulative effect over some years), D may be left in a state of extreme emotional disturbance. Whilst the state endures, D is, given that fear is mixed with anger, likely to take retaliatory action only if and when the provoker is 'off his guard'.[116] As counsel for Kiranjit Ahluwalia put it (as reported by the Court of Appeal[117]), 'women who have been subjected frequently over a period to violent treatment may react to the final act or words by...a "slow-burn" reaction rather than by an immediate loss of self-control'. Alex Reilly expresses it thus:

[L]oss of self-control in anger is traditionally characterised by external signs of rage and, in particular, the extremity of the violent response. Fear might be associated with external signs which are not easily detectable; perhaps being characterised more typically by paralysis and submission, while retaining the ability to response with a single act of homicidal violence.[118]

The immediacy and the loss of self-control dilemmas were identified by the Law Commission, in its Consultation Paper, *Partial Defences to Murder*, although they are not clearly distinguished.[119] On the one hand, as the Law Commission put it, there is a case for saying that, '[t]he defence of provocation elevates the emotion of sudden anger above emotions of fear, despair, compassion and empathy... [and]...in respect of D's with battered women syndrome, provocation may not be a suitable defence because the killer is reacting out of fear or despair'.[120] However, on the other hand, it goes on to say:

It is difficult to distinguish revenge killings, so as to exclude them from this defence. The courts have stretched the subjective requirement, 'loss of self-control', initially in order to

[115] Model Penal Code, art 1.12, discussed in Chalmers (2004). It should be noted that it has for many years been clear that the 'sudden heat of passion' defence in US law, analogous to the provocation defence in English law, is apt (unlike the English provocation defence) to encompass instances in which passion is generated by fear as well as by anger: see the cases discussed in Dressler (2001), at 528, such as *LaPierre v State*, 734 P 2nd 97 (Cal 1958).
[116] I suggest that this is the best characterization of cases such as *Ahluwalia* [1992] 4 All ER 889, *Thornton* [1992] 1 All ER 306, and *Duffy* [1949] 1 All ER 932, amongst others.
[117] *Ahluwalia* [1992] 4 All ER 889, 896 (per Lord Taylor CJ).
[118] Reilly (1997), at 330.
[119] Law Commission (2003), at paras 4.164–4.168.
[120] *Ibid*, at paras 4.164–4.168.

deal with battered women syndrome cases. The wider measure for loss of self-control when applied in other cases . . . raises the question of whether the scope of the defence is too wide, or potentially so. How do gangland killings stay out of the scope of the defence?[121]

(c) Doing away with the loss of self-control requirement?

The Law Commission's answer to these problems was to recommend the removal of the loss of self-control requirement in provocation pleas.[122] However, under its recommendations, a provocation plea would still be disqualified where D acted, 'in considered desire for revenge'.[123] The latter recommendation[124] must be kept in mind, even though ultimately the Government chose to retain the loss of self-control requirement.[125] Under the Law Commission's recommendations, the provocation defence was to still to have an 'old-style' application to instances in which D killed only in response to a 'gross provocation . . . which caused the defendant to have a justifiable sense of being seriously wronged'.[126] However, the defence was also to cover a new set of cases in which D killed in response to a 'fear of serious violence towards the defendant or another'.[127] Under the Law Commission's recommendations, though, in neither of these sets of circumstances was there a requirement to show any kind of loss of self-control, so long as D did not act 'in considered desire for revenge'.[128] The Law Commission's thinking was that by eliminating the subjective element, one instantly escapes (in my terminology) the loss of self-control dilemma, whilst doing at least something to address the immediacy dilemma by excluding calculated revenge killings from the scope of mitigation.

The first point to note is that the scope in practice to give effect to this thinking is little broader than a knife edge. Provoked killings inevitably involve some element of 'desire for retaliatory suffering'.[129] That is why the recommendation (subsequently adopted in the 2009 Act, section 54(4)) only speaks of disqualifying cases in which there was a 'considered' desire for revenge, and not just a 'desire for revenge'. Had section 54(4) eliminated all provoked killing motivated by a desire for revenge pure and simple, it would have paradoxically provided for the elimination of the defence of provocation itself. Secondly, had the loss of self-control requirement been abolished, as the Law Commission recommended, one result of

---

[121] *Ibid*, at para 4.168.   [122] For a detailed discussion, see Mitchell (2011).

[123] Law Commission (2004), at para 1.13.   [124] Adopted by s 54(4) of the 2009 Act.

[125] 2009 Act, s 54(1)(a).   [126] Law Commission (2004), at para 1.13.

[127] *Ibid*. As is now well-known, the Government accepted the latter recommendation by the Law Commission, broadening the defence to include killing through fear rather than anger, more or less in full. The former recommendation it accepted only in a still further restricted form. In addition to the need for provocation such as gave rise to a justifiable sense of being seriously wronged, a further requirement was imposed requiring that the provocation be 'extremely grave' in character. This further requirement virtually eliminates the need for the long-established 'objective test' of whether a person of ordinary temperament, tolerance, and self-restraint might have reacted in a similar way; but that further hurdle was nonetheless still included: 2009 Act, s 54(1)(c).

[128] Law Commission (2004), at para 1.13. See now the 2009 Act, s 54(4).

[129] Horder (1992a), at 60.

the reform would have been that Smith and Hogan's famous example of how a killing, however gravely provoked, must be murder unless there was evidence of a loss of self-control, would no longer be accurate:

A traditional example of extreme provocation is the finding of a spouse in the act of adultery; but if D, on so finding his wife, were to read her a lecture on the enormity of her sin and then methodically to load a gun and shoot her . . . D would be guilty of murder and it would be irrelevant that the jury may think that a reasonable man in like circumstances would lose self-control.[130]

Given that the Government chose to retain the loss of self-control requirement, whether or not the Law Commission would have agreed that Smith and Hogan's example could, in theory, fall within the scope of the provocation as the Law Commission wished to reform it is no longer significant.[131] More important is the fact that the Government did not confine the application of the loss of self-control requirement to old-style provocation cases. The requirement has also been applied to the new kinds of cases that could reduce murder to manslaughter, as recommended by the Law Commission: cases where a loss of self-control was (in the wording of the 2009 Act section 55(3)) attributable to, 'D's fear of serious violence from V against D or another identified person'.

Almost all the attention, in relation to this provision, has understandably focused on its application to cases in which D is a woman who has been violently or psychologically abused over a long period by her partner (V), then kills him.[132] The common law struggled to accommodate such cases within the old provocation defence, for reasons that still have an application under the new law. First, D's reaction in such cases was in all probability motivated not so much by anger and hence by the desire for retaliatory suffering, but more (or exclusively) by fears about V's continued, and perhaps escalating, use of violent or psychological abuse. In many such cases, D would have killed V when he was off his guard, as when asleep or in a drunken stupor.[133] In such cases, there often seems to be little scope for a plea of self-defence, because there may appear to have been little prospect of an imminent attack by V that is necessarily and proportionately pre-empted by the use of lethal violence. Further, although in some such cases there may be evidence of diminished responsibility sufficient to reduce murder to manslaughter,[134] that will be far from true of all such cases. Moreover, even if there is such evidence, D may understandably believe that it would be degrading to rely on it in circumstances where the focus should be, morally and legally, on the terrifying position in which V put D rather than on any (possibly temporary) defects of mental functioning that V's course of conduct produced in D.

---

[130] Smith and Hogan (1999), at 356–7. Obviously, this example would still be murder under the reformed law, but for a different reason: that the only provocation was an act constituting infidelity.

[131] For criticism of this aspect of the recommendations, see Horder (2005), at 133.

[132] See now Edwards (2011), and the helpful discussion in Simester and Sullivan *et al* (2010), at 400–1.

[133] See *Ahluwalia* [1992] 4 All ER 889; *Thornton (No 2)* [1992] 1 All ER 306.

[134] See *Ahluwalia* [1992] 4 All ER 889.

The thinking is, then, that by providing a defence to murder along the lines of section 55(3), the law (a) avoids the risk of mis-describing D's motivation by squeezing it into the old-style provocation category, (b) avoids the risk of degrading D by requiring her to plead diminished responsibility, and also (c) provides a way out of a dilemma confronting those who seek an acquittal on the grounds of self-defence in such cases. The dilemma arises from the need to decide whether to stake everything on a claim to a complete acquittal on self-defence grounds, bearing in mind the risk that the claim may be rejected if jury takes the view that D's lethal reaction was not a necessary and proportionate pre-emptive strike. If that risk turns into reality (in the absence of any basis for pleading old-style provocation or diminished responsibility), D faces conviction for murder. The section 55(3) defence provides an escape from this dilemma, by making provision for a halfway house verdict: conviction for manslaughter in cases where a fear of serious violence stemming from a loss of self-control explains D's actions. These issues have prompted widespread discussion that I will not go further into here, in so far as they apply to abused women.[135] What has been neglected is the application of section 55(3) to other instances in which D responds to a fear of serious violence by killing. A brief examination of such cases reveals weaknesses in section 55(3). Consider this example:[136]

D is a soldier on duty at a checkpoint, at which there have been incidents in which approaching cars have fired at soldiers on duty. D shouts a warning at a car that is heading directly for him at high speed. As the car closes in, D fires a shot that passes harmlessly to the left of the car. The car veers past him to the right, and D fires another six shots through the rear window, killing the driver of the car. It turns out that the driver was merely a young 'joy rider'. When interviewed, D says that he panicked after firing the first shot, but also that at the back of his mind was the thought that the driver might blow up the car, killing others, with a remote control once the driver had passed the checkpoint. D admits he has no explanation for his panic, in spite of his training, or for his belief that the driver might have a remote control device.

My focus here will be on the relevance of a loss of self-control to the analysis of this set of facts. Quite wrongly, English law has for some time permitted D to seek complete acquittal through a claim of self-defence in this situation, even though his belief that his act was necessary to prevent a potentially lethal explosion was not based on reasonable grounds.[137] That being so, there is a good prospect that D will be able to establish a self-defence claim on these facts. Under the Law Commission's recommendations, D could also have pleaded—perhaps in the alternative—'excessive defence', on the basis that he acted out of fear of serious violence, but simply went too far in his reaction. Most noticeably, in making this second plea,

[135] See Edwards (2011); Herring (2011).
[136] Based on a mixture of the facts of *Clegg* [1995] 1 All ER 334 (HL), and *McCann v UK* (1996) 21 EHRR 97.
[137] See now the Criminal Justice and Immigration Act 2008, s 76(3). See, more broadly, the discussion in Leverick (2006), at 160–8; Horder (2004), at 57 fn 40.

under the Law Commission's recommendations there would have been no need for D to rely on the 'panic' element in his or her reaction, because there would have been no need to show that he or she had lost self-control at the time of the killing. By contrast, under section 55(3) of the 2009 Act, the partial defence would be unavailable unless D could show that he or she had lost self-control at the time of the fatal shooting. In theory, this makes D's panic a crucial issue; but what is really added by this requirement? I suggest that nothing useful is added. Section 55(3) reflects an understandable desire to make one concept—loss of self-control—the guiding concept in both provocation and excessive defence cases, given that the two may be combined in a single plea; but the result is confusion. When, as in my example, someone is trained to occupy a role in which they are duty-bound to remain in control, precisely because they are armed and may open fire with lethal intent in some circumstances, how can a 'loss of self-control' even get off the ground as part of their excusatory defence if they do impermissibly open fire and kill?[138] The loss of self-control requirement—an additional ascriptive feature of the partial excuse added to the need to show that serious violence was feared[139]—may in some cases wrongly sideline a powerful underlying normative argument. This is the argument that, in some situations—typically when people are performing certain roles—self-control should never be lost.[140]

The law's understanding of loss of self-control goes wrong in two ways, from the perspective of someone seeking to civilize permissions and excuses. First, the absence of any requirement that a loss of self-control be sudden opens the door to mitigation in too many cases where D has had time to brood on the supposed provocation. This undermines the ideal that in a civilized society people temporize, and restrain their desires for retaliatory suffering through violence. Secondly, the law is now prepared to look with benignity on losses of self-control leading to impermissible killing in the course of defensive or law enforcement action, even when it is a defining feature of D's role *not* to lose self-control in such situations, and to keep his or her head even when others may be losing theirs. Whatever the subjectivist arguments there may be in favour of such a legal position, both developments unacceptably diminish the law's claim to be civilized, as well as humane. They run counter to the hard-won civilizing developments (examined earlier) achieved in the mid-twentieth century, through restrictions on the scope for the permissible use of force, and on the scope of the doctrine of provocation.

---

[138] This point is particularly well explained, in relation to this kind of situation, by Gardner (1998b), at 579–81. As he memorably puts it (at 580), '[o]ur soldier's excuse is not validated by the standards of level-headedness which he tends to live up to, so that he can excuse himself by saying: I've always been a bit of a panicker, so what did you expect?' In my example it is not significant whether D is a 'bit of a panicker' but Gardner's point is well-made nonetheless.

[139] A requirement considered below.

[140] See further, Horder (2004), at 54: 'Surely, for example, the President of the USA should *never* lose his or her temper when one finger is hovering over the nuclear "button", whatever the provocation?'

II. Defective Foundations: the Royal Commission and The 1957 Act

1. Reform issues wrongly rolled up together

The 1957 Homicide Act has set most of the terms for the legal and scholarly debate concerning the scope of murder, and hence of the mandatory penalty for murder, for more than 50 years. The 1957 Act was based to a very significant extent on the recommendations of the Royal Commission on Capital Punishment.[141] The Royal Commission was naturally guided in its deliberations and recommendations by the way that it interpreted its main term of reference, 'to consider and report whether liability under criminal law...to suffer capital punishment for murder should be limited or modified...',[142] that penalty being, 'fixed and automatic'.[143] These terms of reference, like the appointment of the Royal Commission itself, were themselves ultimately the product of a botched and (in any event) half-hearted attempt by the post-war Labour Government to include a clause abolishing the death penalty in the Criminal Justice Act 1948.[144]

Public opinion in post-war Britain strongly supported the death penalty, with almost 70 per cent disapproving even of a temporary suspension.[145] Prominent among 'retentionists' were key sections of the ruling elite: both the judiciary and the House of Lords.[146] The Labour Government was at that time seeking to reduce the power of the House of Lords to delay legislation more generally, on the grounds that the House of Lords 'was not competent to interpret the popular will as against the judgment of the House of Commons'.[147] So, a defeat by the House of Lords on the abolition of capital punishment at a time when, on this issue at least, the House of Lords found itself backed to the hilt (so to speak) by public opinion, was unthinkable. A watered-down clause in the Criminal Justice Bill retaining the death penalty for a narrow range of murders was introduced at one stage, but was decisively rejected even by those who favoured abolition.[148] In the months following the passing of the Criminal Justice Act 1948, the setting up of a Royal Commission was endorsed by the cabinet, with the Commission's remit including

---

[141] Royal Commission on Captial Punishment (1953).   [142] *Ibid*, at 1 (my emphasis).

[143] *Ibid*, at para 144. This obviously meant that, by way of contrast with other crimes, leaving matters of leniency to the sentencing process or to the Home Secretary's discretion to commute the sentence was not adequate to do justice. The death sentence was not, of course, carried out in every case at that time, even if it was mandatory for the judge to pass that sentence following conviction.

[144] See the fascinating account of the history leading up to the appointment of the Royal Commission, in Bailey (2000).

[145] *Ibid*, at 337.

[146] *Ibid*, at 311, 315, and 348.

[147] *Ibid*, at 342.

[148] *Ibid*, at 343–4. The kinds of murder for which the death penalty was to be retained were murder incidental to robbery, burglary, etc committed by gangs, murder in the course of a sexual offence or in using of explosives, murder in resisting or avoiding arrest, escaping from custody, and the like, murder through the 'systematic administration of poison', murdering a prison officer, and committing a second murder.

the limitation but not the abolition of the death penalty.[149] The cabinet's endorsement was no doubt made easier by the fact that the Royal Commission would not be reporting in the lifetime of the existing Parliament. The Royal Commission duly reported in 1953, by which time the Conservative Government—which favoured retention—had been in power for two years. The new Government initially rejected the Royal Commission's recommendations,[150] but was still under pressure to make some reforms to stave off demands for complete abolition of the death penalty. Consequently, it repeated the previous Government's ill-fated approach: retaining the penalty for certain categories of murder in the 1957 Act.[151] However, that approach was to be buttressed by important doctrinal changes, whose effects over time in reducing the application of the death penalty were less likely to be noticed by the public. Not only was the scope of 'murder' to be narrowed in law, but partial defences reducing murder to manslaughter were to be widened. It is against that background that the Royal Commission's recommendations must be understood.

The Royal Commission saw its task as being the liberal duty 'to look for means of confining the scope of that punishment as narrowly as possible without impairing the efficacy attributed to it'.[152] How was this to be achieved? The Royal Commission set out two paths to reform, one more confidently endorsed than the other. The first, fully endorsed, path involved a doctrinal focus both on whether 'certain forms of homicide should be taken out of [the murder] category', and on the provocation defence.[153] The second, less enthusiastically endorsed, path to reform involved a focus on a broader question of 'whether any defects we had found in the existing system could be better remedied by giving either the Judge or the jury a discretionary power to substitute a lesser penalty in the process of trial'.[154] It was the first path that was by-and-large taken by the Government, in shaping the 1957 Act, with such significant consequences for the direction of legal analysis and theorizing in the following 50 years.

Changes to the law involved in the first path to reform included the abolition of the doctrine of constructive malice, a reform that, as we have seen, had been a long-term target of progressive lawyers and scholars for many years.[155] Further, the doctrine of provocation—reducing murder to manslaughter—was not only to

---

[149] Some 50 years later, a Labour Government was to do something rather similar, of course, in setting out the Law Commission's terms of reference for the review of murder. The review was to move forwards on the assumption that the mandatory life sentence was retained for murder: see the discussion in Ch 1 above.

[150] Which included the view that it was unworkable to try to isolate categories of murder suitable for the death penalty.

[151] This time, the categories were murder in the course of theft, by shooting or explosion, in resisting arrest or escaping from custody, the murder of a police officer, the murder of a prison officer by the prisoner, and committing more than one murder: Bailey (2000), at 345–6.

[152] Royal Commission on Capital Punishment (1953), at para 15. The reference to the death penalty's supposed 'efficacy' was a nod in the direction of the Labour Government's view that the death penalty could only be justified on deterrent grounds, and not on retributive grounds: Bailey (2000), at 343.

[153] Royal Commission on Capital Punishment (1953), at para 15.

[154] *Ibid.*

[155] See Ch 1 above; Royal Commission on Capital Punishment (1953), at para 790(4).

be retained, but slightly widened. Provocative words were henceforth to be treated as just as capable as deeds of depriving the reasonable person of self-control, and the old deeds-based 'categories' of sufficient provocation were accordingly to be abolished.[156] However, no analogous defence to murder was to be put in place for 'mercy' killings,[157] howsoever defined, and the Royal Commission rejected a proposal for a partial defence of diminished responsibility.[158] The creation of a new offence of aiding, abetting, or instigating suicide was recommended, to be used in cases of suicide pacts in which the parties intended to die together through mutual assistance.[159] By contrast, it was recommended that suicide pact cases in which the survivor had killed the other party (later referred to by the Law Commission as 'you-then-me' pacts[160]) were to continue to be treated as murder cases.[161] Clearly, these were a very modest set of recommendations, involving (setting on one side the abolition of constructive malice[162]) relatively minor changes to the substantive law.

Having said that, the Royal Commission also floated a more imaginative solution (in its own words, 'a radical departure'[163]) to the problem of murder's, and hence the death penalty's, over-extensiveness.[164] This solution went beyond reform of substantive law doctrine, to include reform of sentencing procedure. In broad terms, there was to be a two-step process. First, the jury would determine whether or not the accused was guilty of murder. If the accused was found guilty of murder then, at the second stage, the recommendation was to allow a jury to find that there were 'extenuating circumstances' explaining or attending the murder.[165] At the second stage, such a finding would mean that the judge could no longer pass the death penalty, but would instead reflect those circumstances in handing down a sentence of imprisonment for life.[166] I will not go through all the advantages and disadvantages of the recommendation discussed by the Royal Commission.[167] Most significantly, the Royal Commission saw this radical solution as a way to stop the spread—that, ironically, it proposed to contribute to itself in its more modest recommendations—of demands for new lesser offences or partial defences

---

[156] *Ibid*, (6).   [157] *Ibid*, (10).   [158] *Ibid*, (27).   [159] *Ibid*, (8).

[160] Law Commission (2005), at para 8.28.   [161] *Ibid*.

[162] I do not think it unfair to set this issue on one side, as the doctrine had been so heavily criticized already, by 1949. It is also arguable that the abolition of constructive malice was not, by 1957, such a radical step. The doctrine had already been significantly narrowed in scope at common law: see *Serné* (1887) 16 Cox 311.

[163] Royal Commission on Capital Punishment (1953), at para 571.

[164] *Ibid*, ch 8.

[165] *Ibid*, at para 594. We saw in Ch 1 above (at the end of section IV) that an attempt was made during the passage of the Coroners and Justice Bill 2009 through the House of Lords to replace the Government's Law Commission-backed proposals with changes along such lines.

[166] The Royal Commission looked at some variations on this recommendation in the Belgium Criminal Code, the South African Criminal Code, and in the Criminal Codes of Pennsylvania, Massachusetts, and New Jersey: see Royal Commission on Capital Punishment (1953), at paras 586–94. The Royal Commission acknowledged that, by substituting 'imprisonment for life' for the death penalty, it would not be substituting a whole life sentence.

[167] See generally, Royal Commission on Capital Punishment (1953), ch 8.

to remove certain types of homicide from the scope of murder. The Commission said (in a passage worth citing at some length):

The signal advantage of the jury discretion is that it would solve our main problem. It would make the law of murder flexible... the courts would be free to impose a sentence of life imprisonment for such offences as 'mercy killings', murders of children by mothers in distressing circumstances not covered by the Infanticide Act, murder committed under provocation of a kind or degree inadequate to reduce the crime to manslaughter or culpable homicide, cases of mental abnormality insufficient to justify a finding of insanity or, in Scotland, of diminished responsibility.... It would also enable the courts... to give such weight as they thought proper to the youth of the offender.[168]

This radical recommendation was *not* intended to replace the narrower doctrinal reforms also being recommended, but to supplement them. Juries were still to consider the expanded doctrine of provocation, the special provisions for infanticide, and the new offence of aiding, abetting, or instigating suicide at the first stage, namely when deciding whether or not D was guilty of murder. So, the recommendation, though imaginative, was perhaps not quite as radical as the Royal Commission believed it to be. Moreover, it was not endorsed with any special enthusiasm. The Royal Commission qualified their endorsement of it by saying as part of its recommendation, '[w]e recognise that the disadvantages of a system of "jury discretion" may be thought to outweigh its merits':[169] hardly an illustration of having the courage of one's convictions.

It is in some ways remarkable that the Royal Commission recommended for handling through 'jury discretion' not only cases of mercy killing and cases of provocation too weak to satisfy the formal requirements for the partial defence, but also cases of infanticide and diminished responsibility[170] falling short of the doctrinal requirements in law for a successful plea. For, in so recommending, the Royal Commission was opening the way for unduly harsh treatment of killings influenced by mental disorder. It was opening the way for cases to occur in which a judge could find that he or she had no alternative but to sentence to death someone believed to be suffering from an abnormality of mental functioning at the time of the offence. This could happen when the jury had convicted of murder and then refused to declare any mitigating circumstances, in spite of clear medical evidence pointing to an abnormality of mental functioning.[171] Ironically, given the liberal, civilizing aims of the Royal Commission in general, to allow for this possibility was to oblige judges to perpetrate a serious moral wrong when handing down death sentences in such cases, notwithstanding the possibility that this penalty might be mitigated at a later stage through the prerogative of mercy. As the dissentients in the decision in *Atkins v Virginia*[172] (subsequently endorsed by a majority in the US Supreme Court[173]) were to put it many years later:

---

[168] *Ibid*, at para 568.   [169] *Ibid*, at para 790(46).
[170] At that time, diminished responsibility was a defence to murder in Scotland, but not in England and Wales.
[171] Royal Commission on Capital Punishment (1953), at para 560.
[172] 260 Va. 375, 534 SE 2nd 312 (2000).   [173] *Atkins v Virginia* 536 US 304 (2002).

It is indefensible to conclude that individuals who are mentally retarded are not to some degree less culpable for their criminal acts. By definition, such individuals have substantial limitations not shared by the general population. A moral and civilised society diminishes itself if its system of justice does not afford recognition and consideration of those limitations in a meaningful way.[174]

In this respect, the Royal Commission failed to distinguish between (i) cases involving reduced *responsibility* for committing murder (through, in this instance, diminished capacity), that meant it would be inhumane to pass the death penalty however terrible the murder, and (ii) cases involving an ascriptive judgement that too little blame can be attached to an offender to warrant the mandatory death penalty for murder.[175] Rules of responsibility relate to the extent or degree to which D was morally active, or only passive, with regard to his or her conduct (here, murder).[176] The greater the extent of an abnormality of mental functioning (or the younger D is), the more passive D is likely to have been, morally speaking, with regard to the commission of murder. It is strongly arguable that any proven degree of moral passivity with regard to D's conduct in killing another makes the mandatory passing of the death penalty nothing short of abhorrent. In that regard, the recommendations of the Royal Commission were not consistent. The Commission rightly recommended that it should no longer be possible to pass the death penalty on those under the age of majority (at that time, 21 years of age).[177] However, the Royal Commission wrongly failed to follow this through by making an analogous recommendation for all those suffering from diminished capacity at the time of the offence. Such a recommendation would have been appropriate, even if the diminution of capacity would not have sufficed to satisfy the requirements of the infanticide offence or (in Scotland) the diminished responsibility defence.[178]

Two important consequences flowed from the way that the Royal Commission developed its more imaginative recommendations as a supplement to, and not a replacement for, the much more modest doctrinal proposals. First, the Commission's lack of real commitment to the more imaginative set of recommendations, as compared with its commitment to the more modest proposals, left the Government greater freedom to adopt the latter, rather than the former, as the foundational structure for the new law. What the Government did was simply make some concession to the more imaginative recommendations, by the expedient of tacking on a few further doctrinal reforms cherry-picked (and if need be modified) from these more imaginative recommendations. So, to begin with, the Government adopted the Royal Commission's recommendations for a widened partial defence of provocation (section 3 of the 1957 Act). The Government did not take either of two more radical courses: either putting provocation on a par with 'mercy' killing,

---

[174] *Atkins v Virginia* 260 Va. 375, 534 S.E. 2d 312, at 325.

[175] On the relevance to the criminal law of the distinction between normative and descriptive rules, and rules of responsibility, see Horder (2004), at 52–8, and n 38 above.

[176] See Horder (2004), at 9–10.

[177] Royal Commission on Capital Punishment (1953), at paras 196–206.

[178] See text at n 168 above.

the latter being thought by the Royal Commission best suited for lenient treatment only through the prerogative of mercy, or giving to the jury the task of deciding if the element of provocation or of mercy in the killing amounted to an 'extenuating circumstance'. Yet, the Royal Commission, in rejecting the suggestion that there should be a partial defence of diminished responsibility, had itself described the partial defence treatment of the provocation issue as nothing more than:

[A] device to enable the courts to take account of a special category of mitigating circumstances in cases of murder and to avoid passing sentence of death in cases where such circumstances exist.[179]

Why, then, continue with the partial defence structure in any form? By recommending retention of that structure for provocation, and by only half-heartedly recommending the more dynamic structure in which the focus was on the jury's role in point of mitigation for sentencing purposes, the Royal Commission itself paved the way for the expansion of partial defences. The Government went on to adopt the partial defence structure to provide a means of reducing murder to manslaughter in both 'die together' and 'you-then-me' suicide pacts (section 4 of the 1957 Act).[180] Additionally, the Government felt free to use the partial defence structure to seek to resolve, at least in part, the ethical problem of judges having to pronounce the sentence of death on mentally disordered offenders. It did this, contrary to the recommendations of the Royal Commission, through further doctrinal reform in the shape of yet another partial defence. This was the defence of diminished responsibility (section 2 of the 1957 Act), borrowed from Scotland, and embodied in provisions later described by Edward Griew as 'altogether a disgrace', and by Buxton LJ as 'disastrous... [and] beyond redemption'.[181]

A much simpler, less adversarial and legalistic structure might have emerged had the Royal Commission, and then the Government, adopted a different scheme. First, instances should have been clearly identified in which it would simply be morally unacceptable to pass the death penalty, however horrific the crime. D's youth (being under the age of majority) or the judge's acceptance of evidence of D's diminished mental capacity,[182] at the time of the offence, should have been placed in this category. These kinds of case should have been treated separately because they concern the rules of responsibility.[183] Secondly, instances should have been identified, perhaps through guidelines to judges, in which too little blame may attach to D, given the circumstances in which the killing took place (provocation;

---

[179] Royal Commission on Capital Punishment (1953), at para 413.

[180] Contrary to the Royal Commission's recommendation for a lesser offence to deal with the former and its recommendation that the latter kind of pact should remain murder in the survivor. The aiding or abetting suicide offence was to come, of course, in the Suicide Act 1961.

[181] Cited in Law Commission (2005), at para 6.36.

[182] I will not argue the point here, but there is a strong case for saying that determinations of whether D is suffering from diminished mental capacity (and if so to what extent) are better dealt with by trial judges than by juries. This is what happens in jurisdictions in which diminished capacity is dealt with as a sentencing matter: see, eg, Victorian Law Reform Commission (2004), ch 5; Hemming (2008).

[183] See Horder (2004), at 52–8, and text at n 175 above.

'mercy' killing; suicide pact, some defensive motivation) to make the death penalty the right penalty. In such cases, cases where an ascriptive judgement of lesser blame makes the death penalty the wrong one,[184] the jury judgement that there were extenuating circumstances would prevent the judge from passing the death penalty. In both sets of instances, what is of great importance, bearing in mind the sorry history of the partial defence structure that was preferred in the 1957 Act, is that questions of degree are better handled. Under a partial defence structure, a great deal can be made to turn on exactly how much provocation there was (whether it might have moved an ordinary person to lose self-control and kill), or on exactly how diminished D's capacity was ('substantial' impairment), in a way that adversarial litigation is not ideally suited to bring out. Moreover, even in cases where it is possible largely to remove questions of degree, as in the definition of 'suicide pacts' for the purposes of the partial defence in section 4 of the 1957 Act, this inevitably involves some arbitrary line-drawing. Perhaps the key question, though, is whether the 1957 Act lived up to the promise of a more civilized law of homicide; arguably, it did not.

2. The 1957 Act and civilized values

I will not go through all the now well-known criticisms of the 1957 Act, or go over the legal twists and turns in the development of the partial defences since that time.[185] I will concentrate instead on a brief examination of the issues central to my main theme, the civilization of the criminal law governing defences. In seeking to fulfil its terms of reference, the Royal Commission was in effect seeking to pursue the liberal common good or strategic concern that I earlier described. This was preventing the spread of over-criminalization and unfair labelling, by reducing or eliminating these phenomena where no deterrent effect would be achieved, or where the taking of retribution would be in almost all circumstances unduly harsh or disproportionate.[186] However, the way in which the 1957 Act took that agenda forward meant that the law failed fully to achieve this goal, whilst at the same time introducing some distinctly uncivilized elements into the working of the partial defences.

(a) Provocation and diminished responsibility

So far as provocation is concerned, the wording of section 3 of the 1957 Act meant that provocation became a largely jury-controlled rather than a judge-controlled excuse for what would otherwise be murder. If there was 'any evidence' of a provoked loss of self-control, then the entire matter of whether the provocation defence (including both factual and evaluative conditions) was made out on the facts had to be put to the jury.[187] This turned out to be a far worse change in

---

[184] For the term 'ascriptive judgement', see n 38 above; Horder (2004), at 52–8.
[185] See, eg, Simester and Sullivan *et al* (2010), at 380–94.
[186] See text at n 15 above.   [187] See n 58 above.

practice than it might have seemed in theory, and the blame can be laid at the door of the higher courts, in virtue of the way in which they interpreted section 3. First, to be consistent with the jury-dominant nature of section 3, the courts should have insisted on a simple approach to the law's understanding of the 'reasonable' person, by whose standards D's reaction was to be judged. The courts could have said that the reasonable man had such characteristics as the jury in the case in question thought it right and fair to take into account in the circumstances (subject to the normal exclusionary rules about self-induced provocation, intoxication, and the like). However, the higher courts were unable to resist the temptation to turn the whole issue into legal battleground, wading into a minute exegesis of the make-up of the reasonable person, in a way that simply encouraged further appeals on points of law, and hence yet further (not always consistent) judicial exegesis. The House of Lords or Privy Council (with reference to and with implications for English law) considered some aspect of the provocation defence—and this is not a complete list—in 1968, 1973, 1978, 1996 (twice), 1997, 2001, and 2005. There have, of course, been a far greater number of Court of Appeal decisions over the last fifty years to add to this. Yet, the law did not improve very much, or become more predictable between the (quite correct) overruling of *Bedder* in *Camplin* in 1978,[188] and the decision in *AG for Jersey v Holley* in 2005.[189]

Further, the phrase, 'any evidence' of a provoked loss of self-control, could easily have been interpreted by the courts to mean 'any evidence of real substance'; that is to say, any evidence worthy of a reasonable jury's consideration. Although such an interpretation would obviously have imported some judicial control over the applicability of the defence into section 3, it is a widespread and perfectly normal kind of judicial control that would not have detracted in a highly significant way from the jury-controlled orientation of section 3. Regrettably, the phrase was not interpreted in this way. The phrase was taken very literally by trial court judges (fearful of appeals) to include even the flimsiest of evidence of provocation.[190] This entailed a number of bizarre consequences at trial. It meant that the defence had to be put to the jury even if, for example, the evidence of the provoked loss of self-control emerged unexpectedly from the prosecution's own case.[191] The defence was also to be put before the jury when, at the end of the forensic part of the trial, the judge decided of his or her own motion that there was some evidence of a provoked loss of self-control, even if neither the prosecution nor the defence had sought to

---

[188] *Bedder* (1954) 58 Cr App R 133; *Camplin* [1978] AC 705.

[189] *AG for Jersey v Holley* [2005] 3 All ER 371 (PC). See further *Faqir Mohammed* [2005] EWCA Crim 1880. For discussion of the way in which the 2009 Act seeks to embody the decision in *Holley*, see Taylor (2011); Elvin (2011).

[190] Trial judges no doubt took their lead from obiter dicta to this effect in the speech of Lord Diplock in *Camplin* [1978] AC 705, at 716.

[191] In the much-criticized decision in *Acott* [1996] 4 All ER 443, the House of Lords sought to row back from this conclusion, at least to some extent, by insisting that there must by a, 'specific act or words of provocation', whether or not this is relied on, as such, at trial. The ruling simply raised more questions than it answered. For example, is the crying of a 17-day-old baby a 'specific act or words of provocation'? Arguably, not. However, the Court of Appeal in *Doughty* [1986] Crim LR 625 thought such a piece of conduct (or event) was something requiring a direction in accordance with s 3.

fight the case on that basis.[192] To compound that particular anomaly, when the judge felt compelled to put the defence to the jury in such circumstances, the jury was in all probability likely to take the defence more seriously precisely because it was the respected impartial official (the judge), and not the 'partisan' counsel for one side or the other, who requested them to consider it. Ironically, all this potential for trial anarchy when evidence of provocation was in issue did not in every case involve a clear benefit to D him or herself. As I have already said, evidence (however thin) that self-control was lost might in some cases have threatened to undermine D's case if his or her main claim was to a complete acquittal on the grounds of self-defence, because it may cast doubt on the reasonableness of D's reaction, in the circumstances.[193]

One of the main new remedies provided by the 2009 Act to address the shortcomings of the wording of section 3 of the 1957 Act was the restoration, by section 54(6), of the judge's power to withdraw the loss of self-control issue from the jury, where a properly directed jury could not reasonably conclude that the defence might be made out. That change was essential. Under the old law, the rule that 'any evidence' of a provoked loss of self-control triggered a requirement to put the defence to the jury had become one of the most criticized aspects of the defence. It meant that too many weak cases reached the jury, some of which—albeit perversely—inevitably succeeded. This aspect of the way the defence operated was something the Law Commission was, as we have seen, keen to eliminate:

The current position does not serve the interests of justice because the need to put the defence to the jury [when there is 'any' evidence of provoked loss of self-control] increases the likelihood that an unmeritorious claim may succeed.[194]

Successful acquittals of murder in weak provocation cases, stemming from the 'any evidence' rule, had begun to bring the law into disrepute, as a threat to civilized values in the sense I have described.[195] What is more, the law was brought further into disrepute, in this respect, in virtue of yet another trial anomaly.

Under the law as it stood in 1957, D lost his or her shield against cross-examination concerning his or her character if he or she cast imputations on the character of a prosecution witness (a 'tit-for-tat' rule).[196] However, it followed that the shield would not be lost if D cast the same kind of imputations on a deceased victim. So, D, even if a proven liar, had an almost completely free hand in both provocation and diminished responsibility cases to introduce as testimonial evidence what he or she believed or imagined that V had done by way of provocation. The prosecution would have little or no opportunity to correct the impression thereby given to the jury of the nature and gravity of the supposed provocation,

---

[192] See Law Commission (2006), at paras 5.15–16. See further the discussion of *Coutts* [2006] UKHL 39, in section III.2.b. below.
[193] Law Commission (2006), at para 5.15.
[194] *Ibid*, at para 5.15. See n 64 above.
[195] See the discussion of *Naylor* in the text at n 60 above. See further, amongst countless other cases, *Mellentin* [1985] 7 Cr App R (s) 9, and *Doughty* (1986) 83 Cr App R 319.
[196] Criminal Evidence Act 1998, s 1(f)(ii).

even when the prosecution strongly suspected D's tale was a pack of lies. That caused understandable outrage amongst victims' families, who may well have known all too well of D's self-serving tendency to exaggerate or of his history of deception, and yet been obliged silently to endure 'legally licensed slander' of a loved one by the person who unlawfully killed (and quite probably, murdered) him or her.[197] Section 31 of the Criminal Justice and Public Order Act 1994 had some ameliorating effect, in that it extended the law to allow the prosecution to claim that D had lost the shield if he or she cast imputations on the character of the deceased victim, as well as on any prosecution witness.[198] However, this change could not deter or affect those of previously good or unknown character who nonetheless made the most of their opportunity to blacken the name of the deceased victim, in the hope of making a favourable impression on the jury.

The negative effect of such unrestrained adversarialism—putting V him or herself on trial post mortem—was not the product only of provocation cases. It could also emerge from diminished responsibility cases, not least when diminished responsibility and provocation were pleaded together.[199] Such a double plea could be little more than a cynical ploy in weak cases, aimed at persuading a jury to consider evidence meant to be relevant only to one of these pleas, as part of a single body of material relevant to both defences. A typical example might be the use of evidence of D's reduced powers of self-control to establish mental abnormality for the purposes of a plea of diminished responsibility, and evidence of a history of V's real or alleged infidelity to establish provocation for the purposes of a provocation plea. The defence hope would be that D would get the unwarranted mix-and-match benefit of both pieces of evidence being wrongly considered by the jury, as part of an overall question they might mistakenly think they had been asked: does D deserve to be convicted of manslaughter only?[200] This could be a particularly attractive strategy where the foundation of D's diminished responsibility claim was that V's allegedly provocative conduct over a long period caused severe depression or jealousy of a pathological kind amounting to an abnormality of mind substantially impairing mental responsibility.[201] Now that, under the 2009 Act, the defences of provocation and diminished responsibility have so significantly diverged, one may ask whether there is still a case for allowing them to be pleaded together, rather than forcing D to make a choice between them.

Adversarialism's negative effects can in fact be found in cases involving a plea of diminished responsibility alone, an area that has not attracted the attention it deserves from partial defence sceptics. A classic example, concerning a murder that took place just before the 2009 Act came into force, is provided by the facts of

---

[197] Hence, this trial anomaly is something to which organizations such as Victim Support have rightly objected: see Law Commission (2005), at para 2.68.

[198] Section 31 had now been superseded by the relevant provisions of the Criminal Justice Act 2003.

[199] See Mackay (1988). For broader discussion of gender politics in diminished responsibility cases, see Horder (2004), at 165–9.

[200] See Mackay (1988).

[201] See Horder (2004), at 165–9.

the unreported case of *Challen*.[202] D bludgeoned her husband to death with a hammer, hitting him 25 times as he sat eating lunch, and then forced cloth into his mouth to prevent him breathing, causing his death. She claimed to have been suffering from depression, caused by her husband's persistent unfaithfulness. Accordingly, the trial did not turn simply on the medical evidence produced by each side, with the defence claiming that she suffered from 'a depressive condition of moderate severity', and the prosecution saying that even if she was depressed, it was not a condition amounting to an abnormality of mind substantially impairing her mental responsibility (as required, under the old law). Central to the trial was V's alleged infidelity, evidence of which D had become seemingly obsessed with uncovering (she had taken to following V, reading his phone and text messages, and so on). The jury rejected her plea of diminished responsibility, and she was convicted of murder. Nonetheless, with the addition of some medical evidence tendered by each side that would not normally be relevant to a provocation plea, the case was effectively run as if it was a provocation case, where D had every incentive to and did seek to make the blackening of V's character central to her case. As many commentators have noted, V's character is in a sense as much 'on trial' in such cases as D herself.[203] One likely side-effect of the tightening up of the provocation defence by the 2009 Act is that we will see many more such cases. Killers with only weak evidence of provocation, or those wishing to rely wholly or mainly on evidence of infidelity, will turn gratefully to the relatively generous new test, in diminished responsibility cases, of whether an abnormality of mental functioning was caused by a 'recognised medical condition'.[204]

The first root cause of the negative effects of adversarialism, generated by a partial defence structure, is the fact that the evidence must be presented in such a way as to generate a 'winner' and a 'loser'.[205] As I have said, this is a defect in the process when excusatory defences turn wholly or mainly on matters of degree, such as the 'gravity' of the provocation, or the extent to which an abnormality of mental functioning 'substantially impaired' D's faculties in a relevant respect. Such matters of degree are not well suited to resolution through an adversarial contest. Following (broadly) the Royal Commission's recommendation, where a jury convicts of murder but reports to the judge that they accept that there was provocation,[206] the question of the degree of the provocation should be relevant only to sentence (with or without a role for the jury), in the way recommended, albeit feebly, by the

---

[202] (Unreported). See *Elmbridge Guardian*, 30 June 2011; <www.bbc.co.uk/news/uk-england-surrey-13877131>.

[203] See Edwards (1996).

[204] 2009 Act, s 52(1). Some leading commentators have denied that the newly minted defence of diminished responsibility is more generous to an accused: see Mackay (2011). That argument seems more relevant to the link between D's conduct and D's medical condition than it does to the breadth of the phrase, 'recognised medical condition'.

[205] In diminished responsibility cases, of course, the problem is arguably worse than in provocation cases because both sides must meet a standard of proof.

[206] Where D pleads guilty the issues would all be ones for the judge, with the assistance of counsel.

Royal Commission.[207] The second root cause of the negative effects of adversarialism is the need for the defence to present the evidence of diminished responsibility or provocation in part by appealing to the sympathy of the jury, whose role not so much in fact-finding but in evaluating D's conduct is pivotal. At trial, this is what has led to unacceptable character assassinations of victims post mortem. By contrast, at the more inquisitorial sentencing stage, whilst there might still be a burden and standard of proof to address, it is possible for both sides—and for the evidence of victims' families—to be considered as part of a more holistic, less antagonistic process.

In that respect, it is worth noting that the Royal Commission's reflections on sentencing processes are a classic indication of how, at that time, the interests of victims and their families did not feature on the mental map of lawyers and law reformers, even when considering the sentencing stage in homicide cases. For example, in considering the role of the prosecution at the stage where extenuating circumstances were considered, as a possible basis for relieving the judge of the duty to pass the death penalty, the Royal Commission said:

> It would, however, be contrary to the recognized traditions of the Bar that counsel for the prosecution should be put in a position where he was pressing for the death penalty. . . . It would therefore seem preferable that he should take no active part in the proceedings on the issue of sentence, but should be present only as *amicus curiae*. He should not call witnesses, or cross-examine witnesses called by the defence; nor should it be his duty to put before the court any information, favourable or unfavourable, about the prisoner's character and antecedents.[208]

This concern predominantly with what might count in the offender's favour, lingered on for decades, and needs to be seen as all-of-a-piece with the law's casual disregard for the interests and suffering of victims and their families in homicide cases right up until the Criminal Justice and Public Order Act 1994 Act,[209] and beyond. The introduction of a degree of civilization into the law in this respect, the treatment of victims and their families with proper concern, as persons capable of suffering and frustration,[210] had to wait some time longer for official backing. This now takes the form of the Victim Personal Statement ('VPS'), considered (at the victim's or family's request) at the sentencing stage. As Victim Support have said of this system:

> The VPS gives victims a voice in the court process and can help to address some perceived imbalances between the victim and the offender. Before sentence is passed there is often a 'plea in mitigation' from the defence counsel seeking the lightest possible sentence. If the VPS is read out at this stage it allows the victim to express the emotional, practical, financial

---

[207] See Royal Commission on Capital Punishment (1953). The position with regard to diminished responsibility is discussed below.

[208] Royal Commission on Capital Punishment (1953), at para 560.

[209] See text at n 198 above.

[210] Dworkin (1977), at 272; see Horder (2004), at 141.

or behavioural impact of the crime. This gives the judge a fuller picture of the harm caused. It is important for victims to be able to describe the effects, as the trial itself focuses only on the evidence.[211]

It is arguable, though, that contrary to the Royal Commission's recommendation, evidence pointing to a diminished responsibility plea should not be treated as a matter where the jury has a role to play (even though a VPS will still be relevant). Just as much as when the death penalty was in issue, it is not acceptable that a jury could be moved—by the horrific nature of the crime, for example—to reject evidence of diminished responsibility and convict of murder without extenuating circumstances, thus obliging the judge to pass the mandatory sentence. The risk of such a result is simply not worth running, for the sake of preserving a role for the jury in such cases. Would we, for example, be willing to contemplate using an argument in favour of the jury's role to press for a lay jury's assessment to be made central to a decision to *release* an offender from prison or hospital, on the grounds that he or she is no longer suffering from an abnormality of mental functioning and is no danger to the public? That seems unlikely. Assuming sentencing decisions should not be turned over to non-judicial experts,[212] it is judges, not juries, who are in a position to be trained reliably and accurately to assess the merits of evidence given by expert witnesses, and the underlying assumptions of their methodology. The Law Commission, though, felt unable to go down this road.[213] To do so would be to give the judge a powerful discretion to avoid passing the mandatory life sentence in cases involving mental disorder and illness. As the Commission was bound by its terms of reference to keep the mandatory life sentence in place, it could not in good faith recommend changes, such as this, that would substantially undermine its mandatory character. However, the Law Commission did observe that:

Medical experts also commonly suggested that the partial defence should be abolished as a trial matter. Instead, they thought discretion should rest with the judge to determine the appropriate sentence post trial, if he or she found that D was suffering from diminished responsibility. This would (in very broad terms) accord with the way in which diminished responsibility is handled in France and Germany: as a sentencing matter only. It is a solution recently endorsed by the state of Victoria.[214]

Only through the introduction of a procedure of this kind will it become more likely that those suffering from abnormalities of mental functioning will in all cases be treated with the concern that they deserve.

---

[211] Victim Support, *Policy Position Statement, Victim Personal Statements* (April 2011), at 2.
[212] See the discussion of the Queensland model, in Law Commission (2005), at paras 6.109–6.116. For discussion of the legal position in France, see Law Commission (2005), at para 6.116.
[213] Law Commission (2006), at paras 5.83–5.106.
[214] *Ibid*, at para 5.94, referring to the Victorian Law Reform Commission (2004), at 241.

(b) Half-completed suicide pacts: a solution in search of a problem?

When the Royal Commission considered how to approach cases of suicide pacts in which one party had survived, it pointed out the relevance of the law governing complicity in crime.[215] As the Royal Commission explained, under the law as it then stood:

> Suicide is a crime . . . and if two persons enter into an agreement to commit suicide and one of them dies in pursuance of the agreement but the other survives, the survivor is guilty of murder, as a principal in the second degree to the self-murder of the other party if he is present at the time when it is committed, or if he is absent, as an accessory before the fact.[216]

As I indicated earlier, in approaching this issue, the Royal Commission distinguished between two kinds of cases, labelled by the Law Commission as 'die together' pacts as opposed to 'you-then-me' pacts.[217] As the Royal Commission observed, in 'you-then-me' pacts the survivor is in fact guilty as a principal in the first degree: he or she intentionally kills the other party before (at best) trying and failing to kill him or herself. In such cases, the Royal Commission thought that D should be guilty of murder, because D 'is directly responsible for [V's] death'.[218] By contrast, in 'die together' pacts, so the argument runs, responsibility is only indirect, with D playing a role only as accessory or as a principal in the second degree; but how convincing is this reasoning? That the Royal Commission was not very committed to making morally pivotal the question whether D's responsibility was direct or indirect, is illustrated by its approach to complicity in murder more generally. Elsewhere in the Report, the Commission addressed the question whether, 'the existing law (the mandatory death penalty for murder) bears too severely on the offender who has not been *directly responsible* for the killing', such as a secondary party in a burglary-turned-murder who merely keeps watch and plays no part in the striking of the final blow.[219] The Royal Commission recommended no change to the law to benefit such an offender, because it would be 'impracticable to make by any definition or rule of law a distinction between the more guilty accomplices and the less guilty'.[220] In other words, a distinction between direct and indirect responsibility is not workable in the complicity context. What was it, then, that turned the distinction from an apparently impracticable one for the law of complicity, to one that was recommended as central to determining the scope of the partial defence of suicide pact?

One reason not to spend too much time looking for an answer to this question (I don't doubt that there might be one[221]) is the unreliability of the conceptual

---

[215] Royal Commission on Capital Punishment (1953), at para 164.   [216] *Ibid*, at para 164.

[217] *Ibid*, at paras 8.19–8.37.   [218] *Ibid*, at para 166.

[219] Royal Commission on Capital Punishment (1953), at para 118 (my emphasis).

[220] *Ibid*. See further Ch 6 above.

[221] In broad terms, 'die together' pacts are ones in which the death of both parties is meant to arise out of the same action or course of conduct, whether or not jointly undertaken, such as consensually holding hands when jumping off a cliff, sitting in a car together whilst it fills with a noxious gas, and so on. By contrast, 'you then me' pacts are ones in which the deaths arise from separate actions (whether

basis on which the Royal Commission drew the distinction between 'die together' and 'you then me' pacts. Its unreliability stems from the inadequacy of the distinction between direct and indirect responsibility, in the hands of the Royal Commission, to do the work it is meant to do in this context. As an example of a 'die together' pact, the Royal Commission gave a set of facts in which 'two old people resolve to end a life of poverty or sickness by gassing or by taking poison, but only one of them dies'.[222] In *Sweeney*,[223] a pact along such lines involved D (who was prone to depression) agreeing with V (who had advanced muscular dystrophy) that they would die in a conflagration in their car. They both took sleeping tablets and paracetamol, and sat together in the car, after D had poured petrol on and set light to it. The intensity of the heat drove them both to seek to escape from the car, but only D—who suffered serious burns in the attempt—managed to do so. D pleaded guilty to manslaughter. This seems clearly to be a case the Royal Commission would regard as a 'die together' pact not involving direct responsibility on D's part for V's death; but how convincing is that analysis? Suppose that V had at no point consented to die with D, and stayed in the car initially only under duress. In that case, it seems certain that D would be regarded as having direct responsibility for V's death. There is an uninterrupted chain of causation linking D's intention to kill both himself and V, D's setting fire to the car, and V's death. Yet, if we change the example back to one in which V consents all along to these self-same actions,[224] there is no reason to change the analysis of how D comes to be responsible for V's death, namely directly. That is true of *Sweeney*, and of many similar cases. In the event, of course, section 4 of the 1957 Act was designed to cover both 'die together' and 'you then me' pacts, even though that entailed offering mitigation to someone who killed through pointing a gun at V's head and pulling the trigger with intent to kill:

4(1) It shall be manslaughter, and shall not be murder for a person acting in pursuance of a suicide pact between him and another to kill the other or be a party to the other being killed by a third person . . .

(3) For the purposes of this section 'suicide pact' means a common agreement between two or more persons having for its object the death of all of them, whether or not each is to take his own life, but nothing done by a person who enters into a suicide pact shall be treated as done by him in pursuance of the pact unless it is done while he has the settled intention of dying in pursuance of the pact.

For the Royal Commission this was the wrong approach, not least because the empirical evidence (albeit thin) tended to show that in 'you then me' pacts D's subsequent efforts to kill himself were more 'half-hearted'.[225] The threat that

---

or not performed by the same person) undertaken sequentially. Having said that, the distinction is not an especially clear-cut one.

[222] Royal Commission on Capital Punishment (1953), at para 164.

[223] (1986) 8 Cr App R (S) 419 (CA), discussion in Law Commission (2005), at paras 8.16–8.18.

[224] Bearing in mind that, of course, consent cannot in law be given to the infliction of lethal or grievous harm, and so has no legal bearing on the status of murder other than as provided for by statute.

[225] Royal Commission on Capital Punishment (1953), at para 176.

implicitly concerned the Royal Commission, then, was to what I have called common good (v), the threat that too many unmeritorious claims will succeed, and to common good (vii), the risk that problems of proof will be intractable.[226] However, not only does section 4 as it stands leave these concerns as very real ones, but its wording and scope raise other difficulties.

The assumption running through the Royal Commission's discussion of suicide pacts seems to be that they involve only two people, one of whom survives. Section 4 does nothing, though, to restrict its application to such cases. D may stand to be convicted of manslaughter only, even in cases involving mass suicide pacts instigated by D as a 'cult' leader who systematically kills every other person (however many there may be) party to the pact, but who then cannot bring himself to commit suicide as agreed.[227] This is hardly the kind of civilizing development in relation to excuses encouraged in other contemporary partial excuse cases such as *Semini*.[228] Further, section 4 relies for its legitimacy, in part, on there having been an understanding by the consenting victim that D will him or herself be committing suicide; but how much moral force does that understanding have? It makes of central importance an express or implied promise by D to kill him or herself: a promise, and an act, with no intrinsic moral value.[229] Finally, the Law Commission has observed that, even if one overlooks these theoretical and scope-based objections to section 4, the gendered nature of its operation in practice needs to be accounted for (as with provocation and diminished responsibility).[230] In cases of homicide-suicide in England and Wales, 75 per cent of the victims are female whereas 85 per cent of the suspects are male; and men who enter into suicide pacts are three times more likely to have been in a caring role prior to the event than men who commit solitary suicide.[231] In a typical case, the man (D) will have been the dominant partner in the relationship, but now fears that he will be unable adequately to fulfil his role as carer for his wife or partner, either because of a deterioration in her health, or in his, or both.[232] Accordingly, the evidence shows that it tends to be the man who takes the lead in the homicide-suicide, with his wife or partner co-operating.[233] The Law Commission is led to the hypothesis that men cope less well in caring roles, but instead of seeking help from outside try to remain in control of the decision-making and the outcome:

A dependent-protective attachment to the spouse and the need to control the relationship are known to play an important role in the chain of events leading to spousal homicide-suicide.[234]

---

[226] For these common goods, see Horder (2004), at 16–17. The 1957 Act, s 4 placed the burden of proof in relation to the suicide pact defence on the survivor, in implicit acknowledgement of the threats to common goods (v) and (vii).

[227] See Law Commission (2005), at para 8.21.

[228] [1949] 1 KB 405, discussed in the text at n 22 above.

[229] Law Commission (2005), at para 8.23.   [230] *Ibid*, at paras 8.68–8.83.

[231] *Ibid*, at para 8.70.   [232] *Ibid*, at para 8.72.   [233] *Ibid*, at para 8.75.

[234] Malphurs, Eisdorpher, and Cohen (2001), at 49.

That is not to cast doubt on the validity of V's consent in all such cases, although in some cases it may well not be completely free and fully informed. The point is that—speculative though it might be, as a suggestion—in these situations V is likely to identify with D's interests and see herself as 'a burden' to him, the removal of which will improve the quality of his life. The taking of control over the situation by D, in killing V (even at V's request), prevents such issues being adequately addressed by health professionals through the provision of counselling or other treatment for both D and V.

Like section 3, section 4 of the 1957 Act reflects the gendered patterns of violence and of its legitimation in the eyes of accused persons and their legal representatives during the twentieth century, even if (unlike section 2) section 4 does not so consistently involve the deployment of an aggressive adversarialism to bring those patterns out. The patterns of violence cannot be much influenced by changes to the structure of the law of homicide; but we are better off with a structure that confronts those patterns in a civilized way. That requires the abolition of the provocation and suicide pact defences, and their replacement with an open and fair system of sentence mitigation, alongside a judge-controlled procedure for cases (following a trial of the facts) in which there is persuasive expert evidence of diminished responsibility influencing D's conduct in killing or being a party to a killing.

III. Excessive Defence: The Final Frontier?

1. Provocation and excessive defence

The Royal Commission did not consider 'excessive defence'[235] as a possible basis for reducing murder to manslaughter, notwithstanding the considerable attention it paid in that regard to provocation, diminished responsibility, 'mercy killing', and suicide pacts. There has always been a respectable body of older legal authority favouring the view that the broader provocation defence is merely an outcropping of a partial defence to murder that had 'excessive defence' at its heart.[236] However, once it became settled that a provocation plea was concerned with provocation such as might move a reasonable person to lose self-control and kill, excessive defence in itself ceased to play such a central role in the defence.[237] This development meant that the provocation defence became at least in one respect wider, and at least in one respect narrower, than the pure excessive defence claim to mitigation of the offence that, historically, underpins it.

In what respect is it wider? In pleading provocation, the nature of any violence used or threatened by V, and not just its degree, may be relevant to a provocation

---

[235] Action taken where some defensive force is permissible, but the action in question goes beyond, in point of proportionality, what is strictly necessary to ward off or negate the threat.

[236] See n 40 above, and Horder (1992a), ch 5.

[237] See *Kirkham* (1837) 8 C & P 115.

plea in a way that it is not relevant—or not quite so relevant—to an excessive defence plea.[238] Here is an example:

V tries to force D to submit to having an object pushed into his or her (D's) anus. Although D could resist this attack by other means, D loses self-control and intentionally kills V.

In this example, it may be the exact nature of the violence threatened by V—not its degree—that best explains D's reaction, and a provocation-based plea is apt to account for such a possibility in a way that a pure excessive defence plea cannot. A pure 'excessive' defence plea is dependent for its merit on a finding that D did not go *too far* beyond what would have fallen within the bounds of reasonableness and hence been permissible conduct in defence of oneself or another. This reflects the predominantly normative basis of the plea.[239] By contrast, the likely relevance of proof of loss of self-control, in a provocation case such as the example just given, is precisely that it can explain, as part of an ascriptive assessment of blame, why the exact nature of the threatened violence led D to go *so far* beyond the level of force that might have been regarded as permissible to meet the threat posed by V.[240]

In what respect is the provocation plea narrower than an excessive defence plea? Answering this question involves building on the analysis just given. A provocation plea hinges on a finding that D had lost control at the time of the offence. By contrast, the focus of an excessive defence is just how far D went beyond what it would have been reasonable to do in defence of oneself or another, *irrespective* of whether or not self-control had been lost at the time of the offence. Where, by intentionally killing, D goes beyond the bounds of what might be considered a reasonable response to the threat, D's conduct may be explained by cognitive or judgmental rather than by volitional factors. The classic case is where D's conduct is motivated by (say) what D mistakenly considered right in the circumstances, irrespective of whether self-control was lost.[241] Naturally enough, the common law recognizes that volitional and cognitive factors come together to shape D's reaction in many situations in which he or she acts in self-defence. So, as Lord Morris famously put it in *Palmer v R*:

If a jury thought that in a moment of unexpected anguish, a person had only done what he honestly and instinctively thought was necessary, that would be the most potent evidence that only reasonable defensive action had been taken.[242]

Implicit in this rightly generous view of how to judge the proportionality of action taken in defence of oneself or another is an understanding that the effect of fear on cognition or judgement—on the understanding and interpretation of events—may

---

[238] That the nature, not just the degree, of violence used or threatened could be a source of grave provocation was well-understood in a society sensitive to slights upon honour: see Horder (1992a), ch 2.

[239] See Horder (2004), at 52–8; see too text at n 38 above.

[240] Obviously, not all provocation cases involve going 'too far' in excessive defence.

[241] See Horder (2004), at 45–8, for an analysis of such a belief, as contrasted with a loss of self-control, in terms of a 'first dimension' to excusing conditions.

[242] *Palmer v R* [1971] 1 All ER 1077 (PC), at 1078.

play a crucial role in how much force D uses to ward off or repel a threat, whether or not self-control is lost in the face of provocation at the time of D's action. In the heat of the moment, I may understand a threat to be greater than I would have done given time for reflection; or, I may think more force is needed than I would have done had I been a disinterested observer, because understandable fear for my own or another's safety is affecting my powers of perception and judgement.[243] This is one of the excusatory elements influencing the scope of the permission to use force in self-defence that comes into play when the permission to act self-defensively arises unexpectedly and D's (re)action is more-or-less spontaneous.

It was the role that fear, rather than anger, may play in leading someone to over-react by using fatal violence that led the Law Commission to recommend that there should be a separate branch of the provocation defence, based on 'fear of serious violence towards the defendant or another', without any additional requirement of 'provocation' or of 'loss of self-control'.[244] The Government chose, by contrast, to make loss of self-control the central feature of both the orthodox provocation and the excessive defence branches of the new partial defence under the 2009 Act. We have already seen how incongruous the loss of self-control requirement is, when the excessive defence plea is employed by a lawfully armed officer who has over-reacted by killing someone perceived to be a threat.[245] An analogous point could be made about the plea when it is employed by the other target group of offenders in this context, battered women.[246] Suppose that a woman kills her abusive husband because she fears serious violence. What justification do we have for insisting that she also have lost self-control at the time of the killing, as well as fearing serious violence, before making it permissible to convict of manslaughter rather than of murder? In such cases, the loss of self-control requirement appears to be doing the work that, in an ordinary self-defence plea, is done by the requirement that there be no way that D could reasonably be expected to escape or negate the threat other than through the use of lethal force. Accordingly, if a battered woman who has killed her abusive husband pleads self-defence, and also pleads excessive defence in the alternative, she will encounter a familiar problem in running the two defences. This is that the evidence of loss of self-control relevant to the second plea may run counter to the evidence relevant to the first plea, namely evidence that her response was within the bounds of that which might be considered reasonable, from someone in her particular circumstances fearing the use of serious violence. In short, the loss of self-control requirement may actually prejudice rather than assist her self-defence plea. In any event, in many such cases, the issue is not whether *ex hypothesi* excessive force was used due to loss of self-control but whether force should have been used *at all*, in the circumstances (an issue addressed below).

[243] For general discussion of this phenomenon in this context, see Horder (2004), ch 2.
[244] Law Commission (2006), at para 5.11. The defence could nonetheless be combined with a more orthodox provocation plea based on anger.
[245] See text at n 136 above.
[246] There is an extensive discussion of the application of the defence in this context in both Law Commission (2005) and Law Commission (2006).

This raises the question of whether the excessive defence plea really warrants legal recognition in the form of a partial defence, even if it is shorn (as the Law Commission suggested it should be) of the loss of self-control requirement. I suggest that it does not. To that end, I will consider the use of the plea in two contexts. First, in so far as the defence may apply to armed officers using lethal force, I will argue that subsuming excessive defence cases within the law of gross negligence manslaughter is the better route to a *via media* between conviction for murder and complete acquittal on the basis of self-defence.[247] This same solution could in theory be applied to cases of battered women who kill their abusers. However, I will argue that the breadth of the right or permission to use defensive force, properly understood, should be exploited to provide a complete defence in some such cases more often than may currently be the case. Shaped in this way, the law is more likely to ensure that, as Lord Bingham put it:

[F]ollowing a fairly conducted trial, defendants should be convicted of offences which they are proved to have committed and should not be convicted of offences which they are proved not to have committed. The interests of justice are not served if a defendant who has committed a lesser offence is either convicted of a greater offence, exposing him to greater punishment than his crime deserves, or acquitted altogether, enabling him to escape the measure of punishment which his crime deserves.[248]

2. Excessive defence and law enforcement

(a) The (ir)relevance of fear of serious violence

The removal of the suddenness requirement in relation to a loss of self-control by section 54(2) of the 2009 Act was in part designed to benefit a battered woman who delayed reacting with lethal violence until her abusive partner was off his guard.[249] In relation to this group of offenders, the introduction of an excessive defence provision in section 55(3) of the 2009 Act is meant to accommodate a feature of her conduct that was never easily accommodated by the old provocation defence. The provision makes room for placing emphasis on the fact that her primary motivation for killing is fear of violence, in circumstances where it is not an easy matter to determine what degree of force used will take one outside the bounds of reasonableness (and hence outside the reach of the complete defence of self-defence). So, suppose that a jury is unwilling to convict of murder, because D feared serious violence, but is also unwilling to acquit on the grounds of self-defence because D appears to have gone too far by killing the abuser. The jury now has the mid-way option of manslaughter by excessive defence. The value of this half-way house solution will be discussed in detail below. The excessive defence provision is, though, general in character. It is not confined to instances in which

---

[247] Whatever problems may attend the law of gross negligence manslaughter itself. On this, see further Herring and Palser (2007).
[248] *Coutts* [2006] UKHL 39, at para 12. The decision in *Coutts* is discussed further below: text at n 259.
[249] See, eg, *Ahluwalia* [1992] 4 All ER 889 (CA).

lethal violence is used in a domestic context, unlike (say) the Domestic Violence Crime and Victims Act 2004. So, the application of the provision to other kinds of example must be considered. A key group of offenders to whom it applies is that of armed officers using lethal violence in the performance of their duties. In discussing the (dis)value of the excessive defence in this context, it would be helpful to focus on an example:

D is a police sniper armed with a high-powered rifle. D has been called to an isolated apartment block in which an armed V is barricaded into an apartment twenty-five floors from ground level (D is positioned on the roof of a nearby block of flats). D has been informed that V is alone in the apartment, and cannot escape through his door. V suddenly appears at his window firing wildly with what is clearly a shotgun. D shoots with intent to cause serious harm and kills V. D admits that he was aware that V was firing a shotgun and that a shotgun posed only a small risk of causing serious harm when fired from so far high up and so far from the nearest neighbouring apartment block. However, D maintains that he thought it right to inflict seriously disabling injuries, because in his view any risk of serious harm being done by V was unacceptable.

Naturally, one would expect D to be following guidance given by police organizations concerning what it is appropriate action in such circumstances.[250] A failure to follow such guidance might count against D, but it would not be decisive because the guidance itself is subject to the laws of the land.[251] How should such a case be approached, addressing the issues germane to the present argument? So far as excessive defence is concerned, I have already suggested that a loss of self-control requirement is superfluous—indeed something of an embarrassment—in such cases, quite apart from the fact that (as we have seen) it sits uneasily, to D's potential detriment, alongside a primary plea that the force used was permissible in self-defence. What, though, of the requirement that D have acted in *fear* of serious violence? I suggest that this requirement is likewise unnecessary, and distracting in this context. An officer opening fire in such circumstances should certainly be motivated by a desire to negate, ward off, or at least minimize an unlawful threat (using the least harmful means that can effectively achieve that goal); but that desire need not itself stem from, or be accompanied by, a fear of serious violence. An excusatory focus on the effect of D's emotions in this kind of example threatens to detract from what should be the main focus: D's use of perception and judgement in guiding his actions. In that regard, an attempt to argue that D's perceptions and judgements, in so far as they were wrong, were (understandably) altered by D's fears, meets almost exactly the same kind of objection that we found earlier in an appeal to loss of self-control.[252] Given that D is a trained firearms officer, it should be one of the defining features of his

---

[250] See National Policing Improvement Agency (2010); <www.westmercia.police.uk/assets/_files/documents/sep_09/wmp_1252486699_Manuel_of_Guidance_Police_Use_.pdf>.

[251] For more detailed discussion, see Rogers (1998).

[252] See n 138 above.

reaction in such a case that it does distort his grasp of what is reasonably permissible in the circumstances.[253]

That is not to say that, in my example, the jury should be asked to do no more than choose between convicting of murder and acquitting on the grounds of self-defence. However, the intermediate option should be gross negligence manslaughter, not manslaughter through excessive defence as defined by the 2009 Act. Why? First, '(gross) negligence' is a concept whose focal concern is not with the impact of D's emotions on his or her reaction, but with the degree to which D departed from an expected standard of conduct. This is a standard by which it is not unfair to judge D when it has been adequately shaped by guidelines giving concrete content to it (as it will have done in this kind of case).[254] So, in my example, a key question will be whether D's killing of V through D's decision to shoot with intent to disable by seriously injuring, in order to negate only a small risk of serious harm coming to an innocent person, was not only unjustified but also a departure from the expected standard of conduct so great as rightly to be regarded as manslaughter.[255] That is a matter on which expert evidence could and should be given at trial,[256] in search of the right outcome. This is because D is on trial for his failure to live up to a carefully crafted set of responsibilities, of which he will have been fully aware, when using firearms. Yet, such evidence would be of much more marginal relevance, if the focus of the trial was merely the question whether D reacted as he did through a *fear* of serious violence.

However, so far as this intermediate option is concerned, an issue arises as to how it should be introduced at trial. It may seem obvious. Surely, one just asks the jury to consider in turn whether D is guilty of murder, guilty of gross negligence manslaughter, or not guilty by reason of self-defence? Unfortunately, matters are not so straightforward. It will be argued in the next section that, perhaps especially when agents of the state are on trial for murder in relation to an incident arising from the purported performance of their duties, there is a compelling case for giving them maximum scope for seeking 'vindication' at trial. That may mean holding back the intermediate option of gross negligence manslaughter, until the jury has first been presented with a stark choice between murder or self-defence, and has failed to agree on one or other of those options. At present, the law is not structured so as to encourage that procedure. Instead, a process is preferred in which the jury considers all three options (murder; gross negligence manslaughter; self-defence) together. I will now suggest that this approach is wrong in this context.

---

[253] See Aristotle, *Ethics*, book 2ii: 'Similarly with courage; it is by habituating ourselves to make light of alarming situations and to face them that we become brave, and it is when we have become brave that we shall most be able to face an alarming situation.'

[254] See n 250 above.

[255] See *Bateman* (1925) 19 Cr App R 8; *Adomako* [1995] 1 AC 171.

[256] As it was in *Adomako* [1995] 1 AC 171, in a different context.

(b) Seeking vindication at trial

When someone pleads self-defence, they seek *ex post facto* vindication of their conduct as lawful, because permissible in the circumstances. The same is true of most cases in which D claims to have acted in prevention of crime.[257] The element of vindication in law is, of course, something missing when someone pleads an excuse, such as loss of self-control, or when they plead that the wrongful harm was done by accident. In a self-defence or prevention of crime case, D is saying, 'Whether or not you like what I did, I had every right to do it in the circumstances, and I ask (and expect) you, the jury, to recognize that fact in your verdict by acquitting me'. Seeking vindication at trial is likely to be of special significance to those whose work by its nature may involve the deliberate infliction of harm, such as the work of armed law enforcement officials.[258] When such officials shoot to kill, their actions take place against, and should be influenced by, a background of public interest concerns it is their duty to protect and promote. By way of contrast with the ordinary citizen who finds that they have to use lethal force in self-defence, lawfully armed officials do not act (or not merely) to protect their private rights. That being so, vindication at trial may be all the more important for them, because there is a sense in which it will be critical to them in labelling terms to establish that, in shooting to kill, they were (in the time-honoured phrase) 'only doing their job', something that sets them apart from the private citizen similarly situated. The issue has not been directly confronted in law, but important clues indicating how it would be addressed are to be found in the decision in the House of Lords in *Coutts*.[259]

In *Coutts*, D claimed that V died in a tragic accident during a sex game in which, with V's consent, he put manual pressure on her neck. By contrast, the prosecution claimed that D was sexually excited by strangulation, and had intended to cause V's death (or to cause her serious harm) in that way. On the one side, there was evidence from previous lovers that D had, with their consent, applied manual pressure to their necks with no ill effects. On the other side, amongst other pieces of evidence, D's claim that he had no interest in violence appeared to be contradicted by prosecution evidence that, both before and after V's death, D had visited pornographic websites showing violence towards women. Further, rather than report V's death immediately, D had placed V's body in a storage facility to which he made repeated visits (suggestive of some necrophilic tendencies), and then a month later taken the body—naked, with a ligature made from tights tied twice around the neck—to some woodland where he set fire to it. D had also prevaricated in answers he gave to the police both before and after the discovery of the body. D was charged with murder. D claimed that V's death was an accident. The trial proceeded on that basis, but at the close of evidence, the judge invited counsel to make submissions on whether he should direct the jury that a verdict of

---

[257] See generally, Horder (2000).   [258] Rogers (1998); Thorburn (2008).
[259] [2006] UKHL 39.

manslaughter was open to them. Prosecuting counsel said that the judge should not do that, because the Crown's case had throughout been that this was a deliberate killing, and nothing else. Consequently, it would be unfair to put the case to the jury on any other basis. Defence counsel agreed, having asked D, 'Do you want us to make representation [on manslaughter], or do you want to roll the dice and be home with Lisa and the boys?' D replied (having heard that the likely sentence for manslaughter would be about fifteen years' imprisonment), that he would indeed prefer to 'roll the dice', by putting the prosecution to its proof on his claim of accidental death. D was convicted of murder and appealed. He said that the judge should have put the option of manslaughter to the jury, because if the jury had rejected his claim of accident and wished to convict him of 'something', given the nature of the Crown's case the only option the jury had was murder. D claimed that was unfair, because it allowed no scope for the jury to remain unsure whether D intended death or serious injury, and yet convict him of manslaughter if they were also sure that V's death was no mere tragic accident.

The Court of Appeal rejected D's appeal.[260] The Lord Chief Justice raised 'two critical features of the case' that, in his view, distinguished it from other authorities.[261] First, there was the fact that both the prosecution and the defence thought it would not be in the interests of a fair trial that manslaughter should be left to the jury. Secondly:

[T]he only basis upon which the jury could convict the appellant of manslaughter was factually wholly different from the case that the prosecution was advancing in order to obtain a conviction of murder. It was not, for example, a case where it would be possible for the jury to come to the conclusion that the appellant was not guilty of murder but guilty of manslaughter on the case for the prosecution.[262]

So far as these final words are concerned, what the Lord Chief Justice has in mind are cases in which, for example, the prosecution's attempt to rebut a defence plea of self-defence involves reliance on evidence that D lost control and inflicted disproportionate force.[263] In such a case, it would be proper (so the argument goes) for the judge to put the option of manslaughter by reason of provocation to the jury. It would be proper, even if provocation had not been at issue during the course of the trial, because the case made by the prosecution in rebutting D's argument itself raises evidence of provocation. In such circumstances, if the jury are presented with only two alternatives, conviction for murder or acquittal on the grounds of self-defence, there may conceivably be a real risk of injustice if the option of manslaughter by reason of provocation is not also considered.[264] One can appreciate the force of this argument, although it was in effect criticized earlier on the grounds that it could entail disproportionate weight being given by the jury to a weak provocation case. However that may be, it is the first part of this passage that is of

[260] *Coutts* [2005] EWCA Crim 52.   [261] *Ibid*, at para 58.
[262] *Ibid*, at para 58.   [263] *Ibid*, at para 62.
[264] The same line of reasoning applies where the evidence of provocation comes out in the course of the defence's case, even if it is not relied on by the defence in making their case: see generally, *Hopper* [1915] 2 KB 431 (HL); *Mancini* [1942] AC 1 (HL); *Bullard v The Queen* [1957] AC 635 (PC).

importance here. As the Lord Chief Justice rightly observes, it would be wrong for the judge to put alternative verdicts to the jury if legal and factual issues central to establishing these verdicts has not been heard or tested in cross-examination. As the Lord Chief Justice went on to say:

[F]or the judge to introduce the possibility of a verdict of manslaughter on these grounds [gross negligence or unlawful-and-dangerous-act] would have transformed the nature of the case that the appellant was required to meet. The jury would not only have had to decide whether the victim may have died in the course of consensual sexual intercourse, but they would also have had to come to a conclusion as to the degree of danger that consensual asphyxial sexual intercourse, as practiced by the appellant, involved.[265]

In the present context, what is vital about these observations is their bearing on a trial involving an armed officer who has intentionally killed. The Lord Chief Justice's comments provide scope for the prosecution and defence in effect to agree that they will run the case as one in which the jury is given a straightforward choice: conviction for murder, or acquittal on the grounds of self-defence. This gives appropriate scope for D to insist at trial on nothing short of vindication for his or her conduct. What could be added to the Lord Chief Justice's observations is that it would be perfectly possible for both sides to be prepared, this issue having been raised at the plea-and-case-management hearing, to make a case for and against conviction for gross negligence manslaughter, but only if the jury initially fail to agree to convict of murder or to acquit on the grounds of self-defence. The issue would then be whether the judge is prepared, when a jury fails to agree on murder or self-defence, to add a count of manslaughter (thus avoiding the need to consider a possible re-trial arising at that point). Such speculation has, though, been rendered idle by the decision of the House of Lords to overturn the decision of the Court of Appeal, and quash D's conviction for murder.[266]

As the passage cited earlier from the House of Lords' judgment indicates,[267] the House of Lords' primary concern—one that shaped its understanding of 'the interests of justice'—was with ensuring that D is neither wrongly acquitted, nor convicted of an offence greater than can be supported by evidence about which the jury is sure. In particular, a court is under a duty to do what it can to ensure that D is not convicted of an offence greater than the evidence can support, simply because the jury feel compelled to convict D of 'something' because they have rejected his or her claim of accident, or his or her claim to have acted in self-defence. Upholding the interests of justice, so understood, entails adopting a rule (subject to exceptions) that the judge should, in cases such as *Coutts*, put the possibility of a manslaughter verdict to the jury even if such a possibility has not been part of the case for either the prosecution or for the defence. As Lord Bingham put it:

The public interest in the administration of justice is, in my opinion, best served if in any trial on indictment the trial judge leaves to the jury, subject to an appropriate caution or warning, but irrespective of the wishes of trial counsel, any obvious alternative which there is

---

[265] *Coutts* [2005] EWCA Crim 52, at para 61.
[266] Coutts was convicted of murder at a re-trial.   [267] See text at n 248 above.

evidence to support. . . . I would also confine the rule to alternative verdicts obviously raised by the evidence: by that I refer to alternatives which should suggest themselves to the mind of any ordinarily knowledgeable and alert criminal judge, excluding alternatives which ingenious counsel may identify through diligent research after the trial.[268]

I will not address here the general difficulties to which this explanation for the House of Lords' decision gives rise, such as its confinement to trials on indictment, or the pivotal role it gives to alternative verdicts 'obviously' raised by the evidence as opposed to alternative verdicts legally applicable on the facts. More significant is the House of Lords' failure to acknowledge that what counts as a rule favouring 'the public interest in the administration of justice' is a matter of weighing competing principles in a particular context.

In this context, the House of Lords paid too little attention to the principle that evidence pointing to conviction for, or to acquittal of, an offence should be led respectively by the prosecution or the defence in a manner best calculated to explain it to the jury, as part of their respective cases. In other words, each possible verdict should be tested through the ordinary forensic process in the course of the trial. In some instances, of course, the possible commission of a lesser included offence may be effectively tested by the forensic process bearing on the greater offence, even when the lesser offence is not specifically addressed by counsel. Such a possibility regularly arises in relation to unlawful-and-dangerous-act manslaughter, on a murder charge.[269] However, in some instances, the way that the respective cases for the prosecution and for the defence come to be made may mean that one or more key legal issues arise in relation to the lesser offence, that do not arise in relation to the greater offence. In such instances, the interests of justice require that the lesser offence is specifically addressed by counsel through the forensic process. As the Court of Appeal indicated, had the judge put the alternative verdict of manslaughter to the jury in *Coutts*, 'irrespective of the wishes of trial counsel' (Lord Bingham's words), D would have had no chance to argue either that V consented to having him squeeze her neck—and that consent was a valid plea in law to that act— or that the way in which he did the act did not amount to 'gross' negligence. It is simply not enough to try to meet this point by saying that, when counsel make their closing speeches, they can, 'address the jury with the knowledge of what the judge will direct'.[270] How can that possibly enable counsel adequately to address the evidence for and against the view that manslaughter was committed, given the way in which D would seek to rebut the prosecution's manslaughter case?

The difficulties to which *Coutts* gives rise may in part reflect the fact that most of the homicide cases relied on in support of the House of Lords' view were cases in which the stark choice was between accident (or lack of intent), and murder. In particular, the House of Lords did not discuss the position of someone—especially an agent of the state—seeking primarily to vindicate their conduct as permissible, through a claim of self-defence or prevention of crime, as the only alternative to

---

[268] *Coutts* [2006] UKHL 39, at para 24.
[269] See Criminal Law Act 1967, s 6(2) and 6(3).
[270] *Coutts* [2006] UKHL 39, at para 24.

murder. Allowing a trial to proceed to its conclusion, so as to preserve this possibility, also serves the public interest in the administration of justice. Further, as suggested earlier, in such cases an alternative verdict of manslaughter by gross negligence can be offered to a jury that has failed to agree on a verdict of murder or of self-defence or prevention of crime. Evidence for and against this alternative verdict, especially expert evidence on whether or not D was negligent and if so, how negligent he or she was, can then be heard prior to further jury deliberation on that verdict.

3. Excessive defence and battered women

(a) The excusatory element in self-defence

I will start this discussion in a roundabout way, by looking at the circumstances in which D may be denied a (partial) defence because, very loosely speaking, there was an opportunity to do something to remedy the situation other than commit the crime in question. We saw earlier that the law appears to be inconsistent in the way that it approaches this issue, and in particular the question whether a defence becomes unavailable if D delays his or her reaction past the point at which there was an opportunity to take some other (non-criminal) course of action instead. In duress cases, it is clear that the excuse will be available only if the threat of death is to be carried out, 'immediately, or almost immediately', if the specified crime is not committed.[271] By way of contrast, in provocation cases, the requirement that loss of self-control be 'sudden' has been abolished.[272] So long as self-control was lost at the time of the killing, it seems no longer to matter that D had a perfectly good opportunity to calm down and master his or her emotions following the final episode of provocation.[273] What is the position in self-defence (or defence of another) cases?[274] Here, there are significant differences between American and English law. American law closely confines the limits of conduct regarded as defensive. It must be conduct that meets a danger that is 'impending, and present, and not prospective or even in the near future'.[275] By contrast, in English and Irish Law, the rules are more flexible and context-dependent.[276] It has been held that a soldier in Northern Ireland was entitled to shoot someone whom he (mistakenly) believed to be a terrorist, to prevent him committing terrorist crimes in the near future, even though there was no suggestion that any such crime was imminent.[277] In *Cousins*,[278] D produced a shotgun and threatened V that he (D) would use it at

---

[271] *Hasan* [2005] UKHL 22. See text at n 82 above.
[272] 2009 Act, s 54(2).
[273] Except in so far as this shows that the 'loss of self-control' was faked or that, when D killed V, it was out of a considered desire for revenge: 2009 Act, s 54(4).
[274] For an authoritative discussion, see now Leverick (2006), ch 5.
[275] Dressler (2002b), at 260.
[276] McColgan (1993), at 517–18.
[277] *Kelly* [1989] NI 341; but for criticism see Simester and Sullivan *et al* (2010), at 774. The ensuing discussion of the case law is taken directly from Simester and Sullivan's helpful exegesis.
[278] [1982] QB 26 (CA), discussed by Simester and Sullivan *et al* (2010), at 774.

some point in the future, unless a close relative of V's withdrew a threat to kill D. It was held that D should have been entitled to plead that his conduct was self-defensive or action in prevention of crime. Finally, in *A-G's Reference (No 2 of 1983)*[279] it was held that D could be lawfully in possession of petrol bombs when he had prepared them solely for the purpose of defending his property against possible looting during a city riot. Which approach is the right one?

English law's more generous criteria for regarding D as eligible to claim self-defence or action in prevention of crime reflect an underlying understanding that the key test is not (by way of contrast with duress) the strict test of whether the threat was imminent. It is the more generous test of whether it is reasonable to expect D to have exploited an opportunity to do other than he or she did, in meeting the threat with (lethal) force.[280] It is in the light of this broader test that one should analyse situations involving an imminent threat:

X suddenly and unexpectedly runs towards me with a knife raised in an aggressive manner and so I ward V off by throwing a nearby brick at him or her.

Such cases are cases in which the relative imminence of the threat provides a strong case for saying either that (a) there was no other choice if the threat was to be negated, or that (b) other choices—such as, for example, simply retreating behind a door and locking it—were perfectly reasonably overlooked in the heat of the moment. Where, because the danger was imminent, I sought spontaneously to negate it in an aggressive way rather than by pausing to think of a possible alternative to aggression, I have a good case for saying that it was unreasonable to expect me to have done otherwise. It is the latter that is the key issue, rather than the issue of whether the threat was imminent.

What is the significance of this discussion in this context? First, I need to explain the differences between the law's approach (on my interpretation of it) to duress or provocation cases, and its approach to self-defence or prevention-of-crime cases. Homicide cases where duress or provocation can be raised as issues are cases involving claims to excuse. The lethal actions in question, however understandable in the circumstances, involve the impermissible violation of another's rights (or of a public interest).[281] Given that the duress and provocation defences always involve, *qua* excuses for action, an impermissible violation of another's rights (or of a public interest), we would need especially compelling reasons to extend their scope to instances in which D had an opportunity to avoid the impermissible violation. In the absence of such reasons, we risk making the law uncivilized, by placing too much ascriptive emphasis on D's personal weaknesses and failings, at the expense of his or her normative duty to avoid impermissible violations of others' rights. By

---

[279] [1984] QB 456 (CA), discussed by Simester and Sullivan *et al* (2010), at 774. It should be noted that, as the authors point out, in both *Cousins* [1982] QB 26 (CA), and in *A-G's Reference (No 2 of 1983)* [1984] QB 456 (CA), the steps taken in self-defence were not intended to be lethal.

[280] See Horder (2002a).

[281] Tadros (2001); Huigens (2004).

contrast, in a case of self-defence or prevention of crime, the question whether V's rights have been permissibly violated is the very question in issue.

In that regard, the law must seek to achieve a balance. On the one hand, even an admitted aggressor should not find his or her aggression met with unnecessary (or disproportionate) force. Accordingly, rules concerning when force may permissibly be used to negate or ward off aggression should reflect this requirement. On the other hand, the law should not adopt a set of rules, like strictly construed imminence or immediacy requirements, which are optimal in general only for (putative) aggressors. Such rules would shift too great a burden of risk on to the (putative) defender. A strict imminence or immediacy requirement may entail the loss of a chance for the (putative) defender to secure a better chance of warding off the threat, by (say) taking time to forearm him or herself before an attack begins. In that respect, of course, a strict imminence or immediacy requirement may also mean that the (putative) defender loses a chance to incorporate a necessary element of surprise into his or her response. Most importantly, in the way that the law strikes this balance, the law may inevitably have to incorporate an excusatory element into the shape and scope of the permission. So far as (dis)proportionality is concerned, the *Palmer* doctrine[282] is an illustration of this. That, in the agony of the moment, one thought of something as reasonable force (excusatory element), may be evidence that it *was* reasonable force (permitted action).[283] So far as the necessity for the use of force is concerned, what matters is whether an opportunity to do otherwise is judged to have been reasonable.[284] In, say, heat-of-the-moment situations, when D uses aggression spontaneously to negate or ward off the threat, we may forgive his or her neglect even of an obvious non-aggressive alternative, as when D fails to shut a door against the aggressor instead of using or threatening violence. We may do this because it would be unreasonable, in the circumstances, to expect and require D to be alert and responsive to such an alternative.[285] In making that judgement, the limits of what may permissibly be done in self-defence are being influenced by an ascriptive consideration, the tendency for people to consider fewer alternatives in the heat of the moment.[286]

Similarly, we may allow D considerable latitude to prepare for and use aggression in other kinds of case. An example is where there are known (as opposed to overlooked) conditions of uncertainty bearing on whether resort to an alternative to aggression is demanded of D in the circumstances:

D, hearing an intruder in the process of breaking in, has time to unlock his or her gun cabinet and arm him or herself with a (lawfully owned) gun, or to telephone the police, but does not have time to do both.

---

[282] See n 242 above.   [283] See text at n 242 above.
[284] For a similar argument, see Leverick (2006), at 102.
[285] I say we 'may' forgive because of course it could be that D is an experienced law officer familiar with the layout of the place in which he or she is under attack, and who can thus be expected to be alert to the door-closing alternative even in the heat of the moment.
[286] For an exploration of this theme, see Horder (2004), ch 2.

We may still allow D to plead self-defence if D (say) goes on to obtain the gun and threaten the intruder with its use. We may do this, even though there was a reasonable opportunity to do otherwise by taking a non-aggressive course in telephoning the police. We may take the view that it would not be reasonable to expect or require D to take the latter course in the circumstances, given that it may take time to get through to the police, the police may not arrive in time, and so on. Naturally, in some circumstances, it will be right to regard such cases as ones in which D may *permissibly* take more than one course of action in response to a threat, one of which involves aggression. However, as when considering the proportionality of force used in accordance with the *Palmer* doctrine,[287] essentially ascriptive, excusatory considerations tend inescapably to blend in with the considerations bearing on permissibility, in the determination of whether the use of force in self-defence or the prevention of crime was necessary. These ascriptive considerations give D a latitude, rightly denied to him or her in duress cases, to choose aggression over non-aggression in some circumstances. The legitimacy of judging D by reference to these considerations is warranted, because they are relevant to the very question whether D was impermissibly violating V's rights. By contrast, in duress (and provocation) cases, that V has had his or her rights impermissibly violated by D's criminal action is not in doubt. In such cases, it follows that there is a compelling argument that the law should not compound the rights violation by giving D's excuse greater latitude, when it comes to the question whether some non-aggressive course of action should have been taken instead. A strictly construed imminence requirement is the way in which English law now reflects this argument, in the way in which it delimits the excuse of duress.[288]

4. Battered women who kill passive abusers

The existing law of self-defence is perfectly capable of accommodating cases in which D responds to a threat of (say) being punched for the umpteenth time by a violent—and more powerful—partner, by shooting or stabbing him to death. Disparities in strength, speed, agility, willingness to use—and history or pattern of use of—physical violence are—alongside the *Palmer* direction,[289] and (if need be) expert evidence[290]—all part of the circumstances the jury should be bound to consider as part of its assessment of whether D's response fell within the bounds of reasonableness. There is no need to complicate this perfectly clear picture by the introduction of a partial defence of excessive defence. However, a troubling feature of some instances in which a battered woman kills an abusive partner is that she may understandably take the opportunity when he is off his guard (asleep, perhaps) to kill him intentionally.[291] Do such cases pose special problems that cannot be addressed through the law of self-defence?

---

[287] See text at n 242 above.   [288] *Hasan* [2005] UKHL 22.
[289] See text at n 242 above.
[290] For a good discussion, in this context, see Stubbs and Tolmie (1999).
[291] See, eg, *Ahluwalia* [1992] 4 All ER 889; *Thornton* [1992] 1 All ER 306.

The first point to note is that the applicability of the excessive defence branch of the new loss of self-control defence under the 2009 Act is far from secure in its application to such cases.[292] To be sure, when D kills in such a case, she may be able to claim that she did so due to fear of serious violence from V. However, admitting an intentional killing of V when he was off his guard will not enhance a claim that this was done whilst self-control was lost. Quite possibly, as evidence in the hands of the prosecution, such an admission (or proof of the fact) will count against such a claim, pointing instead towards the defence-disqualifying finding that D acted from a considered desire for revenge.[293] Moreover, whilst the idea that a 'fear of serious violence' may form part of the basis for reducing murder to manslaughter captures the idea of (not too) excessive defence, it is silent on a crucial question. Does fear of suffering serious violence (if lethal force is not pre-emptively used) at some unspecified time in the future 'count', in the same way as a fear that serious violence will be done more or less immediately? As partial defences have an excusatory basis, the question has in theory the same central relevance that it has in duress cases and should be given the same answer. This is that fears of serious violence to be inflicted so far into the future that there is an opportunity to resort to the authorities, exclude one from the scope of the (partial) defence.[294] Even a loss of self-control at the time of the offence should not allow one to evade this exclusion in excessive defence cases, any more than it would in duress cases. Naturally, a sympathetic jury could bend the partial defence of loss of self-control into a shape that fits the facts as they wish to construe them; but that should not blind us to the underlying difficulties, and in some cases juries may be wrong to take such a sympathetic approach.

By contrast, so-called 'pre-emptive' strikes can fall within the scope of legitimate self-defence if they meet the normal criterion (as I have expressed it), namely that D lacked a reasonable opportunity to take a non-aggressive course of action instead. Accordingly, in some circumstances, the pre-emptive use of violence may be permissible even when V is off his guard. A classic example (modified for present purposes) is given by Aileen McColgan:[295]

D is being held hostage by ruthless terrorists. D is told that she will be killed if a ransom demand is refused, but three such demands—decreasing in amount—have been refused and she remains alive. That night, catching her sleeping guard unawares, she intentionally kills him with a blow on the head, as the only way of making her escape undetected.

For Joshua Dressler, if we are committed to regarding human life as special, we should not regard the deliberate taking of life in self-defence as justified unless it was absolutely necessary on the immediate occasion.[296] This test cannot be satisfied in the example just given, any more than it could in cases where battered women kill passive abusers. Dressler suggests that the defence of duress of circumstances is better suited to deal sympathetically with such cases.[297] That suggestion (were

---

[292] See Simester and Sullivan *et al* (2010), at 400–1.   [293] 2009 Act, s 54(4).
[294] See *Hasan* [2005] UKHL 22.   [295] McColgan (1993), at 517–18.
[296] Dressler (2002b).   [297] *Ibid*, at 275–81.

duress to be extended to cover murder cases) falls foul of the view—defended earlier[298]—that it is precisely in duress cases that we should require D to satisfy a strict immediacy or imminence test, because D's action impermissibly violates V's right not to be killed. Accordingly, Dressler's view runs contrary to the idea that part of what makes self-defensive actions permissible *as such* is that, in themselves, they involve nothing more or less than the negating, avoiding, blocking, or warding off of the threat. By contrast, whilst actions taken under duress of circumstances may equally be intended to negate, avoid, block, or ward off threats, they involve something more, something that is impermissible. Such actions achieve their goal (when offences against the person are in issue) through the invasion of the rights of a person who is him or herself not part of the threat. Suppose D hurls X through Y's glass window, as the only way proportionately to meet X's threat to inflict serious injury there and then on D. D's action is simultaneously self-defensive, so far as the invasion of X's right to personal integrity is concerned, and taken under duress of circumstances, so far as the invasion of Y's property rights is concerned. The same action can thus be permissible respecting the invasion of one person's interests (X), but only excusable respecting the invasion of another person's interests (Y).[299]

A final point, in relation to Dressler's argument. The 'special-ness' of human life cannot prevent its being permissibly terminated in certain circumstances by reference to the same criteria (such as proportionality) that would ground a permission to inflict serious harm, to cause a bruise, to push someone, and so on. On my account, one such criterion is whether D could reasonably be expected to take some alternative course of action, be that inflicting a lesser degree of harm, or adopting a non-aggressive course of action.

How does this analysis help us in the present context? The passive abuser (like the hostage's captor, in McColgan's example) is killed because it is he who poses the danger. He is not an innocent person who has become the instrument through which danger from a different source is being blocked or warded off. It follows that, at least in some important cases, the correct characterization of the action of an abused woman who kills her passive abuser is as the blocking of a danger or threat *as such*. This is an action that is in principle self-defensive. Further, the foregoing discussion suggested that self-defence is broad enough to accommodate some battered women who kill passive abusers, without supplementation by a defence of excessive defence.[300] If the question is whether the killing of a threatening person who was at that moment passive is murder, then in part the answer depends on whether the jury can be sure that there was no *reasonable* opportunity to take a less drastic or non-aggressive course of action. In the right circumstances—perhaps, complete isolation and control of D by a violent and aggressive V, in the time

---

[298] See text at n 281 above.

[299] I accept, of course, that there is a great deal more than could be said about this issue, and about variations on these facts, but such a discussion would take me too far from the central concerns of this chapter.

[300] Bearing in mind, given the infinite variety of possible sets of circumstances, that in some cases where battered women kill, their cases will be better dealt with in other ways: perhaps as ones of diminished responsibility, provocation, murderous revenge, and so on.

leading up to the killing—the prosecution may struggle to satisfy the jury of this, whether D was a hostage or a battered woman. That being so, when put together with other (partial) defences at her disposal, self-defence adequately addresses, 'the problem of battered women who kill' without the need for supplementation by a partial defence of excessive defence.

Bibliography

Alexander, Larry and Ferzan, Kimberley, 'Results Don't Matter' in Paul Robinson, Stephen Garvey, and Kimberley Ferzan, *Criminal Law Conversations* (Oxford: Oxford University Press, 2009).

Allen, Neil, *The Criminal Justice System and Health Care* (Oxford: Oxford University Press, 2007).

Almond, Paul, 'Understanding the Seriousness of Corporate Crime: Some Lessons for the New "Corporate Manslaughter" Offence' (2009) 9 *Criminology and Criminal Justice* 145.

Amos, Andrew, *Ruins of Time Exemplified in Sir Matthew Hale's History of the Pleas of the Crown* (London: V & R Stevens and GS Norton, 1856)

Anon, 'On Codification, and its Application to the Laws of England' (1830) *Foreign Quarterly Review* VI, 333.

Arbous, MS *et al*, 'Mortality Associated with Anaesthesia: a Qualitative Analysis to Identify Risk Factors' (2001) 56 *Anaesthesia* 1141.

Aristotle, *Ethics*, edition of JAK Thomson (London: Penguin Classics, 1955).

Aronson, Mark and Whitmore, Harry, *Public Torts and Contracts* (Sydney: Law Book Company, 1982).

Ashworth, Andrew, 'Transferred Malice and Punishment for Unforeseen Consequences' in Peter Glazebrook (ed), *Reshaping the Criminal Law* (London: Stevens, 1978).

Ashworth, Andrew, 'The Elasticity of *Mens Rea*' in Colin Tapper (ed), *Crime, Proof and Punishment* (London: Butterworths, 1981).

Ashworth, Andrew, 'Taking the Consequences' in Stephen Shute, John Gardner, and Jeremy Horder (eds), *Action and Value in Criminal Law* (Oxford: Oxford University Press, 1993).

Ashworth, Andrew, 'Is the Criminal Law a Lost Cause?' (2000) 116 *Law Quarterly Review* 225.

Ashworth, Andrew, 'Principles, Pragmatism and the Law Commission's Recommendations on Homicide Law Reform' (2007) *Criminal Law Review* 333.

Ashworth, Andrew, 'A Change of Normative Position: Determining the Contours of Culpability in Criminal Law' (2008) 11 *New Criminal Law Review* 232.

Austin, John, *Lectures on Jurisprudence*, edited by R Campbell (London: John Murray, 1879).

Austin, JL, 'A Plea for Excuses' in Michael Corrado (ed), *Justification and Excuse in the Criminal Law* (New York: Garland, [1956], 1994).

Bagaric, M and Edney, R, 'The Sentencing Advisory Commission and the Hope of Smarter Sentencing' (2004) 16 *Current Issues in Criminal Justice* 125.

Bailey, Victor, 'The Shadow of the Gallows: The Death Penalty and the British Labour Government, 1945–51' (2000) 18 *Law and History Review* 305.

Baker, Brenda, 'Provocation as a Defence for Abused Women Who Kill' (1998) XI *Canadian Journal of Jurisprudence* 193.

Baurmann, Michael, *The Market of Virtue: Morality and Commitment in a Liberal Society* (New York: Springer, 2002).

Bentham, Jeremy, 'An Introduction to the Principles of Morals and Legislation' edited by JH Burns and HLA Hart (London: Macmillan, [1789], 1970).

Besse, SK, 'Crimes of Passion: The Campaign against Wife-Killing in Brazil, 1910–1940' (1989) 22 *Journal of Social History* 653–66.

Bingham, Lord Thomas, 'A Criminal Code: Must We Wait For Ever?' (1998) *Criminal Law Review* 694.

Blackstone, Sir William, *Commentaries of the Laws of England*, 4 vols (Oxford: Clarendon Press, 1765–69).

Booth, Cherie, and Squires, Daniel, *The Negligence Liability of Public Authorities* (Oxford: Oxford University Press, 2006).

Bowring, J (ed), *The Works of Jeremy Bentham*, vol 3 (Edinburgh: W Tait, 1838–43).

Brudner, Alan, 'Agency and Welfare in the Penal Law' in Stephen Shute, John Gardner, and Jeremy Horder (eds), *Action and Value in Criminal Law* (Oxford: Clarendon Press, 1993).

Bucy, P, 'Corporate Ethos: A Standard for Imposing Corporate Criminal Liability' (1991) 75 *Minnesota Law Review* 1095.

Burke, James (ed), *Speeches of the Right Hon Edmund Burke: with Memoir and Historical Introductions* (Dublin: Duffy, 1854).

Buxton, Sir Richard, 'Joint Enterprise' (2009) *Criminal Law Review* 233.

Chalmers, J, 'Merging Provocation and Diminished Responsibility: Some Reasons for Skepticism' (2004) *Criminal Law Review* 198.

Chan, Wing-Cheong, Mitchell, Barry, and Yeo, Stanley (eds), *Codification, Macaulay and the Indian Penal Code* (Farnham: Ashgate, 2011).

Clarke, A, Moran-Ellis, J, and Sleney, J, *Attitudes to Date Rape and Relationship Rape: A Qualitative Study* (London: Sentencing Advisory Panel, 2002).

Clarkson, CMV, 'Corporate Culpability' (1998) 2 *Web Journal of Current Legal Issues* 2.

Colvin, Eric, 'Corporate Responsibility and Criminal Liability' (1995) 6 *Criminal Law Forum* 1.

Creedon, Silas, 'Hand Hygiene Compliance: Exploring Variations in Practice between Hospitals' (2008) 104 *Nursing Times* 32.

Criminal Law Commissioners, *Fourth Report* (1839), Parl Pap xix–235.

Criminal Law Revision Committee, *Offences against the Person*, Cmnd 7844 (London: HMSO, 1980).

Cromwell, P, 'Group Effects on Decision-Making by Burglars' (1991) 69 *Psychological Reports* 579.

Cross, Sir Rupert, 'The Reports of the Criminal Law Commissioners (1833–49) and the Abortive Bills of 1853', in PR Glazebrook (ed), *Reshaping the Criminal Law* (London: Stevens and Sons, 1978).

Cumper, Peter and Lewis, Tom, '"Public Reason", Judicial Deference and the Right to Freedom of Religion and Belief under the Human Rights Act 1998' (2011) 22 *King's Law Journal* 131.

Cunningham, Sally, 'Punishing Drivers Who Kill: Putting Road Safety First?' (2007) 27 *Legal Studies* 288.

De Búrca, G, and Gardner, S, 'The Codification of the Criminal Law' (1990) 10 *Oxford Journal of Legal Studies* 559.

Department for Business, Innovation and Skills (DBIS), *Code of Practice on Consultation* (London: BIS, 2008).

Department of Health, *The Use of Antipsychotic Medication for People with Dementia: Time for Action* (London: Department of Health, 2009).

Dilhof, Anthony M, 'Transferred Intent: an Enquiry into the Nature of Criminal Culpability' (1998) 1 *Buffalo Criminal Law Review* 501.

Dressler, Joshua, *Understanding Criminal Law,* 3rd edn (New York: Lexis Publishing, 2001).

Dressler, Joshua, 'Why Keep the Provocation Defence?: Some Reflections on a Difficult Subject' (2002a) 86 *Minnesota Law Review* 959.

Dressler, Joshua, 'Battered women who kill their sleeping tormenters: reflections on maintaining respect for human life while killing moral monsters' in Stephen Shute and AP Simester (eds), *Criminal Law Theory: Doctrines of the General Part* (Oxford: Oxford University Press, 2002b).

Dubber, Mark, 'Penal Panopticon: The Idea of a Modern Model Penal Code' (2000–01) 4 *Buffalo Criminal Law Review* 53.

Du Bois-Pedain, Antje, 'Intentional Killings: The German Law' in Jeremy Horder (ed), *Homicide Law in Comparative Perspective* (Oxford: Hart Publishing, 2007).

Duff, RA, 'Acting, Trying and Criminal Liability' in Stephen Shute, John Gardner, and Jeremy Horder, *Action and Value in Criminal Law* (Oxford: Oxford University Press, 1993).

Duff, RA, *Criminal Attempts* (Oxford: Oxford University Press, 1996).

Duff, RA, *Answering for Crime* (Oxford: Hart Publishing, 2007).

Duff, RA, 'Perversions and Subversions of Criminal Law' in RA Duff *et al* (eds), *The Boundaries of the Criminal Law* (Oxford: Oxford University Press, 2010).

Duff, RA and Marshall, SE, 'Criminalisation and Sharing Wrongs' (1998) 11 *Canadian Journal of Law and Jurisprudence* 7.

Dworkin, RM, *Taking Rights Seriously* (London: Duckworth, 1977).

East, Edward, *A Treatise of the Pleas of the Crown* (London: Butterworth, 1803).

Eastwood, David, 'Men, Morals and the Machinery of Social Legislation 1790–1840' (1994) 13 *Parliamentary History* 190.

Eden, W, *Principles of Penal Law*, 2nd edn (London: Macmillan, 1771).

Edwards, Susan, *Sex and Gender in the Legal Process* (London: Blackstone Press, 1996).

Edwards, Susan, 'Abolishing Provocation and Reframing Self-Defence—the Law Commission's Options for Reform' (2004) *Criminal Law Review* 181.

Edwards, Susan, 'Loss of Self-Control: When His Anger is Worth More than Her Fear' in Alan Reed and Michael Bohlander, *Loss of Self-Control and Diminished Responsibility: Domestic, Comparative and International Perspectives* (Farnham: Ashgate, 2011).

Elvin, Jesse, 'Killing in Response to Circumstances of an Extremely Grave Character' in Alan Reed and Michael Bohlander, *Loss of Self-Control and Diminished Responsibility: Domestic, Comparative and International Perspectives* (Farnham: Ashgate, 2011).

Emmerson, Ben, and Ashworth, Andrew, *Human Rights and Criminal Justice*, 1st edn (London: Sweet & Maxwell, 2001).

Endicott, Timothy, 'Linguistic Indeterminacy' (1996) 16 *Oxford Journal of Legal Studies* 667.

Englund, Tom, 'Higher Education, Democracy and Citizenship—The Democratic Potential of the University?' (2002) 21 *Studies in Philosophy and Education* 281.

Ewing, AC, *The Morality of Punishment* (London: K Paul Trench, 1929).

Farmer, Lindsay, 'Reconstructing the English Codification Debate: The Criminal Law Commissioners, 1833–45' (2000) 18 *Law and History Review*,<www.historycooperative. org/journals/lhr/18.2/farmer.html>.

Farrar, JH, *Law Reform and the Law Commission* (London: Sweet & Maxwell, 1974).

Fifoot, CHS, *Judge and Jurist in the Reign of Victoria* (London: Stevens & Sons, 1959).

Finckenauer, James, 'Public Support for the Death Penalty: Retribution as Just Deserts or Retribution as Revenge?' (1988) 5 *Justice Quarterly* 81.

Finkelstein, Claire, 'Merger and Felony Murder' in RA Duff and SP Green (eds), *Defining Crimes* (Oxford: Oxford University Press, 2005).

Finkelstein, Claire, 'Two Models of Murder: Patterns of Criminalisation in the United States' in Jeremy Horder (ed), Homicide *Law in Comparative Perspective* (Oxford: Hart Publishing, 2007).

Finnis, John, 'On "Public Reason"', Oxford Legal Studies Research Paper No 1/2007, <http://ssrn.com/abstract=955815>.

Fuller, Lon, *The Morality of Law*, revised edn (New Haven: Yale, 1969).

Gardner, John, 'Rationality and the Rule of Law in Offences Against the Person' (1994) 53 *Cambridge Law Journal* 502.

Gardner, John, 'Crime: In Proportion and In Perspective' in Martin Wasik and Andrew Ashworth (eds), *Fundamentals of Sentencing Theory* (Oxford: Clarendon Press, 1998a) 31.

Gardner, John, 'The Gist of Excuses' (1998b) 1 Buffalo *Criminal Law Review* 575.

Gardner, John, 'On the General Part of the Criminal Law' in RA Duff (ed), *Philosophy and the Criminal Law* (Cambridge: Cambridge University Press, 1998c).

Gardner, John, 'Justification under Authority (2010) 23 *Canadian Journal of Law and Jurisprudence* 71.

Garland, David, *Punishment and Modern Society: A Study in Social Theory* (Oxford: Oxford University Press, 1990).

Glazebrook, Peter, 'Structuring the Criminal Code: Functional Approaches to Complicity, Incomplete Offences and General Defences' in AP Simester and ATH Smith (eds), *Harm and Culpability* (Oxford: Oxford University Press, 1996).

Glazebrook, Peter, 'A Better Way of Convicting Businesses of Avoidable Deaths and Injuries' (2002) 61 *Cambridge Law Journal* 405.

Gobert, James, 'What Motivates the White Collar Criminal?: A Critical Look at the Social, Environmental, Political, Economic and Human Factors which Underlie White Collar and Corporate Crime' in H Pontell and G Geis (eds), *International Handbook of White Collar Crime* (New York: Springer, 2007).

Gobert, James, 'The Corporate Manslaughter and Corporate Homicide Act 2007— Thirteen Years in the Making but was it Worth the Wait?' (2008) 71 *Modern Law Review* 413.

Gobert, James and Punch, Maurice, *Rethinking Corporate Crime* (London: Butterworths, 2003).

Gooderham, Peter, '"No-one Fully Responsible": a "Collusion of Anonymity" Protecting Health-Care Bodies from Manslaughter Charges' (2011) 6 *Clinical Ethics* 68.

Gough, Stephen, 'Pre-natal Injury and Homicide Following *Attorney-General's Reference (No 3 of 1994)*' (1999) 62 *Modern Law Review* 128.

Gough, Stephen, 'Taking the Heat out of Provocation' (1999) 19 *Oxford Journal of Legal Studies* 481.

Griffin, Stephen and Moran, Jon, 'Accountability for Deaths Attributable to the Grossly Negligent Act or Omission of Police Force: The Impact of the Corporate Manslaughter and Corporate Homicide Act 2007' (2010) *Journal of Criminal Law* 358.

Halliday, Simon, LLan, Jonathan, and Scott, Colin, 'The Public Management of Liability Risks' (2011) 31 *Oxford Journal of Legal Studies* 527.

Hammond, Anthony, *On the Reduction to Writing of the Criminal Law of England* (London: Butterworth & Son, 1829).

Harding, Christopher, *Criminal Enterprise: Individuals, Organisations and Criminal Responsibility* (Cullompton: Willan, 2007).

Harris, James, *Law and Legal Science* (Oxford: Clarendon Press, 1979).

Hart, HLA, *The Concept of Law* (Oxford: Clarendon Press, 1961).

Hart, HLA and Honoré, AM, *Causation in the Law*, 2nd edn (Oxford: Clarendon Press, 1985).

Hawkins, William, *A Treatise of the Pleas of the Crown* (London: Sweet, 1824).

Hayek, FA, *The Road to Serfdom* (London: Macmillan, 1944).

Hemming, Andrew, 'It's Time to Abolish Diminished Responsibility, the "Coach and Horses" Defence Through Criminal Responsibility for Murder' (2008) 10 *University of Notre Dame Australia Law Review* 1.

Herald of Free Enterprise Report of the Court, No 8074 (London: Department of Transport, 1987).

Herring, Jonathan, 'The Serious Wrong of Domestic Abuse and the Loss of Self-Control Defence' in Alan Reed and Michael Bohlander, *Loss of Self-Control and Diminished Responsibility: Domestic, Comparative and International Perspectives* (Farnham: Ashgate, 2011).

Herring, Jonathan and Palser, E, 'Gross Negligence Manslaughter and the Duty of Care' (2007) *Criminal Law Review* 17.

Hershovitz, Scott, 'Legitimacy, Democracy and Razian Authority' (2003) 9 *Legal Theory* 201.

Hogan, Brian, 'Comment' (1978) *Criminal Law Review* 597.

Holland, Winifred, 'Murder and Related Issues: an Analysis of the Law in Canada' in Jeremy Horder (ed), *Homicide Law in Comparative Perspective* (Oxford: Hart Publishing, 2007).

Home Office, *Making Punishments Work; Report of a Review of the Sentencing Framework for England and Wales* (London: Home Office, 2001).

Home Office, *Summary of Responses to Corporate Manslaughter: The Government's Draft Bill for Reform* (London: Home Office, 2005).

Home Office, *Corporate Manslaughter and Corporate Homicide: A Regulatory Impact Assessment of the Government's Bill* (London: Home Office, 2006).

Home Office, *Together We Can End Violence against Women and Girls: A Strategy* (London: Home Office, 2009).

HomRag, Public *Opinion and the Penalty for Murder* (Waterside Press: Hook, 2011).

Horder, Jeremy, 'The Problem of Provocative Children' (1987) *Criminal Law Review* 655.

Horder, Jeremy, *Provocation and Responsibility* (Oxford: Oxford University Press, 1992a).

Horder, Jeremy, 'Autonomy, Provocation and Duress' (1992b) *Criminal Law Review* 706.

Horder, Jeremy, 'Provocation and Loss of Self-control' (1992c) 108 *Law Quarterly Review* 191.

Horder, Jeremy, 'The Duel and the English Law of Homicide' (1992d) 12 *Oxford Journal of Legal Studies* 419.

Horder, Jeremy, 'Re-Thinking Non-Fatal Offences against the Person' (1994) 14 *Oxford Journal of Legal Studies* 335.

Horder, Jeremy, 'A Critique of the Correspondence Principle in Criminal Law' (1995) *Criminal Law Review* 759.

Horder, Jeremy, 'Two Histories and Four Hidden Principles of *Mens Rea*' (1997a) 113 *Law Quarterly Review* 95.

Horder, Jeremy, 'Gross Negligence and Criminal Culpability', (1997b) 47 *University of Toronto Law Journal* 495.

Horder, Jeremy, 'On the Irrelevance of Motive in Criminal Law' in Jeremy Horder (ed), *Oxford Essays in Jurisprudence*, 4th Series (Oxford: Oxford University Press, 2000).

Horder, Jeremy, 'Killing the Passive Abuser: A Theoretical Defence' in Stephen Shute and AP Simester (eds), *Criminal Law Theory: Doctrines of the General Part* (Oxford: Oxford University Press, 2002a).

Horder, Jeremy, 'Strict Liability, Statutory Construction and the Spirit of Liberty' (2002b) 118 *Law Quarterly Review* 459.

Horder, Jeremy, Criminal Law' in Peter Cane and Mark Tushnet (eds), *The Oxford Handbook of Legal Studies* (Oxford: Oxford University Press, 2003) 226.

Horder, Jeremy, *Excusing Crime* (Oxford: Oxford University Press, 2004).

Horder, Jeremy, 'Reshaping the Subjective Element in the Provocation Defence' (2005) 25 *Oxford Journal of Legal Studies* 123.

Horder, Jeremy, 'Judges' Use of Moral Arguments in Interpreting Statutes', in Timothy Endicott, Joshua Getzler, and Edwin Peel (eds), *Properties of Law: Essays in Honour of Jim Harris* Oxford: Oxford University Press, 2006).

Horder, Jeremy and Hughes, David, 'Comparative Issues in the Law of Homicide' in Jeremy Horder (ed), *Homicide Law in Comparative Perspective* (Oxford: Hart Publishing, 2007).

Horder, Jeremy and McGowan, Laura, 'Manslaughter by Causing Another's Suicide' (2006) *Criminal Law Review* 1035.

Hostettler, John, *Politics and Law in the Life of Sir James Fitzjames Stephen* (Chichester: Barry Rose, 1995).

House of Commons' Justice Committee, *Joint Enterprise* (11th Report of Session, 2010–12).

Huigens, Kyron, 'Duress is not a Justification' (2004) 2 *Ohio State Journal of Criminal Law* 313.

Husak, Douglas, 'Partial Defences' (1998) XI *Canadian Journal of Law and Jurisprudence* 167.

Husak, Douglas, *Overcriminalisation* (Oxford: Oxford University Press, 2008).

Jones, TH, 'Causation, Homicide and the Supply of Drugs' (2006) 26 *Legal Studies* 139.

Kamenka, E and Tay, A, 'Beyond Bourgeois Individualism: the Contemporary Crisis in Law and Legal Ideology' in Eugene Kamenka and RS Neale (eds), *Feudalism, Capitalism and Beyond* (London: Edward Arnold, 1975).

Kantorowicz, Ernst H, *The King's Two Bodies: A Study in Mediaeval Political Theology* (New Jersey: Princeton University Press, 1957).

Katyal, Neal Kuma, 'Conspiracy Theory' (2003) 112 *Yale Law Journal* 101.

Kettler, D and Meja, V, 'Their "Own Peculiar Way": Karl Mannheim and the Rise of Women' (1993) 8 *International Sociology* 5.

Kettler, David, Meja, Volker, and Stehr, Nico, *Karl Mannheim* (London: Tavistock, 1984).

Krey, Volker, *German Criminal Law: General Part*, vol 3 (Kohlhammer Studienbücher: Sttutgart, 2002).

Kutz, Christopher, *Complicity* (Cambridge: Cambridge University Press, 2007).

Lacey, Nicola, Wells, Celia, and Quick, Oliver, *Reconstructing Criminal Law*, 3rd edn (London: Butterworths, 2003).

Law Commission, *Law Com No. 89: The Mental Element in Crime* (London: HMSO, 1978).

Law Commission, *Annual Report, Law Com No. 107* (London: HMSO, 1981).

Law Commission, *Report to the Law Commission on the Codification of the Criminal Law, Law Com No. 143* (London: HMSO, 1985).

Law Commission, *A Criminal Code for England and Wales*, 2 vols (London: HMSO, 1989).

Law Commission, *Assisting and Encouraging Crime,* Consultation Paper No 131 (London: HMSO, 1993).

Law Commission, *Law Com No. 237: Legislating the Criminal Code: Involuntary Manslaughter* (London: HMSO, 1996).

Law Commission, *Partial Defences to Murder,* Consultation Paper No 173 (2003a).

Law Commission, *Children: Their Non-accidental Death or Serious Injury (Criminal Trials) A Consultative Report, Law Com No. 279* (London: HMSO, 2003b).

Law Commission, *Children: Their Non-accidental Death or Serious Injury (Criminal Trials), Law Com No. 282* (London: HMSO, 2003c).

Law Commission, *Partial Defences to Murder, Law Com No. 290* (London: The Stationary Office, 2004).

Law Commission, *A New Homicide Act for England and Wales?* Consultation Paper No 177 (London: The Stationary Office, 2005).

Law Commission, *Murder, Manslaughter and Infanticide, Law Com No 304* (London: The Stationary Office, 2006).

Law Commission, *Participating in Crime, Law Com No 305* (London: The Stationary Office, 2007).

Leader-Elliot, Ian, 'Recklessness and Moral Desiccation in the Australian Law of Murder' in Jeremy Horder (ed), *Homicide Law in Comparative Perspective* (Oxford: Hart Publishing, 2007).

Leader-Elliot, Ian, 'Sudden Fight, Consent, and the Principle of Comparative Responsibility in the Indian Penal Code' (2010) *Singapore Journal of Legal Studies* 282.

Leverick, Fiona, *Killing in Self-Defence* (Oxford: Oxford University Press, 2006).

Loader, Colin and Kettler, David, *Sociology as Political Education* (New Brunswick: Transaction Publishers, 2002).

Lobban, Michael, *'How Benthamic Was the Criminal Law Commission?'* (2000) 18 *Law and History Review* 427.

Lord Chancellor's Department, *Proposals for English and Scottish Law Commissions* (London: TSO, Cmnd 2573, 1965).

Lovibond, Sabina, *Ethical Formation* (Cambridge Mass: Harvard University Press, 2002).

Lukes, Steven, *Power: A Radical View,* 2nd edn (London: Palgrave Macmillan, 2005).

Mackay, RD, 'Pleading Provocation and Diminished Responsibility Together' (1988) *Criminal Law Review* 411.

Mackay, RD, 'The New Diminished Responsibility Plea: More than Mere Modernisation?' in Alan Reed and Michael Bohlander, *Loss of Self-Control and Diminished Responsibility: Domestic, Comparative and International Perspectives* (Farnham: Ashgate, 2011).

Malphurs, JE, Eisdorpher, C, and Cohen, D, 'A Comparison of Antecedents of Homicide-Suicide and Suicide in Older Married Men' (2001) 9 *American Journal of Geriatric Psychiatry* 49.

Mannheim, Karl, 'Competition as a Cultural Phenomenon' in Bryan S Turner (ed), *Essays on the Sociology of Knowledge: Karl Mannheim: Collected English Writings,* vol 5 (London: Routledge & Kegan Paul, [1928] 2000).

Mannheim, Karl, *Ideology and Utopia* (London: Routledge & Kegan Paul, [1936], edited by Bryan S Turner, 1997).

Mannheim, Karl, *Freedom, Power and Democratic Plannning* (London: Routledge, 1951).

Marshall, B, Webb, B, and Tilley, N, 'Rationalisation of Current Research on Guns, Gangs and other Weapons: Phase 1' (London: Jill Dando Institute of Criminal Science, 2005).

Marx, Karl, *Early Writings* (London: Harmondsworth, 1975).

McColgan, Aileen, 'In Defence of Battered Women Who Kill' (1993) 13 *Oxford Journal of Legal Studies* 508.

Mid Staffordshire NHS Foundation Trust Inquiry, vol 1 (London: The Stationary Office, 2010).

Miles, Jo, 'The Coroners and Justice Act: making a "dog's breakfast" of homicide reform' (2009) 10 *Archbold News* 5.

Mill, JS, *On Liberty* (Indianapolis: Bobbs-Merrill, [1859] 1955).

Miller, John, 'Report from the Select Committee on Criminal Laws' (1820–21) 24 *Quarterly Review* 232.

Ministry of Justice, *Murder, Manslaughter and Infanticide: Proposals for Reform of the Law*, CP 19/08 (London: Ministry of Justice, 2008).

Ministry of Justice, *Murder, Manslaughter and Infanticide: Proposals for Reform of the Law; Summary of Responses and Government Position*, CP(R) 19/08 (London: Ministry of Justice, 2009).

Misak, Cheryl, 'Pragmatism, Emipricism and Morality' in Sabina Lovibond and SG Williams (eds), *Identity, Truth and Value: Essays for David Wiggins* (Oxford: Oxford University Press, 1997).

Mitchell, Barry, 'Public Perceptions of Homicide and Criminal Justice' (1998) 38(3) *British Journal of Criminology* 453.

Mitchell, Barry, 'Further Evidence of the Relationship between Legal and Public Opinion on the Law of Homicide' (2000) *Criminal Law Review* 814.

Mitchell, Barry, 'Minding the Gap in Unlawful and Dangerous Act Manslaughter: A Moral Defence of One-punch Killers' (2008) 72 *Journal of Criminal Law* 537.

Mitchell, Barry, 'More Thoughts about Unlawful and Dangerous Act Manslaughter and the One-punch Killer' (2009) *Criminal Law Review* 502.

Mitchell, Barry, 'Loss of Self-Control under the Coroners and Justice Act 2009: Oh No! in Alan Reed and Michael Bohlander, *Loss of Self-Control and Diminished Responsibility: Domestic, Comparative and International Perspectives* (Farnham: Ashgate, 2011).

Mitchell, Barry and Roberts, Julian, 'Public Attitudes Towards the Mandatory Life Sentence for Murder: Putting Received Wisdom to the Empirical Test' (2011) *Criminal Law Review* 456.

Mitchell, Barry and Roberts, Julian, *Exploring the Mandatory Life Sentence for Murder* (Oxford: Hart Publishing, 2012).

Model Criminal Code Officers' Committee Report, *General Principles of Criminal Responsibility* (Canberra: Criminal Law Officers Committee of the Standing Committee of Attorneys-General, 1992).

Moore, Michael, *Placing Blame* (Oxford: Clarendon Press, 1997).

Morgan, Neil, 'The Fault Element of Offences' in Wing-Cheong Chan, Barry Mitchell, and Stanley Yeo (eds), *Codification, Macaulay and the Indian Penal Code* (Farnham: Ashgate, 2011).

Morgan, R, 'Privileging Public Attitudes to Sentencing?' in JV Roberts and M Hough (eds), *Changing Attitudes to Punishment* (Cullompton: Willan, 2002).

Morris, Terence and Blom-Cooper, Louis, *Fine Lines and Distinctions: Murder, Manslaughter and the Taking of Human Life* (Hook: Waterside Press, 2011).

National Policing Improvement Agency, *Manual of Guidance on the Management, Command and Deployment of Armed Officers*, 2nd edn (London: NPIA, 2010).

New South Wales Law Reform Commission, *Partial Defences to Murder: Provocation and Infanticide* (Report 83, 1997).

Norrie, Alan, 'The Coroners and Justice Act 2009—Partial Defences to Murder (1) Loss of Self-Control' (2010) *Criminal Law Review* 275.

Nourse, Victoria, 'Passion's Progress: Modern Law Reform and the Provocation Defence', 106 *Yale Law Journal* 1331 (1997).

Nuffield Council on Bioethics, *Human Bodies: Donation for Medicine and Research* (London, 2011) <www.nuffieldbioethics.org/donation/donation-our-ethical-framework>.

Office of the Leader of the House of Commons, *Post-legislative Scrutiny: The Government's Response* (London: Office of the Leader of the House of Commons, 2008) <http://www.justice.gov.uk/lawcommission/docs/lc302_government_response.pdf>.

Ormerod, David, *Smith and Hogan: Criminal Law,* 11th edn (Oxford: Oxford University Press, 2005).

Ormerod, David and Fortson, Rudi, 'Drug Suppliers and Manslaughters (Again)' (2005) *Criminal Law Review* 819.

Pearce, LM, Knowles J, Davies, GP, and Buttress, S, *Dangerous Driving and the Law: Road Safety Research Report No. 26* (London: Department for Transport, 2002.)

Pedain, Antje, 'Intention and the Terrorist Example' (2003) *Criminal Law Review* 579.

Perry, Stephen R, 'Judicial Obligation, Precedent and the Common Law' (1987) 7 *Oxford Journal of Legal Studies* 215.

Postema, Gerald, *Bentham and the Common Law Tradition* (Oxford: Clarendon Press, 1986).

Postema, Gerald, 'Classical Common Law Jurisprudence (Part II)' (2003) 3 *Oxford University Commonwealth Law Journal* 1.

Pound, Roscoe, 'The Need for a Sociological Jurisprudence' (1907) 19 *Green Bag* 607.

Quick, Oliver, 'Prosecuting "Gross" Medical Negligence: Manslaughter, Discretion and the Crown Prosecution Service' (2006) 33 *Journal of Law and Society* 421.

Quick, Oliver, 'Medical Killing: Need for a Specific Offence?' in CMV Clarkson and Sally Cunningham (eds), *Criminal Liability for Non-Aggressive Death* (Aldershot: Ashgate Publishing, 2008), 155.

Radzinowicz, Sir Leon, *A History of the English Criminal Law*, vol 1 (London: Stevens, 1948).

Radzinowicz, Sir Leon, 'Sir James Fitzjames Stephen and His Contribution to the Development of the Criminal Law' (London: Selden Society Lecture, 1957).

Rawls, John, 'The Idea of an Overlapping Consensus' (1987) 7 *Oxford Journal of Legal Studies* 1.

Raz, Joseph, *The Authority of Law* (Oxford: Clarendon Press, 1979).

Raz, Joseph, *The Morality of Freedom* (Oxford: Clarendon Press, 1986).

Raz, Joseph, *Practical Reason and Norms* (Oxford: Clarendon Press, 1990).

Raz, Joseph, *Engaging Reason* (Oxford: Oxford University Press, 1999).

Reason, J, 'Safety in the Operating Theatre—Part 2: Human Error and Organisational Failure' (2005) 14 *Quality Safety Health Care* 56.

Reed, Alan and Bohlander, Michael, *Loss of Self-Control and Diminished Responsibility: Domestic, Comparative and International Perspectives* (Farnham: Ashgate, 2011).

Reed, Alan and Wake, Nicola, 'Sexual Infidelity Killings: Contemporary Standardisations and Comparative Stereotypes' in Alan Reed and Michael Bohlander (eds), *Loss of Self-Control and Diminished Responsibility: Domestic, Comparative and International Perspectives* (Farnham: Ashgate, 2011).

Reilly, Alex, 'Loss of Self-Control in Provocation' (1997) 21 *Criminal Law Journal* 320.

Roberts, Julian, *Public Opinion and Sentencing: Surveys by the Canadian Sentencing Commission; Research Reports of the Canadian Sentencing Commission* (Ottawa: Canadian Department of Justice, 1988).

Roberts, Julian, 'Public Opinion, Crime and Criminal Justice' in M Tonry (ed), *Crime and Justice: A Review of Research*, vol 16 (Chicago: University of Chicago Press, 1992).

Roberts, Julian, 'Public Opinion and Sentencing Policy' in S Rex and M Tonry (eds), *Reform and Punishment: The Future of Sentencing* (Cullompton: Willan Publishing, 2002).

Roberts, Paul H, 'Justice for All: Two Bad Arguments (and Several Good Suggestions) for Resisting Double Jeopardy Reform' (2002) 6 *International Journal of Evidence and Proof* 197.

Robinson, Paul H, 'Should the Criminal Law Abandon the *Actus Reus-Mens Rea* Distinction?' in Stephen Shute, John Gardner, and Jeremy Horder (eds), *Action and Value in Criminal Law* (Oxford: Oxford University Press, 1993).

Robinson, Paul H, Cahill, M, and Mohammed, U, 'The Five Worst (and Five Best) American Criminal Codes' (2000) 94 *Northwestern University Law Review* 1.

Robinson, Paul H and Darley, John M, 'Objectivist and Subjectivist Views of Criminality: A Study in the Role of Social Science in Criminal Law Theory' (1998) 18 *Oxford Journal of Legal Studies* 409.

Robinson, Paul H and Kurzban, Robert, 'Concordance and Conflict in Intuitions of Justice' (2007) 91 *Minnesota Law Review* 1829.

Robinson, Paul H, Goodwin, Geoffrey P, and Reisig, Michael D, 'The Disutility of Injustice' (2010) 85 *New York University Law Review* 1940.

Rock, Paul, *After Homicide: Practical and Political Responses to Bereavement* (Oxford: Clarendon Press, 1998).

Rogers, Jonathan, 'Justifying the Use of Firearms by Policemen and Soldiers: a Response to the Home Office's Review of the Law on the Use of Lethal Force' (1998) 18 *Legal Studies* 486.

Rogers, Jonathan, 'The Law Commission's Proposed Restructuring of Homicide' (2006) *Journal of Criminal Law* 223.

Royal Commission, *The Law Relating to Indictable Offences* (Report and Draft Code Bill), Cmnd 2345, 1879; Parl Paps (1878–79) XX 169.

Royal Commission on Capital Punishment, *Report*, Cmnd 8832 (London: HMSO, 1953).

Royal Commission on Transport (1928–30), *The Control of Traffic on Roads*, Cmnd 3365 (London: HMSO, 1929).

Russell, N and Morgan, R, *Sentencing of Domestic Burglary; Research Report 1* (London: Sentencing Advisory Panel, 2001).

Sampson, Anthony, *An Anatomy of Britain* (London; Hodder & Staughton, 1962).

Saunders, TJ, *Plato's Penal Code* (Oxford: Clarendon Press, 1991).

Sayre, FB, 'Mens Rea' (1932) 45 *Harvard Law Review* 974.

Scarman, Lord, *Law Reform: The New Pattern* (London: Routledge & Kegal Paul, 1968).

Scheffler, Samuel, *Human Morality* (Oxford: Oxford University Press, 1992).

Schofield, P and Harris, J, *'Legislator of the World': Writings on Codification, Law and Education* (Oxford: Oxford University Press, 1998).

Select Committee on Criminal Laws (1819) *Parliamentary Papers VIII*, 585.

Sellers, Mortimer, 'Republican Impartiality' (1991) 11 *Oxford Journal of Legal Studies* 273.

Sharp, F and Otto, M, 'A Study of the Popular Attitude Towards Retributive Punishment' (1909) 20 *International Journal of Ethics* 314.

Sharp, Granville, *Remarks on the Opinions of some of the Most Celebrated Writers on Crown Law, Respecting the due Distinction between Manslaughter and Murder* (London: B White, 1773).

Sheridan, L, 'Charity versus Politics' (1973) 2 *Anglo-American Law Review* 47.

Shute, Stephen, Gardner, John, and Horder, Jeremy, *Action and Value in Criminal Law* (Oxford: Oxford University Press, 1993).

Simester, AP, 'Intention Thus Far' (1997) *Criminal Law Review* 704.

Simester, AP, 'Can Negligence be Culpable?' in Jeremy Horder (ed), *Oxford Essays in Jurisprudence, 4th Series* (Oxford: Oxford University Press, 2000).

Simester, AP, 'The Mental Element in Complicity' (2006) 122 *Law Quarterly Review* 578.

Simester, AP and Sullivan, GR, *Criminal Law: Theory and Doctrine,* 2nd edn (Oxford: Hart Publishing, 2003).

Simester, AP, Sullivan, GR, Spencer, JR, and Virgo, GJ, *Criminal Law: Theory and Doctrine*, 4th edn (Oxford: Hart Publishing, 2010).

Simons, Kenneth W, 'The Relevance of Community Values to Just Deserts: Criminal Law, Punishment Rationales and Democracy' (2001) 28 *Hofstra Law Review* 635.

Slapper, G, and Tombs, S, *Corporate Crime* (London: Longman, 1999).

Smith, Sir John, 'Codification of the Criminal Law': (1) The Case for a Code' (1986) *Criminal Law Review* 285.

Smith, Sir John, 'Criminal Liability of Accessories: Law and Law Reform' (1997) 113 *Law Quarterly Review* 453.

Smith, Sir John and Hogan, Brian, *Criminal Law*, 9th edn (London: Butterworths, 1999).

Smith, Sir John and Hogan, Brian, *Criminal Law*, 10th edn (London: Butterworths, 2005).

Smith, Sir John and Hogan, Brian, *Criminal Law*, 11th edn (London: Butterworths, 2008).

Smith, KJM, *James Fitzjames Stephen* (Cambridge: Cambridge University Press, 1988).

Smith KJM, 'Macaulay's Utilitarian Penal Code: An Illustration of the Accidental Function of Time, Place and Personalities in Law Making' in WM Gordon and TD Fergus (eds), *Legal History in the Making* (London: Hambledon Press, 1991).

Smith, KJM, *Lawyers, Legislators and Theorists* (Oxford: Clarendon Press, 1998).

Spencer, John, 'Road Traffic Law: A Review of the North Report' (1988) *Criminal Law Review* 707.

Spencer, John, 'Intentional Killings in French Law' in Jeremy Horder (ed), *Homicide Law in Comparative Perspective* (Oxford: Hart Publishing, 2007).

Spencer, John, 'The drafting of Criminal Legislation: Need it be so Impenetrable?' (2008a) 67 *Cambridge Law Journal* 585.

Spencer, John, 'Messing Up Murder' (2008b) *Archbold News* 5.

Spencer, John and Pedain, Antje, 'Approaches to Strict and Constructive Liability in Continental Criminal Law' in AP Simester (ed), *Appraising Strict Liability* (Oxford: Oxford University Press, 2005).

Stanton-Ife, John, 'Horrific Crime' in RA Duff *et al* (eds), *The Boundaries of the Criminal Law* (Oxford: Oxford University Press, 2010).

Stephen, Sir James, 'Law Reform', *Saturday Review*, 2 February 1856, 252.

Stephen, Sir James, *A History of the Criminal Law of England*, vols 1–3 (London: MacMillan & Co, 1883).

Stephen, Sir James, *Digest of the Criminal Law* (London: MacMillan & Co, 1887).

Stephen, Sir James, *Horae Sabbaticae*, 3rd Series (London: Macmillan, 1892).

Stevenson, CL, *Ethics and Language* (New Haven: Yale University Press, 1944).

Stubbs, Julie and Tolmie, Julia, 'Falling Short of the Challenge? A Comparative Assessment of the Australian Use of Expert Evidence on Battered Woman Syndrome' [1999] *Melboune University Law Review* 27.

Sullivan, GR, 'Corporate Killing—Some Government Proposals' (2001) *Criminal Law Review* 31.

Sullivan, GR, 'First Degree Murder and Complicity—Conditions for Parity of Culpability between Principal and Accomplice' (2007) 1 *Criminal Law and Philosophy* 271.

Sullivan, GR, 'Participating in Crime: Law Com No 305—Joint Ventures' (2008) *Criminal Law Review* 19.

Tadros, Victor, 'The Characters of Excuse' (2001) 21 *Oxford Journal of Legal Studies* 495.

Tadros, Victor, *Criminal Responsibility* (Oxford: Oxford University Press, 2005a).

Tadros, Victor, 'The Distinctiveness of Domestic Abuse: a Freedom-Based Account' in RA Duff and SP Green (eds), *Defining Crimes* (Oxford: Oxford University Press, 2005b).

Tasmanian Law Reform Institute, *Criminal Liability of Organisations,* Final Report No 9 (Hobart: Tasmanian Law Reform Institute, 2007).

Taylor, Richard, 'Jury Unanimity in Homicide' (2001) *Criminal Law Review* 283.

Taylor, Richard, 'The Nature of Partial Defences and the Coherence of (Second Degree) Murder' (2007) *Criminal Law Review* 345.

Taylor, Richard, 'The Model of Tolerance and Self-Restraint' in Alan Reed and Michael Bohlander, *Loss of Self-Control and Diminished Responsibility: Domestic, Comparative and International Perspectives* (Farnham: Ashgate, 2011).

Thorburn, Malcolm, 'Justifications, Powers and Authority' (2008) 117 *Yale Law Journal* 1070.

Thring, Lord Henry, *Practical Legislation* (London: J Murray, 1902).

Tov-Ruach, L, 'Jealousy, Attention and Loss' in A Rorty (ed) *Explaining Emotions* (Berkeley: University of California Press, 1980).

Tur, RHS, 'Criminal Law and Legal Theory' in W Twining (ed), *Legal Theory and the Common Law* (Oxford: Blackwell, 1986).

Turner, JWC, *Kenny's Outlines of Criminal Law*, 16th edn (Cambridge: Cambridge University Press, 1952).

Turner, JWC, *Russell on Crime*, 12th edn, vol 1 (London: Butterworths, 1964).

Victim Support, *Coroners and Justice Bill: A Missed Opportunity for Victims of Crime* (London: Victim Support, 2009).

Victorian Law Reform Commission, *Defences to Homicide*: *Options Paper* (Melbourne: Victorian Law Reform Commission, 2003).

Victorian Law Reform Commission, *Defences to Homicide* (Melbourne: Victorian Law Reform Commission, 2004).

Von Hirsch, Andrew and Simester, AP (eds), *Incivilities: Regulating Offensive Behaviour* (Oxford: Hart Publishing, 2006).

Waldron, Jeremy, 'A Right to Do Wrong' (1981) 92 *Ethics* 21.

Waldron, Jeremy, 'A Rights-based Critique of Constitutional Rights' (1993) 13 *Oxford Journal of Legal Studies* 18.

Wasik, Martin, 'Sentencing in Homicide' in Andrew Ashworth and Barry Mitchell (eds), *Rethinking English Homicide Law* (Oxford: Oxford University Press, 2000) 177.

Weber, Max, *The Theory of Social and Economic Organisation*, AM Henderson and Talcott Parsons, trans (New York, Oxford University Press, 1947).

Wells, Celia, 'The Criminal Law Revision Committee: Offences Against the Person: Homicide' (1980) 43 *Modern Law Review* 681.

Wells, Celia, 'Swatting the Subjectivist Bug' (1982) *Criminal Law Review* 209.

Wells, Celia, 'Manslaughter and Corporate Crime' (1989) 139 *New Law Journal* 931.

Wells, Celia, *Corporations and Criminal Responsibility*, 1st edn (Oxford: Oxford University Press, 1993).

Wells, Celia, *Corporations and Criminal Responsibility*, 2nd edn (Oxford: Oxford University Press, 2001).

Wells, Celia, 'Corporate Crime: Opening the Eyes of the Sentry' (2010) 30 *Legal Studies* 370.

White, SM, 'Corporate Manslaughter' (2008) 63 *Anaesthesia* 210.

Williams, Bernard, *Moral Luck* (Cambridge: Cambridge University Press, 1982).

Williams, Glanville, *Criminal Law: The General Part*, 2nd edn (London: Stevens, 1961).

Williams, Glanville, *Textbook of the Criminal Law*, 2nd edn (London: Stevens, 1983).

Wilson, Harold, *Purpose in Politics: Selected Speeches* (London, Weidenfeld & Nicholson, 1964).

Wilson, William, 'Murder and the Structure of Homicide' in Andrew Ashworth and Barry Mitchell (eds), *Rethinking English Homicide Law*, (Oxford: Oxford University Press, 2000).

Wilson, William, 'The Structure of Criminal Homicide' (2006) *Criminal Law Review* 471.

Wilson, William, 'A Rational Scheme of Liability for Participating in Crime' (2008) *Criminal Law Review* 3.

Wirth, Louis, 'Preface' in Karl Mannheim, *Ideology and Utopia* (London: Routledge & Kegan Paul, 1936).

Zimring, Franklin E, 'Populism, Democratic Government, and the Decline of Expert Authority: Some Reflections on Three Strikes in California' (1996–97) 28 *Pacific Law Journal* 243.

Index

abortion 5, 64, 110, 111, 201–2
academics *see* scholars
accidental killing 42, 245, 246, 248
administrative-bureaucratic systems 53, 54, 67
   see also regulatory model
adultery *see* infidelity
adversarialism 232, 233, 234
agent-neutral /agent-specific approaches 190, 191
aggravated vehicle taking 77
Ahluwalia, Kiranjit 218
anaesthesia-related deaths 121, 123, 125
armed forces 135, 137, 138, 139
   see also police operations
Aronson, Mark 133
arson 143
Ashworth, Andrew 24, 26, 29, 30, 167, 181
assisted dying 85
attempted murder 181
Austin, JL 204
Austin, John 18, 19, 20, 21, 44
Australia
   industrial manslaughter 117
   Model Criminal Code 125, 126, 127, 128
   Tasmanian Law Reform Institute 125, 133, 134, 139
Automobile Association 35

Bagaric, M, and Edney, R 62
battered women 214, 215, 218, 242
   excessive defence against passive abusers 252–5
Bentham, Jeremy 7, 68, 69, 107, 108, 164, 171
Blackstone, Sir William 66, 68, 69, 155
bureaucratization 53, 54, 67
   see also regulatory model
Burke, Edmund 57, 60n
Buxton, Sir Richard 161, 228

Californian Penal Code 109
capacity-sensitive negligence test 59
capital punishment *see* death penalty
Care Quality Commission 119, 120, 122, 123
causal remoteness 186
causation doctrine 192, 193, 194
chance medley doctrine 203
child victims 83, 84, 211
citizenship 58, 63
   see also stakeholders
civil liberties 111, 112
civilizing process 200–5, 208, 212, 213, 216, 222, 229, 234, 239
codification 9, 13, 16

benefits and limitations 106–8
complicity law 162–5
draft criminal code 42–5
traditional-codificatory ideal 69–70
   aims and elements 75
   allocation of offences 76, 78
   reform proposals inspired by common law principles 70–2
Committee of Inquiry in the Criminal Laws (1819) 7–11, 53
common law
   aims and elements 75
   impact of regulatory model 72–4
   reconciliation with regulatory model 86–8
   reform proposals 70–2
   traditional crimes 67, 68, 76, 78
      creation of new context-specific offences 79–80, 86, 112
complicity *see* joint criminal ventures
consent defence 20–1
   suicide pacts 238, 239
constructive malice 224
corporate manslaughter 74, 76, 86–7, 109
   Australia: industrial manslaughter 117
   corporate culture 116, 120, 121, 122, 125, 126, 127, 128, 129, 130, 135–6, 137, 138, 139
   cost factors 119, 131
   duty of care 117–19
   fatal injury rate in Britain 114–15
   health services 115
      negligent NHS Trusts 119–24, 125, 127, 128, 129
   Marxist presuppositions 115, 116, 123
   proving fault under the 2007 Act 124–30
   public bodies 114, 115–19
      joint ventures with private organizations 133
   public sector exemptions 130
      decisions based on public policy 130–4
      military 135, 137, 138, 139
      police 135, 137, 138, 139
      prisons 131–2, 135, 136, 137
   senior management 114, 126
correspondence principle 42, 46
Criminal Law and Legal Policy Unit (CLLPU) 32–4
Criminal Law Revision Committee (CLRC) 16
   public consultation 35–8
   recommendations for homicide 38–42, 44
criminalization 201, 229
Cross, RA 12
culpable homicide 20, 71, 93

- <u>Negligence</u> — previous.
  proved re. delegation bit.
  -> no mention Cory

  ↓ moved
  by

  Northern Ship .... Qu. is where)
  that influence came from .